Lecture Notes in Computer Science 1516

Edited by G. Goos, J. Hartmanis and J. van Leeuwen

Springer

Berlin
Heidelberg
New York
Barcelona
Budapest
Hong Kong
London
Milan
Paris
Singapore
Tokyo

Wolfgang Ehrenberger (Ed.)

Computer Safety, Reliability and Security

17th International Conference, SAFECOMP'98
Heidelberg, Germany, October 5-7, 1998
Proceedings

Springer

Series Editors

Gerhard Goos, Karlsruhe University, Germany
Juris Hartmanis, Cornell University, NY, USA
Jan van Leeuwen, Utrecht University, The Netherlands

Volume Editor

Wolfgang Ehrenberger
Fachhochschule Fulda
Fachbereich Angewandte Informatik
Postfach 12 69, D-36012 Fulda, Germany
E-mail: ehrenberger@informatik.fh-fulda.de

Cataloging-in-Publication data applied for

Die Deutsche Bibliothek - CIP-Einheitsaufnahme

Computer safety, reliability and security : 17th international
conference ; proceedings / SAFECOMP '98, Heidelberg, Germany,
October 5 - 7, 1998. Wolfgang Ehrenberg (ed.). - Berlin ; Heidelberg
; New York ; Barcelona ; Budapest ; Hong Kong ; London ; Milan ;
Paris ; Singapore ; Tokyo : Springer, 1998
    (Lecture notes in computer science ; Vol. 1516)
    ISBN 3-540-65110-1

CR Subject Classification (1991): D.1-4, E.4, C.3, F.3, K.6.5

ISSN 0302-9743
ISBN 3-540-65110-1 Springer-Verlag Berlin Heidelberg New York

© Springer-Verlag Berlin Heidelberg 1998
Printed in Germany

Typesetting: Camera-ready by author
SPIN 10692744   06/3142 – 5 4 3 2 1 0   Printed on acid-free paper

Preface

Computers and their interactions are becoming the characteristic features of our time: Many people believe that the industrial age is going over into the information age. In the same way as life of the beginning of this century was dominated by machines, factories, streets and railways, the starting century will be characterised by computers and their networks. This change naturally affects also the institutions and the installations our lives depend upon: power plants, including nuclear ones, chemical plants, mechanically working factories, cars, railways and medical equipment; they all depend on computers and their connections. In some cases it is not human life that may be endangered by computer failure, but large investments; e.g. if a whole plant interrupts its production for a long time. In addition to loss of life and property one must not neglect public opinion, which is very critical in many countries against major technical defects.

The related computer technology, its hardware, software and production process differ between standard applications and safety related ones: In the safety case it is normally not only the manufacturers and the customers that are involved, but a third party, usually an assessor, who is taking care of the public interest on behalf of a state authority. Usually safety engineers are in a better position than their colleagues from the conventional side, as they may spend more time and money on a particular task and use better equipment. On the other hand, in addition to the costumer's wishes, they have to take into account the demands of assessors and regulators, who may reject their final product.

It has been the purpose of the SAFECOMP conference series to review the state of science and technology of safety related computing and provide a constructive exchange of ideas, opinions and visions among experts.

Since the SAFECOMP conferences have been running over nearly 20 years now, one may make some comparisons. This year's contributions are characterised by a large share of formal approaches and formal methods; it seems that deterministic views are coming to dominate over probabilistic ones. Another characteristic is that the hardware problems as such seem to be more or less solved; the contributions submitted in 1998 are dealing mainly with system aspects and with software aspects.

I hope that the reader of this book gets important information on how to make computer controlled systems safer at lower cost.

Fulda, Germany
August 1998

Wolfgang Ehrenberger

International Programme Committee

S. Anderson - UK
R. Bloomfield (EWICS Chair) - UK
F. Dafelmair - D
W. Ehrenberger (IPC Chair) - D
J.Gorski - PL
P. Joannou - CDN
F. Koornneef - NL
Ch. Mazuet - F
G. Rabe - D
B. Runge - DK
I. Smith - UK

H. Bezecny - D
S. Bologna - I
G.Dahll - N
H. Frey - CH
G. Hockey - UK
J. Järvi - FIN
R. Lauber - D;
M. van der Meulen - NL
J. Rainer - A
F. Saglietti - D
J. Zalewski - USA

P. Bishop - UK
G. Cleland - UK
P. Daniel - UK
R.Genser - A
D. Inverso - USA
K. Kanoun - F
V. Maggioli - USA
A. Pasquini - I
F. Redmill - UK
E. Schoitsch - A

Local Organising Committee

C. Harms   R. Lauber   H. Rampacher   W. Ehrenberger

Contents

Medical Informatics

Formal Methods II - Languages and Verification

Applications

List of Contributors

R. Belschner
Daimler Benz AG
FT2/EA, HPC T721
D - 70546 Stuttgart

Piergiorgio Bertoli
Istituto per la Ricerca Scientifica
  e Tecnologica (IST)
I - 38050 Povo, Trento

Gino Biondi
Ansaldo Segnalamento Ferroviario
Via dei Pescatori 35
I -16129 Genova

Sandro Bologna
ENEA C.R. Casaccia
Via Anguillarese 301
I - 00060 Roma

Rocco Bove
ENEA C.R. Casaccia
Via Anguillarese 301
I - 00060 Roma

Aarnout Brombacher
University of Technology
P.O. Box 513
NL - 5600 MB Eindhoven

Alessandro Cimatti
Istituto per la Ricerca Scientifica
  e Tecnologica (IST)
I - 38050 Povo, Trento

Ferdinand J. Dafelmair
TÜV Energie- und Systemtechnik
Westend Street 199
D - 80686 Munich

Vincent David
LETI (CEA - Advanced
  Technologies)
DEIN - CEA/Saclay
F - 91191 Gif sur Yvette Cedex

Jean Delcoigne
LETI (CEA - Advanced
  Technologies)
DEIN - CEA/Saclay
F - 91191 Gif sur Yvette Cedex

Fokko van Dijk
Holland Railconsult
P.O. Box 2855
NL - 3500 GW Utrecht

E. Dilger
Robert Bosch GmbH
Postfach 106050
D - 70049 Stuttgart

Giovanni Dioppa
ENEA C.R. Casaccia
Via Anguillarese 301
I - 00060 Roma

Rolf Drechsler
Albert-Ludwigs-University
Institute of Computer Science
Am Flughafen 17
D - 79110 Freiburg im Breisgau

Wan Fokkink
University of Wales Swansea
Singleton Park
Swansea SA2 8PP
United Kingdom

Alceu Heinke Frigeri
Fachbereich Elektrotechnik
Fernuniversität
Elberfelderstrasse
D - 58095 Hagen

T. Führer
Robert Bosch GmbH
Postfach 106050
D - 70049 Stuttgart

W. Geisselhardt
Gerhard-Mercator-University
Duisburg
Dept. of Dataprocessing
Faculty of Electrical Engineering
D - 47057 Duisburg

Fausto Giunchiglia
Istituto per la Ricerca Scientifica
  e Tecnologica (IST)
I - 38050 Povo, Trento

Janusz Gorski
Department of Applied Informatics
Technical University of Gdansk
Narutowicza 11/2
PL - 80-952 Gdansk

Timm Grams
Fachhochschule Fulda
Fachbereich Elektrotechnik
Marquardstraße 35
D - 36039 Fulda

S. Gritzalis
Department of Information and
  Communication Systems
University of the Aegean
30 Voulgaroktonou Street
GR - 11472 Athens

Wolfgang Halang
Fachbereich Elektrotechnik
Fernuniversität
Elberfelderstraße
D - 58084 Hagen

B. Hedenetz
Daimler Benz AG
FT2/EA, HPC T721
D - 70546 Stuttgart

Maritta Heisel
Institut für Verteilte Systeme
Fakultät für Informatik
Otto-von-Guerike-Universität
Magdeburg
D - 39016 Magdeburg

H. Hilmer
Gerhard-Mercator-University
Dept. of Information Processing
Faculty of Mechanical Engineering
D - 47057 Duisburg

Philippe Hilsenkopf
Framatome IT/LA
Tour Framatome
F - 92400 Courbevoie

Kevin Hollingworth
Centre for Software Reliability
Department of Computing Science
University of Newcastle upon Tyne
NE1 7RU
United Kingdom

Andrew Hutchison
Department of Computer Science
University of Cape Town
Private Bag
7700 Rondebosch
South Africa

J. Iliadis
Department of Information and
   Communication Systems
University of the Aegean
30 Voulgaroktonou Street
GR - 11472 Athens

Peter Isacsson
Q-Labs AB
Ideon Research Park
S - 22370 Lund

Silvije Jovalekic
University of Applied Science
Jakobstraße 6
D - 72458 Albstadt

Jeff Joyce
Raytheon Systems Canada, Ltd.
13951 Bridgeport Road
CAN-Richmond, BC V6V 1J6
Canada

P. Kan
Department of Computing
Imperial College
180 Queens Gate
London SW7 2BZ
United Kingdom

Niels Kirkegaard
IFAD
Forskerparken 10
DK - 5230 Odense

Bert Knegtering
Honeywell Safety Management
   Systems
P.O. Box 116
NL - 5223 AS 's-Hertogenbosch

H.-D. Kochs
Gerhard-Mercator-University
Duisburg
Deptartmt. of Information Processing
Faculty of Mechanical Engineering
D - 47057 Duisburg

Gea Kolk
Holland Railconsult
PO Box 2855
NL - 3500 GW Utrecht

Floor Koornneef
Delft University of Technology
Safety Science Group
Kanaalweg 2b
NL - 2628 EB Delft

K. Lano
Department of Computing
Imperial College
180 Queens Gate
London SW7 2BZ
United Kingdom

M. Lenord
Gerhard-Mercator-University
Deptartmt. of Information Processing
Faculty of Mechanical Engineering
D - 47057 Duisburg

Evelyne Leret
EDF/DER
6, quai Watier
BP 49
F - 78401 Chatou

Peter Liggesmeyer
Corporate Technology
Siemens AG
Otto Hahn Ring 6
D - 81730 München

Arndt Lindner
Institut für Sicherheitstechnologie
Forschungsgelände
D - 85748 Garching

Nicolas Martin-Vivaldi
Q-Labs AB
Ideon Research Park
S - 22370 Lund

Agathe Merceron
Basser of Computer Science
University of Sydney
Madsen Building F09
Sydeney NSW 2006
Australia

Bas A. de Mol
Academic Medical Center
Deptmt. Cardiopulmonary Surgery
Meibergdreef 9
NL-1105 AZ Amsterdam Zuidoost

Giorgio Mongardi
Ansaldo Segnalamento Ferroviario
   (ASF)
Via dei Pescatori 35
I - 16129 Genova

Benny Graft Mortensen
IFAD
Forskerparken 10
DK - 5230 Odense

B. Müller
Robert Bosch GmbH
Postfach 106050
D - 70049 Stuttgart

Monika Müllerburg
GMD
Schloss Birlinghoven
D - 53754 Sankt Augustin

Bartosz Nowicki
Department of Applied Informatics
Technical University of Gdansk
Narutowicza 11/2
PL - 80-952 Gdansk

V. Oikonomou
Department of Informatics
T.E.I of Athens
Ag.Spiridonos St.
GR - 12243 Aegaleo

Alain Ourghanlian
EDF/DER
6, quai Watier
BP 49
F - 78401 Chatou

Philippe Paris
Framatome IT/LA
Tour Framatome
F - 92400 Courbevoie

G. Michele Pinna
Dipartimento di Matematica
Universita degli Studi di Siena
Via del Capitano 15
I - 53100 Siena

Carmen Porzia
Ansaldo Segnalamento Ferroviario
Via dei pescatori, 35
I - 16129 Genova

Thomas Ringler
University of Stuttgart
Instistute for Industrial Automation
and Software Engineering
Pfaffenwaldring 47
D - 70569 Stuttgart

Bernd Rist
Eff-Eff Company
Joh.-Mauthe-Str. 14
D - 72458 Albstadt

Dario Romano
Ansaldo Segnalamento Ferroviario
(ASF)
Via dei Pescatori 35
I - 16129 Genova

Martin Rothfelder
Corporate Technology
Siemens AG
Otto Hahn Ring 6
D - 81730 München

Heinrich Rust
Lehrstuhl für Software Systemtechnik
BTU
Postfach 101344
D - 03013 Cottbus

Krysztof Sacha
Warsaw University of Technology
Institute of Control and Computation
Engineering
ul. Nowowiejeska 15/19
Pl - 00-665 Warszawa

Amer Saeed
Centre for Software Reliability
Department of Computing Science
University of Newcastle upon Tyne
NE1 7RU
United Kingdom

Francesca Saglietti
Institut für Sicherheitstechnologie
Forschungsgelände
D - 85748 Garching

A.Sanchez
CINVESTAV-Guadalajara
Abdo Postal 31-438
Guadalajara 45550
Mexico

Thomas Santen
Institut für Verteilte Systeme
Fakultät für Informatik
Otto-von-Guerike-Universität
D - 39016 Magdeburg

Erwin Schoitsch
Österreichisches Forschungszentrum
Seibersdorf
A - 2444 Seibersdorf

Gerald Sonneck
Österreichisches Forschungszentrum
Seibersdorf
A - 2444 Seibersdorf

J. Steiner
University of Stuttgart
Institute for Industrial Automation
    and Software Engineering
Pfaffenwaldring 47
D-70569 Stuttgart

Lorenzo Strigini
Centre for Software Reliability
City University
Northampton Square
London EC1V 0HB
United Kingdom

Fernando Torielli
Ansaldo Segnalamento Ferroviario
    (ASF)
Via dei Pescatori 35
I - 16129 Genova

Paolo Traverso
Istituto per la Ricerca Scientifica
    e Tecnologica (IST)
I - 38050 Povo, Trento

Paul van de Ven
Holland Railconsult
P.O. Box 2855
NL - 3500 GW Utrecht

Bas van Vlijmen
Utrecht University
Heidelberglaan 8
NL - 3584 CS Utrecht

Michael Wallbaum
Department of Computer Science 4
University of Technology
Ahornstrasse 55
D - 52056 Aachen

Kirsten Winter
GMD FIRST
Rudower Chaussee 5
D - 12489 Berlin

Ken Wong
University of British Columbia
Department of Computer Science
CAN-Vancouver, BC V6T 1Z4
Canada

Formal Methods I

Analysis and Specification

CoRSA - A Constraint Based Approach to Requirements and Safety Analysis

Kevin Hollingworth and Amer Saeed

Centre for Software Reliability, Dept. of Computing Science, University of Newcastle upon Tyne, NE1 7RU, UK. E-mail:K.J.Hollingworth@ncl.ac.uk

Abstract. In this paper a novel approach for safety analysis of embedded systems is proposed, based on modelling and analysing a system in terms of constraints.

The main contributions of the reported work are: the introduction of a notation for modelling entities of the physical environment and controller, based on expressing state transition models as constraints; and providing procedures for the analysis of these models by resolution of a series of constraint satisfaction problems. In addition the work provides a systematic framework for modelling and analysis in terms of constraints, and can be realised in a constraint based programming language.

1 Introduction

In this paper a novel approach for safety analysis is proposed, based upon modelling embedded systems in terms of state transition model, expressed as a set of constraints. Procedures are then defined for the analysis of liveliness and safety properties of such constraint models based upon the resolution of constraint satisfaction problems.

Within the development life-cycle, of embedded systems, studies and experience suggest that the requirements phase is the major source of errors leading to unacceptable levels of risk [1]. Safety analysis offers the potential to determine whether the risk associated with a computing system is acceptable in relation to overall system risk, in the context of defined failure assumptions [2]. The objectives of safety analysis during the phase of requirements analysis are two fold: i) provide evidence that the risk associated with the requirements specification is acceptable; ii) provide guidance for the inclusion of risk reduction strategies, thereby producing more robust requirements specifications.

1.1 Safety Analysis for Embedded Systems

Approaches proposed for safety analysis can be placed into three groups.

Modified safety techniques. Variants of traditional safety analysis techniques have been proposed for software specifications and have been developed for most stages of the software development cycle, including: FMECA for requirements specifications [3], modified HAZOPs for designs [4], FTA for source code [5].

These techniques were developed for models of conventional technologies to examine the relationships between failure behaviours and hazards, these techniques are less effective for software models.

Formal techniques. Formal techniques have been advocated for several stages in the development of embedded systems [6, 7, 8, 9]. These studies have shown benefits can arise from the application of formal techniques. However, they have also illustrated some of the drawbacks. The particular needs of safety properties have not been used to simplify the analysis, nor have efficient procedures been identified for the modelling and analysis of failure behaviours.

Novel techniques. Techniques based on a combination of formal and safety analysis techniques have been proposed [10, 11, 12].

None of the approaches provide a coherent automated method for modelling and analysis of safety properties and failures, for the early stages of the development of embedded systems.

1.2 Constraint Based Approaches for System Development

A constraint satisfaction problem (CS-problem) consists of a set of variables, for each variable a domain and a set of constraints restricting the values that the variables can take. A solution to a CS-problem is where all the variables are assigned a value and the constraints evaluate to true.

The relationship between constraint satisfaction and model checking can be viewed as an examination of a state space in order to determine the validity of specified properties. Early application of constraints to system development was to model security rules and real-time distributed systems [13, 14].

More recently, constraint satisfaction has been proposed as an approach for confirmation of consistency and verification of established modelling notations [15, 16].

CoRSA: Language and Analysis Techniques For the development of the Constraint based approach to Requirements and Safety Analysis (CoRSA), the conceptual framework proposed by the ATMOSPHERE project [17] is adopted. The languages and techniques of CoRSA will be based on the notions of constraints and resolution of a constraint satisfaction problem (CS-problem).

CoRSA: Modelling
The behaviour of a system will be modelled as a set of constraints describing a state-transition system, three categories of constraints are defined. The behaviour of a model will be partitioned into modes (normative and failure), similar to the approach used for Interactors [10]. Time is represented in the model by interpreting the states of the system as time slices, each being associated with a unit of time [14].

CoRSA: Analysis
The consistency of a CoRSA model will be determined by ensuring that there

is at least one solution to the CS-problem, obtained by the composition of all the constraints.

The verification and safety analysis of a CoRSA model can be conducted by using a fix-point definition to obtain all the reachable states of the CoRSA model, and confirm that these states exclude system hazards.

Case Study: Gas Burner The gas burner benchmark example [6, 8, 18] is extended by including some redundant components to explore safety analysis for a simple fault-tolerant system.

The plant of the gas burner, typically, consists of the following components:a gas chamber, in which concentration of gas can build up and an inlet pipe. The plant interface consists of; a flame sensor, which detects the presence of a flame; a flow sensor, which detects whether or not gas is flowing; an on/off safety valve that can be used to stop gas flowing into the chamber. The control system monitors the gas chamber and regulates the flow of gas.

Section 2, provides an overview of the language and process model. Section 3, presents an overview of the realisation of CoRSA in a constraint based programming language (CBL). Finally, Section 4 draws some conclusions and outlines directions for future work.

2   The CoRSA Approach

In this section, we present the CoRSA approach to the analysis of safety requirements. The presentation is structured into three parts, firstly the language.

2.1   The CoRSA language

Firstly the block template notation will be discussed, the textual language will then be introduced.

The block template notation Figure 2 shows a CoRSA block template. Once a template has been produced for the system this can easily be transformed into a CSP via the CoRSA textual language. Within the template the Declarations section contains all the information needed to define the variables and domains. The Modes section declares a number of labels for behaviour modes. At least three modes will always be defined these being INIT, GLOBAL and HAZARDS. The definition of the mode constraints are placed in the Constraints section.The INIT mode contains all initial state constraints, the Global mode contains those constraints that are always used. The Hazards mode contains all the constraints describing the system's hazards. All modes are divided into transition and invariant constraints. Finally other modes define particular behaviour traits.

CoRSA textual language The fields of a CoRSA template are completed using a simple textual language. This language enables an analyst to define constraints over the value of declared variables in their current and or successor state. A primitive constraint is a mathematical expression over the variables; primitive constraints can be composed using the standard logical operators. The underlying semantics of this textual language is in terms of a set of current/successor state pairs. A program in the CoRSA textual language defines a CS-problem. A completed CoRSA template can be translated into a number of programs in the textual language, the execution of these programs corresponds to the analysis of the CoRSA template.

2.2   CoRSA Analysis Procedures

CoRSA and state transition models A CoRSA template can be related to a state transition model, M, as a 5-tuple :-

$$M = \langle InitialState, MInvState, MTransPairs, HInvState, HTransPairs \rangle$$

where $InitialState$ is the set of current/successor state pairs satisfying the initial state constraints, $MInvState$ is the set of states satisfying the invariants, $MTranPairs$ is the set of current/successor state pairs that satisfy the transitions, $HInvState$ is the set of states satisfying the hazard invariants and $HTranPairs$ the set of current/successor state pairs satisfying the hazard transitions.

The set of all traces for machine M can be defined as: -

$$Trace[[M]] = \{tr \; \epsilon \; (MInvState \cap MTransPairs)^* \qquad (1)$$
$$|tr(0) \; \epsilon \; InitialState \wedge \; \forall i \; \epsilon\{1,\dots,len(tr)\}$$
$$: (tr(i-1)(2) = tr(i)(1))\}$$

The set of all reachable pairs of machine M can be defined as: -

$$Pair[[M]] = \{P \; \epsilon \; MInvState \; | \; \exists \; tr \; \epsilon \; Trace[[M]] : \qquad (2)$$
$$\exists \; i \; \epsilon\{0,\dots,len(tr)) : P = tr(i) \; \vee \; P = (tr(i-1)(2), tr(i)(1))\}$$

Analysis of safe behaviour

- Postulate a set of invariants $PInv$ that characterises the fixed point for the set of states. $PostulateInv$ and $PostulateInv'$ denote the sets of states that satisfy $PInv$ in the current and successor states.
- Confirm that the initial state satisfies the fixed point invariants

$$InitialState \; \subset \; PostulateInv \qquad (3)$$

- Confirm that $PInv$ is a fixed point, $PInv$ is a fixed point iff: -

$$(MTransPairs \; \cap \; MInvState \; \cap \; PostulateInv) \; \subset \; PostulateInv' \quad (4)$$

- $FPair$ is a set of current and successor state pairs that define a fixed point

$$FPair[[M]] = MInvState \; \cap \; MTransPairs \; \cap \; PostulateInv \quad (5)$$

Hazardous behaviour For a machine M we can define hazardous behaviour: -

$$Hazard[[M]] = HTransPairs \cup HInvState \cup HInvState' \qquad (6)$$

It is sufficient to show that: -

$$FPair[[M]] \cap Hazard[[M]] = \{\} \qquad (7)$$

The approach adopted, in equations 5–9, is similar to the incremental invariance rule proposed by Manna and Pneuli [19].

Analysis as a CS-problem Recall, the domain of a CS-problem is a pair of states. The checks in Section 2.2, see Equations 3,4 and 7, can be expressed by showing no solution exists for: -

- the initial state constraints and the negated constraints for the postulated invariants in the current state.
- the transition constraints, invariant constraints, the postulate invariant constraints for the current state and the negated constraints for the postulated invariants in the successor state.
- finally, the transition and invariant constraints, the postulate invariant constraints for the current and successor states, and the hazard constraints.

2.3   CoRSA Process Model : A Case Study

The activities of CoRSA, see Figure 1, start with the external and elicitation activities and progress through to analysis.

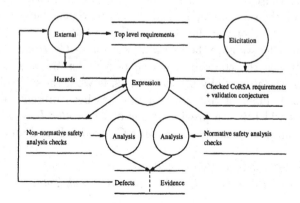

Fig. 1. CoRSA Process Model

CoRSA external activities produce a set of hazard definitions. This is achieved through performing preliminary hazard analysis on the top level requirements. As defects in the top level requirements may be highlighted by subsequent analysis activities, the external activities include a rectification process that corrects any defects found. Preliminary hazard analysis for the gas burner was conducted resulting in the following hazard being identified:- *If there is a gas leak for more than ten consecutive states there is a hazard state.*

CoRSA elicitation activities model the top level requirements in terms of the CoRSA templates and establish validation conjectures. The product of this modelling can then be automatically checked, using a CBL, for consistency using validation checks. Defects found are fed back otherwise a checked CoRSA requirements and validation conjectures document is produced.

For the plant the following variables have been identified:- *Gas* which represents whether the gas is on or off, *Flame* which represents whether there is a flame or not, *Leak* (initially set to no) which indicates a leak, *Leak Total* (initially set to 0) which is the number of units the gas burner has been leaking for and *Old Leak Total* (initially set to 0) which contains the previous *Leak Total*. A constant has also been identified this being *Maximum Leak Duration* and is set at 10 time units.

For the plant a number of invariants have been identified these include:-
There is a Leak if and only if the Gas is on and there is no Flame (PI1)
If there is a Leak then Leak total is equal to the Old Leak Total plus 1 (PI2)
If there is no Leak then the Leak Total is reset to 0 (PI3)

Also the following transition has been identified:-
The Old Leak Total in the next state equals the current Leak Total (PT1)

For the plant interface we have the following variables:- *Gas Sensor* (initially set to no) which senses the presence of gas or not, *Flame Sensor* (initially set to no) which senses the presence of a flame or not and *Safety Valve* (initially set to off) which is a valve that can shut the gas off as a safety precaution.

For the controller we have the following variables:- *Controller Leak* (initially set to no) which is the controllers notion of whether there is a leak or not, *Controller Leak Total* (initially set to 0) which is what the controller perceives to be the total number of time units a leak has been present and *Controller Old Leak Total* which is the previous value of *Controller Leak Total*. Also the following constant has been identified:-*Max Controller Leak Duration* (set to 6) units.

Invariants over the controller include :-
If there is no Controller Leak then the Controller Leak Total is reset to 0 (CI3)

The transitions for the plant interface include:-
The Gas Sensor in the next state is equal to the current state of Gas (IT1)

Finally the remaining transitions over the controller and plant are CT1, CT2 , CT3 (see Figure 2). Note that in Figure 2 a variable without an apostrophe appended denotes the current state and with denotes the successor state.

Variables *Leak, Leak Total, Old Leak Total, Gas Sensor, Flame Sensor, Controller Leak Total* and *Controller Old Leak Total* are set to an initial value of 0. These constraints will be referred to as In1,In2,In3,In4,In5,In6 and In7. The *Safety Valve* is set to an initial value of 1 (open) and the constraint will be referred to In8. The CoRSA template for the case study can be seen in Figure 2.

CoRSA expression activities are concerned with the expression of information needed to perform safety analysis, this includes the expression of hazards, failure behaviours, normative and non-normative safety analysis checks. This information is expressed as a program in the CoRSA textual language. These programs are in the form of a CS-problem.

Following is the hazard identified for the gas burner in terms of the CoRSA language:- $Inv : (LeakTotal >: MaximumLeakDuration)$.

Also a number of invariants must be postulated before analysis can be performed, these postulated invariants are:-
If the Leak Total > 0 then the Controller Leak
    Total must be >= The Leak Total - 1   (IP1)
If Leak Total > Maximum Leak Duration - 1
    then the Gas must be off   (IP2)
If Controller Leak Total > Maximum Controller Leak
    Total + 1 then Safety Valve should be on   (IP3)

Now the normative safety analysis checks can be stated in terms of the CoRSA language :-
```
Declarations Decl
not(Current:IP1 and Current:IP2 and Current:IP3) and (Current:In1 and
Current:In2 and ... and In8)
```
and checked by showing there are no solutions to the given constraints. The other checks can be shown to be similar.

CoRSA analysis activities translate the CS-problems produced by the expression activity into CBL programs and execution produces either evidence that the specifications are safe or a number of defects.

3   Realisation and Analysis

In this section an overview of the realisation of CoRSA in a CBL, namely OZ [20], will be presented in terms of normative safety analysis checks for the case study. This will be followed by a discussion of non-normative safety analysis checks.

```
┌─ Declarations ──────────────────────────┌──────────────┐────┐
│                                          │  GAS-BURNER  │    │
│                                          └──────────────┘    │
```

Constants:

Maxleakduration	10	Maximum Leak Duration
Maxcleakduration	6	Maximum Controller Leak Duration

Variables:

Gas	Bool	Gas On/Off
Flame	Bool	Flame yes/no
Leak	Bool	Leak yes/no
Ltotal	Int	Total consecutive leaks
Oltotal	Int	Old leak total
Sgas	Bool	Gas Sensor On/Off
Sflame	Bool	Flame sensor yes/no
Safetyvalve	Bool	Safety valve open/shut
Cleak	Int	Controller leak
Coltotal	Int	Controller old leak total
Cltotal	Int	Controller leak total

Modes:

NORMATIVE	Normal behaviour
NON-NORMATIVE1	Gas sensor failure
NON-NORMATIVE2	Safety Valve fails

── Constraints ──

GLOBAL

Invariants:

iff:	Gas=1 and Flame=0	action: Leak=1	PI1
if:	Leak=1	action: Ltotal=Oltotal+1	PI2
if:	Leak=0	action: Ltotal=0	PI3
iff:	Sgas=1 and Sflame=0	action: Cleak=1	CI1
if:	Cleak=1	action: Cltotal=Coltotal+1	CI2
if:	Cleak=0	action: Cltotal=0	PI3

Transitions:

action: Oltotal'=Ltotal			PT1
action: Coltotal'=Cltotal			CT3
action: Sflame'=Flame			IT2
if:	Safetyvalve=0	action: Gas'=0	CT1

INIT

action:	Leak=0	action:	Ltotal=0	action:	Oltotal=0
action:	Sgas=0	action:	Sflame=0	action:	Safetyvalve=1
action:	Cltotal=0	action:	Coltotal=0		

HAZARDS

action: Ltotal > Maxleakduration

NORMATIVE

Transitions:

action: Sgas'=Gas			IT1
if:	Cltotal>Maxcleakduration	action: Safetyvalve'=0	CT2

NON-NORMATIVE1

Transitions:

action: Sgas'=0			IT1
if:	Cltotal>Maxcleakduration	action: Safetyvalve'=0	CT2

NON-NORMATIVE2

Transitions:

action: Sgas'=Gas			IT1
if:	Cltotal>Maxcleakduration	action: Safetyvalve'=1	CT2

Fig. 2. Gas Burner Template

3.1 Normative Safety Checks

The First step in producing the OZ code from the gas burner template is the expression of the *Constants* and *Variables* sections. To simplify the code two variables have been used for each variable name on the template. The first variable, appended with the number 1, represents the current state while the same name with a number 2 appended represents the successor (or next) state. An OZ code extract for integer (in this example a range), boolean and constant declarations for the gas burner is:-

```
BooleanCurrent[Gas1 Flame1 Leak1 Safetyvalve1] = BooleanCurrent
BooleanNext[Gas2 Flame2 Leak2 Safetyvalve2] = BooleanNext
RangeCurrent[Ltotal1 Oltotal1 Cltotal1] = RangeCurrent
RangeNext[Ltotal2 Oltotal2 Cltotal2] = RangeNext
Time[Maxcleakduration] = Time
{FD.dom 0#1 BooleanCurrent}
{FD.dom 0#1 BooleanNext}
{FD.dom 0#200 RangeCurrent}
{FD.dom 0#200 RangeNext}
Maxcleakduration = 6
```

Once all the variables have been declared the constraints over these can be implemented. First the initial state constraints can be added:-

```
% Initial state constraints
Leak1=:0          Ltotal1=:0   Oltotal1=:0
Safetyvalve1=:0  Cltotal1=:0
```

The global invariants PI1 and PI2 can now also be implemented. Note that, as invariants hold over both the current and successor states, two constraints are required for each invariant. Also PI1 is an example of an `iff` in the CoRSA template while PI2 is an example of an `if`:-

```
% Plant Invariant Constraint 1 - PI1
{FD.equi {FD.conj Gas1=:1 Flame1=:0} Leak1=:1 1}
{FD.equi {FD.conj Gas2=:1 Flame2=:0} Leak2=:1 1}
% Plant Invariant Constraint 2 - PI2
{FD.impl Leak1=:1 Ltotal1=:Oltotal1+1 1}
{FD.impl Leak2=:1 Ltotal2=:Oltotal2+1 1}
```

An example of global transitions, in this case CT1 and PT1, are shown as:-

```
% Controller Transition Constraint 1 - CT1
{FD.impl Cltotal1 >: Maxcleakduration Safetyvalve2=:0 1}
% Plant Transition Constraint 1 - PT1
Oltotal2=:Ltotal1
```

Once all constraints are entered, including postulated invariant constraints, OZ can be used to perform the safety analysis checks by feeding the program to the solver. To perform the normative safety analysis check stated in terms of the CoRSA language, we can see that not all the constraints are required. The constraints not required by the check are therefore commented out. The solver is then used to resolve the CS-problem. If no solution is returned then the check has been passed. If a solution is obtained through solving the CS-problem then the result can be used to either correct problems in the code or to reason about the specification.

3.2 Non-normative Safety Checks

Non-normative analysis checks are performed in a similar way to normative. If, for example, constraints IT1 and CT2 in the NON-NORMATIVE1 section are used instead of those in the NORMATIVE behaviour section the constraints simulate a gas burner where the gas sensor has failed. Performing the safety analysis checks will then show that the system is not safe. Given the results it can be easily shown that the system can be made more robust by adding a pressure sensor and the appropriate constraints. First a new variable, *Psensor*, is added. The pressure sensor is intended to indicate when the pressure in the gas chamber breaches a particular threshold. In this case we will assume that the pressure in the chamber is proportional to that of `Ltotal` and that we want the sensor to toggle when it reaches the value of *Maxleakduration-limit*. To include the behaviour of the pressure sensor the following constraint has to be added to the normative section of the template:-

`if:Ltotal>=(Maxleakduration-limit) action:Psensor=1 (PS1).`

Also the constraint CT2 must be altered in the normative and non-normative behaviour mode sections as well as adding two new non-normative modes. CT2 in the normative section should be altered to:

`if:Cltotal>Maxcleakduration or Psensor=1 action:Safetyvalve'=0`

CT2 should also be altered similarly in the NON-NORMATIVE1 and NON-NORMATIVE2 sections. The new non-normative modes are NON-NORMATIVE3, where the pressure sensor fails and NON-NORMATIVE4, where the pressure sensor and gas sensor fails. The pressure sensor can be made to behave non-normatively by altering the constraint PS1, in NON-NORMATIVE3 and NON-NORMATIVE4, to:

`action:Psensor=0.`

The gas burner can now be shown to tolerate the failure of the gas sensor or pressure sensor by performing the checks on behaviour modes NORMATIVE, NON-NORMATIVE1 and NON-NORMATIVE3. To show that the gas burner is not robust enough to tolerate both the gas sensor and pressure sensor failing the checks must be performed using the behaviour mode NON-NORMATIVE4; NON-NORMATIVE2 is not tolerated due to the valve failure.

4 Concluding Remarks

4.1 Discussion of Example

The example demonstrates several of the basic features of CoRSA: modelling (expression of simple initial, invariant and transition constraints) and analysis (derivation of the basic checks).

History Variables. The simplified gas burner study can be extended to the classical example, in which a hazard occurs if the gas has leaked for more than 20% of the last 60 time units. A boolean array of 60 slots could be used to record the leak history, two variables would be declared `CurrentHistory` and `OldHistory`.

Failure Mode Variables. Safety analysis, with respect to a particular class of failures, can be defined by introducing auxiliary variables for the failure modes and constraints. For example, for the gas sensor (`Sgas`) and pressure sensor (`Psensor`), two boolean variables are introduced GM and PM. The behaviour of the sensors are predicated on the value of the mode. For `Sgas` we would have the following transition constraints:

```
if: GM=0 action:Sgas'=Gas
if: GM=1 action:Sgas'=0
```

Similar transitions would be added for `Psensor`. Another variable (SF) could be introduced to model total number of sensor failures (assuming the flame sensor does not fail) by addition of the following invariant: `action: SF=GM+PM`. This could be used to define the failure assumptions: no sensor failures, SF=0; at most one sensor failure, SF<=1.

4.2   Conclusions and Future Work

A systematic and incremental approach to modelling and analysis of safety properties is provided by the process model and the axiomatic style of the CoRSA textual language. The formulation of the CoRSA semantics provides an intuitive conceptual model and enables CoRSA to exploit analysis procedures for transition systems [21]. The CoRSA template supports modelling and analysis by organisation of the constraints into fields based on the checks and terms of the elements of a state transition model.

A key strength is that the analysis checks encoded in a CoRSA template can be translated into a series of executable CS-problems in a CBL. During the resolution of a CS-problem if unexpected solutions are identified these can be used to debug the CoRSA template, thereby providing a systematic approach to rectification. Once a CoRSA model has been expressed and analysed exploration of different failure assumptions and risk reduction strategies is supported by the flexibility of the notation.

An object-oriented variant of CoRSA is under investigation. The results of this work will be applied to a large-scale case study of a fuel management system.

On the expressibility of CoRSA, the main issue is better support for the expression and analysis of basic timing constraints [22], currently it is planned to provide such support through a macro notation. The CoRSA and other state-oriented models, e.g. Statecharts [23] and or event-oriented models e.g. Petri Nets [24] is a topic of further study.

Finally an objective comparison providing evidence on the improvement provided by CoRSA over alternative candidate methodologies needs to be performed. The gas burner example will be used as the basis for this comparison.

Acknowledgements

Kevin Hollingworth is funded as a CASE Research Student by the EPSRC and BAe Airbus Ltd.

References

[1] R. R. Lutz. Analyzing software requirements errors in safety-critical, embedded systems. In *Proceedings of the IEEE Symposium on Requirements Engineering*, pages 126–133, San Diego, California, January 1993.

[2] A. Saeed, R. de Lemos, and T. Anderson. Safety analysis of requirements specifications for safety-critical software. In *ISA Transactions*, volume 34, pages 283–295, 1995.

[3] R.Lutz and R.Woodhouse. Experience report: Contributions of SFMEA to requirements analysis. *ICRE*, 1996.

[4] J.A. McDermid and D. Pumfrey. A development of hazard analysis to aid software design. In *Proceedings of the Ninth Annual Conference on Computer Assurance (COMPASS '94)*, pages 17–25, Gaithersburg, MD, July 1994.

[5] N. G. Leveson, S. S. Cha, and T. J. Shimeall. Safety verification of Ada programs using software fault trees. *IEEE Software*, pages 48–59, July 1991.

[6] J.M. Rushby. Formal methods and certification of critical systems. Technical Report CSL-93-7, SRI International, Menlo Park, CA., December 1993.

[7] B. Dutere and V. Stavridou. Formal requirements of analysis of an avionics control system. *IEEE Transactions on Software Engineering*, SE-23(1):267–278, May 1997.

[8] A. P. Ravn, H. Rischel, and K. M. Hansen. Specifying and verifying requirements of real-time systems. *IEEE Transactions on Software Engineering*, SE-19(1):41–55, January 1993.

[9] R. de Lemos A. Saeed and T. Anderson. The role of formal methods in the requirements analysis of safety-critical systems: a train set example. In *Proceedings of the 21st Symposium on Fault-Tolerant Computing*, Montreal, Canada, June 1991.

[10] M. Cepin et al. An object-based approach to modelling and analysis of failure properties. In P. Daniel, editor, *16th International conference on Safety Reliability and Security (SAFECOMP'97)*, pages 281–294, York, UK, September 1997. Springer-Verlag.

[11] C.J.Garrett, S.B.Guarro, and G.E.Apostolakis. The dynamic flowgraph methodology for assessing the dependability of embedded siftware systems. *IEEE Transactions on Systems, Man and Cybernetics*, 25(5):824–840, May 1995.

[12] J.D.Reese and N.G.Leveson. *Software Deviation Analysis*. PhD thesis, UCI, 1996.

[13] F. C. Furteck. *Constraints and Compromise*, pages 189–204. Foundations of Secure Computation. Academic Press, 1978.

[14] F. C. Furteck. Specification and verification of real-time, distributed systems using the theory of constraints. In W. Bibel and R. Kowlaski, editors, *5th Conference on Automated Deduction*, pages 110–125, Les Arcs, France, July 1980. Springer-Verlag.

[15] Y. Lebbah. Consistency checking by type inference and constraint satisfaction. In P. Daniel, editor, *16th International conference on Safety Reliability*

and Security (SAFECOMP'97), pages 253–264, York, UK, September 1997. Springer-Verlag.

[16] S. Lajeunesse and A. Rauzy. Using the constraint programming system Toupie for qualitative analysis of industrial systems failures. In *ESREL'97 International Conference on Safety and Reliability*, pages 2021–2028, Lisbon Portugal, June 1997.

[17] K. Kronlof, editor. *Method Integration: concepts and case studies.* John Wiley and Sons Ltd, 1993.

[18] J. Gorski and B.Nowicki. Safety analysis based on object-oriented modelling of critical systems. In E. Schoitsch, editor, *15th International conference on Safety Reliability and Security (SAFECOMP'96)*, pages 46–60, Vienna, Austria, October 1996.

[19] Z.Manna and A.Pnueli. *Temporal Verification of Reactive Systems: Safety.* Springer-Verlag, 1995.

[20] M. Muller et al. *DFKI OZ*, 1995.

[21] Z.Manna and A.Pnueli. *Models for Reactivity*, volume 30. Acta Informatica, 1993.

[22] B. Dasarathy. Timing constraints of real-time systems: Constructs for expressing them, methods of validating them. *IEEE Transactions on Software Engineering*, SE-11(1):80–86, January 1985.

[23] D. Harel. Statecharts: A visual formalism for complex systems. *Science of Computer Programming*, 8:231–274, 1987.

[24] J.L.Paterson. *Petri Net Theory and the Modeling of Systems.* Prentice-Hall, 1981.

An Agenda for Specifying Software Components with Complex Data Models

Kirsten Winter[1], Thomas Santen[1], and Maritta Heisel[2]

[1] GMD FIRST,Rudower Chaussee 5, D-12489 Berlin, Germany,
kirsten.winter@first.gmd.de, santen@first.gmd.de
[2] Otto-von-Guericke-Universität Magdeburg, Fakultät für Informatik, Institut für Verteilte
Systeme, D-39016 Magdeburg, Germany, heisel@cs.uni-magdeburg.de

Abstract. We present a method to specify software for a special kind of safety-critical embedded systems, where sensors deliver low-level values that must be abstracted and pre-processed to express functional and safety requirements adequately. These systems are characterized by a *reference architecture*. The method is expressed as an *agenda*, which is a list of activities to be performed for setting up the software specification, complemented by validation conditions that help detect and correct errors. The specification language we use is a combination of the formal notation Z and the diagrammatic notation statecharts. Our approach not only provides detailed guidance to specifiers, but it is also part of a more general engineering concept for engineering safety-critical embedded systems that was developed in the ESPRESS project, a joint project of academia and industry.

1 ESPRESS: Engineering of Safety-Critical Embedded Systems

The work we present in this paper has been carried out in the context of the ESPRESS project during the last two years[1]. In ESPRESS, we investigate development methods for software to be used as part of safety-critical embedded systems. We favor the application of formal methods for this purpose. Even though every software-based system potentially benefits from the application of formal techniques, their use is of particular advantage for the development of safety-critical embedded systems, because the potential damage operators and developers have to envisage in case of malfunction may be much worse than the additional costs of applying formal techniques in system development.

Figure 1 shows the basic ESPRESS process model. The agenda presented in this paper guides the development of a requirements specification. Such a requirements specification is further validated and serves as a basis for safety analyses, test case generation, and software design.

We use the ESPRESS notation μSZ [1] to express the specifications developed with our agenda. This notation provides a semantically well-defined combination of the Statemate languages [6] (namely statecharts and activity charts), the formal specification language Z [15], and an extension of Z by temporal logics [2]. The Statemate languages and Z have been chosen for ESPRESS because of their relevance in industrial

---

[1] The ESPRESS project is a cooperation of industry and research institutes funded by the German ministry BMBF ("Förderschwerpunkt Softwaretechnologie", grant 01 IS 509 C6).

development process | **methodological guidance**
                                           | **of development steps**

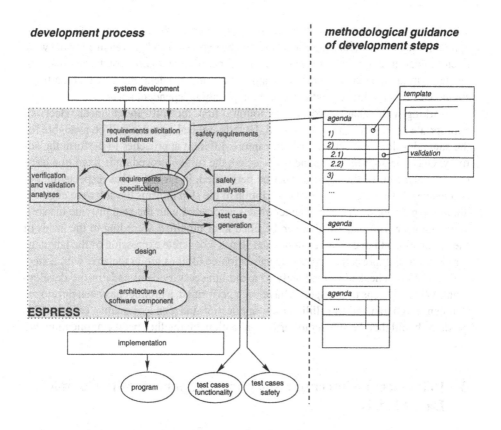

Fig. 1. Basic ESPRESS process model

contexts and their fairly good tool support. For reasons of space, we cannot systematically explain μSZ and its constituting languages; we only give an informal explanation of the constructs used in this paper as they appear.

2 Agendas

An agenda [7] gives guidance on how to perform a specific software development activity. It consists of a list of steps to be performed when carrying out some task in the context of software engineering. The result of the task will be a document expressed in a certain language. Agendas contain informal descriptions of the steps. With each step, *templates* of the language in which the result of the task is expressed are associated. The templates are instantiated when the step is performed. The steps listed in an agenda may depend on each other. Usually, they will have to be repeated to solve the given task. Agendas are presented as tables, see Figure 5. Agendas may be nested, and we call the "super-steps" *stages* (see Table 1).

Agendas are not only a means to guide software development activities. They also support quality assurance because the steps of an agenda may have validation conditions associated with them. These validation conditions state necessary conditions that the artifact must fulfill in order to serve its purpose properly. When formal techniques are applied, some of the validation conditions can be expressed and proven in a formal way. Such validation conditions are marked "⊢". Since the validation conditions that can be stated in an agenda are necessarily application independent, the developed artifact should be further validated with respect to application dependent needs.

Working with agendas proceeds as follows: first, the software engineer selects an appropriate agenda for the task at hand. Usually, several agendas will be available for the same development activity, which capture different approaches to perform the activity. Once the appropriate agenda is selected, the further procedure is fixed to a large extent. Each step of the agenda must be performed, in an order that respects the dependencies of steps. The informal description of the step informs the software engineer about the purpose of the step. The templates associated with the step provide the software engineer with patterns that can be filled in or modified according to the needs of the application at hand. The result of each step is a concrete expression of the language that is used to express the artifact. If validation conditions are associated with a step, they should be checked immediately to avoid unnecessary dead ends in the development. When all steps of the agenda have been performed, a product has been developed that can be guaranteed to fulfill certain application-independent quality criteria. This product should then be subject to further validation, taking the specific application into account.

3   Reference Architecture: Software Components with Complex Data Models

A reference architecture describes a class of software components that share common principles. We sketch the reference architecture for embedded software components with complex data models, henceforth called CDM reference architecture. An instance of this class of software components, the safety-controller of a traffic light system, serves us to illustrate the agenda for that reference architecture. We introduce the traffic light system in Section 4.

Software components of embedded systems often have a relatively simple data model. Although a mathematical model of the requirements of such a system may be complex, e.g., a system of differential equations, and the resulting software may involve non-trivial algorithms, it is often possible to express the functional requirements as a direct relation between the values of controlled variables, which are measured by sensors, and values of manipulated variables. Examples are small automotive controllers, such as cruise control systems, or controllers of household appliance. In earlier work, we identified two reference architectures, called *cyclic software component* and *active sensors*, for systems with a simple data model. Agendas for these systems are described in [5, 9].

In the present paper, we consider software components that are characterized by the fact that the sensors deliver low-level values (e.g., sequences of "on" and "off" values), and for which no theory exists that relates them to the high-level notions as they are used by domain experts in their discourses about the problem domain. In such a situation, we cannot easily describe the requirements for a software component by a direct relation between sensor values and actuator commands. Instead, the sensor values must first be abstracted and interpreted appropriately to deduce the state of the technical system in which the software is embedded and which is modeled on a higher level of abstraction. Sometimes it is necessary to accumulate several consecutive sensor inputs. We use the term *controlled entities* to name the higher-level notions that represent abstractions of sensor value variations over time.

The relation between sensor values and actuator commands is then divided into two relations, one relation between sensor values and controlled entities, and a second relation between controlled entities and actuator commands. The CDM reference architecture shown in Figure 2 reflects these considerations. The two outermost components map technical data (e.g., a lamp being *on* or *off*) to "logical" data suitable for specifying the software component (e.g., a lamp being *on*, *off* or *flashing*). The specification of the software component that determines logical actuator commands based on logical sensor values consists of two parts: the *internal domain model* and the *regulator*.

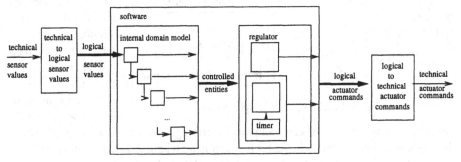

Fig. 2: The CDM reference architecture

The internal domain model derives the values of controlled entities. These entities describe the state of the controlled system in terms that are adequate to specify the control task on a level of abstraction as it is used by domain experts. The regulator specifies a relation between controlled entities and actuator commands in a "direct" way (similar to the relation between sensor values and actuator commands in simpler systems).

4 Case Study: Traffic Light Safety-Control

Most traffic light systems today are controlled by software. The software controller usually consists of two largely independent modules (see Figure 3): the phase control program and the safety controller. The phase control program receives signals about traffic flow from various sensors in the streets and sends commands to the switchboard to turn on and off the signal heads.

The second module, the safety controller, is responsible to guarantee that the *real* signals as shown by the signal heads allow only safe traffic flow at any time. To this end, it monitors not only the commands produced by the phase control, but it also receives sensor data from the signal heads about their current state relative to the last received switch command.

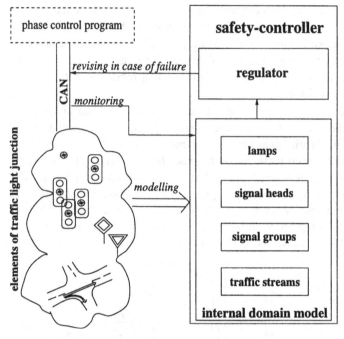

Fig. 3: Entities of a traffic light system

Figure 4 illustrates the interaction between phase control, safety control, and the switchboard. The upper half of the timing diagram shows the normal operation of the traffic light control. Every 500 ms, the phase control issues a burst of commands to the switchboard. The switchboard acknowledges these commands with a delay of less than 100 ms, which is the time the sensors in each lamp need to determine its working state. Acknowledgments come in pairs describing the state of the lamp relative to the latest switching command: one bit for each lamp tells whether it is unintentionally on (*uon*), a second bit whether it is unintentionally off (*uoff*). If neither an *uon* nor an *uoff* is acknowledged, then this indicates that the signal head shows the intended signal. If both bits are set, then faulty sensor data are received. The switchboard may also issue *uon* and *uoff* messages spontaneously if a failure occurs in the otherwise silent time between two command bursts.

The safety controller monitors all commands and acknowledgments. If it detects an unsafe state, it issues appropriate commands to the switchboard to re-establish a safe situation (see bottom of Figure 4). Our task is to specify such a controller with the following general requirements:

1. The controller is generic: it is parameterized with data describing the configuration of a traffic light junction.
2. The controller must detect all unsafe signal conditions. In particular, it may not assume that the phase control commands lead to safe signal conditions.
3. The controller must take appropriate action to establish a safe situation, such that an unsafe situation does not last for more than 300 ms.

The major objective of the specification is to *precisely* capture the meaning of a "safe condition" of a traffic junction *in general*, i.e., not for a particular junction only, but for an (almost) arbitrary configuration of lanes, traffic lights, etc. A detailed analysis of the problem reveals that it is appropriate to base a judgment on the junction's safety condition on the signals issued for the different *traffic streams*. A traffic stream is the logical entity of all vehicles (or pedestrians) entering and leav-

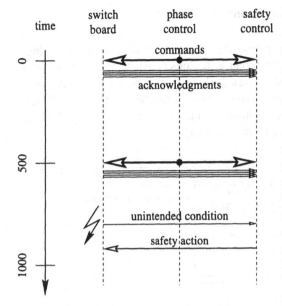

Fig. 4: Interaction between the modules

ing the junction at the same points, e.g., the stream of vehicles entering at one point and turning left. Several traffic streams may share the same lane. Based on this abstraction, judging the safety condition of a junction amounts to considering the concurrently open traffic streams and the timing requirements between opening and closing traffic streams.

The safety controller can judge the safety condition only based on its observation of the switching commands of the phase control and acknowledgments of the switchboard. To specify the action of the safety controller depending on the states of traffic streams, we first must describe how the flow of information about states of single lamps can be assembled to an *internal model* of the traffic junction in terms of useful abstractions such as signal heads (consisting of several lights), signal groups (which work synchronously), and traffic streams. This is actually the most complex part of the task.

The next section introduces an agenda to specify software components with such a complex data model and illustrates the application of the agenda to the case study.

5 Agenda for Software Components with Complex Data Models

The CDM agenda consists of three stages, shown in Table 1. In the first stage, the embedding of the software in its environment must be defined. This stage consists of defining the technical and the logical software interfaces, and the mappings between them. It is performed as described in [5],

Stage
1 Context embedding
2 Controlled entities
3 Software model construction

Table 1: Stages of the CDM agenda

and will not be discussed further in this paper (see [8] for a complete description). Stage 2 is characteristic for the CDM reference architecture that needs complex data models. It is described in more detail in Section 5.1. In the third stage, the internal domain model and the regulator must be specified (see Figure 2). Again, only the internal domain model is characteristic for the CDM reference architecture and hence discussed in more detail in Section 5.2. As for the specification of the regulator, we only note that it may contain two different kinds of components. "Passive" components are triggered by a change of some controlled entity, whereas "active" components are activated internally by the regulator when an internal timer times out.

5.1 Sub-Agenda for the Definition of Controlled Entities

The internal domain model has to construct the controlled entities based on the logical sensor values. The regulator must produce the logical actuator commands from the controlled entities, see Figure 2. Figure 5 shows the agenda for defining controlled entities. First, the appropriate entities must be identified and given a Z type ($CEtype_1, \ldots CEtype_n$). Step 2.1 also contains a template for an activity chart defining the overall data flow that occurs in the software component.

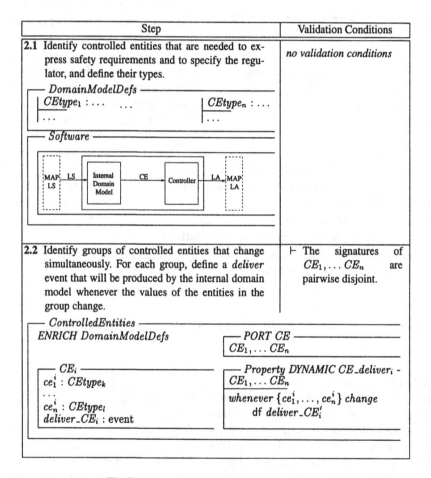

Fig. 5. Sub-agenda for definition of controlled entities

Step 2.2 defines the dynamics that must occur in connection with controlled entities: when the values of the controlled entities change, the regulator must be notified, because it may be necessary that new actuator commands must be determined. This is achieved by generating *events* that will cause the regulator to take appropriate actions. It is not necessary to define an event for each controlled entity. Instead, events are defined for *groups* of controlled entities that may change their values simultaneously, i.e., if one entity of the group changes its value, then the others *may* also change their values.

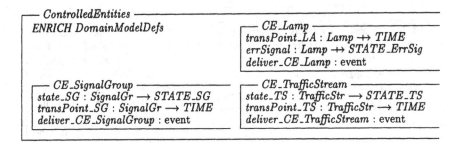

Fig. 6. Controlled entities for the safety

The schema *ControlledEntities* defines a *process class*. Process classes are the structuring entities of μSZ. They are containers for sets of plain Z declarations, of schema definitions, and of Statemate statecharts and activity charts. The schema definitions inside a class may have assigned certain *roles*. For example, the role of schema definitions introduced with the keyword *PORT* is to describe data variables that can be shared by a process with its environment.

In the process class *ControlledEntities*, the grouping of controlled entities is defined using the schemas CE_i. These groups of entities are collected in the port schema CE. The schema with the keyword *Property DYNAMIC* expresses that an event *deliver_CE_i* must be generated (df $deliver\_CE_i'$) whenever one of the corresponding controlled entities has changed its value.

Safety Controller. Step 2.1 of the CDM agenda requires us to identify entities that allow us to describe the requirements on the safety controller at an adequate level of abstraction. This task encompasses a detailed requirements analysis, and for the safety controller, it needed considerable effort to find a suitable set of entities that allows us to clearly express the control task. We found three important groups of failures that the safety controller may need to react to (c.f. Figure 3):

1. For single lamps, the controller must evaluate *uoff* and *uon* messages to record failures, and detect sensor failures such as omissions of acknowledgments and inconsistent sensor data.
2. For signal groups, the controller must decide whether a sequence of signals is admissible (e.g., in Germany, a transition from "red" to "green" must always go via a combined "red-and-yellow" signal) and whether timing constraints for single signals are satisfied.
3. For traffic streams, the controller must evaluate the safety of simultaneously open streams, and it must monitor intermediate green times, which are required, e.g., between closing a stream and opening a crossing stream that turns left.

In Step 2.1, we define the types describing the information about lamps, signal groups, and traffic streams, that the regulator needs to evaluate the three groups of failures. In Step 2.2, we use these types to specify three groups of controlled entities, as shown in Figure 6. The data of a particular traffic light junction are parameters to our specification. Therefore, the components of the groups *CE_Lamp*, *CE_SignalGroup*, and *CE_TrafficStream* are *functions* mapping identifiers of lamps, etc., to states or transition points. The transition point is the most recent point in time when the state of an element changed. The type *STATE_ErrSig* has four elements: *ok*, *uoff*, *uon*,

Step	Validation Conditions
3.1.1 Identify abstraction layers of controlled entities, and associate exactly one such layer to each controlled entity. ── *AbstractionLayer$_i$* ──────── **ENRICH** *ControlledEntities* ┌── **PORT** *CELayer$_i$* ─────── ce_j^k : ... ... *deliver_CE$_j$* : event	⊢ If a port *CELayer$_i$* contains a controlled entity ce_j^k, and it is the port of the maximal abstraction layer index i that contains controlled entities of the group CE_j, then it also contains the event *deliver_CE$_j$*. ⊢ Each controlled entity is contained in exactly one port *CELayer$_i$*
3.1.2 Identify the interface between each pair of consecutive layers, and the internal data for each layer. The input port of *layer$_1$* are the logical sensor values. ── *Interface_0_1* ──── ── *Interface_i_i + 1* ──── **ENRICH** *LogicalSensors* ┌── **PORT** *IF_i_i + 1* ── *IF_0_1* ≅ *LS* ... *update_model$_i$* : event ── *AbstractionLayer$_i$* ──────────── **ENRICH** *Interface_i − 1_i* **INPUT** *IF_i − 1_i* **ENRICH** *Interface_i_i + 1* ┌── **DATA** *State$_i$* ──── ┌── **INIT** ... ──── ...	*no validation conditions*

Fig. 7. Steps for Stage 3: definition of abstraction layers

and *fail*, which describe the possible constellations of acknowledge messages (*fail* indicating that both, a *uoff* and a *uon* message have been received). The functions in *CE_lamp* are partial, because acknowledgment messages arrive sequentially, in groups of twelve, from the switchboard. The domains of these functions are the identifiers of lamps for which an acknowledgment has been received after the last command burst from the phase control. Transition points need to be evaluated by the regulator to find missing acknowledgments.

The functions in the other two groups are total, because they describe the complete state of the junction, which is accumulated from incoming messages about state changes of lamps. The types $STATE\_SG$ and $STATE\_TS$ are parameters to the specification, because the concrete information to evaluate safety of a junction depends on the legal context: what is tolerable in one community may not be legal in another.

5.2 Specification of the Internal Domain Model

Stage 3 of the CDM agenda (cf. Table 1) consists of two steps: specifying the internal domain model, and specifying the regulator. We consider only specifying the internal domain model, for which the sub-agenda is given in Figures 7 and 8.

Having identified the necessary controlled entities, and decided on their types and dynamics in Stage 2 of the agenda, we must now specify how the controlled entities can

Step	Validation Conditions
3.1.3 Specify the behavior of each abstraction layer.	⊢ If *AbstractionLayer$_i$* changes data in *IF_i_i* + 1, then df *update_model$_i$*. ⊢ *AbstractionLayer$_i$* reacts to *update_model$_{i-1}$* events, i.e. the corresponding statechart performs a state transition. ⊢ If *AbstractionLayer$_i$* changes entities in *CELayer$_i$*, then it also generates the corresponding *deliver* events. ...
3.1.4 Assemble abstraction layers into the internal domain model. 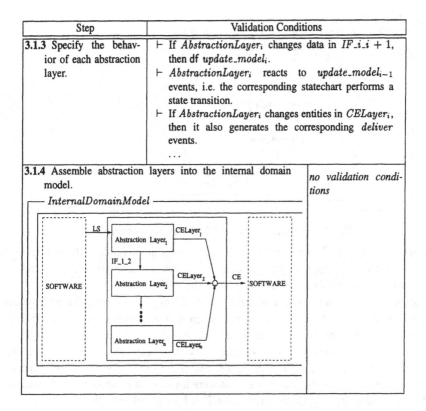	*no validation conditions*

Fig. 8. Steps for Stage 3: structure of the internal domain model

be obtained from the logical sensor values. This is the purpose of the internal domain model.

We begin by identifying appropriate *abstraction layers* in Step 3.1.1. Controlled entities that can be derived directly from the logical sensor values belong to the first layer *AbstractionLayer$_1$*, whereas controlled entities that are defined in terms of other controlled entities belong to a higher abstraction layer.

In Step 3.1.2, we must decide what kind of information must be propagated from one level to the next one. This information is collected in the port schemas *IF_i_i* + 1. An event *update_model$_i$* notifies the next abstraction layer when relevant information changes. Furthermore, each abstraction layer may have a memory, e.g., for accumulating values. This results in a local state *State$_i$*.

So far, we have modeled the data aspects of the abstraction layers. It remains to specify their behavior, which is the purpose of Step 3.1.3. We distinguish two kinds of behavior: an abstraction layer may either immediately react to an *update_model$_i$* event, or it may buffer incoming values and only take action when some internal condition is fulfilled. These alternatives are discussed in Section 5.3. Step 3.1.4, finally, is automatic and consists in assembling the abstraction layers in a cascade-like manner, see also Figure 2.

Safety Controller. While the order of Steps 3.1.1 through 3.1.4 describes their logical dependencies and is appropriate when developing a specification, it is easier to explain

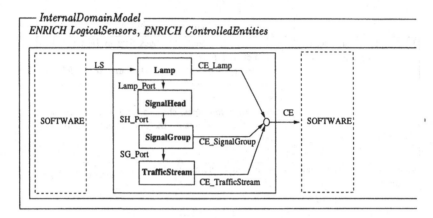

Fig. 9. Internal domain model for the safety controller

the resulting product in the reversed order: The internal domain model of the traffic light safety controller, shown in Figure 9, is a cascade of abstraction layers, which resembles the informal "entity-relationship" analysis sketched in Figure 3.

The entities of the lowest abstraction layer are **Lamps**. They are grouped together to **SignalHeads**. Several signal heads form a **SignalGroup**, each of which determines the state of one or more **TrafficStreams**. The state of the elements of one abstraction layer determines the state of the following layer. The relevant data are transmitted along the interfaces, namely *Lamp_Port*, *SH_Port* and *SG_Port*. Three of the four internal data layers deliver the controlled entities that were introduced in Section 5.1. The union of all controlled entities yields the interface *CE*, which is linked to the regulator.

5.3 Alternatives for the Definition of Abstraction Layers

We discuss two approaches to Step 3.1.3. The templates for both fulfill most of the verification conditions of that step by construction.

Table 2 shows a template for an abstraction layer that *immediately* reacts to the event $update\_model_{i-1}$. The statechart describing its behavior has only one state, called *working*. Whenever the event $update\_model_{i-1}$ occurs, the operation *Update_Layer$_i$* is invoked. As indicated by the prefix Δ, this operation may change the internal data of the abstraction layer and the values of its outgoing interfaces. If the interface information

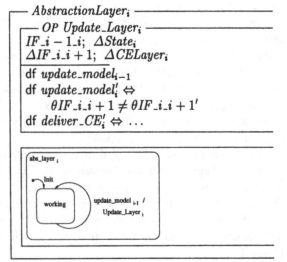

Table 2: Steps for Stage 3: template for immediate reaction

changes ($\theta IF\_i\_i + 1 \neq \theta IF\_i\_i + 1'$), then the next abstraction layer must be notified by generating an *update_model*$_i$ event (df *update_model*$'_i$). Similarly, *deliver_CE*$_i$ events notify the regulator about changed controlled entities.

Table 3 shows the template for *buffered abstraction layers*. They behave differently than immediately reacting layers, although the corresponding state-charts look the same for both. The operation *Update_Layer*$_i$ is a composition of the operations *Fill_Buffer*$_i$ and *Process_Buffer*$_i$. The operation *Fill_Buffer*$_i$ works only on the internal state of the abstraction layer and its input interface $IF\_i - 1\_i$. The operation *Process_Buffer*$_i$ does nothing if a predicate *trigger*$_i$ defined on the internal state is false, as indicated by the prefix Ξ. If the trigger predicate is true, the operation *Generate*$_i$ computes new values for the controlled entities.

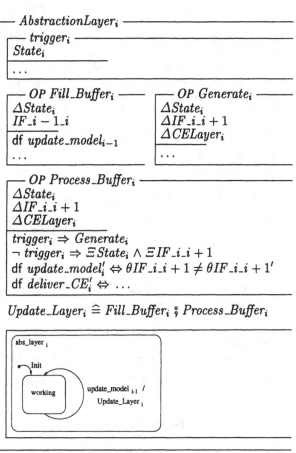

Table 3: Steps for Stage 3: template for buffered behavior

Similar to the immediately reacting abstraction layer, the operation *Process_Buffer*$_i$ generates an event *update_model*$_i$ to indicate that data of the output interface have changed.

For this variant of an abstraction layer, we have the validation conditions that the operation *Fill_Buffer*$_i$ eventually leads to a state satisfying *trigger*$_i$, and that the operation *Generate*$_i$ falsifies *trigger*$_i$.

Safety Controller. The abstraction layer *SignalGroup* contributes to computing the current state and the transition points of the signal groups in the system. Incoming data are states and transition points of the signal heads. They are available at port *SH_Port*. Outgoing data are the current states and transition points of the signal groups as defined in *SG_Port*. The port *CE_SignalGroup* contains the controlled entities enabling the regulator to monitor the sequence of phases as well as the duration of each phase (cf.

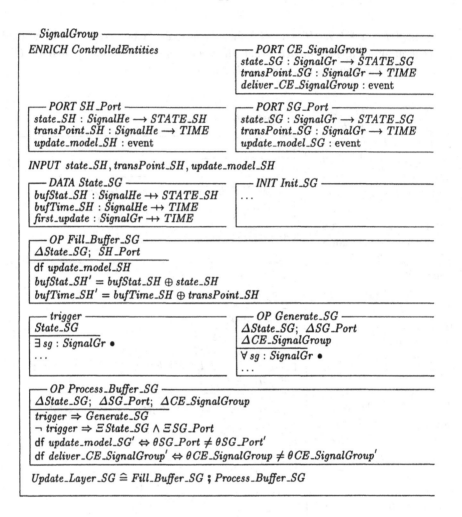

Fig. 10. The abstraction layer of signal groups

Figure 9). In this case the controlled entities are the same as the outgoing data, i.e. the ports *CE_SignalGroup* and *SG_Port* are the same except for the generated events.

The incoming values for signal heads have to be buffered because they are delivered sequentially instead of simultaneously. The specification shown in Figure 10 is an instance of Table 3. Whenever the event *update_model_SH* is read from the incoming port *SH_Port*, the operation *Update_Layer_SG* is performed. This operation is a composition of the operations *Fill_Buffer_SG* and *Process_Buffer_SG*. The shape of the statechart, which is omitted here, is exactly the one of the chart in Table 3.

The operation *Fill_Buffer_SG* just adds the data read from the incoming port *SH_Port* to the buffer functions called *bufStat_SH* and *bufTime_SH* by functional overwriting. The operation *Process_Buffer_SG* assembles the buffered values when *trigger* is satisfied. This is the case if there exists a signal group whose update information is complete, or whose transition point was set more than a certain time span ago. If *trigger* is not satisfied, then the data remain as they are. In case of change, two events

```
┌─ TrafficStream ──────────────────────────────────────────────────────
│ ENRICH ControlledEntities
│ ┌─ PORT SG_Port ──────────────┐  ┌─ PORT CE_TrafficStream ────────────┐
│ │ state_SG : SignalGr ↛ STATE_SG │  │ state_TS : TrafficStr ↛ STATE_TS │
│ │ transPoint_SG : SignalGr ↛ TIME │  │ transPoint_TS : TrafficStr ↛ TIME │
│ │ update_model_SG : event        │  │ deliver_CE_TrafficStream : event │
│ └────────────────────────────┘  └─────────────────────────────────┘
│ INPUT state_SG, transPoint_SG, update_model_SG
│ ┌─ OP Update_Layer_TF ─────────────────────────────────────────────
│ │ SG_Port;  ΔCE_TrafficStream
│ ├──────────────────────────────────────────────────────────────────
│ │ df update_model_SG
│ │ df deliver_CE_TrafficStream' ⇔ θCE_TrafficStream ≠ θCE_TrafficStream'
│ │ state_TF' = interpret_signal_TF ∘ state_SG ∘ signals_TF
│ │ transPoint_TF' = transPoint_SG ∘ signals_TF
│ └──────────────────────────────────────────────────────────────────
└──────────────────────────────────────────────────────────────────────
```

Fig. 11. The abstraction layer of traffic streams

update_model_SG and *deliver_CE_SignalGroup* report about the new values along the outgoing ports.

An example for unbuffered immediate reaction is given with the highest abstraction layer of the cascade, namely the process class *TrafficStream* in Figure 11. The update operation determines the current values of the traffic streams according to the actual data of the signal groups which control them. Incoming data are defined in the port *SG_Port*. The states and the transition points of the traffic streams are the controlled entities which are delivered to the regulator via the port *CE_TrafficStream*. The behavior is cyclic as before but there is no need to store values as internal data, because the values of all signal groups are determined simultaneously.

The updating operation is activated each time the event *update_model_SG* is read from the input port. It computes the data for the actual state and transition point for each traffic stream in accordance with the signal groups that give the signals to them. To determine the actual state value means to interpret the signal from the signal group in terms of opening or closing. Both functions *interpret_signal_TF* and *signals_TF* are external functions described by the planning documents. The event *deliver_CE_TF* is generated if there is any change of data.

6 Related Work

The use of formal methods to specify software for safety-critical embedded systems is not uncommon, see e.g. [10–12]. However, few approaches provide an explicit method-ology to develop formal specifications. Related to this aim is the work of Souquières and Lévy [14]. They support specification acquisition with *development operators* that reduce *tasks* to subtasks. However, they do not consider safety-related issues, and the development operators do not provide means to validate the developed specification.

More agendas that support the specification of software for safety-critical embedded systems can be found in [5, 9]. There, different reference architectures and formalisms are supported. More details of the traffic light system can be found in [8, 13].

7 Conclusions

The requirements for safety-critical embedded systems can be non-trivial. In these cases, we cannot assume that highly abstract requirements are easily captured as a direct relation between sensor values and actuator commands.

Without formal specification techniques, the relation between high-level requirements and low-level sensor data often is established only in the design and implementation phases and in an ad hoc manner. This results in a gap between high-level requirements documents and low-level design and implementation documents. Consequently, errors in mapping high-level requirements to low-level data are either detected very late in the development process, or not at all. It is very hard to certify the safety of systems developed in that way.

Our approach avoids these problems by proposing to

1. Set up a formal requirements specification before beginning with the design and implementation of the software component.
   In this way, functional and safety requirements for the software component are stated explicitly and unambiguously.
2. Define the abstract notions, which are used to express requirements, in terms of low-level sensor data formally and early in the software development process.
   In this way, we establish a direct connection between the requirements analysis and the software modeling phases. As a result, the requirements are adequately reflected in the software model.

For the traffic light safety controller, finding appropriate abstract notions to characterize safe states of a traffic junction (such as signal groups and traffic streams) was a crucial point in developing an adequate specification, because these abstractions are not documented in the domain specific literature [3, 4].

In addition, we have identified a *systematic way of procedure* to achieve the abstraction of low-level values to high-level concepts. This systematic way of procedure and the formal nature of our specification language force software developers to analyze the system much more thoroughly than this is the case for traditional software engineering approaches. For example, classifying controlled entities into groups that may change simultaneously (see Step 2.2 of Figure 5) forces the specifier to carefully reconsider all the controlled entities introduced in Step 2.1.

Following the CDM agenda leads to a *clean architecture* of the software component. The clear cascade-like organization of abstraction layers leads to well structured and comprehensible specifications even for complex applications.

The validation conditions associated with the steps of the agendas ensure that the specification fulfills certain *quality criteria*. All of the validation conditions presented in this paper can be expressed formally and be demonstrated with machine support. Without formal techniques, such a rigorous validation of the specification would not be possible.

Apart from making *design knowledge* explicit and re-usable, an agenda provides a *documentation* of the specifications developed with it. Each part of the specification can be mapped to a step of the agenda that explains its purpose. In this way, the *evolution* of specifications is facilitated considerably.

The traffic light case study has provided a proof of concept for the approach presented in this paper. It is not an academic example but a real-life industrial application. Safety controllers for traffic light systems are highly non-trivial. The complete formal specification [13] is 50 pages long, and an informal analysis document takes another 21 pages. A first version of the formal specification had been developed without using the agendas presented in this paper. Revising this first version to make it conform to the agenda resulted in eliminating some ad hoc solutions and has lead to a better structured and more comprehensible specification that can be adjusted to new requirements in a systematic way.

References

1. R. Büssow, H. Dörr, R. Geisler, W. Grieskamp, and M. Klar. μSZ – ein Ansatz zur systematischen Verbindung von Z und Statecharts. Technical Report TR 96-32, Technische Universität Berlin, 1996.
2. R. Büssow and W. Grieskamp. Combinig Z and temporal interval logics for the formalization of properties and behaviors of embedded systems. In R. K. Shyamasundar and K. Ueda, editors, *Asian '97*, LNCS 1345, pages 46–56. Springer-Verlag, 1997.
3. Deutsche Elektrotechnische Kommission im DIN und VDE (DKE). DIN Norm VDE 0832 – Straßenverkehrs-Signalanlagen (SVA), 1990.
4. Forschungsgesellschaft für Straßen- und Verkehrswesen. Richtlinien für Lichtsignalanlagen – RiLSA, 1992.
5. W. Grieskamp, M. Heisel, and H. Dörr. Specifying safety-critical embedded systems with Statecharts and Z: An agenda for cyclic software components. In E. Astesiano, editor, *Proc. ETAPS-FASE'98*, LNCS 1382, pages 88–106. Springer-Verlag, 1998.
6. D. Harel, H. Lachover, A. Naamad, A. Pnueli, M. Politi, R. Sherman, A. Shtull-Trauring, and M. Trakhtenbrot. Statemate: A working environment for the development of complex reactive systems. *IEEE Transactions on Software Engineering*, 16(4), 1990.
7. M. Heisel. Agendas – a concept to guide software development activites. In R. N. Horspool, editor, *Proc. Systems Implementation 2000*, pages 19–32, London, 1998. Chapman & Hall.
8. M. Heisel, T. Santen, and K. Winter. An agenda for software components with complex data models. Technical report, GMD FIRST, 1998. to appear.
9. M. Heisel and C. Sühl. Methodological support for formally specifying safety-critical software. In P. Daniel, editor, *Proc. 16th SAFECOMP*, pages 295–308. Springer-Verlag London, 1997.
10. J. Jacky. Specifying a safety-critical control system in Z. *IEEE Transactions on Software Engineering*, 21(2):99–106, 1995.
11. J. McDermid and R. Pierce. Accessible formal method support for PLC software development. In G. Rabe, editor, *Proc. 14th SAFECOMP, Belgirate, Italy*, pages 113–127, London, 1995. Springer-Verlag.
12. A. Ravn, H. Rischel, and K. Hansen. Specifying and verifying requirements of real-time systems. *IEEE Transactions on Software Engineering*, 19(1):41–55, 1993.
13. T. Santen and K. Winter. Sicherung einer Lichtsignalanlage in μSZ. Technical report, GMD FIRST, 1998. to appear.
14. J. Souquières and N. Lévy. Description of specification developments. In *Proc. of Requirements Engineering '93*, pages 216–223, 1993.
15. J. Spivey. *The Z Notation – A Reference Manual*. Prentice Hall, 1992.

Safety in Production Cell Components: An Approach Combining Formal Real Time Specifications and Patterns*

Heinrich Rust**

Lehrstuhl für Software Systemtechnik, BTU Cottbus

Abstract. Application of formal methods alone does not ensure safety properties of the systems modeled. This powerful strategy must be complemented by provisions which help to check adherence of the model to the system in question. We propose to use a pattern based approach to increase the structure in formal models of concurrent systems and in this way to make them more easily understandable. The method is applied in a distributed real time specification of a belt component in a production cell which used the HyTech notation. Several specification patterns have been identified; they regard global structure, the use of variable restrictions, of synchronization labels, and the use of locations.

1 Introduction

This paper deals with the following questions: How can concurrent real time specifications increase safety of built systems? How can they be structured? What are the important components? What concepts should notations support explicitly for good understandability?

We investigate these questions in the context of specifying a component of a production cell. Production cell components and their associated control programs are a good application field to try out formal specification and verification methods for several reasons:

- Correctness of the system (control software in combination with controlled hardware) is safety relevant.
- Different interacting system components of a production cell are best modeled separately. Thus, it can be checked how well a notation supports concurrency.
- Analysis of the throughput of the cell and functionality depending on absolute timing makes it sensible to do quantitative analyses.
- Tolerances in system parameters might make it necessary to model nondeterminism.

---

* Submitted for presentation at SAFECOMP'98

** Reachable at: BTU, Postfach 101344, D-03013 Cottbus, Germany; Tel. +49(355)69-3803, Fax.:-3810; rust@informatik.tu-cottbus.de

Thus, case studies modeling production cell components can reveal several important features and shortcomings of a method. In [LL95], several case studies involving a production cell have been reported.

1.1 Safety assurance of concurrent real time systems

The functionality of a production cell is best described as a concurrent real time system. We consider multi-method approaches necessary for safety assurance. In the last years, tools and concepts have been developed in different fields of computer science which can be put together to go a step forward in the direction of higher integrity systems.

We will describe a combination of two concepts to enhance safety of systems: Using a formal description technique, and using patterns (cf. [GHJV94,CS95,BMR⁺96]) to structure the description. We focus on the analysis phase, before the system is deployed. In this phase, safety analyses will have to deal with a model of the system considered, and they will have to check two key properties of these models:

- Is a system which is represented by the model safe, or does the model show safety problems?
- Does the model fit the reality? Or better: Is the model faithful in those respects which are used for safety analyses?

Formal modeling techniques are useful to check these two properties in the following way:

- A tool based on a formal modeling technique might make it easy to check a redundantly modeled system for consistency. This is the main strategy followed, for instance, in model checkers or proof support system, where a description of the system and a specification of expected behaviours are combined into a redundant description whose consistency can be checked fully or partly automatically.
- The fact that a notation is defined formally, i.e. with mathematical exactness, forces modeling decisions to be taken which might seem unnecessary when a less exactly defined notation is used. The model is better defined, and incompatibilities between model and reality will become clearer when they are not allowed to stay implicit and hidden by a friendly interpretation, but are forced to become explicit.

The use of a formal notation is not per se sufficient to ensure compatibility of a system and its model. This comparison process is not itself formalizable if the system is part of the real world. Thus, humans have to use their judgement. Formality of a notation has a positive role in this process by forcing exact interpretations, but it also has a negative role because the description of all detailed interpretation decisions takes a lot of space. Thus, the models tend to become intellectually unmanageable.

1.2 Properties of patterns

Patterns can help when a system description is very large. We define patterns as recurring structures which are perceived as a whole. The perceived size of a system depends on the number of components and the relations a reader has to understand. Patterns decrease these numbers by perceiving several previously separately considered elements as a unit.

The pattern concept was developed during the last years in the software engineering community as 'design patterns for object oriented systems'. Object oriented design patterns are reusable structures in designs. What makes them interesting?

- We just mentioned the most important point: Patterns make chunking easier in perception and thinking about designs. 'Chunking' is a concept from cognitive psychology. It means that several distinct elements are perceived and mentally represented as a unit.
- They make recognition of structures easier and in this way enhance understanding.
- Useful patterns can be frozen in the syntax of a description notation.
- Syntactically fixed patterns can automatically transport some aspect of a good design practice to programmers which learn to use the notation.
- Patterns encapsulate typical design problems and successful solutions for them.

We transfered the notion of object oriented design patterns to concurrent hybrid specifications. We used the notion in the construction of a formal model of a transport belt in a production cell, i.e. we applied a formal modeling notation to the problem, and we emphasized the search for structural patterns during this construction.

Casais [Cas94] also applied the pattern concept in the description of a production cell. In his case study using Eiffel, he identified "synchronization patterns" which were useful in the connection of different physical components of the production cell with each other.

1.3 The modeling notation

In the work we report here, we use HyTech [HHWT95], a tool for modeling concurrent linear hybrid systems and for proving properties about these systems. 'Hybrid' means that HyTech allows to model both continuous and discrete aspects of the system, 'linear' means that the continuously changing components are modeled with variables having piecewise constant derivatives. With these variables, HyTech allows to model time behaviour quantitatively.

The HyTech system encompasses three components:

- a language for modeling concurrent linear hybrid systems,
- a language for formulating algorithms to prove properties of the modeled system,

– and an interpreter which allows to execute the proof programs in the context of a modeled system.

In the present work, we will focus on use of the modeling language. Important features of the modeling language are the following:

– A system is described in a modular way as a collection of finite automata.
– The automata can communicate via signals. This communication is based on CSP-like synchronization labels.
– There is the possibility for communication based on shared access to globally visible analogue variables.
– Locations have invariants and transitions have guards. These are conjunctions of linear inequalities over the global variables.
– When a component automaton is in a given location, the possible development of the global variables can be restricted by a linear predicate over the time derivatives.
– There are several mechanisms for modeling discrete system transitions. All are associated with transitions of the component automata:
  • Each transition changes the active location of a control automaton. This can additionally change the restrictions for time derivatives of global variables.
  • A transition with a synchronization label can only be taken if all parallel automata having the synchronization label in their alphabet also perform a transition labeled with this synchronization label.
  • When a transition is taken, the values of global variables may be reset.

We do not consider verifications made possible in HyTech in this paper.

2 The transport belt

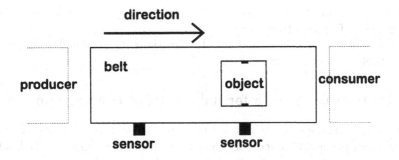

Fig. 1. The belt

We illustrate our approach by modeling a transport belt of a production cell (cf. Fig. 1). The transport belt we consider has the following set of physical features:

- The belt can be moving and can be stopped. The direction of movement is fixed. Thus, we can distinguish an end from where objects are fed to the belt and an end to which objects are transfered. We will call them the producer end and the consumer end.
- The belt is equipped with two sensors for objects. One sensor is positioned near the producer end, the other near the consumer end. Each sensor has two sensitivity radii. The smaller radius defines the region in which an object is sensed safely, the larger radius defines the region out of which an object is never sensed. In the region between the larger and the smaller radius, the transitions of the sensor from the off-state to the on-state and vice versa occur.
- The belt has a length and a speed (when switched on).

The control program of the belt fetches objects from the neighbour at the producer end, transports them to the consumer end, and transfers them to the neighbour positioned at that end. It might be described in the following way.

- Wait until the producer wants to transfer an object.
- Tell the producer that the transfer can start.
- Start belt motion.
- Wait until the object has been transfered to belt.
- Tell the producer that the transfer has been accomplished.
- Transport object to other end of belt.
- Stop belt motion.
- Tell the comsumer that an object is to be transfered.
- Wait for the consumer to tell that the transfer can start.
- Start belt motion.
- Wait till the consumer tells that transfer has been accomplished.
- Stop belt motion.
- Start program at the beginning.

The context of the belt consists of two neighbours:

- There is a producing neighbour. Its functionality is modeled as repeated transfer of objects to the belt.
- There is a consumer neighbour. Its functionality is modeled as repeated receipt of objects from the belt.

3 Pattern usage in a formal model of the transport belt

This section describes our HyTech model of the transport belt. We structured the model description into several sections. The first section contains declarations of symbolic constants, e.g. for the belt's length, its speed, the positions of the sensors and their radii. The second section contains the declaration of several global variables. One represents the position of the object on the belt, the others are used in special testing automata to represent the time the system spends in critical situations. The following section contains automata declarations.

As an example for an automaton, we give in Fig. 2 the model of a sensor. The logic is the following:

– The automaton has three locations:
  • `loc_off_before` represents situations in which there is an object on the belt positioned before the sensor, while the sensor is off.
  • `loc_on` represents situations in which the sensor is on.
  • `loc_off_after` represents situations in which the sensor is off and the object is positioned after the sensor. This is the initial configuration.
– The automaton uses three synchronization labels:
  • `s1_b1_sAon` is generated when the automaton passes from location `loc_off_before` into the location `loc_on`. This signal indicates a switch from the off- to the on-state.
  • `s1_b1_sAoff` is generated when the automaton passes from location `loc_on` into location `loc_off_after`. This signal indicates a switch from the on- to the off-state.
  • The signal `s1_bA_to_b1` indicates that a new object has been put on the belt. It can be received when the automaton is in location `loc_off_after` and makes the automaton move to `loc_off_before`.
– Invariants and guards of the automaton involve several symbols:
  • `b1_pos` is the current position of the object on the belt.
  • `b1_sensApos` is the (fixed) position of the sensor on the belt.
  • `sensor_radius_min` and `sensor_radius_max` are the minimal and maximal radii determining the ranges in which objects are recognized.
– Invariants of the locations are given behind the keyword **while** in each location description. They describe conditions which must hold while the automaton is in the associated location:
  • The invariant of `loc_off_before` describes that the sensor might stay off as long as the object did not yet enter the inner radius around the sensor position.
  • The invariant of `loc_on` describes that the sensor may stay on until the object leaves the outer radius of the sensor.
  • The trivially true invariant of `loc_off_after` describes that there is no position-induces restriction for the time the sensor may stay off.
– Every location is associated with a **wait**-expression given in braces. Here, restrictions for the time derivatives of the global variables can be given. We do not restrict any of these variables in the sensor automaton described, thus all restrictions are trivially empty.
– Each transition is described in a **when**-expression. In our example, each location has exactly one transition. After the keyword **when**, the guard is given. After the keyword **sync**, a synchronization label is given, and after the keyword **goto**, the name of the target location is given.
  The guard in `loc_off_before` determines that the sensor can only switch to the on-state when the object has reached the inner circle. If the minimal radius is strictly smaller than the maximal radius, this together with the invariant defines the transition to happen nondeterministically some time between the moment the object reaches the outer radius and the moment the object reaches the inner radius. Invariant and guard in `loc_on` are used in a similar way.

```
1  automaton b1_sensA
2     synclabs:
3        --These signals are output by the automaton.
4        sl_b1_sAon,sl_b1_sAoff,
5        --This signal is received by the automaton.
6        sl_bA_to_b1;
7
8     --Initially,we assume to be in the off-state after the sensor
9     --  and the plate is not on the belt.
10    initially loc_off_after;
11
12    --In this state,the sensor is off because the plate is too far
13    --  before the sensor.
14    loc loc_off_before:
15       --We stay here as long as the plate has not reached the
16       --  minimal range of the sensor.
17       while b1_pos <= b1_sensApos-sensor_radius_min  wait {}
18       --After the plate has reached the maximal sensor range,we
19       --  can generate an on-signal and go to the on-state.
20       when b1_pos >= b1_sensApos-sensor_radius_max
21          sync sl_b1_sAon goto loc_on;
22
23    --We can stay here as long as we are in the on-state,that is,
24    --  as long as the plate is in the maximal sensor range.
25    loc loc_on:
26       while b1_pos <= b1_sensApos+sensor_radius_max  wait {}
27       --We can leave this state whenever the plate leaves the
28       --  minimal sensor range.
29       when b1_pos >= b1_sensApos+sensor_radius_min
30          sync sl_b1_sAoff goto loc_off_after;
31
32    --This location represents the situations where the plate
33    --  is far after the sensor.
34    loc loc_off_after:
35       --We can stay in this state indefinitely.
36       while True  wait {}
37       --We leave this state when another plate is put onto the belt.
38       when True  sync sl_bA_to_b1  goto loc_off_before;
39 end
```

Fig. 2. An example automaton: A sensor

3.1 Patterns involving global structure

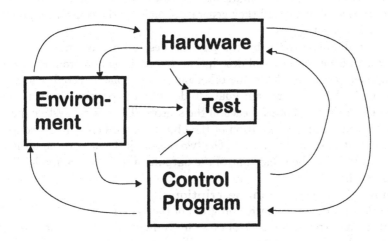

Fig. 3. Structure and information flow in system description

The first set of patterns we found helpful in developing our model concerns the structure of the description. Some of the component automata belong more closely to each other than to others. The HyTech notation does not support hierarchical structure of automata, so this structure cannot be expressed explicitly.

We used the strategy to split up the total functionality of the model into four automata sets with clearly defined responsibilities, different structural properties (like nondeterminism or the input property), and different interactional patterns with each other.

For each of the patterns, we give a name, the problem it solves, a description of the static structure and the interactions, and we refer to an example in our case study.

- **Name: Subsystem description**
  Problem: Design a structure of interacting automata for the description of a subsystem and its interfaces.
  Static structure: Split the description of the subsystem into the following four groups: Hardware, control program, interface to environment, test automata. Figure 3 shows a description of the global structure and the information flows between the components of the specification.
  Interactions: A subsystem interacts with its environment. This has to fulfill the interface description specified in the environment automata.
  Example: The whole specification of the transport belt is given as a subsystem description.
- **Name: Hardware description**
  Problem: Model physical properties of the production cell component.

Static structure: Use a set of automata which are allowed to be deterministic to model systems. Use analog variables to model continuous quantities.
Interactions: These automata react to signals from the control program and the environment, and they generate signals for the control program and the environment.

The variables controlled by the physical descriptions are not read by automata outside the physical description. Information flow from the physical component of the model to the other model components is only via signals.
Example: We use three automata to describe the physical system, one for the belt motion and one for each of the sensors. The critical system quantity in our case is only the position of the object on the belt. This is controlled by the belt motion automaton. The two sensors just react to the position of the object on the belt and control the outputs of the physical model, i.e. the sensor values.

- **Name: Control program description**
  Problem: Model the control program of the system.
  Static structure: The control program is modeled with one or several automata. To be implementable, we will expect the control program to be deterministic. There can be no multiple possibilities for transitions taken in the automaton set.
  Interactions: The control program interacts via signals with the control programs of the neighbouring production cell components, it generates signals for the physical model, and it receives signals from the physical model.
  Example: We use just one automaton for the control program. It defines the standard algorithm.

- **Name: Environment description**
  Problem: A set of automata describe the environment of modeled system. They can be interpreted as defining the protocols which the model production cell component expects its neighbours to use.
  Static structure: These automata are allowed to be nondeterministic to express both nondeterminism and incompleteness of knowledge about the context.
  The context automata must model both the relevant context for the physical system and the relevant context for the control program.
  Interactions: The context automata interact with both the control program of the production cell element modeled, and with the physical representation.
  Example: We describe the environment of the belt using two automata, one describing the protocol which the upper neighbour uses when he feeds a new object, and one describing the protocol the lower neighbour uses when receiving an object.

- **Name: Test automata**
  Problem: A set of automata are there for checking correctness conditions of the component.
  Static structure: These automata are restricted to be pure input automata. This means that they may not restrict the rest of the model in any way: All signals in the alphabet of a test automaton must be receivable at any time,

and global variables read in any other automaton may not be restricted in any way by a test automaton.

Interactions: Test automata may interact with any other automaton, but only in a reading manner, because they may not influence the development of the system..

Example: We define some automata which check that during transfer of an object from one neighbour to another, both belts are moving.

3.2 Patterns involving variable restriction

The Hytech notation enforces no restrictions regarding the influences on the value change of global variables in different automata. We found it helpful to associate each global variable to an automaton in which it is controlled, and to avoid influencing this variable in any other automaton.

A variable is defined to be restricted in an automaton if the wait-expression of any location of the automaton references the time derivative of the variable, or if there is a value assignment for the variable in some transition of the automaton.

We define one relational patterns a variable and a set of automata can have. We give a name, a problem, the solution taken in the pattern, and an example of its use.

- **Name: Input/Output variables**

  Problem: Some analog quantities are controlled in just one part of the system. Their values may be used in one or several other components of the system, but the speed of their change and their discrete value changes are only restricted in one subsystem.

  Solution: Represent the quantity with a variable or a set of variables. Represent the subsystem which controls the physical quantity as a set of closely associated automata, and represent all other subsystems as sets of associated automata. Let only the first set of associated automata do discrete assignments to the variables or restrictions of the derivatives. The other automata sets may only refer to the variables reading.

  Example: We represent the position of an object on the belt as an analog variable. This is controlled by a part of the hardware description of the system. It is read in the automata describing the sensors, which also belong to the hardware description.

3.3 Patterns involving synchronization

Synchronization labels can be used in different ways in the system. They represent discrete signals for interprocess communication, but unlike one would expect for signals, HyTech abstracts from the property that they are either generated or only received in an automaton. But this is a valuable structural information:

– **Name: Input/output signals**

Problem: An event occurs in one subsystem. Other subsystems can react to this event, but they can not restrict the generating subsystem. How is this modeled?

Solution: Some synchronization labels are used only as inputs in an automaton. This means that the automaton must in every configuration be able to perform a transition labeled with this label. This implies that the automaton does not restrict the rest of the system to perform transitions involving this synchronization label. Some synchronization labels are used as input signals in all but one automaton. Such a label represents an output signal of the one automaton which restricts it.

Examples: In the sensor automaton above, the label `sl_bA_to_b1` represents almost an input signal. It is not really an input signal because there are configurations of this automaton in which the signal cannot be received, but seen globally, this is not a problem, since the control program and the environment model prevent this signal from being generated in the environment.

We use true input signals in the test automata.

We use output signals in a lot of places, e.g. in the communication of the physical model of the belt with the controller: The signals `sl_b1_sAon` and `sl_b1_sAoff` are output signals of the automaton modeling a sensor of the belt. They are only referenced in one further automaton, the one describing the control program.

– **Name: Input automata**

Problem: Some automata are in no way allowed to influence the possible developments in the rest of the systems.

Solution: An automaton in which all synchronization labels are used as input signals and which further does not restrict any global variable read in any other automaton, we call it an input automaton. An input automaton can never restrict the development of the rest of the system in any way.

Example: We use input automata for the test automata we talked about in Sec. 3.1.

– **Name: Multiply restricted signals**

Problem: Input and output signals are a good solution to create a clear structure in the communication patterns of a concurrent system, but they are not always the most concise solution to a synchronization problem. Imagine, for example, two control programs of adjacent belts. There is a synchronization point in which the upstream belt tries to start the transfer of a belt, and the downstream belt tries to start the receipt of a belt. We model this synchronization point with a synchronization label in our approach.

This label can not represent an input signal for the downstream belt, since it might not be ready when the upstream belt wants to initiate the transfer. Vice versa, the same is true.

Solution: We must allow that labels is restricted in both control program automata.

This usage pattern of a signal puts less structure into the system, but we want to allow it nevertheless.

Example: We use multiply restricted signals in the communication of control programs of neighbouring production cell components.

3.4 Patterns involving locations

We can have different patterns for the usage of locations:

- **Name: Deterministic automata**
  Problem: Some automata represent control programs. These have to be implementable.
  Solution: We defined deterministic locations as those on which the invariant of the location and the guards and the input labels of the transitions together have the effect that the reaction to every event is deterministic. An automaton containing only deterministic locations is called a deterministic automaton.
  Example: The control program of the belt is modeled with a deterministic automaton.
- **Name: Error locations**
  Problem: Sometimes, an automaton needs a location which detects erroneous system configurations.
  Solution: This is a location into which an automaton moves when it detects an error condition, and which is never left after it has been entered.
  Example: We made use of this pattern in our test automata.

4 Summary

A case study in which a transport belt of a production cell was described with the modeling language of the tool HyTech has been performed. It demonstrated several opportunities to apply the concept of patterns in the development of a specification of a transport belt.

Why is this a contribution to enhancing the integrity of systems?

These techniques help to structure specifications of hybrid systems. This additional structure helps the constructor to build better systems and it helps the reader to understand the system better.

How can we build on these results? Two directions seem promising:

- We would like to have a notation which, via its syntax, supports important usage patterns for a hybrid system description notation.
- We would like to associate specific proof obligations rules with different patterns. Thus, a pattern could encompass both constructive and verificational knowledge.

Acknowledgements

I thank Claus Lewerentz for the discussions concerning form and content of this paper.

44

References

[BMR+96] Frank Buschmann, Regine Meunier, Hans Rohnert, Peter Sommerlad, and Michael Stal. *Pattern-Oriented Software Architecture – A System of Patterns*. John Wiley and Sons, Chichester, 1996.

[Cas94] Eduardo Casais. Eiffel: A reusable framework for production cells developed with an object-oriented programming language. In Claus Lewerentz and Thomasn Lindner, editors, *Case Study "Production Cell"*, chapter XV, pages 241–256. FZI, Karlsruhe, 1994.

[CS95] James O. Coplien and Douglas O. Schmidt, editors. *Pattern Languages of Program Design*. Addison-Wesley, Reading,Massachusetts, 1995.

[GHJV94] Erich Gamma, Richard Helm, Ralph Johnson, and John Vlissides. *Design Patterns: Elements of Reusable Object-Oriented Software*. Addison Wesley, Reading/Massachusetts, 1994.

[HHWT95] Thomas A. Henzinger, Pei-Hsin Ho, and Howard Wong-Toi. A user guide to HyTech. In *Proceedings of the First Workshop on Tools and Algorithms for the Construction and Analysis of Systems (TACAS)*, LNCS 1019, pages 41–71. Springer-Verlag, 1995.

[LL95] Claus Lewerentz and Thomas Lindner. *Formal Development of Reactive Systems*. Springer-Verlag, Berlin,Heidelberg, 1995.

Safety Properties Ensured by the OASIS Model for Safety Critical Real-Time Systems

Vincent David[1], Jean Delcoigne[1], Evelyne Leret[2], Alain Ourghanlian[2],
Philippe Hilsenkopf[3], Philippe Paris[3]

[1] LETI (CEA - Advanced Technologies) DEIN - CEA/Saclay
91191 Gif sur Yvette Cedex - France
david@albatros.saclay.cea.fr
[2] EDF/DER 6, quai Watier - BP 49
78401 Chatou - France
[3] Framatome IT/LA Tour Framatome
92400 Courbevoie - France

Abstract. The main focus of this paper is the problem of ensuring safety properties such as timeliness in safety critical systems. We introduce the OASIS model and its associated techniques to model both real-time tasks and to ensure determinism and dependability concerns when tasks are executed in parallel. By this approach we will show some formal aspects of our real-time task model and also how this result is used to ensure that the timeliness property and the sizing can be achieved on a safety critical real-time study case.

1. Introduction

The CEA, with EDF and Framatome, works out a plan of R&D, named OASIS, which mainly deals with the dependability of complex safety critical I&C systems in nuclear power plants. The trouble is to realize real-time critical systems which are more intricate than today's and easier to implement and to test. It must also be safer but still be according to the international standard ISO/CEI-880. In the safety critical domain, the design and the implementation of real-time systems are still challenging concerns. Real-time constraints induce not only the presence of timing constraints, such as deadlines dictated by the environment, but also an increasing application complexity, such as the management of different time-scale entities [11]. The presence of these constraints complicates the solution of many problems that are well understood if no timing constraint has to be considered. Both the logical and temporal correctness [12] must be proved as soon as possible. The agreement between the dependability concerns and the designing, the implementing or the executing methods has to be demonstrated, thanks to determinism and predictability properties.

We can identify two common approaches to design and to implement safety critical applications: a "sequential" approach and a "parallel" approach. They have different properties concerning the performance and safety aspects. The former corresponds to the loop programming technique. The existing safety critical applications are still mainly realized with this ad-hoc technique. It can ensure a range of safety properties for the software, but if they are used to design complex applications where there are numerous different time-scales, the system will be considerably oversized. The "synchronous approach" [7] is a well-defined implementation of this technique. On the other hand, the parallel implementation of multitasking matches the historical Dijkstra's works and more recently the works on CSP [5] from which derive the Occam and Ada languages. The more significant benefit of these approaches is the high level of application complexity they afford through the use of real-time monitors. But determinism and predictability properties are no more guaranteed and analytic verifications are more difficult.

Numerous works are also dealing with ensuring the timeliness property thanks to the definition and implementation of real-time task and communication scheduling algorithms [10]. Kopetz's work [6] deals with the time-triggered approach to design distributed fault tolerant real-time systems based on a static pre-run-time scheduling. Its implementation corresponds to a "sequential" execution model in our preceding classification. Fault tolerance and parallelism mechanisms that are developed inside one processor, don't match the focused problem for designing a safety critical real-time system that will be oversized.

The use of parallelism techniques (e.g. multitask programming) in the design and the implementation steps of safety critical systems, while still ensuring strong safety properties, is the main focus of our approach. The OASIS approach [2][3] proposes rules and methods for safety critical application engineering. It allows to design and to implement parallel programs with fully deterministic and predictable behaviors and thus to guarantee specified dependability properties.

2. The OASIS model

The OASIS approach is object-based: processing and data are encapsulated in the same structure, and data have only one writer (the owner task). Few assumptions are made about task nature. We suppose first that the number of system tasks is off-line fixed, and secondly that all iterative algorithms are bounded by known limits.

The main idea of the OASIS approach is, first of all to form and to work out multitask programs which are sporadic or cyclic, regular or irregular (i.e. conditional), with entirely deterministic and predictable behaviors, and then to demonstrate that some properties of well functioning (safety, liveliness and timeliness) descended from the specifications of the system can be proved and are in harmony with the constraints of qualification defined by safety standards and recommendations. Apart from the fact that the warranty of the deterministic behaviors ensures a safer programming of complex systems, test phases are more significant and the warranty of physic properties connected to operational safety of the system is a priori established.

2.1. Fundamental principles

In the OASIS approach, an application is viewed as a set Ω of communicating tasks that interact to achieve their functionality and real time is managed by a time-triggered architecture. The processing of each task is synchronous at particular time and the visible lasting value is independent from the target. The decomposition in tasks corresponds exactly to the processing that should be executed in parallel. In a time-triggered (or TT) approach, a system observes the environment and initiates its processing at recurring predetermined instants. In OASIS these instants are points of the globally synchronized time of the TT system.

With each task ω in the system, we associate a real-time clock H_ω that represents the set of physical instants where the input and output data are or can be observed. The joining of all clocks H_ω for each ω in Ω, is the definition of the system real-time clock H_Ω. The H_Ω clock includes all the observable instants of the system and is global, fundamental to the whole system. In our approach, we only manipulate regular real-time clocks (i.e. periodic clocks). We can then construct the smallest regular clock that includes all H_Ω instants. From now on, we consider that these two clocks are equivalent and we note both H_Ω. So, we deduce the new H_ω from the global clock, i.e. H_Ω, by exhibiting a factor K_ω and a shifting Δ_ω such as: $H_\omega = K_\omega * H_\Omega + \Delta_\omega$.

Time can be manipulated through the advance instruction (*ADV*). The instruction *ADV(k)* in the task code indicates that the next activation instant will be its current instant plus k H_ω periods. An *ADV* instruction splits the task code into two parts: the part of code (a processing) before and the part of code after the *ADV* instruction. A task is viewed as series of processing that have precedence relationships. Thus, we can declare the task's future instants (i.e. activation instants) and both earliest start date and latest end date (i.e. deadline) of each processing. For example, in the following code series:

```
{...processing_1; ADV(sta); processing_2; ADV(end);}
```

sta in fact represents the earliest start date and *end* the latest end date of *processing_2*. So, we introduce the apparent or formal duration of the processing '*processing_2*' as being the value of *end-sta* in H_ω periods. Formal duration is unvarying. This contributes to ensure the independence of the target computer system and by the way the absolute predictability of the real-time system.

2.2. Communication mechanisms

There are two modes of communication between tasks (common modes that we usually meet). The first mode is implicit, it is the use of exposed variables (also called temporal data flow), the second mode is explicit, it is the sending of messages.

2.2.1. Temporal data flow

The notion of temporal variable is directly associated with the time management. A temporal variable is a real-time data flow associated with an internal (encapsulated) variable of a task (which is the owner of this data) and driven by the real-time clock of the task. At each step of this clock, a new value is added to the flow. If the instant of the clock corresponds to an instant of the *ADV* instruction, the current value of the interior data will be at the top of the flow, else the top of the flow will be duplicated.

The owner task of a temporal variable X can declare it to be shown. Then reader tasks can access to anterior values of the variable X; each reader has to show the number (i.e. the depth) of value it needs to consult. A reader can only access to these anterior values at its local clock instant (time coherency, see figure 1). At any time, the visible values of a shown variable depend only on the instant of the reading task.

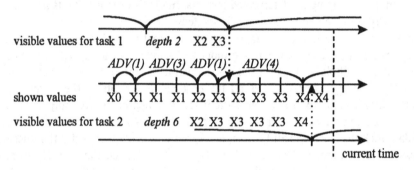

Fig. 1. Visible values of a temporal data flow

The reference to the anterior value can be made straight by indexing. This definition of the temporal variable seems similar to the works of H.R. Callison [1].

2.2.2. Send of messages

The OASIS model permits exchange by message too. Each time a message is sent, a date of visibility of the message is introduced. We associate to each queue of messages, a maximum number of steps (in the task clock) in order to accomplish each message from its date of visibility. An overstepping of this number may correspond to a failure of the task and the OASIS run-time will then release a specified procedure.

An issuing task sends a message to a queue of a task, and specifies its visibility instant. The addressee will know the message only when the clock reach the visibility instant of the message and consequently it can consume it from this instant only. The introduction of the visibility instant, or release instant, secures a temporal coherence of the mechanism. By specifying the order of the messages in a queue, the running becomes independent of the system of communication. After the arrangement by visibility instant, messages of a queue can be ordered by the name of issue and last by order of transmission at the issuer. It assumes a total order on the messages in each file.

From these known static elements, we can deduce automatically a safe bound of the number of messages that the system must store in each file. The behavior of the model is by the way deterministic, safe and unvarying with regard to the implementation.

2.3. Formal aspects of the real-time task model

For coding and programming applications with the OASIS approach, we need to express the particular primitives of the real-time task model (the *ADV* instruction and other specific features like communication). Languages, like C or Ada, have qualified compilers and are used for programming real-time applications. They commonly don't need such primitives. So, we have defined a ΨC (resp. ΨAda) dialect above the C language (resp. the Ada language). This dialect is a semi-formal language that contains all the formal aspects of the OASIS approach. Since it is not the subject of the paper we will not describe it further. Nevertheless, we will use in this paper a pseudo-code notation similar to a reduced Ψ-dialect for describing real-time task code.

Each real-time task has no termination and can be represented as a main "for ever" loop that encapsulates the task processing. They have always timing constraints on their code execution. In the OASIS approach, it means that the tasks have at least one *ADV* instruction to describe their timing constraints.

2.3.1. Definition of task state-transition diagrams

We use a formalism based on graph theory to represent a state-transition diagram for each task. At each state, we associate a vertex. At each transition, we associate an oriented edge. We finally obtain a symbolic graph where each vertex is an observable state of the task (corresponding to one *ADV*) and each edge is the processing executed between two *ADV* instructions. We will see that it allows us to describe more precisely the timing behavior of a task and to facilitate the identification of possible conception mistakes on the timing constraints (see figure 2 and 3).

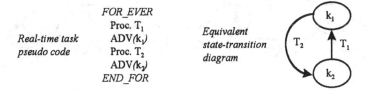

Fig. 2. Equivalent state-transition diagram

When there is a conditional instruction with an *ADV* instruction in the "then" or the "else" body, there are two exit edges at the vertex. We only consider the IF...THEN...ELSE...ENDIF case in this paper. The presence of an *ADV* instruction in a conditional processing makes the state-transition diagrams more complex: it introduces a new vertex and can greatly increase the number of edges in the graph (see figure 3).

A graph represents the symbolic execution of a task, i.e. all the possible execution paths of a task as if it was separately executed on a processor. By construction, there exists an unique edge for a given processing and an unique vertex for a given *ADV* instruction. So, for a given task there exists one and only one state-transition diagram and there is an equivalence relationship between state-transition diagrams and task codes. We can equivalently describe a task by its code or by its symbolic state-transition diagram.

2.3.2. Illustration

Let two tasks ω_1 and ω_2 which communicate together such as $H_{\omega1} = H_\Omega$ and $H_{\omega2} = 3.H_\Omega$ (one period of $H_{\omega2}$ is equal to three periods of H_Ω). The task ω_2 processes data that are sent by the message of the task ω_1 when data are ready (a simple producer / consumer case). We give their formal code description and their corresponding state-transition diagrams in the following figure.

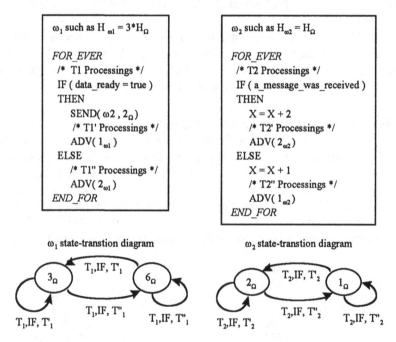

Fig. 3. Description of ω_1 and ω_2 tasks

To send messages, we use a simplified primitive SEND(ω, δ) where ω is the addressee task and δ is the date of visibility (in the unit of the global clock H_Ω): the visibility instant is equal to the current instant of the clock of the issuer increased by δ. The task ω_2 has a shown variable X and ω_1 consults its last value: when ω_2 receives a message, it increases the current value of X by 2 units, else just by one unit. We also suppose that the processing, that depend on the presence or absence of the message sending instruction, have not the same timing constraints. We will further consider that processing T2 is also including the test and consumption of messages. The non-explained processing are put between the symbol /* and */. Each processing fulfills the assumptions made in section 2.

2.3.3. Analysis of the example
To analyze the temporal behavior of this study case above, let just have a look at the time diagram on figure 4 which corresponds to a given scenario (for ready data). Let X_C the current value of X and $X_{/\omega}1$ its shown value to $\omega1$.

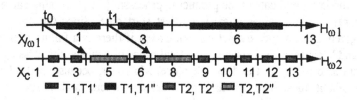

Fig. 4. A possible time diagram

Between the two instants t_0 and t_1, the clock of $\omega1$ is at the instant t_0. So, during the running of T1 and T1', $X_{/\omega}1 = X_C(t_0) = 1$ (even if X changes its current value between t_0 and t_1), whatever the message is actually sent between t_0 and t_1, it is noticed like have been sent at t_0 of the clock of $\omega1$ and will be visible from the instant $(t_0 + 2\Omega)$. At the instant t_1, the instant of last bringing up to date is $(t_0 + 2\Omega)$, we have $X_{/\omega}1 = X_C(t_0 + 2\Omega) = 3$ (value at the top of the flow at the instant t_1).

3. Ensured properties

Determinism is one of the basic properties of OASIS. In our context, determinism means that the behavior is single and unvarying. It has also a direct impact on test troubles of real-time systems. In test phase, the system runs with a known number of test sets or scenarios. Then, if we want to analyze or to explain the results of the tests, determinism is necessary. When an observer repeats an input scenario, it is seen differently by the real-time system which scans the environment at its own rhythm (usually some nanoseconds). The time scale at which a TT system observes the environment is perfectly known, and it can be defined correctly. Replay a scenario is to present once more the entrance data on the same slice of time of the TT system.

Another basic sight of determinism in the OASIS approach is that any processing has constant visible lasting value. Each task has a behavior independent of the target architecture. Then we can realize an off-line sizing of all the physical supplies which are necessary for the running. Due to unvarying behavior, adding (or suppressing) a task which has no direct interaction with other tasks, doesn't affect the application behavior. To a modular decomposition corresponds a modular real-time behavior.

3.1. Safety

This property is verified when we are able to demonstrate that some non-authorized system malfunctions (mainly connected with parallelism in our approach) are impossible. One of the most significant characteristics of the safety is the data coherence. There are two kinds of interactions: the temporal variables and the messages. For the first communication category, the new value is actually shown only after the latest end date of the producing processing. A processing can only read the temporal variable values after its earliest start date. Since the architecture is time-triggered, incoherence cannot happen except if there is a failure. For the same grounds and because of the existence of a total order in a queue, the message passing mechanism also preserves the data coherence. Moreover, because of the hypothesis we made about these two mechanisms, message queue and temporal variable memory requirements can be sized off-line and no memory saturation can occur.

3.2. Liveliness

In our context, a system is lively when all tasks can always become ready. In the OASIS approach, liveliness property is intrinsic. Indeed, the only blocking instruction is the *ADV* instruction. When the processing (corresponding to the code preceding the *ADV* instruction) is ended, the task wait only the future activation instant defined by the *ADV* instruction before beginning a new processing. So, deadlock can't exist in OASIS. Liveliness property demonstration is then included in the timeliness property demonstration (see next section).

3.3. Timeliness

This property (temporal correctness) is verified if and only if all the critical task processing are always executed in a timely manner. This property always verified in the design phase has to be demonstrated when we are executing the application (some tasks could miss their processing deadlines). This verification is directly connected with the target computer sizing problem.

In the OASIS approach, all timing constraints, such as deadlines, are clearly expressed in the design phase. All these constraints are calculated on the same global real-time clock. We also know processing upper bounds for each real-time task (in the application domain we consider, each processing has a bounded duration and an upper bound can be exhibited). To schedule and execute these tasks on the target computer, we can then use the results of the deadline-driven scheduling techniques [8]. These techniques are efficient, rigorous and optimal if the programming model is adequate. Indeed, we only need to calculate processor load and to make an off-line analytic verification of linear inequalities. It allows us to calculate necessary and sufficient conditions to guarantee that task on-line scheduling still ensures the timeliness property (see section 4).

Timeliness is also significant as a performance measure for real-time systems [4]. When evaluating performances of real-time systems, a binary qualitative criterion is the timeliness satisfaction, the ability to meet all deadlines. We share the same point of view and the verification of this criterion can be directly done as we will show it.

4. Timeliness and sizing verification

If we know the basic features of the target computer, it is possible to size the resources that are necessary to correctly execute an application. Our approach is based on an off-line analysis of all interactions between all the tasks, to guarantee that the deadline-driven on-line scheduling ensures timeliness. If we are in the single processor case, we are interested in knowing if the processor is best-suited (e.g. if its utilization factor is near and less than one); in the multiprocessor case, the problem is to determine the number of processors and their interconnection topology that are necessary. We will further only consider the single processor case in this paper.

4.1. Mathematical verification

To verify if a task can be executed separately on a processor, we can define the processor load it generates on a given processor. A real-time task ω_i is constituted by series of processing we identify in its state-transition diagram. For each processing j, we know its execution time upper bound (on a given processor) τ_{ij} and its lasting value δ_{ij}. From now on, processing execution time will designate the upper bound of the processing execution time, i.e. its WCET (worst case execution time). We first define the processing load ρ_{ij} as the ratio between its execution time and its lasting value: $\rho_{ij} = \tau_{ij} / \delta_{ij}$. For a task ω_i, we can then define its load ρ_i, as the maximum of its processing loads: $\rho_i = \max_j(\rho_{ij})$. Finally, the inequality $\rho_i < 1$ is fulfilled if and only if the task ω_i can be executed on the given processor.

Let $\Omega = \{\omega_i / i \in I\}$ be the set of tasks of the application. With previous results, we have a sufficient and necessary condition to execute one task on a given processor. We could extend these results to Ω. We then define a set of necessary conditions for each task in Ω, that we name elementary necessary conditions (ENC):

$$\forall i \in I, ENC_i: \rho_i < 1 \tag{1}$$

In our case, we can also define a sufficient condition for the correct execution of the set of tasks Ω, based on the deadline-driven scheduling analysis:

$$\text{Sufficient condition [8]: } \Sigma_i \, \rho_i < 1 \tag{2}$$

If we only use this sufficient condition, some correct cases could be ignored or conversely, it could lead to a great oversizing of the target computer. Indeed, this sufficient condition (2) doesn't take into account the behaviors of the tasks: all tasks are considered as totally asynchronous.

In real-time systems, synchronization points in time are numerous; task timing behaviors may not be ignored. In our approach, we can have more accurate results than with the common sufficient condition. Our solution, well-suited for the OASIS approach, is based on the following theorem, which is a refinement of the sufficient condition (2):

Theorem. At each TT time interval of the system, the sum of every parts of execution times of all active task processing (i.e. executed in the TT time interval) must be less than the interval duration.

This theorem constitutes a necessary and sufficient condition of the OASIS model, because (2) becomes a necessary and sufficient condition if at any time we replace the general factor load ρ by the actual load rest.

4.2. A simple example

We introduce here a frequent example that illustrate how the mathematical verification is achieved. Let two tasks that are periodically synchronized at the beginning and at the end of their execution, as shown on figure 5

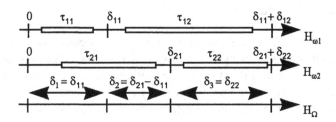

Fig. 5. Time diagrams of two task periodically synchronized

So, we obtain the following set of inequalities (see figure 5 and 6) :

$$\exists\, \alpha \in [0, 1], (\tau_{11} + \alpha.\tau_{21}) / \delta_1 \leq 1 \tag{3}$$
$$\exists\, \beta \in [0, 1], (\tau_{22} + \beta.\tau_{12}) / \delta_3 \leq 1$$
$$((1 - \alpha).\tau_{21} + (1 - \beta).\tau_{12}) / \delta_2 \leq 1$$

Only α and β are the free variables of the system. If this linear inequality system has a solution, the two tasks can be correctly executed on the same processor, i.e. the timeliness property will be guaranteed. If we replace the right member of the inequalities by a free variable k (k in the real domain), and we search the minimum value of k for which the system still has a solution, we will obtain the « true » task load generated by these two tasks if they are executed on the same processor (this method shapes the problem as a resolution of a set of inequalities of linear algebra; the expression of this problem and its resolution are simple and well known).

The unique equivalent state-transition diagram (called composition graph) deduced from the equivalent state-transition diagrams of these two tasks is shown on figure 6. From the initial state-transition diagrams, we are able to build this graph automatically and as well to generate and to solve the corresponding inequality system, but this aspect will not be further described in this paper.

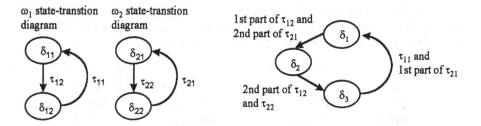

Fig. 6. The state-transition diagrams and the unique equivalent composition graph

We should finally notice that the WCET of the processing (τ_{ij}) can be calculated with existing results [9].

5. A study case

Let the operational application which is a software management of a safety device. This system, sometimes called « ébulliomètre », supervises, displays data and signals alarms connected with the state of the core in nuclear power plant. Its mission is to prevent the risk of appearance of bubbles of steam in Water Pressurized Reactor. There exist two identical systems which are not synchronized. They exchange their data taken from the environment, and their results from their own computations, to ensure coherent results and to identify failures. Each of it should first takes the data from the environment and compares a first group of results. While it should continue on computing with the last received results, it should send its own results towards the other one. Finally, it should display the possible alarms if an anomaly is detected.

5.1. Presentation of the example

To illustrate the principles of OASIS model presented above we consider a typical application from the example of an « ébulliomètre ». We introduce a printer to edit historical traces, and an operator which may act on supervision parameters, and may choose mode traces. We suppose that there exist two main lines or ways of communication. The first line is used to exchange the data with the other system, the second line is used to communicate with the operator. We call this model of application MESC. The intervening of a human operator during a computing cycle makes the management of this system intricate. It must be correctly taken into account. OASIS must do a safe gathering between the elements which communicate but which also evolve in an asynchronous way. Each MESC still be an asynchronous element of the environment for the other MESC.

The global functioning is based on a main periodic set of tasks with a period DurCycle. The figure 7 represents the functioning, during a cycle, of different tasks which form the supervisor processing. The inputs from the core are called *pumps*, *pressures* and *thermocouples*. The outputs are *sending* (data to the other MESC), *printing* (data to the printer) and *alarms* (data to the screen). It should be noticed that the data for *sending* are exchange by a message just after *computation1*.

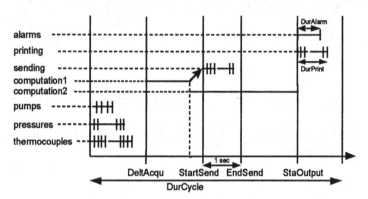

Fig. 7. Time diagram of the supervision cycle

This functioning is directly deduced from the specification of the clock and the date of visibility of the message. We should remark that *computation1* and *computation2* are two consecutive processing in the computation task. This cut off comes from a timing constraint due to a *send* (an exchange by message) during the computation.

The tasks called operator and receiver are independent and asynchronous compared to the main cycle. To obtain the global functioning we should superpose the time diagrams of the operator task and the receiver task which are not take into account in the main cycle.

5.2. Sizing verification

We can now apply the calculation rules of the section 4. We remind that the aim is to warranty a safe sizing of the computation supply with a sufficient condition (SC), but also to obtain a correct sizing (else, concerning this problem, we fall in the case of standard oversizing of complex systems which are loop implemented, directly or not by a static scheduling). We should notice that all the periodic activities are indexed on the time diagram of the main supervision cycle shown on figure 7. On the other hand, the remainder of the application (i.e. the receiver task and the operator task) shows asynchronous activities compared to the main set of tasks. So, we can already say that it is quiet unreal to analyze closely (with a time-driven scheduling) the composition of the receipt and operator processing with the supervision processing.

They correspond in fact to input/output activities on low rated lines (about 1000 bytes per second).

Let u_1, the maximum load due to the supervision terms, and u_2 and u_3 the respective maximum load due to the receipt and operator, then $u_1+u_2+u_3 \leq 1$ is a sufficient condition (SC) very close to the necessary and sufficient condition (NSC), because u_2 and u_3 give a low contribution compared to u_1. We are now going to u_1, with the hypothesis that all ENC_k (which give the simple terms; some of them will be recalled hereafter) are verified.

On the first interval [0, DeltAcqu], we haven't make any particular hypothesis about the acquisition rhythms of the following data, *pump, pressure, thermocouple*.

So we simply have:

$$u_1^{\ 1} = \tau_{pump}/\delta_{pump} + \tau_{pressure}/\delta_{pressure} + \tau_{thermocouple}/\delta_{thermocouple} \tag{4}$$

On the second interval [DeltAcqu, StartSend]:

$$\exists \alpha \in [0,1] \text{ such as } u_1^{\ 2} = (\tau_{computation1} + \alpha . \tau_{computation2})/(\text{StartSend}-\text{DeltAcqu}) \tag{5}$$

On the third et forth intervals [StartSend, EndSend] and [EndSend, StaOutput]:

$$u_1^{\ 3} = \tau_{emission}/\delta_{emission} \tag{6}$$

$$u_1^{\ 4} = (N_c . \tau_{emission} + (1-\alpha) . \tau_{computation2})/(\text{StaOutput}-\text{StartSend}) \tag{7}$$

where N_C is the maximum number of bytes to emit.
And on the fifth interval, like for u_1 :

$$u_1^{\ 5} = \tau_{alarm}/\delta_{alarm} + \tau_{printing}/\delta_{printing} \tag{8}$$

So $u_1 = \max_i u_1^{\ i}$, from which the requested SC,

$$\max_i u_1^{\ i} + u_2 + u_3 \leq 1 \tag{9}$$

which warrants a safe and correct sizing (CS), very close to the NSC for that application.

6. Conclusions

So far the development constraints for critical systems in nuclear field are more about means to use than objectives to reach. We used loop programming and prohibited the use of interruption to obtain a deterministic and predictable behavior for the system. One of the objectives of the OASIS approach is to show that there exist other means to develop critical system. So we try to shift the constraints from means to objectives.

The model presented in this paper ensures, by its principle, some important safety properties as the coherence of the data and an unvarying and deterministic real-time behavior. The main benefits of our approach deal with the dependability and parallelism adequacy issue and the computer sizing problem. We saw that timeliness is a significant part of performance evaluation for safety critical real-time systems. In this context, the computer sizing problem is very significant, and the timeliness verification is strongly connected with. The absolute determinism is a necessary element to the pertinence of the tests. That's why the analytic and test work necessary to the qualification of the system will be easier with OASIS. Moreover, with a simulation of time (TT), the unvarying behavior in regard to the implementation allows us to produce earlier actual execution traces in the working out of the software (that's an important benefit to help the design).

Works on the OASIS project have a more global span than the works presented here. Its technical objectives are to propose a complete chain of development: language, compilation & simulation tools, safety embedded run-time are under development. These former works deal with fault-tolerant problems and techniques (such as fault-checking and fault-confining) in order to ensure the required level of reliability and safety. To reach this security level, the OASIS run-time is designed on a dedicated microkernel which is strictly limited to the necessary functions and it ensures memory protection between different elements of the application. It can detect some failure, stop immediately the failing processing and then, it can keep a correct running of the rest of the application.

OASIS and its run-time gives actual multitask functioning which is closed to the flexibility we obtain with standard asynchronous approaches which are not deterministic. Moreover, OASIS is not limited by standard loop programming technique based on static pre-run-time scheduling. The level of safety reached is superior (or equal) to those obtained when using a loop programming technique (in an ad-hoc manner or automatically) associated with static scheduling.

References

1. Callison, H.R.: A time-sensitive object model for real-time systems. ACM Trans. on Software Engineering and Methodology, Vol. 4, n°3 (1995) 287-317
2. David, V., Aussaguès, C., Cordonnier, C., Aji, M., Delcoigne, J.: OASIS: a new way to design safety critical applications. 21st IFAC/IFIP Workshop on Real-Time Programming, Gramado, Brazil (1996)
3. David, V., Aji, M., Delcoigne, J., Aussaguès, C., Cordonnier, C.: Le modèle de conception OASIS/ҰC pour les systèmes temps-réel complexes critiques. Real-Time &Embedded Systems, TEKNEA, Paris (1996)
4. Halang, W.A., Gumzej, R., Colnaric, M.: Measuring the performance of real-time systems. 22nd IFAC/IFIP Workshop on Real-Time Programming, Lyon, France (1997)
5. Hoare, C.A.R.: Communicating Sequential Processes. Prentice-Hall International (1985)
6. Kopetz, H.: The Time-Triggered approach to real-time systems design. Predictability Dependable Computing Systems (Randell, B., Laprie, J.-C., Kopetz, H., Littlewood, B.) (1995) 53-78
7. Le Guernic, P., Benveniste, A., Bournai, P., Gautier, T.: SIGNAL: a data-flow oriented language for signal processing. INRIA, Research Report-378 (1985)
8. Liu, C.L., Layland, J.W.: Scheduling algorithms for multiprogramming in a hard real-time environment. Journal of the ACM, Vol. 20, n°1 (1973) 46-61

9. Puschner, P.P., Schedl, A.V.: Computing maximum task execution times - a graph-based approach. Real-Time Systems, Vol. 13, n°1 (1997) 67-92

10. Ramamritham, K.: Allocation and scheduling of complex periodic tasks. IEEE Proceedings of the ICDCS (1990) 108-115

11. Stankovic, J.A.: Misconceptions about real-time: a serious problem for next-generation systems. IEEE Computer, Vol. 21, n°10 (1988) 10-19

12. Stankovic, J.A., Ramamritham, K.: What is predictability for real-time systems? Real-Time Systems, Vol. 2, n°4 (1990) 247-254

Linking Hazard Analysis to Formal Specification and Design in B

K. Lano, P. Kan*, A. Sanchez**

Abstract. Once a hazard analysis of a system has been undertaken and a list of safety properties that it must satisfy derived, can this be used to obtain properties which a software controller for the system must satisfy? In addition, what evidential value for the safety of a system are proofs of correctness of a formal specification of its software components? We will examine these issues in the context of a specification and development technique for the B formal specification language, which has been used to specify and design discrete event control systems for batch-processing plants. A simple example is used to illustrate the ideas. The results obtained from a larger case study are also presented.

1   Introduction

Although standards such as Defence Standard 00-55 [11] and IEC 1508 [4] regard formal methods and formal proof as highly desirable for safety-critical systems, such methods may not contribute to the safety or reliability of a system, if they are applied without analysis of the relationship between the system properties and the software properties [15, 9]. The situation is akin to that of naive proofs of program correctness which take no account of the actual boundedness of datatypes of real programs [2], so yielding incorrect conclusions about the results or termination of programs.

   This paper demonstrates how to establish strong relations between specification correctness and desired system properties such as safety invariants of a class of discrete-event systems. Hazard Analysis techniques are used to identify safety properties which are incorporated as part of the specification set of a given system. Formal techniques are then used to synthesize and implement the control logic satisfying, among some other system invariants, the established safety properties. Section 2 describes the method, Section 3 discusses how system safety properties can be related to specification properties, and Section 4 reports on an industrial case study of a flexible production cell.

2   Method for Reactive Control System Specification

The following steps are taken to specify a controller for a discrete event system described in terms of a set of actuators and sensors, and required reactions to

---

 * Dept. of Computing, Imperial College, 180 Queens Gate, London SW7 2BZ, UK. kcl@doc.ic.ac.uk. Phone: 0171 594 8246. Fax: 0171 581 8024.
** CINVESTAV-Guadalajara, Apdo Postal 31-438, Guadalajara 45550, Mexico

events detected by the sensors, and invariants that the state of the system must satisfy [6].

1. Produce component models – describing the events each device (sensor or actuator) generates or responds to. These models are given as state machines.

2. Formalise: (i) required reactions to events; (ii) safety properties/invariants.

3. Produce data and control flow diagram (DCFD) of entire control system, showing all signals from sensors to the controller and all commands from the controller to actuators.

4. Partition DCFD where possible into a set of controllers each managing a disjoint set of actuators.

   We may need to group actuators together (that is, make a set of actuators be controlled by single controller) if required invariants link their states (eg: gas valve open ⇒ air valve open, in the gas burner system) – the controller is responsible for trying to maintain the invariant by sending control signals in a correct order, or responding to sensor events that break the invariant.

5. Specify controllers in B: each input event responded to by the controller has a corresponding operation which describes that response (for each possible mode of the controller).

   The invariant of each controller expresses local control invariants for the particular collection of sensors and actuators that it manages.

6. Specify sensors/actuators in B: these specifications represent the controllers *inferred knowledge* about the physical system, on the basis of events it has received and produced.

7. Implement controller using B library components. Procedural controller synthesis [14] is used to derive the control algorithms (ordering of actuator signals) required for each event response.

8. Implement sensor/actuator specifications – these will be linked eventually to actual physical devices.

9. Specify and implement an 'outer level' component which detects input events (eg: by polling sensors, by extraction from message queues, etc) and notifies the controller that they have occurred. This is usually defined in terms of the controller modes, following [5].

Animation can be applied to the controller specifications to check that the specified behaviour is actually what the user intends, and that it avoids hazard scenarios.

Proof can be applied to specifications to check internal correctness of machines and interfaces: ie, that the invariants of the machines are maintained by their operations, and that operations are called only in situations where their preconditions hold. Proof can be applied between specifications and implementations to check that the implemented response behaviour meets the specifications[3].

2.1 Procedural Controller Synthesis (PCS)

PCS is a technique developed to synthesise controllers for discrete event systems, using as inputs the component models, and logical constraints on the states which the controller can reach [14]. The controllers are expressed as finite state machines (FSMs). PCS produces a control algorithm in terms of a sequence of control commands (represented as solid transitions on the FSMs and DCFD) to components in response to input events (represented as dashed transitions). These sequences of commands can be directly translated into implementations of the B controller operations which define responses to the input events. An example of a procedural controller is given in Figure 6.

PCS produces a finite state machine which has only *wait* states (characterised by having all outgoing transitions 'dashed' or uncontrollable) or intermediate response states (characterised by having a single controllable outgoing transition). Wait states are represented in the diagram by ovals – they represent points where the controller is waiting for further input/uncontrollable events. They also correspond to states established by completed control reactions (and hence, in the case study, to the modes of **GasBurner**).

2.2 Example: Gas Burner

The process to be controlled in the case study is the simplified burner system of [13, 14] shown in Figure 1. It consists of the following process items: an on/off valve to feed air (av); an on/off valve to feed fuel (gv); a flame igniter (ig); a flame detector (fd); an on/off switch to start/stop the operation of the burner (sw). The component FSMs of the valves, ignitor and flame detector are shown in Figure 2 and the data and control flow diagram of the system is given in Figure 4. The switch FSM is isomorphic to that for the flame detector.

The objectives of the control system for the burner are to (i) start it up, maintain it with an ignited flame and to shut it down when requested, in the safest possible way and (ii) to deal with abnormal and emergency conditions that may arise during operation. In order to maximise the life of the igniter, it must be used only when the system must ignite (this is an *operational invariant*). The initial state of the system is when all valves are closed, and the rest of the components are off.

From a fault tree analysis of hazards such as "explosive concentration of fuel present" (Figure 3) we can derive invariant properties of the burner system which must be maintained to eliminate or reduce these hazards. Here a necessary invariant is that the air valve must always be open if the gas valve is open. For the controller, this means that the conjunction of the two states marked with a *

---

[3] Although proof of temporal properties is outside the scope of the B tools at present.

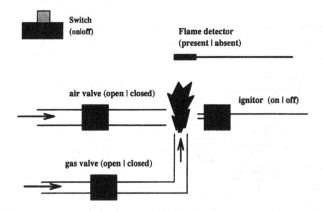

Fig. 1. Gas Burner Components

Gas Burner: Domain Model

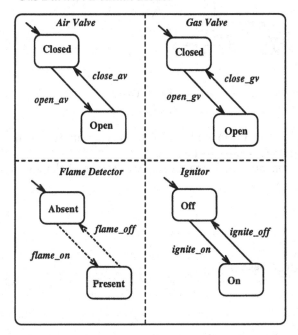

Fig. 2. Component FSMs

must not be allowed to occur. Similarly, from the hazard "unintended ignition" we can derive the invariant that the air valve must always be open if the flame is present. We assume that device failures are detected by individual device controllers, rather than by the overall controller. An example of a system in which device failures are also managed by the controller, is described in [6]. It must be possible to embed (via a statemachine morphism [7]) the FSM models of components used by procedural controller synthesis into those used by the hazard

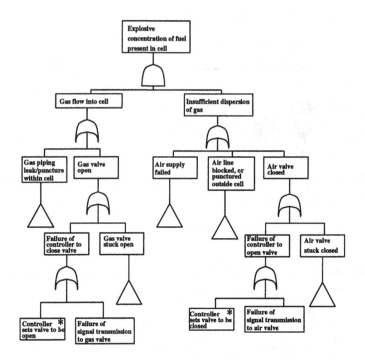

Fig. 3. "Explosive Concentration" Fault Tree

analysis, in order that the hazard conditions identified by hazard analysis can be related directly to the desired controller behaviour.

The B versions of the component models are direct translations of the state machines. For example, the gas valve is:

```
MACHINE GasValve
SEES GB_Types
VARIABLES gvstate
INVARIANT gvstate: GVState
INITIALISATION  gvstate := gv_closed
OPERATIONS

  open_gv =
     PRE gvstate = gv_closed
     THEN
       gvstate := gv_open
     END;

  close_gv =
     PRE gvstate = gv_open
     THEN
       gvstate := gv_closed
     END

END
```

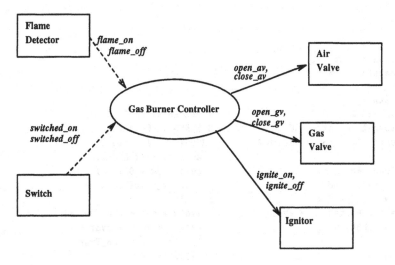

Fig. 4. Gas Burner DCFD

We can therefore formalise the operational invariant as:

$$\textbf{istate} = \textbf{on} \;\Rrightarrow\; \textbf{gvstate} = \textbf{gv\_open}$$

and the two safety invariants as

$$\textbf{gvstate} = \textbf{gv\_open} \;\Rightarrow\; \textbf{avstate} = \textbf{av\_open}$$
$$\textbf{fdstate} = \textbf{present} \;\Rightarrow\; \textbf{avstate} = \textbf{av\_open}$$

The complete reaction to events is specified in a B machine **GasBurner**, in terms of the intended changes to actuator states (left hand side of Figure 5).

The invariant of **GasBurner** expresses the meaning of the various controller modes (**idle, running, try_ignite, flushingon, flushingoff**) which have been identified. Because of the simplicity of the system, and the invariant links between actuator states, we have chosen to control all the actuators with a single controller.

The controller maintains a record (**fdstate** and **swstate**) of the most recent information it has about the sensor states.

A procedural controller for the system is given in Figure 6. Component states are given in the order (**air valve, gas valve, ignitor, flame detector, switch**). For each of the five components there are two possible states, so there are 32 states in the unconstrained system. Only 14 of these are allowed to occur by the procedural controller. It can be seen that the operational invariant and the first safety invariant hold at all of these states, whilst the invariant **fdstate** = **present** $\Rightarrow$ **avstate** = **av_open** only fails at one state.

From the procedural controller we can derive the definitions of implementation operations given in **GasBurnerI** (right hand side of Figure 5).

Finally, we specify the 'outer level' in terms of a periodically executed sampling operation, which detects events and changes the controller mode appropriately (left hand side of Figure 7). This is implemented by testing and comparing

```
MACHINE  GasBurner
...
VARIABLES
  avstate, gvstate, istate,
  fdstate, swstate, cstate
INVARIANT
  avstate: AVState &
  gvstate: GVState &                      IMPLEMENTATION GasBurnerI
  istate: IState & swstate: BOOL &        REFINES GasBurner
  fdstate: FDState & cstate: CState &     IMPORTS GB_Actuators,
                                            swstate_Vvar(BOOL),
  (cstate = idle  =>                        cstate_Vvar(CState),
     avstate = av_closed &                  fdstate_Vvar(FDState)
     gvstate = gv_closed &                INVARIANT
     istate = off & fdstate = absent &      swstate = swstate_Vvar &
     swstate = FALSE) & ...                 cstate = cstate_Vvar &
                                            fdstate = fdstate_Vvar
  (istate = on  =>                        INITIALISATION
              gvstate = gv_open) &          swstate_STO_VAR(FALSE); ...
  (gvstate = gv_open =>                   OPERATIONS
              avstate = av_open) &          switched_on =
  (fdstate = present =>                      VAR cs
              avstate = av_open)             IN
INITIALISATION                                 cs <-- cstate_VAL_VAR;
  avstate := av_closed ||                      swstate_STO_VAR(TRUE);
  gvstate := gv_closed ||                      IF cs = idle
  istate := off || fdstate := absent ||        THEN
  swstate := FALSE || cstate := idle             c_open_av;
OPERATIONS                                       c_open_gv;
  switched_on =                                  c_ignite_on;
    PRE swstate = FALSE                          cstate_STO_VAR(try_ignite)
    THEN                                       ELSE
      swstate := TRUE ||                         IF cs = flushingoff
      IF cstate = idle                           THEN
      THEN                                          cstate_STO_VAR(flushingon)
        avstate := av_open ||                    END
        gvstate := gv_open ||                  END
        istate := on ||                      END;
        cstate := try_ignite
      ELSE                                   ....
        IF cstate = flushingoff
        THEN                                 END
          cstate := flushingon
        END
      END
    END;

  ....
END
```

Fig. 5. Specification and Implementation of Gas Burner Controller

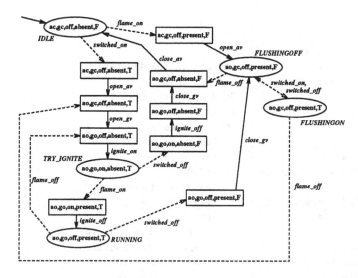

Fig. 6. Procedural Controller for Gas Burner

the previous (**oldfd** and **oldsw**) values of sensor states and the new values (**newfd** and **newsw**) provided as input to the sampling operation (right hand side of Figure 7). Executable code (in a small subset of C) can then be generated.

3 Formalising and Proving Safety Properties

Hazard analysis techniques such as HAZOPS [12] and fault tree analysis [9] will yield safety invariants **Inv**$_S$ which the *controlled system* must satisfy at all times in order to avoid hazardous situations. In contrast, the B specification of the system controller has an *internal model* of the system (Figure 8). If **cstate** represents the actual state of component **C** (for example, the position of a valve, or the presence of a voltage), then there is a corresponding variable **cstate'** modelling the controllers' knowledge of the state of component **C**, based on the events it has received from **C** and the commands it has sent to **C**.

These variables will not have the same value at all times; **cstate'** may be out of date wrt **cstate** because of delays in sensors detecting changes in **cstate**, delays in transmitting the occurrence of such events to the controller, and delays in the controller response to these events. On the other side, the controller may anticipate the change of state in an actuator by setting **cstate'** = **val** before the physical system reaches state **cstate** = **val**. Thus **Inv**$'_S$ (the internal version of **Inv**$_S$ formed by replacing **cstate** by **cstate'**) will only be an approximation to **Inv**$_S$.

The internal model may also be simpler than the actual component state, that is, there may be a non-trivial embedding of the internal model into the component model used by hazard analysis. Figure 9 shows the more detailed valve model used in hazard analysis. This means [7] there is an *abstraction function* **i** which maps concrete states and transitions to abstract ones. In this case study,

```
MACHINE GBOuter
...
VARIABLES mode, oldfd, oldsw
INVARIANT mode: CState &              IMPLEMENTATION GBOuterI
  oldfd: FDState & oldsw: BOOL & ...  REFINES GBOuter
INITIALISATION                       SEES GB_Types, Bool_TYPE
  mode := idle || oldsw := FALSE ||   IMPORTS GasBurner
  oldfd := absent                    INVARIANT mode = cstate &
OPERATIONS                             oldsw = swstate &
  sample(newfd,newsw) =                oldfd = fdstate
    PRE newfd: FDState & newsw: BOOL OPERATIONS
    THEN                               sample(newfd,newsw) =
    IF newfd = oldfd & newsw = oldsw     VAR ofd, osw
    THEN skip /* No events */          IN
    ELSE                                   ofd <-- get_fdstate;
      oldsw := newsw ||                    osw <-- get_swstate;
      oldfd := newfd ||                    IF newfd = ofd &
      IF mode = idle                         newsw = osw
      THEN                               THEN skip
        IF newfd = present &               /* No events detected */
           newsw = TRUE                  ELSE
        THEN mode := flushingon            IF newfd = present &
/* Both events can only occur if              ofd = absent
   unintended ignition happens --        THEN flame_on
   assume  flame_on  occurs first. */    ELSE flame_off
        ELSE /* Just one event: */       END;
        IF newfd = present &             IF newsw = TRUE &
           newsw = FALSE                    osw = FALSE
        THEN mode := flushingoff          THEN switched_on
        ELSE mode := try_ignite           ELSE switched_off
        END                               END
      END                               END
    ELSE   ....                        END
      /* Other cases of mode */
    END                                END
    END

END
```

Fig. 7. Outer Level Specification and Implementation

we map the concrete valve states **open**, **failed_open**, **repairing_open** and **closing** of Figure 9 to the abstract **open**, and the states **closed**, **failed_closed**, **repairing_closed** and **opening** to the abstract **closed**. The mapping should be constructed so that

$$\mathbf{Inv'_S(i(cstate))} \;\Rightarrow\; \mathbf{Inv_S(cstate)}$$

That is, if the controller guarantees an invariant $\mathbf{Inv'_S(i(cstate))}$ on the abstract internal state, this ensures that safety invariant holds for the concrete external state.

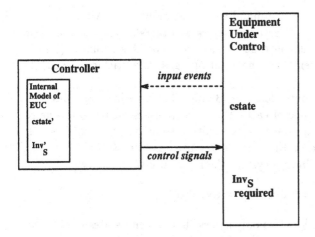

Fig. 8. System and Controller Relationship

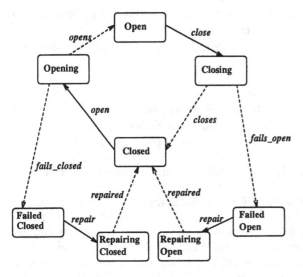

Fig. 9. Extended Valve Model

Since the invariants of B machines only express the properties of those machine states which arise when no operation is executing, these invariants do not constrain the states during operation execution. In the procedural controller model of Figure 6, new input events which occur during a control response are deferred by the procedural controller (and hence the B implementation) until the end of the control response, so the controllers record of sensor states may be out of date during this response.

If we assume that the actuator commands are synchronous (ie, the controller has to wait for the command to complete), the model of the state of an actuator will be up to date after a command to it has completed[4]. After a control response, the internal records of actuator states will therefore match actual actuator states until the next uncontrolled event occurs on this actuator (failures can be modelled as input events, eg: the event of a gas valve sticking closed, etc, as in Figure 9).

In terms of procedural controllers, the B controller invariant *only* describes the properties of the *end* states of each of these response sequences (ie, the so-called 'wait states' where the software is awaiting some input signal from the controlled system). In Figure 6 these are represented as oval states.

For example, in the gas burner system the internal invariant $\mathbf{Inv'_S}$

$$\mathbf{gvstate'} = \mathbf{gv\_open} \;\Rightarrow\; \mathbf{avstate'} = \mathbf{av\_open}$$

is provable in **GasBurner**, but this only shows that the end states of reactions obey this predicate. We can deduce that $\mathbf{Inv_S}$ also holds for the corresponding abstract external system states at all times when the controller is waiting for input events, since this property involves only actuator states, and there are no input events originating from these actuators.

Applying the abstraction mapping i to the concrete component states, we have that $\mathbf{Inv_S(i(cstate))}$ here is

$$\mathbf{gvstate} \in \{\mathbf{gv\_open, gv\_closing,}$$
$$\mathbf{gv\_failed\_open, gv\_repairing\_open}\} \;\Rightarrow$$
$$\mathbf{avstate} \in \{\mathbf{av\_open, av\_closing, av\_failed\_open,}$$
$$\mathbf{av\_repairing\_open}\}$$

which ensures that the hazards due to valve settings or failures identified in Figure 3 cannot arise.

$\mathbf{Inv'_S}$ can be guaranteed to hold for the synthesised procedural controller, since it is selected from within a space (the *controller superstructure*) of controllers which always maintain the required static invariants. We can demonstrate that the derived B controller implementation maintains the invariant during controller operation executions, by defining a **GB_Actuators** machine with interface the atomic valve actions, suitably constrained to maintain the invariant:

```
c_open_gv  =
    PRE avstate  =  av_open & gvstate  =  gv_closed
    THEN open_gv
    END ;

c_close_av  =
    PRE gvstate  =  gv_closed & istate  =  off &
        avstate  =  av_open
    THEN close_av
    END
```

[4] We could assume that the command completes when the device driver confirms that the physical action has succeeded, via some additional sensor which we abstract from in our model of the device.

The invariant of **GB_Actuators** contains the first safety constraint. This constraint can be proved to be preserved by the constrained operations, under the assumption that they are executed only when their preconditions hold: the preconditions express that **open_av** is executed before **open_gv**, and **close_gv** is executed before **close_av**.

Similarly for the invariant **istate = on $\Rightarrow$ gvstate = gv_open**. But the second safety property

$$\textbf{fdstate} = \textbf{present} \Rightarrow \textbf{avstate} = \textbf{av\_open}$$

whilst established by each response of **GasBurner** (ie, it holds at each wait state in Figure 6), may be false in the actual environment for time periods between an occurrence of the **flame_on** event and its detection and the completion of response **open_av** by the controller.

If we assume a polling implementation with a cycle period of τ time units, then the (environment) property **fdstate = present $\Rightarrow$ avstate = av_open** can fail for a duration of $\eta + \tau + \mathbf{D} + \eta'$ where:

- η is the delay between the event of flame becoming present and the flame detector detecting this;

- $\mathbf{D}$ is the deadline of the **sample** operation within each period: $\mathbf{D} \leq \tau$, and it can be proved that the duration of **sample** (as given in **GBOuter** above) can be at most $\mathbf{D}$;

- η' is the delay between the command signal being sent and the air valve opening. If this command is synchronous then this delay is subsumed in $\tau + \mathbf{D}$.

$\tau + \mathbf{D}$ is the maximum delay in the controller response to the **fdstate := present** event: this event may occur just after a polling of the flame detector has been performed, so is not dealt with for the duration τ of one cycle, and is only detected at the beginning of the next cycle. The reaction must then complete within time $\mathbf{D}$.

Figure 10 shows the relationship between the external and internal component states for the gas burner.

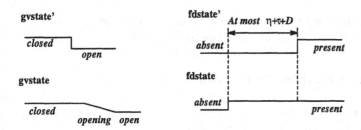

Fig. 10. Example Relationships between Internal and External States

Alternatively the controller may ignore the event for one cycle because it is busy dealing with other events. We require that the controller does not become overloaded, that is, it can always deal with the maximum number of events that may be detected in a cycle (in the gas burner case, this is 2) within that cycle or the next. In particular, the design of **GBOuter** assumes that at most *one* state transition will occur in each monitored component of the system, in a given polling cycle.

If we can place a lower bound t_C on the time for which the condition **fdstate = present** remains true once it becomes true, and remains false once it becomes false, then this approach ensures that no such events are missed if $\tau + D < t_C$.

In general we can derive the following assertions about the controlled system from the formal proof of correctness of the corresponding safety invariants in the B specification, provided that $Inv'_S(i(cstate)) \Rightarrow Inv_S(cstate)$:

- If an invariant Inv'_S refers only to actuator states, and none of these actuators can change state apart from as a result of control signals from the controller, with all control signals being synchronous, then Inv_S will be true at all time points where the controller is idle. If in addition, we can prove Inv'_S at the level of granularity of individual command signals, and ensure that the controller implementation respects the ordering constraints implied by Inv'_S at this level (ie: operations of **GB_Actuators** are always called within their preconditions by **GasBurnerI**), then Inv_S also holds at all time points whilst the controller is active.

- If Inv'_S depends on the state of components which are the source of input events to the controller, then we can limit the time for which Inv_S fails to hold to a maximum period of $\eta + \tau + D$ by a polling implementation with cycle time τ, deadline D and maximum delay η between occurrence of an event that falsifies Inv_S and its detection by the controller, provided that:

  - No more than a single event arises from a given sensed component in a cycle, and the reaction to all events detected in a given cycle can always complete within time D of the start of the cycle;

  - The sensed condition remains false for at least time $t_C > 0$ once it becomes false, and true for at least this time when it becomes true, and $\tau + D < t_C$.

Scheduling theory will be needed to ensure the adequacy of the design, if several controllers/samplers are executing on the same processor [3].

4 Case Study: Flexible Production Cell

The approach was applied to the flexible production cell [10, 8]. The following safety properties for the system were determined:

1. no collisions of cranes and of crane grippers with other components;

2. blanks should only be deposited into a free processing unit or onto a free belt, and must not run off the end of the feed belt.

The procedural controller for the system is divided into the following separate controllers:

1. The feed belt, which takes inputs from the belt blank sensor, the blank reader, the crane gripper and position sensors, and generates outputs to the belt motor and reader.

2. The cranes, taking input from the crane position and grip sensors and the processing unit blank sensors (in order to determine the completion of successful remove and add actions), and generating outputs to the grip and position actuators and the crane magnets.

3. The processing units, taking input from the crane grip and position sensors and the system clock, and outputs to the tool actuator of the processing unit.

A controller **CellController** coordinates the actions of the cranes and processing units, and interacts with a schedular component. The DCFD for this controller is shown in Figure 11. Two levels of outer controllers are used to poll

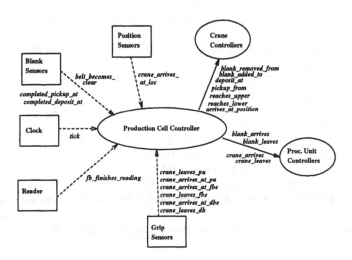

Fig. 11. DCFD of Production Cell Controller

events and direct them to either the feed belt controller or the cell controller.

Conclusions

We have described a systematic development process for safety critical control systems, combining control engineering techniques and formal methods. We have described how properties established for the formal specification can be related to safety properties of the equipment under control, and the limitations of such relationships.

References

1. J. Abrial. *The B Book: Deriving Programs from Meaning*, Cambridge University Press, 1996.
2. I. Currie, *NewSpeak: a reliable programming language*, Chapter 6 of *High-integrity Software*, C. Sennett (Ed.), Pitman, 1989.
3. H Gomaa. *Software Design Methods for Concurrent and Real-time Systems*. Addison Wesley, 1993.
4. IEC, *IEC 1508 Functional Safety: Safety Related Systems*, draft, 1995.
5. International Society for Measurement and Control. *Batch Control Models and Terminology*, ISA-S88.01-1995, 1995.
6. K. Lano, S. Goldsack, A. Sanchez, *Formal Development of Event-Driven Controllers for Process Manufacturing Systems*, in *Industrial-Strength Formal Methods*, M. Hinchey, J. Bowen (eds), Academic Press, 1998.
7. K. Lano, *Refinement and Safety Analysis*, in SAFECOMP '97, Springer-Verlag, 1997.
8. K. Lano, P. Kan. *Design of Flexible Production Cell*, ROOS Project Internal Report, Department of Computing, Imperial College, 1997.
9. N. Leveson, Chapter 15 of *Safeware: system safety and computers*, Addison-Wesley, 1995. ISBN 0-201-11972-2.
10. A. Lötzbeyer, R Mühlfeld, *Task Description of a Flexible Production Cell with Real Time Properties*, FZI, Karlsruhe, 1996.
11. Ministry of Defence, *Defence Standard 00-56*, Issue 2, http://www.seasys.demon.co.uk/, 1996.
12. Ministry of Defence, *Interim Defence Standard 00-58*, Issue 1, http://www.seasys.demon.co.uk/, 1996.
13. I. Moon, G. Powers, J. R. Burch and E. M. Clarke. *Automatic Verification of Sequential Control Systems using Temporal Logic*, American Institute of Chemical Engineers (AIChE) Journal, 38(1) :67–75, January 1992.
14. A. Sanchez. *Formal Specification and Synthesis of Procedural Controllers for Process Systems*, Springer-Verlag. Lecture Notes in Control and Information Sciences, vol. 212. 19 96.
15. Neil Storey, Chapter 11 of *Safety-Critical Computer Systems*, Addison-Wesley, 1996.

Management

and Human Factors

Controlling your Design through your Software Process

Nicolás Martín-Vivaldi and Peter Isacsson

Q-Labs AB, Ideon Research Park
S-223 70 Lund, Sweden
{nmv, pi}@q-labs.se

Abstract. The software industry has identified the need for processes. Problems with low quality, productivity, predictability and reliability and too long cycle times have increased the interest in processes. Another reason for the increased interest is the understanding of the relationship between the development process and the qualities of the product.

This paper discusses different levels of formality for describing a process and describes a practical method for transforming a process to a stricter level of formality. It includes practical experiences from transforming a implicit development process, via semiformal notation, to a formal and executable process model. The right level of formality and detail in a process model is decided by many different factors. This paper describes different ways to represent your processes and gives help in how to choose between the alternatives. It also gives guidelines for how to transform your process model to representations of higher formality.

1 Introduction

Today there is a common understanding of the correlation between the software development process and the resulting reliability of the developed product. The more critical the safety of the software product is, the more will be gained by focusing on the process and the understanding of the process. As the size and complexity of the software products is growing beyond the possibility for exhaustive system and acceptance testing, the industry focus more on preventive actions. Attention is on introducing quality assurance steps into the development process as early and as often as feasible, to relieve final testing.

Looking at the characteristics of software development one can draw some conclusions regarding the necessity to understand the development process. Each software product is unique, which implies that the development process must be adapted to meet the requirements of the product. Software development is a creative, intellectual exercise rather than manufactural, which implies that the development process as well is variable and thereby must be understood and modelled explicitly. Methods applied in the development process are mainly human based, which implies that the effectiveness and efficiency is dependent on the individuals involved. All these characteristics of software development points clearly to the need for explicitly defining the process that is used for the development. Without a documented description of the process none of the characteristics can effectively be addressed.

Using the process as a communication tool for the individuals in the development projects requires that the process is both unambiguous and easy to understand. The right level of formality and detail required to encompass both these requirements spreads from totally implicit, undocumented processes to formal processes with automated execution support. This paper will describe how to transform a process description from implicit to more formal descriptions.

2 Different use of Process Models

The use of the process models depends heavily on the awareness the organisation has regarding what the organisation represents as such. The process is a part of the organisation's total memory of experience and thereby a base for organisational learning. The process is a vehicle for providing products with a expected or even predicted level of reliability. A maturing process will evolve not only by improving its performance, but also by understanding the right level of formality for different purposes of the organisation.

Having an informal process model might be sufficient in new, quickly growing organisations that is still creating its market and its business. As a company grows the greater the cost will become to spread information about the normal, repeated activities. The need for a more formal process model arises. It can be argued that in organisations with a continuous high level of change the need for processes should be less. This can be shown to be correct only to some extent. The importance for any organisation is to understand what is and what is not changing, and thereby what activities to be or not to be described and documented. Understanding the right level of formality and the right amount of information in a process model is the target for providing cost/effective support.

To produce safety critical software will require a more formal definition of the process. As the requirements of the software increases, the process will have to be supported more formally. Higher demands on defect free software at the same time as more people will be involved to produce it, will also require more formal support. The semi-formal and formal process models provides a way to allow the knowledge of the organisation to be applied by the individual.

3 Process Models

A process can be described using different levels of formality and detail. This paper divides them with respect to how formal they are specified.

3.1 Implicit model

The lowest level of process maturity is characterized by:
- no documentation of the process exist. The work is performed according to what the individuals experience as efficient or like they always have done.
- the documented process is not followed at all. The process has not been updated according to how work is performed and the implicit process only lives in the memory of the individuals which also probably differ between different people.

In other words the reality is undocumented. The process is heavily dependent on the efforts of individual people. The characteristics of an implicit model are that it can represent several aspects of the process (applicability), it can also easily be tailored (flexibility) and also be used "as is" for a large set of processes (robustness). The drawbacks are that it is very difficult for an beginner to quickly, clearly and accurately understand the content (readability) and the process can as stated above be interpreted in different ways in by different individuals (relative formality).

3.2 Informal model

The next step is when there exist a textual process, and it is followed. A well described process model will allow people to have a more similar view of the process. Though, still the structure and completeness of this kind of process model can be of different quality. This sort of process description is called informal.

With an informal process model it is easy to represent details and also abstractions (scalability) since you do not have a predefined template you must follow. It is also relatively easy to maintain the process description since the notification is not so specified.

On the other hand it is less applicable, since the process description do not give any support in covering the different aspects. It is also harder for beginners to become quickly competent without extensive training (learnability). This is due to that the process description is not specified harder to follow the main theme and also not fully clear what it means (relative formality).

3.3 Semi-formal model

In the semi-formal model the structure is much more consistent. The model is template based, according to software standards and sometimes illustrated with legends. Checklists exist to give support and to ease the usage of the processes both in awareness and correctness.

Compared to a informal model it is even easier to maintain the process description since it has more structure but is still not so complex to update as a formal model. The *readability* is also high due to that you can specify the training. Checklists and legends make the learning better.

With respect to *robustness* the semi-formal is not so good. It is harder to describe a process with a more specific notation. Scalability is by the same reason not well described, different levels are always difficult to describe if one in the same time wants to be strict on the level of details.

3.4 Formal model

In a formal model there must be no ambiguity about any entities of the process. This makes it possible to make the model enactable. There exist both graphical and plain code implementation possibilities.

With a formal model there is no ambiguity, the *relative formality* is very high, it is also a format that has a high *learnability*, the enactment facilitates the understanding and there is clear definitions.

The negative aspects are *flexibility* and *scalability*. It is hard with a formal notation to describe details and abstraction. The *flexibility* is varying depending on the kind of formal model but still, it is not as simple to tailor, it is too complex. It is hard to handle in a living process but the goal of automated support is really a promising challenge.

3.5 Summary of models

When summarising the different models one can not (unfortunately) say that there is one that is better that the other. It all depends on the environment, resources, history and goal of the organisation.

- **Environment**. The environment can be very different even within an organisation. Are the processes static or dynamic? Are there often changes? Are there a broad set of processes? What are the characteristics of the processes, long-time/short-time, iterative/nonrepeating, how many people are involved using the same process?
- **Resources**. What resources is available? Are the involved people trained in the process? Will there be people allocated to work with the process description? The cost for the different model vary in the same way as the *relative formality*.
- **History**. What kind of notation exist today? What experience in process engineering exist? One can not escape from ones history, it really takes effort to define and maintain semi-formal and formal models, specially if you have no experience.
- **Goals**. The immediate and long term goal of the organisation must be considered. There must be a motivation for why the chosen model must be used and maintained.

Through answering these questions and statements you will have more reason when deciding which process model that is the most suitable one for your organisation.

The reliability of the product is related to *relative formality*. The product is dependent of its process, see chapter 2. The more relative *formality* the easier it is to follow and understand the process. This though is no assurance for that the processes are followed but it gives help to the involved people to learn, understand and maintain the processes. Another aspect is that we can not improve our process (product) if we do not understand the process that is to be followed. Below follows a summary of the different process models and their characteristics.

Table 1. The different models compared relatively (4 is high and 1 is low)

Characteristics	Implicit	Informal	Semi-formal	Formal
Scalability	4	3	2	1
Applicability	4	1	2	3
Flexibility	4	3	2	1
Readability	1	3	4	2
Maintainability	1	3	4	2
Learnability	1	2	3	4
Robustness	4	3	2	1
Relative Formality	1	2	3	4
Product Reliability	1	2	3	4

4 Transformation of process models

This chapter present guidelines how to transform your process model into a more specific model. If you have an implicit or Informal model and want to transform it directly to a formal model we still recommend to go via a semi-formal model. The step between the Informal model and the formal model is too far. In order to span the gap the transformation must go via a semi-formal description. The semi-formal model then offers:

- a high-level design to facilitate the implementation of a informal model in the formal model.
- an easier way to define stringent transformation rules, since the semi formal model is much more specified than an ordinary informal model.
- earlier discovery if the informal model is insufficient or defective.

The transformation can be illustrated by the picture below.

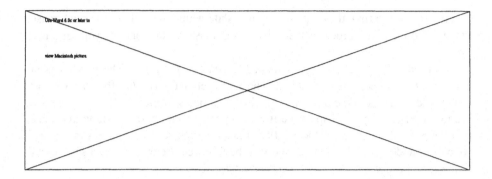

Fig. 1. An illustration of the transformation chain.

The shaded arrow between the Implicit and Informal models represent that there is no guidelines in this paper presenting how to do this transformation. This is due to that this activity is too arbitrary. There is no specified outline of a informal model so this activity can be performed in either way.

The Semi-formal model is just one of many possible realisation of the Implicit/Informal model. It is dependent on what template the semi-formal The template extorts the elements that specifies the process, such as entry/exit criteria or activities, which simplifies the modelling into the formal model. The steps presented in the following chapters are dependent on the model to be used. In our case we have developed guidelines for the semi-formal model, PERFECT template description [12] and for the formal model Process Weaver [1]. The summarized guidelines in this paper are described in detail in [13].

4.1 Implicit and Informal model to Semi formal description

This guideline is for how to transform a Informal or Implicit model into the Semi-formal model, PERFECT template description. It could easily be transformed to fit another semi-formal model.

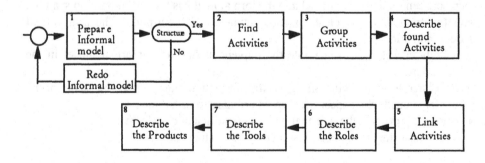

Fig. 2. The transformation steps from Informal model to Semi-formal notation.

1. **Prepare Informal model**. Identify general concepts, for example activity, entry/exit criteria, choice, interruption, resume, return, iteration and roles. If the Informal model lacks most of the concepts, the model may need to be rewritten before continuing the transformation. If it is an implicit model that is to be transformed this step will be to get the involved people into a room where they will perform the following steps (2-8) together. The size of the group should not be greater than 7. A facilitator is also needed, he/she will be able to take a look from outside and to keep the discussion focused.

2. **Find activities**. An activity within a process is a part of the process that leads to a result. In this step, the activities and sub-activities involved in the process are identified.

3. **Group activities**. The activities found in the previous step will be grouped hierarchically and a picture of the activity structure is drawn.

4. **Describe found activities**. The contents of this step is to analyse the activities in the model and write a description.

5. **Link activities**. In this step, the activities are linked together logically. With the help of the entry/exit criteria, activities are linked to find:

- Parallelism. Can two or more activities be performed at the same time?
- Synchronization. Does an activity depend on outputs of more than one activity?
- Iteration. Does some activity have to be iterated?
- Return. Is it necessary to go back to a previous activity?
- Interruption resume. Consider two parallel activities, does a sub-activity in one of the activities depend on a sub-activity from the other activity?

6. **Describe the roles**. Roles found in step 3 will be described by the name of the role, in which activity the role is presented, the object of the role and how the role is appointed.

7. **Describe the tools**. Tools found in step 3 are described by defining the name and writing a short description of the tool.

8. **Describe the products**. In this step, the products (documents) are described by: a description of the main object for the product, and a determination of the attributes needed to describe the product. A diagram showing the relations between the products are made.

4.2 Semi-formal to Formal model

These guidelines are for how to implement the Semi-formal model in a Formal description. The implicit/Informal model must not be forgotten. If only the Template description were to be used, information would be lost since the Template might not cover all information from the Informal model. The Formal model used in this case is Process Weaver [1] and this transformation guidelines must be tailored for chosen formal description. Figure 3 shows an overview of the steps. When implementing the applications in Process WEAVER one must understand that **it should be considered**

as ordinary software development. All actions done to prevent errors in ordinary software development should be performed.

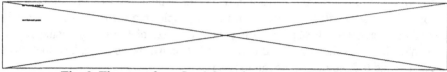

Fig. 3. The steps from Semi-formal to Process WEAVER.

1. **Define roles**. The process can either be very specified or unspecified in the meaning of roles. Very specified means that all roles from the template description are defined into the Process WEAVER and unspecified means that the roles are grouped into a team. The team leader is the only role and he delegates the tasks to the team members.
2. **Create part of Process WEAVER method**. The first time this step is entered, the top level of the process is created. Then for each time the step is entered sub-activities are added to activities.
3. **Implement refined activities**. Refined activities control the terminal activities and terminal activities organize the users' work.
   Step 2 and 3 should be iterated until the activities in the template description are no further decomposed.
4. **Implement terminal activities**. When there are only terminal activities in the method graph, they will be implemented in cooperative procedures with work-contexts.
5. **Make Work Context**. This is the final representation of an activity with variable guidelines, input and output documents.

4.3 Summary of transformation steps

In a process there are several concepts, like activities and roles, that must be described. To summary the transformation steps here is a table over the different process concepts and in which step in the guidelines they are taken care of.

Table 2. The numbers show in which steps the transformation is performed.

General Concepts	to	Semi-formal	to	Formal
Activity	2	Activity	3, 4	Cooperate Procedure
Entry/Exit criteria	4	Entry/Exit criteria	3, 4	Co-shell, Procedure condition button
Choice	5	Inclusive Or	3, 4	Control buttons or Co-shell
Interruption	5	Interruption	3, 4	Wait for state or condition
Resume	5	Resume	3, 4	Fulfilled Wait criteria
Return	5			Handled as iteration

Iteration	5	Loop of activities	3, 4	Loop of C-P until condition fulfilled
Roles	4, 6	Roles	1	Roles
Work Instructions			5	Infotext in work contexts
Synchronisation	5	And In	3, 4	Many places to one transition
Parallelism	5	and Out	3, 4	One transition to many places
Resources	4, 7	Tools and doc.	3, 4	Objects in Work contexts
Product	4, 8	Product	5	Task

5 Experience

Our experience is derived from several projects transforming implicit processes into informal or semi-formal models or informal models into semi-formal descriptions. In one occasion we have transformed a specific part of a Semi-formal description into a formal description.

First we transformed a implicit development process for telecom systems into the Cleanroom inspired Eqlabs process [10, 11], a template based description. Later we transformed a specific part into the formal notation of Process WEAVER to see in what degree automated support that was possible.

When transforming the implicit model there was problems with finding the right number of abstraction levels. Too few implies too much information on each level. Too many will make the process model harder to understand for the process user. The Semi-formal notation (see figure 4) focused on activities and products but the relation between the different activities and products were not so clearly defined. Resources was neither well defined in the implicit model.

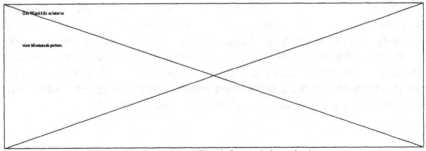

Fig. 4. The resulting Semi-formal description.

When implementing the formal model it was soon discovered that Process WEAVER needed the roles to be more specified than they were. It was not specified who was responsible for the different activities so we solved that by letting a whole team be the lowest level of granularity. The teamleader then got the automated support and divided the work between the team.

Another problem was interruption-resume. It was not clear what to do when you needed to redo a process step. Three times there was possibilities (see ð in figure 5) for redoing a process step. But what was not described were if the step was to totally redone or only specific parts. Here we had to go back to the authors of the Eqlabs process to understand the content of the rework.

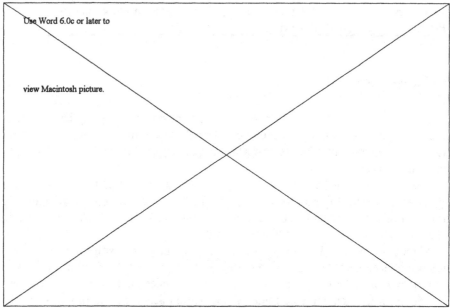

Fig. 5. The Semi-formal description transformed into Formal description.

Parallelism was pretty well described in the Semi-formal model but synchronisation points were lacking. Eqlabs did not define specific synchronisation point, those were supposed do be ongoing through the development. In Process WEAVER it possible to implement generic events but it makes the model much more complex.

Otherwise the other general concepts were well described. It was striking how easy it was to handle the activities and criteria (even though the criteria was not explicitly defined) when a sound level of abstraction is obtained.

6 Further work

We have identified the following areas as possible future work:
- **Capturing a implicit process.** When capturing a implicit process are there some specific aspects to consider compared to when analysing a Informal model?
- **Mapping between semi-formal and formal models**. If a specific formal notation is to be used it will imply some prerequisites on the semi-formal model to make the transformation possible.

- **Studies of general concepts**. Empirical studies on the general process concepts to determine their necessity. Which are the most important and in which order should they be introduced?

7 Conclusion

The importance of having the development process under control, can be affirmed by many of our customers. Having solely an implicit process model can be a risk for the organisation, the reliability of the products will be unnecessarily dependent on each individual and his/hers actions. The possible benefits of more formal process models and automated support is clear, but today it is difficult to make the benefits of a formal model greater than the cost for defining and maintaining the model. In this paper we have shown the transformation steps to go from an implicit or informal process, via semi-formal models to a formal process model. Each step makes the model more unambiguous but also more rigid. Depending on each company's objectives and unique situation, the level of formality must be decided, inbetween the implicit ant the formal.

Our experience show that an Semi-formal, template-based model often is the most suitable alternative for software companies of today. It will make the organisation more robust against errors made by individuals as well as being easier to learn, apply, maintain with still high relative formality and product reliability. For companies with high product requirements the level of formality should be increased, at least for specific parts of the process. This is a promising area for future research with specific focus on safety critical applications.

8 References

1. Christer Fernström. "PROCESS WEAVER: Adding Process Support to UNIX." In Proceedings of the second international conference on the software process, Berlin, Germany. IEEE Press, February 1993.
2. Noureeddine Belkhatir, Jacky Estubier and Walcélio L.Melo. "Software Process Model and Work Space Control in the Adele System." In Proceedings of the second international conference on the software process, Berlin, Germany. IEEE Press, February 1993.
3. Peter H. Feiler and Watts S. Humphrey. "Software Process Development and Enactment: Concepts and Definitions." In Proceedings of the second international conference on the software process, Berlin, Germany. IEEE Press, February 1993.
4. Peter H. Feiler. "Software Process Support in Software Development Environments." Proceedings of the 5th international Software Process Workshop, Maine, USA. IEEE Press, October 1989.
5. H. Dieter Rombach. "A FRAMEWORK FOR ASSESSING PROCESS REPRESENTATIONS." Proceedings of the 5th international Software Process Workshop, Maine, USA. IEEE Press, October 1989.

6. Reidar Conradi, M. Letizia Jaccheri and Cristina Mazzi. "Variability of Process Models, and the EPOS Solution." Proceedings of the 8th international Software Process Workshop, Wadem, Germany. IEEE Press, March 1993.

7. Eric S.K. Yu and John Mylopoulos. "Understanding "Why" in Software Process Modelling, Analysis and Design" Proceedings of the 16th international conference on Software Engineering, Sorrento, Italy. IEEE Press, May 1994.

8. Peter Kawalek. "The Process Modelling Cookbook" University of Manchester, British Telecommunications, September 1991.

9. William H. Ett and Shirley A.Becker. "Evaluating the Effectiveness OF PROCESS WEAVER as a Process Management Tool: A Case Study". Proceedings of the third symposium on Assessment of Quality Software Development Tools, Washington, USA. IEEE 1994.

10. Henrik Cosmo. "Process Description for Function Design" N/TI-93:145, Ericsson, 1993, restricted availability.

11. Henrik Cosmo. "Document Instruction for Function Design" N/TI-93:147, Ericsson, 1993, restricted availability.

12. Perfect Consortium. "Perfect Booklets"., PERFECT Esprit-III Project 9090, May 1994.

13. Nicolás Martín-Vivaldi. "Process Modelling in Process WEAVER", Q-Labs 94:0467, November 1994.

Operator Errors and Their Causes

Timm Grams

Fachhochschule Fulda, Fachbereich Elektrotechnik,
Marquardstraße 35, D-36039 Fulda

Abstract. The *normative model of operator behaviour* constitutes the frame-work for the description of typical operator errors (i.e. deviations from the norm) and their causes. The normative model of operator behaviour will be based on the *decision under risk*. By this the methods of technical risk assessment, economic decision theory and psychology can be utilised in the assessment of operator behaviour. This view on operator errors is basically a technical one. The notion of operator error does not imply who is to blame for it. The normative model is meant to serve as a basis for an analysis of operator errors by means of psychological experiments, and the formulation of guidelines for the design of man-machine communication and user interfaces.

1 Intoduction: Operator errors in the view of a normative model

Usually the term *operator error* is used synonymously with human error. A *human error* is defined as a failure on the part of the human to perform a prescribed act (or the performance of a prohibited act) within specified limits of accuracy, sequence, or time, which could result in damage to equipment and property or disruption of scheduled operations. It is an out-of-tolerance action, where the limits of acceptable human performance are defined by the system (Salvendy, 1997; Swain, 1989).

This definition implies that the criteria for operator errors are given by the machine or - more specifically - by its *specification:* "Each specification takes aim at two directions. It separates areas of responsibility from one another. On one hand it specifies for development, design and production the performances which the system has to provide under certain conditions, and on the other hand it tells the operator and user what he has to do to obtain these performances from the system.

Whether a system is actually useful and harmless does not only depend on whether it operates in accordance with the specification, but also on the extent to which it can be properly operated by people with their inherent and acquired capabilities and weaknesses.

The assessment of utility and risk must also take account of possible operator errors, i. e. violations of the specification by the user, in addition to faults in the system" (VDI/VDE 3542/4, 1995).

The safety specification of a machine including the specification of its fault tolerance should guarantee a low risk of injury or damage to the public and to the environment. In this sense the safety related operator actions should aim at an optimum low risk. This leads to a more specific definition of operator errors. In this paper an *operator error* is conceived to be an avoidable increase of risk caused by the operator.

2 Risk

Risky Maneuvers are not only known from operating plants and systems with great potential for hazards (Perrow, 1984). We know them from every day life too: Often we are accepting high risk paid by a rather modest yield. Fig. 1 shows the relevant terms and measures of risk in both the fields of *Technical Risk Assessment* and *Decision under Risk.*

R	Risk, Expected Damage (or Loss)
i	Event (Caused by a Failure)
p_i	Probability of Event i
x_i	Loss due to Event i
X	Random Damage
s	(Subjective) Severity Function
$R_{\text{objective}} = E[X] = \Sigma_i\, p_i\, x_i$	
$R_{\text{subjective}} = E[s(X)] = \Sigma_i\, p_i\, s(x_i)$	

Fig. 1. Risk

The term *operator* will be used for pilots, drivers, operators of technical plants, etc. Operators have to make decisions: Typically they have to weigh the yield of some action against its risk and to compare the outcome with that of alternative actions (or the non-actions).

For simplicity we are taking only two alternatives into consideration. The alternatives are called A and B, and the random damage (cost, loss) is called X and Y respectively. The mean value of the random variable X - shortly: the expected damage - is denoted by $E[X]$ and will be called *objective risk* of alternative A. Thus an order of preference is defined. Alternative A is preferable to B if and only if $E[X] < E[Y]$.

In the course of technical risk assessment the objective risk is used as a measure. But there is evidence that we can draw wrong conclusions if we rely on the objective risk as the only rational measure.

To demonstrate this, the *Saint Petersburg Game* serves us well. This game and the inherent paradox have been considered within the field of decision theory and economics. One of most influential texts in this field is that of von Neumann and Morgenstern (1944). A philosophical and mathematical treatment can be found in Carnap's work (1959). The psychological aspects of decision making are treated in the work of Kahneman and Tversky (1979, 1982). The Saint Petersburg Paradox can be found in Székely's book (1990, pp. 34).

Daniel Bernoulli described the game in the year 1738: A coin is thrown until the tail appears for the first time. Let n be the number of trials. The gambler then receives 2^n monetary units from the gambling casino. What amount of money should we risk for taking part in the game?

The alternatives offered by the Saint Petersburg Game are (fig. 2):

A Abstention from taking part in the game: In this case the impending cost is equal to the possible payment that cannot be realised. Then the random loss is given by a random variable X of values 2, 4, 8, ... and the respective probabilities 1/2, 1/4, 1/8, ... The n-th value equals 2^n and the corresponding probability equals $1/2^n$. The expected loss - the objective risk - amounts to $E[X] = 2*1/2 + 4*1/4 + 8*1/8 + ... = 1 + 1 + 1 + ... = \infty$.

B Taking part in the game: Now the loss is equal to the stake y. The loss can be conceived to be a random variable Y which assumes value y with probability 1 (such a random variable is called deterministic). The objective risk of this alternative is equal to $E[Y] = y$.

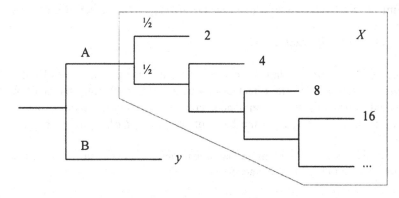

Fig. 2. The Decision Event Tree of the Saint Petersburg Game

Fig. 2 shows the Decision Event Tree (DET) of the game. The branches of the first level of the tree are corresponding to the decisions. Each decision branch is taken as the root of an event tree. The event tree represents the consequences of the decision - the random loss. To each branch of the event trees the (conditional) probability of traversing this branch is assigned. The quantity of loss or damage is notified at the end of the finally approached leaf.

On the basis of objective risk calculations alternative B will be chosen: Whatever the stake y will be, the objective risk will always be smaller than that of alternative A. But most people will only put up to 10 monetary units at stake. This decision is in contrast to the one based on objective risk calculations - and seems to be a rational one, indeed. This contradiction is the so called *Saint Petersburg Paradox*.

To solve the Saint Petersburg Paradox the mathematician Daniel Bernoulli introduced the so called *utility function u:* If z is an objective utility, then the subjective utility is denoted by $u(z)$.

In technical risk assessment we have to deal with damage, loss, or cost. To reformulate the *decision under risk* accordingly we have to replace the utility function by the *severity function s*. The *subjective risk* of a decision A with random loss X is defined to be the expected subjective damage $E[s(X)]$.

The order of preference is now defined through the subjective risk: Alternative A is preferable to B if and only if $E[s(X)] < E[s(Y)]$.

3 The normative model of operator behaviour

The notion of *Decision Event Tree* (DET) is taken as a primary classification scheme for *operator errors*. The DET Model consists of the following elements:

- a *decision tree*, for example the simple one from fig. 3 offering only two alternatives,
- consequential probabilistic *event trees* for each leaf of the decision tree,
- the assignment of a nonnegative value of cost or *damage* to each leaf of the event trees, and
- a (subjective) *severity function s*.

The DET can be derived from available *risk assessment* data and fault trees by the following *transformation rule:* The effect of an operator error effecting the state of some component is equivalent to a component failure leading to the same mode of (non-) operation. This assumption is the basis of the *concept of impact* (Dearden, Harrison, 1996).

The DET usually has to deal with more than one undesirable event and in general a lot of alternatives have to be taken into account.

Example: The decision tree in fig. 3 reflects a certain situation seen by the operator of a power plant. Let the action under consideration be the opening of a certain valve. The above sketched decision tree can be completed to the DET of fig. 4. The action "opening of valve no. 5" may be rewarded by a yield $y = 1$. To express it in terms of cost: Keeping the valve closed (no action branch) is accompanied by the loss y.

On the other hand the opening of the valve has some *impact* on the plant: The probability of the undesirable event "boiler overheat" rises from $q = 0.000242$ to $p = 0.00044$. The assumed damage resulting from a boiler overheat may amount to the value $x = 10^5$.

The random cost associated with the "action"-branch of the decision tree (opening the valve) is denoted by X and the "no action"-branch defines the random cost Y.

The expectation value of random cost is called *objective risk*. The objective risk values of the alternatives under consideration are $E[X] = 44$ and $E[Y] \approx 25$. As the risk associated with the "no action"-decision is lower than the one associated with the opening of the valve, the valve should be kept closed.

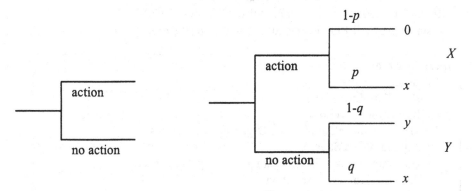

Fig. 3. Decision Tree   **Fig. 4.** Decision Event Tree

Due to a psychological principle - the *overweighting of certainty* - the severity function can usually be assumed to be concave (see the following section). A concave function fulfilling the conditions $s(0) = 0$ and $s(y) = y$ is given by $s(x) = y \cdot \ln(x/x_0+1)/\ln(y/x_0+1)$. This severity function reflects the original Bernoulli formulation of the utility functions (Carnap/Stegmüller, 1959, pp. 124 ff.).

With the given severity function and under the assumption $x_0 = 0.2$ and $y = 1$ we have $s(10^5) \approx 7.32$. The *subjective risk* is now given by $E[s(X)] = 0.00322$ and $E[s(Y)] \approx 1$. Under the preference order of subjective risk the valve should be opened.

4 Causal analysis of operator errors

Fig. 5 shows a classification scheme of operator errors. It represents a personal selection and comprises the most important and typical error causes. Systematic representations (mostly restricted on subareas and with specific aims) can be found in the books on *human factors:* Salvendy (1997), Reason (1990), Rasmussen/Duncan/Leplat (1987). Many of the thinking traps causing operator errors are the sources of programming errors too (Grams, 1988, 1990).

This paper concentrates on the cognitive causes of operator errors. This class of faults usually are committed by emotionally relaxed, well rested and healthy operators acting in an optimum environment. Apparently these faults are the extremely nasty ones. And it is the highly complex and poorly understood human thinking contributing to these faults, and thus making them so unpleasant.

There are several taxonomies for operator errors and their causes, for example the following:

– Norman's Action Cycle (Norman, 1990)
– Heuristics (Kahneman/Slovic/Tversky, 1982)

- Errors in Planning and Decision Making (Dörner/Schaub, 1994)
- Norman's Classification of Slips (Norman, 1981)
- Evans' Selective Scrutiny Model (Evans, 1989)
- Reason's Generic Error-Modelling System (Reason, 1990)
- Rasmussen's Skill-Rule-Knowledge Framework (Reason, 1990)

Operator Error
Situational Factors
Bad Work Environment
Information Overload
Physical, Emotional, Social, and Organisational Factors
Fatigue/Illness/Stress
Uncommunicative, Demotivating Working Atmosphere
Poor Education or Instruction
Cognitive Delusions (Thinking Traps)
Selective Attention (Tunnel Vision, Search Light Principle)
Psychological Set (Einstellung Effect)
Mechanization of Thought and Operation (Luchins)
Functional Fixity (Duncker)
Risk Acceptance
Overestimation of Law and Order (Prägnanz Tendency)
Linear Cause Effect Thinking
Biases and Faults in Inductive Reasoning
Inductive Reasoning Error
Failure to apply Modus-Tollens
Overestimation of Confirmative Information (Confirmation Bias)
Availability Heuristic (Kahneman/Tversky)
Representativeness Heuristik (Kahneman/Tversky)

Fig. 5. Causes of Operator Errors (causes in italics are described in detail within the text)

In the following sections some of the error causes are described in detail. In fig. 5 these are written in italic letters.

4.1 Risk Acceptance

Materials on risk perception can be found in Fritzsche (1986, pp. 128 ff., p. 145) and Perrow (1984). Important contributions to the psychology of decision preferences are from Kahneman and Tversky (1979 and 1982).

Due to a psychological principle - the *overweighting of certainty* - the severity function can usually be assumed to be strictly concave. This results in the *inequality of risk acceptance* $s(E[Z]) > E[s(Z)]$ for any nondeterministic random cost Z. The random (nondeterministic) cost is considered to be less threatening than the deterministic cost with equal objective risk.

The inequality of risk acceptance generally holds under the following preconditions (Fritzsche, 1986, S. 123-149):

- the danger is well known,
- the risk is accepted voluntarily, and
- the decision maker has some influence upon the risk.

Following Bernoulli a logarithmic severity function $s(x) = k \ln(x/x_0)$ will be chosen: This strictly concave function can be taken as a model of risk acceptance. The values of the constants k and x_0 have no influence on the order of preference. The value $s^{-1}(E[s(X)])$ and the random loss X are equivalent with respect to the subjective risk. The *equivalent risk* of the Saint Petersburg Game is equal to 4. This is the maximum amount (in monetary units) an average person would put at stake.

4.2 Inductive Reasoning Error 1: Failure to apply Modus-Tollens

There had been a *persistent leak* of reactor coolant before the outburst of the Three Mile Island (TMI) accident. This leak was known to be *small* and the operators thought it would not affect the main operation. But the leakage created ambiguous temperature indications in the drain piping. The indications disguised a *serious leak of coolant*. This was one of the causes of the eventual disaster (Rubinstein/Mason, 1979; Norman, 1990, pp. 43-44).

Let H_1 and H_2 denote the two hypotheses "small leak" and "serious leak", and E be the observation "high temperature in the drain piping". The logical structure of the error is given by the following pseudo-deduction: From the premises "H_1 implies E" and "E" follows the conclusion "H_1". The operators obviously did not take into consideration alternative premises. Unfortunately they ignored "H_2 implies E".

The thinking trap leading to the error is the *bias toward plausible reasoning* combined with the linear cause effect thinking. Furthermore: The "small leak"-hypothesis has supposedly been chosen because of *availability* (see section 4.4). Evan's *belief bias* (1989) and the *reluctance to think through disjunctions* (Shafir, 1994) can also be conceived to be deeper causes of the bias toward plausible reasoning.

Overlooking hypotheses results in false mental modelling and overly simple representations of the Decision Event Tree. During the TMI accident the decision branch and the branches of the event trees taking the hypothesis H_2 into account were possibly missing in the operator's mental model of the situation.

A famous psychological experiment that enlightens the role of inductive reasoning when deductive reasoning is more appropriate is known as *Wason's Selection Task* (Anderson, 1995). Four cards were placed in front of subjects:

| E | K | 4 | 7 |

All cards have letters on one and numbers on the other side. The task was to judge the validity of the rule: "If a card has a vowel on the one side, then it has an even number on the other". The subjects were asked to turn over only those cards necessary to prove the correctness of the rule.

Result of the psychological experiment: During a large number of experiments it has been found that 89 % of subjects select E correctly, however, 62 % of the subjects also chose to turn over the 4, which is not informative since whatever symbol the other side would carry, it could not falsify the rule. Only a minority chose to turn over the E and the 7, which is the logically informative choice since an odd number behind the E or a vowel behind the 7 would have falsified the rule.

Analysis: Our tendency to inductive reasoning, to drawing conclusions extending the matter, works according to the following scheme: If a theory or hypothesis H allows to predict an event E, and if the event E on the basis of the current knowledge is of low probability, then the theory H becomes more believable if the event E is observed. Shortly: From "H implies E" and "E is true" follows "H becomes more believable". We tend to enrich this inductive reasoning with more decisiveness. We are biased to interpreting it in a deductive way: From "H implies E" and "E is true" we conclude "H is true". We don't differentiate clearly enough between "From H follows E" and "From E follows H". This thinking trap is called *failure to apply modus-tollens* (Anderson, 1995).

4.3 Inductive Reasoning Error 2: Overestimation of Confirmative Information

The TMI mishap shows: The operator's task is to imagine hypotheses and to assess their probabilities. Some operator errors can be attributed to overlooking hypotheses (probability 0) or to assessing the probabilities incorrectly. What are the mechanisms leading to systematic errors in the assessment of hypothesis probabilities?

One of the mechanisms becomes clear through the *Harvard Medical School Study* (Hell/Fiedler/Gigerenzer, 1993). The following description was presented to the subjects of the experiment: A test for a certain disease may be given. Let the base rate of the disease be 1/1000 - i. e.: one out of one thousand persons is actually ill. Five percent of the test results are incorrect. Specifically the false positive rate amounts to 5%. The subjects are asked to give the probability of illness for a person tested positive.

Result of the psychological experiment: The answer given by most of the subjects (professors, physicians and students) is "95%". The correct number can be derived through the use of the Bayes formula: Let the hypothesis of being ill be denoted by H and the positive test result by E. Then the probability $P(H \mid E)$ of being ill under the condition of a positive test result is given by

$$P(H|E) = \frac{P(E|H) \cdot P(H)}{P(E|H) \cdot P(H) + P(E|\neg H) \cdot P(\neg H)} = \frac{0.95 \cdot 0.001}{0.95 \cdot 0.001 + 0.05 \cdot 0.999},$$

being less than 2%. This is in strong contrast to most of the answers.

Apparently a thinking trap is present, the so called *confirmation bias* (i. e. overestimation of confirmative information). The experiment demonstrates an inferential error similar to the one described above where the conclusion "from H follows E" has been mistaken for "from E follows H". With the Harvard Medical School Study it is the disease that is taken as a cause of the positive test result. In this case the backward conclusion from the test result on the cause is plausible, at best; but we take the cause for granted and thus exaggerate the plausible reasoning and take it as a deduction: "From H (the disease) follows most likely E (the positive test result)" is mistaken for "From E (the positive test result) follows most likely H (the disease)". The failure to apply modus tollens as well as the confirmation bias can be conceived to be *inductive reasoning errors.*

4.4 Inductive Reasoning Error 3: Heuristics

The research of Tversky and Kahnemann concerns the mechanisms and heuristics leading to erroneous probability assessment for hypotheses. As the two main causes they have found the *Availability Heuristic* and the *Representativeness Heuristic* (Kahneman/Slovic/Tversky, 1982; Nisbett, 1993).

Availability Heuristic: Items coming into mind most easily are estimated of being more likely than others. For example let a word be sampled at random from an English text. Is it more likely that the word starts with "r" or that "r" is the third letter? Words starting with an r (like road) are remembered more easily than words with an r at the third position (like car). Most people judge words that begin with a given consonant to be more numerous than words in which the same consonant appears in the third position. But the opposite is true: Consonants, such as "r" or "k" are more frequent in the third position than in the first. Apparently the availability heuristic has played some role in the TMI mishap: The hypothesis that has been preferred by the operators was the well known small leak and not the possible serious leak of coolant.

Representativeness Heuristic: The following psychological experiment has been undertaken: Subjects were given a description of *Linda* ("Linda is 31 years old, single, outspoken, and very bright. She majored in philosophy. As a student, she was deeply concerned with issues of discrimination and social justice, and also participated in anti-nuclear demonstrations.") Then the subjects were asked which of the statements upon Linda are judged to be more probable, namely "Linda is a bank teller" (T) or "Linda is a bank teller and is active in the feminist movement" (T&F). An astonishing 87% of the subjects selected the second statement (T&F) to be more likely. That contradicts the rules of logic and probability because the probability of the conjunct of two propositions (T&F) cannot be greater than the probability of one part of it (T). One of the causes of such fallacies is judged to be the *representativeness heuristic:* The probability of that a person belongs to a certain group is evaluated by the degree to which the person is *representative* of this group. To put it more shortly: We tend to read more into a description than is justifiable. Possibly this effect can be blamed for some operator errors: The operator draws too far going conclusions from his observations.

5 Conclusions and Outlook

The situation as perceived by the operator can be described by a *subjective* decision event tree. Situation awareness (Endsley, 1995) can be conceived to be the resemblence of this subjective model to the normative model described above.

It is hypothesized that operator errors typically are caused by incomplete situation awareness, i. e. deviations of the subjective model from the normative one. The structure of the proposed normative model - the DET - thus can be taken as a classification scheme for operator errors and their causes. With respect to the DET the following causes of operator errors can be distinguished:

1. Overestimation of yield y
2. Underestimation of damage x
3. Wrong modelling of consequences: Underestimation or neglect of impact p-q
4. Risk acceptance: Concavity of s
5. Alternatives disregarded: Narrow decision tree

The main issue is covered by the third error class "Wrong modelling of consequences": Wrong modelling of the event tree results from false mental models of the physical world, mainly the errors in *inductive reasoning*.

The fifth class embraces unperceived or ignored decision situations. The decision tree thus may narrow down to a single branch.

During further work the proposed classification scheme will serve as a guide to the analysis of operator errors by means of psychological experiments. This should result in a *descriptive model* of operator behaviour. On the basis of the descriptive model the formulation of countermeasures and guidelines for interface design can be undertaken.

Acknowledgement

The work was supported by the "Stiftung Volkswagenwerk".

References

Anderson, J. R.: Cognitive Psychology and Its Implications. Freeman, New York, Oxford 1995

Carnap, R.; Stegmüller, W.: Induktive Logik und Wahrscheinlichkeit. Springer, Wien 1959

Dearden, A. M.; Harrison, M. D.: Impact as a Human Factor in Interactive System Design. (In Redmill, F.: Anderson, T. (Eds.): Safety-critical Systems: The Convergence of High Tech and Human Factors. Proc. of the 4th Safety-critical Systems Symposium, Leeds 1996. Springer, London 1996, S. 184-199)

Dörner, D., Schaub, H.: Errors in Planning and Decision-making and the Nature of Human Information Processing. Applied Psychology: An International Review 43 (1994) 4, 433-453

Endsley, M. R.: Toward a Theory of Situation Awareness in Dynamic Systems. Human Factors 37 (1995) 1, 32-64

Evans, J. ST. B. T.: Bias in Human Reasoning: Causes and Consequences. Lawrence Erlbaum Associates, Publishers, Hove and London (UK) 1989

Fritzsche, A. F.: Wie sicher leben wir? Risikobeurteilung und -bewältigung in unserer Gesellschaft. TÜV Rheinland, Köln 1986

Grams, T.: Thinking Traps in Programming - A Systematic Collection of Examples. SAFECOMP '88. IFAC Proceeding Series 1988, Number 16. Pergamon Press, 95-100

Grams, T.: Denkfallen und Programmierfehler. Springer, Heidelberg 1990

Hell, W.; Fiedler, K.; Gigerenzer, G. (Hrsg.): Kognitive Täuschungen. Fehl-Leistungen und Mechanismen des Urteilens, Denkens und Erinnerns. Spektrum Akademischer Verlag, Heidelberg, Berlin, Oxford 1993

Kahneman, D.; Slovic, P.; Tversky, A. (eds.): Judgment under uncertainty: Heuristics and biases. Cambridge University Press, Cambridge CB2 1RP, 1982

Kahneman, D.; Tversky, A.: Prospect Theory: An Analysis of Decision under Risk. Econometrica, 47 (March, 1979) 2, 263-291

Neumann, J. von, Morgenstern, O.: Theory of games and economic behavior. Princeton 1944

Nisbett, R. E.: Rules for Reasoning. Lawrence Erlbaum, Hillsdale, N. J., 1993

Norman, D. A.: Categorization of Action Slips. Psychological Review 88(1981)1, 1-15

Norman, D. A.: The Design of Everyday Things. Double Day Currency, New York 1990

Perrow, C.: Normal Accidents. Living with High-Risk Technologies. Basis Books, New York 1984

Rasmussen, J.; Duncan, K.; Leplat, J.: New Technology And Human Error. Wiley 1987

Reason, J.: Human Error. Cambridge University Press 1990

Rubinstein, E.; Mason, J. F.: The accident that shouldn't have happened. The technical blow-by-blow. IEEE spectrum (November 1979), 32-48

Salvendy, G. (Edt.): Handbook of Human Factors and Ergonomics (2nd edition). John Wiley, New York 1997

Shafir, E.: Uncertainty and the difficulty of thinking through disjunctions. Cognition 50 (1994) 1-3, 403-430

Swain, A. D.: Comparative Evaluation of Methods for Human Reliability Analysis. Gesellschaft für Reaktorsicherheit, Garching, 1989

Székely, G. J.: Paradoxa. Klassische und neue Überraschungen aus Wahrscheinlichkeitsrechnung und mathematischer Statistik. Harri Deutsch, Thun, Frankfurt/M. 1990

VDI/VDE-Guideline 3542/4 (July 1995): Safety terms for automation systems.: Reliability and safety of complex systems (terms)

Security

A Performance Comparison of Group Security Mechanisms

Andrew Hutchison[1] and Michael Wallbaum[2]

[1] Department of Computer Science, University of Cape Town,
Private Bag, 7700 Rondebosch, South Africa
hutch@cs.uct.ac.za
[2] Department of Computer Science 4, Aachen University of Technology,
Ahornstr. 55, 52056 Aachen, Germany
wall@i4.informatik.rwth-aachen.de

Abstract. This paper presents the results of a performance evaluation of group security mechanisms achieving different qualities of protection. It is shown that there is a tradeoff between performance and quality of protection but also that scalability needs special consideration in the design of group authentication protocols.

By using the distributed graphical editor MultiGraph as a testbed, the measurements give a good indication of the feasibility of secure synchronous distributed group applications. The measurements revealed that the delays introduced by the security services are well acceptable for MultiGraph.

1 Introduction

In recent years there has been a growing interest in software supporting group interaction. As commercial organisations are starting to make use of this technology the demand for security services in group applications is increasing. In the course of a diploma thesis [Wall97] two multi-party extensions of the Generic Security Service Application Programming Interface (GSS-API) [Li93,Li97] were investigated. The GSS-API facilitates the addition of security services to new or existing applications but only supports peer to peer communication. Extending the interface towards secure multi-party communication is conceived a reasonable approach to provide for security in group applications [BaCo96,Hut97].

The available implementations of group-extended GSS-APIs encapsulate different group security mechanisms, namely different group authentication and key distribution protocols. The Australian Distributed Systems Technology Centre (DSTC) implemented the proposal presented in [BaCo96] using a mechanism offering weak *origin group authentication*, whereby only the initiator of the authentication process authenticates to the other peers. In contrast the proposal presented in [Hut97] was implemented using DSTC's GSS-API as a framework but offers Hutchison's strong *complete group authentication*, whereby each group member resolves its mutual suspicion of each other group member.

While previous research has proposed group security solutions, this is the first attempt we are aware of to systematically quantify and contrast security and performance aspects on the basis of experimental results. The two mechanisms were evaluated according to these criteria using the distributed graphical editor MultiGraph [Kra95] as a testbed.

Section 2 presents the investigated authentication protocols. In Sec. 3 the testbed, i.e. MultiGraph and the test-suite, is briefly described to prepare for the subsequent presentation of the evaluation results. A conclusion and outlook on the subject is given in Sec. 5.

2   The Investigated Group Authentication Protocols

Both investigated mechanisms are based on the authentication server (AS) referred to as *AuthServ* included in DSTC's distribution of the GSS-API. AuthServ provides simple password based client authentication using a three-level key hierarchy and employs TCP/IP sockets for communication with its clients. Confidentiality and integrity services are provided by the DES cipher in CBC-mode [NBS77] and the MD5 message digest algorithm [Riv92]. Unlike other authentication servers, AuthServ keeps track of the currently established security contexts and their group key in the so-called session cache. This special feature is required by DSTC's authentication protocols.

Both mechanisms actually employ two distinct protocols for static and for dynamic authentication. *Static* group authentication protocols establish trust within a group according to the desired quality of authentication. To remove suspicion between a group and a *newly arrived member*, it is possible to re-authenticate the enlarged group using the static protocol. But this is costly in terms of the number of exchanged messages and can be avoided by employing a *dynamic* protocol which considers and takes advantage of the existing state of trust within the group.

The investigated protocols will now be described as far as required for subsequent discussion of evaluation results. A more detailed presentation of the complete group authentication protocols can be found in [Hut95]; DSTC's protocols are covered in [Wall97].

2.1   Static Origin Authentication

The authentication and key distribution protocol implemented in DSTC's GSS-API achieves origin group authentication. Figure 1 shows an example run of the protocol with three communicating parties (A, B and C) and the authentication server. Principal A acts as the initiator and distributor during authentication. In the first step A requests a ticket from the AS and informs it that A, B and C will form a group (1). The ticket's main function is to securely convey the group key. In requesting the ticket A assures the AS of its identity by encrypting the request in K_A, the master key known only to A and the AS. To ensure freshness, the request also contains a timestamp t_G which AuthServ subsequently also uses

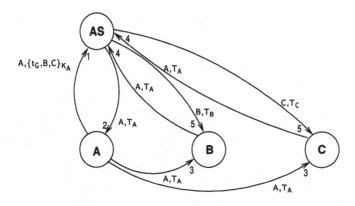

Fig. 1. DSTC's static origin authentication.

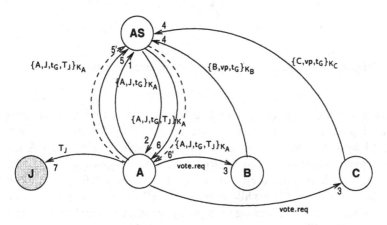

Fig. 2. DSTC's dynamic origin authentication.

to reference the correct session cache entry.[1] AuthServ responds to the request by sending A, T_A to A (2) with the ticket T_A containing $\{K_G, B, C, t_G\}_{K_A}$.

The ticket and the name of the initiator is then passed to the other group members B and C (3), who return the token to the AS (4). The AS then creates T_B and T_C thus implicitly authenticating the initiator A to B and C – if A initiated the authentication protocol, there must be a corresponding entry in the session cache and A must be authenticated to AS. In round (5) the tickets, e.g. $T_B := \{K_G, A, t_G\}_{K_B}$ for peer B, are transferred to the corresponding peers.

2.2 Dynamic Origin Authentication

An example illustrating DSTC's dynamic origin authentication protocol is shown in Fig. 2. The protocol not only provides for authentication of the group coordinator to a newly arrived member but also controls group admission by means

---

[1] Note that time is not synchronised in the current implementation of this mechanism.

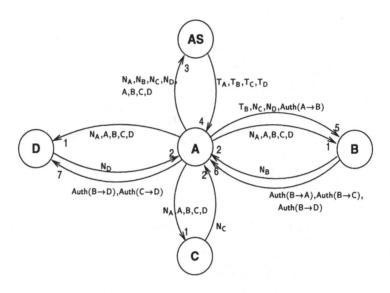

Fig. 3. Hutchison's static complete group authentication protocol.

of a voting scheme. Principal A sends a message to AuthServ requesting the addition of peer J (1). AuthServ responds by sending J's ticket T_J which is not passed to J until the voting procedure is completed (2). Then A informs the other group members of the addition implicitly requesting a vote (3). The other group members state their vote preference vp by sending an appropriate message to the AS (4). Meanwhile A polls the AS to query the vote result (5). AuthServ responds with a message indicating whether voting is still in progress or completed (6). When all members have stated their preference, the result is signalled to A by the token returned from the AS. The ticket received in round 2 of the protocol is then transferred to the new group member J.

A potential problem of DSTC's protocols is the possibility of the principals simultaneously approaching the AS. In combination with the AuthServ's inability to service incoming requests in parallel this holds the potential danger of AuthServ becoming a bottleneck. This conjecture will be corroborated by the results of the performance analysis.

2.3 Static Complete Authentication

An example illustrating Hutchison's static complete authentication protocol considering four parties and an AS is shown in Fig. 3. In this protocol A acts as the initiator and coordinating principal during the authentication. The first protocol step is that A requests nonces from the other group members. A nonce is a random number used as proof of the freshness of messages, since direct correlation can be made between requests containing the random number as a challenge and replies which must contain this challenge to be accepted as fresh. Along with the nonce request A distributes the group membership and N_A, a nonce

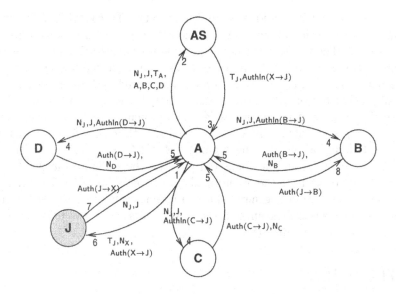

Fig. 4. Hutchison's dynamic complete group authentication protocol.

of its own (1). After collecting the nonces from all other group members (2), A sends the nonces and the group composition to the AS, requesting tickets for all members (3). The AS includes the received nonces into the appropriate tickets, assuring the group members of their ticket's 'freshness'. The generated tickets $T_A, T_B, T_C; T_D$ are sent back to A (4).

A then sends each of the other members X_i its ticket together with an authenticating segment $Auth(A \rightarrow X_i)$ from A to that member X_i and the other member's nonces(5). Using the obtained information, authenticating segments are constructed for each other group member and these are sent to A (6). In Fig. 3 flows (5) and (6) are only shown to/from A and B, although equivalent flows also occur between A and the other group members. A then has the task of distributing the collected authenticating segments to the relevant recipients (7). Figure 3 shows this distribution from A to D, although similar flows occur to B and C. In this way all parties are authenticated to all other parties through the coordination of A.

2.4 Dynamic Complete Authentication

The last investigated protocol is Hutchison's dynamic complete group authentication protocol, which removes mutual suspicion between a completely authenticated group of principals and a joining peer, thus incrementally achieving a completely authenticated enlarged group. In contrast to DSTC's dynamic protocol, group admission is not an explicit part of the protocol but it can easily be integrated.

Figure 4 shows a joining peer J conducting incremental authentication with existing group members A, B, C and D. In this scheme J supplies the coordinating principal A with its identity and nonce (1). The coordinating principal contacts the AS with the name and nonce of the joiner, also passing its own ticket, T_A (2). The ticket is required by the AS to recover the group key, K_G, contained within it – unlike AuthServ, the AS is not expected to store the group key. A new ticket, T_J, is then created for J and passed back to A together with a set of *AuthIn* tokens[2] (3). Peer A distributes J's nonce and the *AuthIn* tokens to the existing group members (4). The principals reply by sending back authenticating segments $Auth(X \rightarrow J)$ together with nonces N_X to be used by J for constructing authenticating segments $Auth(J \rightarrow X)$ (5). A collects the responses from the group members and passes J the assembled authenticating segments and nonces from the other members, as well as its ticket T_J (6). J uses the received information to generate authenticating segments assuring the group members of J's identity. The authenticating segments are sent to principal A (7), which then distributes them (8).

3 The Testbed

The implementations of the protocols presented above were encapsulated in group-extended GSS-APIs and in this fashion integrated into the distributed graphical editor MultiGraph [Kra95]. MultiGraph realises completely symmetric and independant application instances connected by a multicast communication channel. All users can contribute to the joint drawing while identical copies of the drawing are maintained by each user's instance.

3.1 MultiGraph's Transport Protocol

The employed communications protocol stack consists of the unreliable *IP multicast* [Dee89] at the network layer and the Multicast Transport Protocol 2 (MTP-2) [BOGKS94,Sei94] at the transport layer. MTP-2 is a revised version of MTP [AFM90], providing globally ordered, reliable, rate controlled and atomic transfer of messages to multiple recipients. MTP-2 defines a closed multicast group called a *web*. Only members of the multicast group can send to the web which is identified by a sequence of characters.

Three different member roles are defined by MTP-2: master, producer and consumer. The *master* provides the message ordering for all members in the web and observes rate control. *Producers* send data in messages after obtaining a token from the group master. *Consumers* receive these messages and request retransmissions of packets that did not arrive.

To ensure ordering, reliability and atomicity the master assigns every message a state, which can be either pending, accepted or rejected. When the master grants a producer a token allowing it to send a message, that message's status is set to *pending*. On receipt of the token, the producer sends the message to all

---

[2] These contain information used to resolve mutual suspicion between a member and the joiner.

consumers, which store the message until they learn that the master set its status to *accepted*, because it received the message as well. If the master did not receive a message correctly its status is set to *rejected* which obliges all consumers to drop the message.

The status of messages is propagated by *message acceptance records* sent periodically by the master to all web members. Only when the status of a message is set to *accepted* will a consumer deliver the message to its application.

3.2 Experimental Setup

To investigate the performance and scalability of the above group authentication protocols several series of experiments were carried out, all measuring the service-delay, i.e. the difference in time between requesting an operation (e.g. to join a group security context) and completing this operation on all involved processes.

The environment for the performance tests consisted of seven UNIX-work-stations (ranging from Sun Sparc Classic to Sparc 5) connected by a lightly loaded Ethernet-LAN. Six workstations were used to run instances of Multi-Graph, while one workstation served as host for the AS.

For measurements involving up to six MultiGraph-instances, each instance was started on a different host. Due to the lack of available workstations, running multiple instances on one host was unavoidable. When more than six instances were started, the load was distributed evenly amongst the hosts. To avoid bursts of CPU-usage while performing static authentication, it was also taken care of that tokens sent by the initiating peer were destined for acceptors on alternating hosts. Furthermore, the nth instance was always started on the same host.

4 Results

Having described the investigated protocols and the testbed, the experimental results are now presented and analysed. To investigate scalability all experiments were carried out for group sizes $\mid G \mid = \{1, ..., 15\}$ and each experiment was repeated five times to gain confidence in the results – the following graphs display the averages over these five runs.

4.1 The Static Authentication Protocols

Figure 5 shows the minimum and maximum times needed to achieve static origin and complete group authentication, i.e. the difference in time from initiating authentication to completion of the first and last member respectively.

The Static Origin Authentication Protocol. For up to eight instances of MultiGraph the minimum and maximum origin authentication times for $\mid G \mid > 1$ rise linearly from 0.24 s to 0.28 s and 0.57 s to 0.73 s respectively. This slow increase can be attributed to the higher processing time of the AS having to

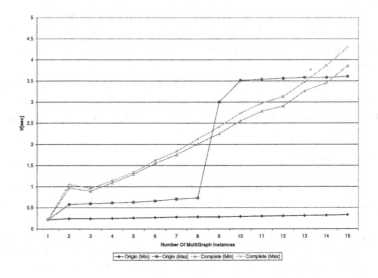

Fig. 5. Static group authentication.

verify the name and credential of each group member requesting its ticket. The minimum times are taken by the initiating peer, which signals completion after passing its ticket to the acceptors. These will then have to transfer the received ticket to the AS and process the returned token, thus needing more time to finish the authentication protocol.

For more than eight members the origin authentication protocol behaves quite unexpectedly, as can be seen in the graph. The maximum times needed to establish a security context rise by more than 3 s, which at first was attributed to system resource limitations. But this cannot explain such an immense increase in authentication time; instead the AS proved to be a bottleneck in the origin authentication protocol as will now be explained.

The initiator's ticket is sent to the group via multicast. This ticket will be delivered to all acceptor's instances *simultaneously*, after the web-master (i.e. the MTP-2 demon at the initiator's site) has received the message and announced the *accepted* message status to the other web-members. The acceptors then (nearly) simultaneously try to establish a TCP-connection to the AS to request their own ticket. Since the server does not spawn a new process on an incoming connection request, only one peer can be served at a time. The peers whose connection request failed will try again but only after waiting for a certain amount of time which increases after each failed request, eventually reaching several seconds.

This 'queueing' occurs twice – once for retrieving the ticket and once for letting the AS verify the GSS-API credential before requesting the ticket. It has to be noted, that for security reasons this separate credential verification is not necessary, since it could be done at ticket-generation time.

The Static Complete Authentication Protocol. Using the complete group authentication protocol, this problem is not encountered since all members' tickets are retrieved by a single request of the initiator and credential verification is done once at ticket-generation time. As for origin authentication the authentication times for increasing group sizes (for $|G| > 2$) rise linearly from 1 s to around 4 s. Again the increased processing time of the server, needing to verify the names and credentials of each member and to create their tickets, contributes to this fact. Additionally, each member instance itself spends more time for verification of other members authenticating segments. In comparison to origin authentication the higher effort for complete authentication explains the generally longer delays.

The corresponding minimum and maximum times are very close (within less than 0.5 s), because each peer has to participate in every round of the protocol – a peer with little processing power or long communication delays can delay the whole authentication process. Again the minimum times are taken by the initiating peer, which has fully authenticated after it has passed the tokens of the last round to the acceptors. The acceptors complete authentication, once they processed their respective token.

Two special cases need to be explained, namely complete authentication with one and two peers. Groups with one member need considerably less time, since they do not need to interact with other group members and can stop at round (4) of the protocol skipping rounds (1) and (2). Surprisingly, context establishment with two peers requires more time than with three peers, which can be attributed to the MTP-2 protocol. When two peers set up a security context using the complete authentication protocol, the last message is sent by the acceptor, namely the segment authenticating the acceptor to the initiator. To send this message, the acceptor's MTP-2 demon must request a token from the master of the web, which runs on the initiator's host, causing a delay. This need not be done for groups with more than three members, since then the last message is sent by the initiator whose demon is master of the web and thus has instant access to the tokens.

4.2 The Dynamic Authentication Protocols

The measurements for dynamic group authentication present nearly the same picture as for static authentication. Figure 6 depicts the delays measured for groups of two or more members.[3]

The Dynamic Origin Authentication Protocol. For origin authentication the AS again proves to be a bottleneck for groups with more than nine members. Here the reason is the voting on the addition of a new member. The increase in time is only 2 s instead of 4 s because credential verification does not take place.

With nine or less group members the minimum and maximum times for origin authentication are independent of the group size. For $|G| < 10$ the minimum and

---

[3] A group has to consist of at least one member before joining can take place.

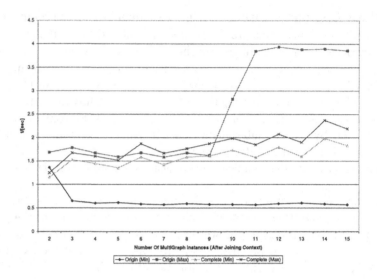

Fig. 6. Dynamic group authentication.

maximum times have constant values around 0.6 s and 1.6 s, the only exception being a group size of two. For groups with a cardinality greater than two, the minimum values displayed are those of the acceptors, who have completed their part of the authentication procedure after casting a vote on the addition of the joining peer. For $| G | = 2$ the minimum time belongs to the coordinating peer, since it has finished the protocol once it has received a ticket from the server and transferred it to the joining peer. The joining peer will only have completed the authentication protocol once having received and processed this ticket.

The gap of more than one second between minimum and maximum times is caused by the polling procedure of the coordinating peer. The coordinating peer has to collect the voting result from the AS. To avoid flooding the server with unsuccessful requests the coordinator's process is suspended for one second, after which usually all votes will have been registered.

The Dynamic Complete Authentication Protocol. As in the static case, the times for dynamic complete group authentication show a slight linear dependency on the group size. The minima and maxima are again very close and slowly rise from about 1.25 s to around 2 s. Here, in contrast to the protocol achieving origin authentication, the joining peer takes the least amount of time, since it has completed the protocol once the authenticating segments have been sent to the coordinator. The peers accepting a new member to the group finish last, since they have to wait for their respective authenticating segment to be passed on by the coordinator.

Despite the five repetitions of the measurements, the displayed curve is not very smooth. This is caused by the experimental setup, which used a fixed mapping between the nth MultiGraph instance and its host. The local minima are always located at those points where an instance running on a fast host joins the context. This can be explained, by the high computational effort of the joining instance. It has to unpack its ticket, verify the authenticating segments and create itself authenticating segments for the other members in the group. In contrast, the other members only have to create and verify *one* authenticating segment. The general increase in authentication time is again due to the rising effort in creating and verifying authenticating segments.

For origin and complete authentication it has to be noted, that in the case of an unauthenticated group one-time static authentication is always 'cheaper' in terms of time than successively adding all the members to the context using dynamic authentication. On the other hand adding a single new member to an established context using the dynamic protocols is more efficient than reauthenticating the enlarged group.

When comparing the times for conferences using complete and origin authentication, it can be said that the weaker origin authentication protocol does not save time compared to the complete authentication protocol. This can definitely be said for groups with more than nine members. Even for smaller groups the negligible time savings do not justify chosing the weaker quality of authentication. The relatively poor performance of the origin authentication protocol is not inherent to this quality of authentication itself but rather to the implementation. The same quality of authentication could be achieved by using the dynamic complete authentication protocol and skipping rounds (4), (5) and (7) of the protocol. No polling would be necessary and the AS would be approached just once, thus most likely achieving better performance.

4.3 Impact On MultiGraph

In performing the measurements it was primarily aimed at determining the performance and scalability of the authentication protocols. A second point of interest was the impact of security services on the *usability* of a distributed editor such as MultiGraph. In an experiment not to be discussed here, the simple assumption was proven, that the times required for pure authentication are simply added to the nearly constant times for joining an unsecured conference.[4]

In a last experiment investigating usability, the overhead of integrity and confidentiality services on conference operations, i.e. on creating objects on the canvas, was measured. Before this overhead is analysed, it has to be noted that the version of the MTP-2 demon used for the experiments shows a different behavior than that used by Krause in [Kra95]. While Krause reports slightly increasing times for an increasing number of group members, the new demon shows relatively constant times for group sizes greater than two. This seems to be an improvement at the expense of groups with one and two members, since here the measured delays are considerably greater than those in [Kra95] and those here for $|G| > 2$.

---

[4] In the discussed testbed, joining a MultiGraph conference with an empty document took about 3 s.

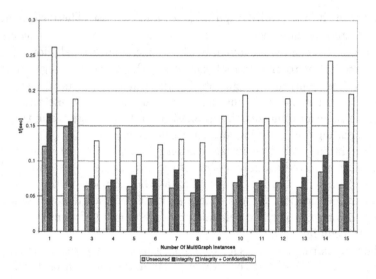

Fig. 7. Drawing an ellipse with different qualities of protection.

Despite this, Fig. 7 gives a good indication of the involved overhead for different security services. It shows that the *integrity service* is relatively inexpensive in terms of time, since a message protected by integrity has only a slightly larger latency than an unsecured message – the maximal difference measured is less than 0.05 s. This cannot be said for the *confidentiality service*, since on average a message protected with integrity and confidentiality needs almost twice the time of an unprotected message. This difference grows for nine and more group members, which can be attributed to the increasing number of instances per host competing for the CPU when decrypting a message.

A delay of one second is considered a reasonable upper limit for 'good responsiveness' of synchronous distributed editors. Even when using integrity *and* confidentiality services, this limit is not nearly reached. The maximal time of around 0.25 s is reached for $| G | = 1$ and $| G | = 14$ and these cases cannot even be seen as representative for reasons stated above. In summary, it can be said, that the integrity and confidentiality services offered by the DES and MD5 implementation of DSTC's GSS-API do not degrade the usability of MultiGraph.

5 Conclusion

This paper has presented a comparison between different group authentication protocols and reported on the performance of secured versions of the distributed graphical editor MultiGraph.

The origin authentication protocols show an almost constant delay over an increasing number of group members for group sizes of up to eight. Beyond this point the AS proves to be a bottleneck of these protocols, increasing the delay by several seconds when validating credentials and registering votes. This underlines the fact that an AS should solely be responsible for generating keys and tickets and that the number of transactions should be kept to a minimum.

Since the complete authentication protocols approach the AS just once, this problem does not arise here. These protocols exhibit a slight linear dependency on the group size, but for the tested sizes the delay was moderate. An experience gained from examining the closely related minimum and maximum times is that the complete authentication protocol is only as fast as the slowest involved peer. Excluding 'slow' peers from the authentication process would speed up the process. The excluded peers could later be dynamically added to the security context.

Employing the authentication protocols in MultiGraph it has been discovered that the added overhead for both qualities of authentication does not make system response times unacceptable. This can especially be said for the integrity and confidentiality services used to protect conference operation requests. Subjective evaluation of the performance has shown that a user can hardly distinguish a secured from an unsecured conference.

Though the measured delays were very moderate it must be kept in mind, that the measurements were done in a LAN – it can safely be assumed that delays for groups spread over a WAN are considerably greater. A solution to this problem could be a distributed authentication server topology, bundling local activities and reducing the amount of long-distance communication.

References

[AFM90] S. Armstrong, A. Freier, K. Marzullo. Multicast Transport Protocol. IETF RFC 1301 (February 1990).

[BaCo95] D.P. Barton, L.J. O'Connor. *Implementing Generic Security Services in a Distributed Environment.* CRC for Distributed Systems Technology, Brisbane, Australia (April 1995).

[BaCo96] D.P. Barton, L.J. O'Connor. *A Design and Implementation of Secure Multiparty Sessions.* CRC for Distributed Systems Technology, Brisbane, Australia (May 1996).

[BOGKS94] C. Borman, J. Ott, H.-C. Gehrcke, T. Kerschat, N. Seifert. *MTP-2: Towards Achieving the S.E.R.O. Properties for Multicast Transport.* Proceedings of the Third International Conference On Computer Communications and Networks (1994).

[Dee89] S.E. Deering. *RFC1112: Host Extensions for IP multicasting.* SRI Network Information Center (August 1989).

[Hut95] A. Hutchison. *Group Security in Distributed Systems.* Inaugural-Dissertation, University of Zurich, Zurich, Switzerland (1995).

[Hut97] A. Hutchison. *gGSS-API: a Group Enhanced Generic Security Service.* Proceedings of the Thirteenth International Information Security Conference (IFIP/SEC '97), Copenhagen, Denmark (1997).

[Kra95] W. Krause. *Untersuchungen von Gruppenkommunikationsmechanismen zur Entwicklung eines verteilten Graphikeditors.* Diploma Thesis, Aachen University of Technology, Germany (1995).

[Li93] J. Linn. *Generic Security Service Application Programming Interface*. IETF RFC 1508, Geer Zolot Associates (September 1993).

[Li97] J. Linn. *Generic Security Service Application Programming Interface, Version 2*. IETF RFC 2078, OpenVision Technologies (January 1997).

[NBS77] NBS. *Data Encryption Standard. FIPS PUB 46*. National Bureau of Standards (1977).

[Riv92] R.L. Rivest *The MD5 Message Digest Algorithm*. Network Working Group RFC (April 1992).

[Sei94] N. Seifert. *MTP-2: Multicast-Transportprotokoll Version 2*. Diploma Thesis, Technical University of Berlin, Germany (1994).

[Wall97] M. Wallbaum *Investigation And Evaluation Of A Group-Extension To The GSS-API*. Diploma Thesis, Aachen University of Technology, Germany (December 1997).

Towards Secure Downloadable Executable Content: The JAVA Paradigm

J.Iliadis[1,2] S.Gritzalis[1,2] V.Oikonomou[2]

[1] Department of Information & Communication Systems, University of the Aegean,
Research Unit, 30 Voulgaroktonou St., Athens GR-11472, GREECE
tel: +30-1-6456688, fax: +30-1-6448428, email: {jiliad, sgritz}@aegean.gr

[2] Department of Informatics, Technological Educational Institute (T.E.I.) of Athens,
Ag.Spiridonos St., Aegaleo, GR-12243, GREECE
tel: +30-1-5910974, fax: +30-1-5910975, e-mail: sgritz@acm.org

Abstract. Java is a programming language that conforms to the concept of downloadable, executable content. Java offers a wide range of capabilities to the application programmer, the most important being that a program may be executed remotely, without any modification, on almost any computer regardless of hardware configuration and operating system differences. However, this advantage raises a serious concern : security. When one downloads and executes code from various Internet sources, he is vulnerable to attacks by the code itself. A security scheme must be applied in order to secure the operations of Java programs. In this paper, the Java security scheme is examined and current implementations are evaluated on the basis of their efficiency and flexibility. Finally, proposed enhancements and upcoming extensions to the security model are described.

1. Introduction

The concept of downloadable executable content is not a new one. The explosion in use of the World Wide Web we are currently experiencing coupled with rapid evolution of the JAVA programming language has given insights into downloadable executable content and at the same time raised some important security issues.

JAVA is an object-oriented language that has been developed and distributed by Sun Microsystems. The main advantage of this language over other object-oriented languages is that the JAVA binary code may be executed on a wide variety of systems, without any modification. This is achieved through the *JAVA Virtual Machine* (JVM), a software program that simulates an imaginary virtual machine [Sun, 1997a], [Sun, 1997b]. The virtual machine insulates the application from differences between underlying operating systems and hardware and ensures cross platform compatibility among all implementations of the JAVA platform. This capability has offered JAVA wide acceptance from the community of application programmers, especially those who implement applications to be deployed in the Internet. However, security issues arise when a user downloads and executes a piece of code from a (possibly untrusted) network source. The user's system is vulnerable to any kind of attack, deriving from the executable content. JAVA has been surrounded by a specific security scheme, from the first release. The latter has undergone major alterations with respect to both its content (libraries, capabilities, structure) and its security mechanisms, the past few years. Now, in the new versions, JAVA promises that through its new designed security mechanism, it provides a secure environment for downloadable executable content that under specific circumstances can make use of a system's resources without compromising their availability and integrity.

This paper addresses the security problems associated with the JAVA programming language and provides some solutions for them. Section 2 provides a brief overview of the problems that would arise when running untrusted programs without providing a secure environment are investigated, section 3 takes a closer look at the solution provided by the JAVA security model. Current implementations as well as upcoming extensions are presented in section 4, where their efficiency and flexibility are evaluated, and proposed enhancements are discussed in section 5. Finally in section 6 concluding remarks are presented.

2. General Security Issues

Downloadable, executable content is the idea of downloading data that is actually code to be executed. The execution of downloadable content should be surrounded by a thorough security and safety scheme because downloadable, executable content (in contrast with traditional applications) could derive from untrusted or even unknown sources and as such it could misuse system's resources. The essence of the problem is that downloading and running JAVA code without placing any restrictions in resources availability, can provide a malicious program with the same ability to mischief as a hacker who had gained access to the host machine.

Hostile applets are a kind of Web-embedded JAVA programs that perform such hostile activities against Web users. An important part of creating a secure and safe environment for a program to run in is identifying the assets that we are concerned about and providing the classes of potential attacks that may occur. Therefore any program can do each of the following [Bank, 1995] [Gritzalis, 1991]:

- attack the *Integrity* of the system
- violate the user's *Privacy*
- limit system resources *Availability*
- achieve user's *Annoyance*

An extreme solution to the above mentioned problems would be to completely confine any downloaded executable content within the Web browser that is running it, hence not permitting any usage of the underlying system's resources. Nevertheless, such a solution is not a feasible one since one grants access to system's resources in order to make a program useful. By implication, one has to carefully consider what system resources and to what extent may be made available to a downloaded executable content, from within a browser, without endangering the system's security and at the same time guaranteeing the usefulness of the executable content.

3. JAVA Security

The Java Development Kit (JDK) is the official JAVA implementation from Sun. In JDK1.1 the downloaded code is executed in a customisable "sandbox", in order to protect the users from hostile applets. This model restricts the actions of an applet in a dedicated area of the web browser. Within its "sandbox" the applet may do anything it wants but cannot gain access to the user's file systems, network connections or other resources. The *sandbox* is made up of several systems that range from the applet security manager to the basic features of the JAVA language and JAVA Virtual Machine (JVM).

The JAVA language enhances safety [Sun, 1997c] by eliminating features like pointers and runtime casting to prevent illegal access to memory. In addition, security is provided by the JAVA simulator (interpreter) during the load and verification of JVM code. The JAVA interpreter inside JVM has three main tasks:

- code loading, performed by the class loader
- code verification, performed by the bytecode verifier
- code execution, done by the runtime system.

Applets are loaded from the network by the applet *Class Loader* which receives the bytecode instruction stream and converts it into internal data structures that represent the applet's classes. It then calls the verifier to check the class files, and creates a namespace where places all the applet's classes. A unique namespace exists for each network source, thus preventing untrusted applets from gaining access to more privileged, trusted parts of the system.

The Class Loader invokes the *Bytecode Verifier* before running a newly imported applet. The verifier subjects each applet class to a number of tests: Checks the bytecode to ensure that it does not forge pointers, violate access restrictions or access objects using incorrect type information and performs any other actions needed to prove that the applet will not be allowed to corrupt part of the security mechanism or to replace part of the system with its own code.

The *Security Manager* is an abstract class that enforces the boundaries around the sandbox. Whenever an applet tries to perform an action which could corrupt the local machine or access information (like the above mentioned actions), the JVM first asks the security manager if this action can be performed safely. If the security manager approves the action, the virtual machine will then perform it. Otherwise, the virtual machine raises a security exception and writes an error message to the JAVA console.

JDK1.2 includes a set of new features [Gong, 1997a], [Gong, 1997b] which introduce another modus operandi for the JAVA security system. JDK 1.2 will consist of the following new protection mechanisms: security policy, access permissions, protection domains, access control checking, privileged operation and JAVA class loading and resolution.

The security policy introduced by JDK1.2 is instantiated at JVM startup and may be altered a posteriori via secure methods. If no policies have been defined, a policy that conforms with the original "sandbox" operation is instantiated. Policies may be loaded either from the local file system or even from the Web. The policy comprises of a mapping between properties of the running code (the URL of the code and the code signature) and a set of permissions granted to that code. If a piece of code carries more than one signatures then the permissions it is entitled to are computed as the sum of permission each signature is entitled to. The permissions of an execution thread are calculated as an intersection of the permissions of all the callers of that thread.

There is a complete set of typed and parameterized access permissions contained in the JDK1.2 abstract class java.security.Permission. Furthermore, there are two abstract classes named java.security.PermissionCollection and java.security.Permissions which contain homogeneous and heterogeneous collections of permissions, respectively. One of the most important methods in this class is the "implies" method. a.implies(b)=true means that if one is granted the permission a then it is also granted the permission b.

JDK1.2 introduces the concept of *protection domains* [Gong, 1998]. The latter form the cornerstone of the new security features included in JDK1.2. A protection domain consists of all the objects that correspond to a principal who has been authorised by the system. Permissions may no longer be granted in JDK1.2 to classes but to protection domains.

Every class may belong to one domain only. The JAVA runtime maintains the mappings between classes and domains as well as between domains and permissions. It is possible to prevent the communication between different domains. When such a communication is necessary it may be performed either indirectly through system code, or directly if all the participating domains allow it. One of the future adjustments pertinent to the protection domains is the inclusion and usage of user authentication and delegation information, in order to be able for a piece of code to have different permissions when executed by different principals.

If a thread transverses more than one domain while executing, the permissions it is entitled to are computed based on the principle of least privilege. According to the latter, when the thread enters a domain which possesses fewer permissions then the previous one, it is entitled to these rights, while when it enters a domain which possesses more permissions than the previous one, it is entitled to the permissions of the previous domain.

Until JDK1.1, the code that performed access controls had to know the status of all it's callers; these checks had to be performed by the programmer. JDK1.2 introduces a new class called AccessController which simplifies this process. JDK1.2 uses "lazy evaluation" of the permissions of an object. When an object requests access to a resource, the programmer may call the checkPermisssion method of this class, thus having the system itself perform the access control on behalf of the programmer. For backward compatibility reasons, the SecurityManager usage is still allowed.

There are cases when a piece of code wishes to use the permission it is entitled to itself, although the status of the code's callers prohibit it. In such a case, the programmer may use the beginPrivileged and endPrivileged methods in the

AccessController class and have his code use the aforementioned permissions. If in such a case the code calls another piece of code, the latter loses the privilege of the former.

The Classloader class has been replaced by the SecureClassloader. The latter can distinguish system classes from others and impose the designed security policy to the latter. In JDK1.2 policy restrictions apply both to applets and applications. In order to impose the security policy to locally installed applications too, a new class has been introduced, called java.security.Main.

As we have already mentioned, it is the purpose of Javasoft to include in following JDK revisions, user authentication information in the security policy. This will provide the means to run the code with different permissions, depending on who's behalf the code is running. User authentication information inclusion and usage has already been tested and performed to a certain degree [Balfanz, 1997].

JDK1.2 and most of the emerging JAVA security frameworks applications depend on the existence of a public key infrastructure. It is an obvious necessity for these frameworks to support the widely accepted standards for Public Key Infrastructures (PKI) and for the security mechanisms that surround them, such as X.509v3 certificates, Secure Socket Layer (SSL), HTTP Secure (HTTPS), Secure MIME (S/MIME) and Secure Lightweight Directory Access Protocol (LDAPS).

4. Security Extensions

The JDK 1.2 includes support for digital signatures (authentication, integrity) and message digests, key management, certificate management and access control. The *JAVA Cryptography Architecture* refers to the framework for accessing and developing cryptographic functionality for the JAVA platform. The official JAVA implementation by Sun includes an implementation of the NIST DSA algorithm, the MD5 and SHA message digest algorithms.

JDK 1.2 provides a security tool, the *javakey*, whose primary use is to generate digital signatures for archive files (JAR files) which enable the packaging of class files. To sign an applet the producer first creates a JAR file and then creates a digital signature based on the contents of the JAR. JDK1.2 also provides a tool called *keytool*, which is used to manage the *keystore*. The latter is a database for private and public keys and their respective certificates. The keystore may resides at the same repository with the policy; it is either stored on a local drive or at a remote repository, accessible via the Web. There is also a new tool available in JDK1.2, called PolicyTool, which is a graphical user interface that one may use in order to generate, import or export a security policy.

Since the ability to encrypt the data prior to being transferred is very important, APIs for data encryption are contained in a *JAVA Cryptography Extension*, as an add-on package to JDK.

Recently, new policy enforcement methods, secure code distribution and JAVA firewall blocking methods have been found and some of them implemented. These are presented in the following paragraphs.

4.1 Policy Enforcement Methods

Once the code is authenticated to the system, that is associated with a principal, then the code is subject to the policy defined for that principal. To enforce this policy, three secure methods have been found [Wallach, 1997]:

- *Capabilities:* Unforgeable pointers which can be safely given to user code
- *Extended stack introspection:* Information about the principals can be included in the stack
- *Name space management:* Restricting or changing an applet's namespace

Capabilities

Fundamentally, a capability is an unforgeable pointer to a controlled system resource. To use a capability, a program must have been first explicitly given that capability, either as part of its initialisation or as the result of calling another capability. Every top level class of an applet could be given by the system an array of capabilities (pointers to objects). Then the applet would be able to use whenever it wishes these capabilities. The objects that are referenced by the capabilities may implement and enforce their own, internal security policy, by checking the parameters with which they are called. The JAVA runtime would have to be modified in order to make private all the methods which handle system resources directly or indirectly. It is only the capabilities themselves (the referenced objects) that should have access to these methods.

Capabilities are easy to implement in JAVA, because of the underlying infrastructure. Systems that support "capabilities" have been researched. One of these is the JAVA Electronic Commerce Framework [Goldstein, 1996], which provides a security platform, complimentary to the one that JAVA is using right now, able to implement complex trust relationships between entities.

Extended Stack Introspection

This policy enforcement method has already been implemented in commercial browsers, such as Netscape Communicator 4 and Microsoft Internet Explorer 4 and in the JDK1.2. There are three primitives that must be implemented for this method:

- enablePrivilege(target)
- disablePrivilege(target)
- checkPrivilege(target).

Every system resource must be associated with a target. Before the system allows the use of a system resource, it should perform a checkPrivilege on the specified target. When a thread, associated with a principal, asks for a system resource it should perform an enablePrivilege on the specified target. The security policy will then decide whether that principal is entitled to use this target and the system will or will not grant the privilege to the code. After the thread has finished using this system resource it must execute a disablePrivilege. If the programmer omits the latter, the privilege should be discarded automatically. This can be done by storing the enabled privilege in a hidden and protected field of the method that created it. The checkPrivilege primitive should check the stack and judge whether a privilege must be given or not based on the *least privilege* rule, in order to prevent trusted code from calling untrusted code and passing the latter the privileges of the former.

Name Space Management
It is a method to enforce a security policy by replacing or hiding the classes that are visible by a program. There has to be a mapping between the applets (and their respective signers) and the namespaces that each applet will be able to see. Hiding a class from the namespace means that the applet may not be able at alto use it, while replacing the class with another (possibly a subclass of the latter) provides a means for controlling even more the way that the applet will call and use the methods contained in the aforementioned class.

Let's assume that we created a subclass S of class C and a method M which overrides the respective method of class C. Method M of subclass S may be providing limited use of the resources that method M of class C provides normally to an applet. If we bind the name of S to C, then the applet that will call method M will have at it's disposal a limited, functional set of resources, although it will believe it has gained access to the full set of resources it has asked for.

4.2 Secure Code Distribution
Secure code distribution [Zhang, 1997] is one of the security issues that concern the JAVA community. There are various approaches to authentication for secure code distribution. One of them is the signed applets. The JAVA class file format is extensible. It is possible to add new attributes to the latter, without influencing the current structure or workflow of the classloaders. These new attributes can contain signatures for the applet which can be verified, provided that the user possesses the certificate of the entity who signed the applet. After the verification the security manager may grant certain rights to the applet, depending on the trustworthiness of the author or of the person who has signed the applet. The level of trust, and therefore the amount and species of rights that should be granted to the applet, that each user preserves for each applet author or signer can be defined a priori by forming a local security policy, accessible from the user through the browser and protected by all means available (e.g. filesystem rights) to the Operating System. Secure code distribution is already supported by Javasoft's JAR specification. A JAR is an archive encapsulating, with proprietary methods, signed or unsigned classes and other files (e.g. sounds).The signature can be verified by the JDK infrastructure, providing thus a secure authentication means for the distribution of applets.

The success of the JAR secure code distribution scheme heavily depends on the existence of a public key infrastructure, based on widely accepted standards. Code signing provides a way for securely authenticating the source or even the author of the applet to the final user. However, the choice of rights or the choice of "trusted" signers or authors is still a decision that must be taken by the user, prior to executing the applet. One should not exclude the possibility of hostile code, deriving from a source or being signed by someone that a user considers to be "trusted". Furthermore, code signing provides no additional security layer for those applets that are considered to be "untrusted". They are still executed in the limited sandbox environment, and the local system's safety depends on the existing security infrastructure.

4.3 Confining the Use of JAVA in a Network Domain

An organisation may wish to ban all JAVA incoming traffic from the Internet, but wishes also to deploy and use JAVA applets internally, in the domain of the organisation. This may be achieved by blocking the JAVA applets at the firewall [Martin, 1997]. However it is a complex task and up to now no solution has proven to be complete, apart from locking all the browsers' preferences in the organisation's internal domain in such a way so they will not be able to interpret JAVA. However, the latter would render the browsers incapable of interpreting JAVA while operating in the organisation's internal domain too.

Blocking JAVA applets at the firewall can be performed by implementing a number of strategies in order to assure that applets do not penetrate the internal network, or if they do, they are not executed at all at the local machines. The first strategy should be the rewriting of the <applet> tag by a proxy, wherever this is found. It could be in an HTTP transmission, or in mail or news messages (HTML enabled mail and news clients exist in the market currently). Rewriting the <applet> tag will cause the client to ignore the existence of the java applet in the message. It should be mentioned though that Javascript may be used in order to create the <applet> tag just before the page is viewed in the browser, rendering the above blocking useless. Another strategy that must be implemented is the blocking of the CAFEBABE signature. Every JAVA class file begins with this 4-byte signature, [Sun, 1997b] so it is possible to block all java classes as soon as they reach the proxy. However, if SSL or JAR files are used, these countermeasures are rendered useless, since the <applet> tag or the CAFEBABE signature will pass undetected, through the proxy. In addition, another strategy that has to be implemented is to set the proxy to reject all files which have an extension ".class". However, if classes arrive at the firewall archived (JAR, Zip) the ".class" extension would not be detected.

If one decides to implement the aforementioned strategies, he should take under consideration the possibility of accidentally blocking useful information, e.g. files whose first 4-byte signature is CAFEBABE but are not JAVA classes or files that contain the "<applet>" string but do not call any JAVA applets (could possibly be a JAVA security paper, in HTML format) or even blocking files that end in ".class" but do not consist of JAVA classes.

5. Proposed Enchancements

The runtime should provide a configurable audit system which would allow system administrators to study the circumstances under which each type of attack has been occurred. As a minimum, files read and written from the local file system should be logged, along with network usage.

Limiting system resources (degradation of service) is still an open issue. The JAVA community is not so concerned about it, though it is one of the easiest to exploit

JAVA security leaks. The JDK should limit the level to which an applet may use system resources.

The security user interfaces we have witnessed so far demand too frequently from the user to take security-related decisions, based on security and system resources information he is provided with upon asked. The number of questions towards the user should be limited as much as possible. This can be achieved by having the site administrator define a system-wide policy and leave the user with a few questions to be asked. Asking the user too many questions sometimes presents an impact quite opposite than the one we wish. The user starts pressing "OK" to any question that comes up, either because he is tired of answering ('authorisation fatigue') to all these questions or because he might not understand the nature of a security related question. The latter imposes new limits on the way that JAVA security providers have to ask questions to end users. These questions should be simple enough for an end user to understand, but at the same time they have to encapsulate in these all the security-related information that has to be contacted to the user. For instance, instead of asking the user whether he wishes to grant the permission to this *word processing* applet to open a system dictionary, use system fonts or grant write permission to the filesystem (at least to a directory of the filesystem), the question could be "Grant this application with *word processing* rights?". Finally, privileges granted or denied to applets (signers) should be stored in order to be looked up automatically the next time an applet arrives that carries a signature by the same signer.

Secure code distribution has evolved; one may identify securely the signer of the code he downloads. Furthermore, JAVA has the ability to enforce a security policy, by using the capabilities model, extended stack introspection and name space management. However, the methods and tools needed in order to define a system-wide policy have not yet been developed. It is up to the user to define the policy used against a certain piece of JAVA code, based on the digital signatures it carries. The end-user should be able to see and define only a part of the policy, enforced upon a piece of JAVA code. In an organisation, a network-wide policy should be designed by the network administrator and the administrators of the local networks.

A central repository, possibly a Directory or a Web Server, could be used in order to store the security policy. The later will be formed by three entities : a system-wide policy by the network administrator, a local policy by the administrators of the local networks of the organisation and the end-user. The policy each of these entities will define will be *based on the signer of JAVA code and on the Certificate Authority which certifies the signers signature* . The network administrator must be given the right to decide on matters such as whether JAVA code may be downloaded to computers inside the organisations network and whether it may access computers other than the one it is downloaded to. The local network administrators should be able to define in which computers JAVA has the right to access the hard disks or other magnetic storage devices and also define quotas, when access to hard disks is allowed; he should also have the right to define which users should be able to download and execute JAVA and to which computers. Finally, the end-user should be left with few choices to make on the JAVA-related security policy, because he may not have the necessary technological background. He should have to answer to questions such as

"Grant game-related privileges to this code?", forming thus the lower layer of the security policy. The inclusion of a configurable security policy in JDK1.2 provides with the capability of grouping certain permissions. The PolicyTool can be used in order to enable the network administrator and the local administrator to store their JAVA-related security policy decisions in the central repository. The PolicyTool may be used by the end-user too in order to define the lower level of the security policy, for his machine. The PolicyTool has to be modified in order to allow to the above three individuals to have access to a specific set of permissions only, as described in the previous paragraphs. As far as the end-user is concerned, the permissions he must select to grant to specific principals should be have a high-level nature, such as "Typical game-related privileges". The latter may be formed by a collection of carefully selected low-level permissions.

6. Conclusions

Remote execution of code has been an attractive and popular approach. JAVA programming language revolutionised the programming world three years ago within nine adjectives; the third one was *Secure*. With the JavaSecurity API, JAVA 1.1 is building on the foundation of previous versions and afford us more flexibility to do what we want, even though it is widely accepted that security, unfortunately but not surprisingly, can never be completely guaranteed.

Digital signatures have been a major contribution to the development of JAVA security. They provide the necessary infrastructure in order to define and enforce a JAVA-related security policy, based on the signature carried by a piece of JAVA code and on the Certificate Authority that certifies that signature.

The flexible security policy introduced in JDK1.2 provides an integrated method in order to grant specific permissions to applets, based on the signatures carried by the latter.

A fundamental research topic [McGraw, 1996] is a new approach to the way the Access Control List model works. The perspective idea is to provide a secure and safe way to implement mature Remote Method Invocation (RMI) facility. RMI will be possible with a strong ACL system in place.

The security scheme that surrounds the remote execution of Java code has undergone a significant number of modifications and adjustments. However, the underlying JAVA architecture has only been altered to a minor degree. This is due to the open architecture that characterises the Java programming language. This is essential in downloadable, executable content. The security scheme may evolve; it may be modified or adjusted according to new findings. The underlying architecture and the applications themselves should not be altered.

References

[Balfanz, 1997] D.Balfanz, L.Gong, (1997) "Secure Multi-Processing in Java".
[Bank, 1995] "Java Security", available at
   http://www-swiss.ai.mit.edu/~jbank/javapaper/javapaper.html

[Felten, 1997] E.W.Felten, D.Balfanz, D.Dean, D.S.Wallach, (1997) "Web Spoofing: An Internet Con Game",
Proceeedings of the 20th National Information Systems Security Conference.

[Goldstein, 1996] Goldstein T., (1996) The Gateway Security Model in the Java Electronic Commerce Framework, JavaSoft, available at
http://www.javasoft.com/products/commerce/jectf_gateway.ps

[Gong, 1997a] L.Gong, M.Mueller, H.Prafullchandra, R.Schemers, (1997) "Going Beyond the Sandbox: An Overview of the New Security Architecture in the Java Development Kit 1.2",
Proceedings of the USENIX Symposium on Internet Technologies and Systems.

[Gong, 1997b] L.Gong, (1997)"New Security Architectural Directions for Java", *Proceedings of IEEE COMPCON.*

[Gong, 1998] L. Gong, R. Schemers (1998) 'Implementing Protection Domains in the Java Development Kit 1.2", Proceedings of the 1998 Network and Distributed Systems Security Symposium, Internet Society

[Gritzalis, 1991] Gritzalis D., (1991) *Information Systems Security*, Greek Computer Society Publications (in Greek).

[Martin, 1997] Martin D., Rajagopalan S., Rubin A., (1997) Blocking Java Applets at the Firewall, *Proceedings of the SNDSS 1997 Symposium on Network and Distributed System Security*, pp.123-133, IEEE Computer Society Press.

[McGraw, 1996] McGraw G., Felten E., (1996) *Java Security Hostile Applets, Holes and Antidotes*, J. Wiley & Sons Inc.

[Sun, 1997a] Sun Microsystems, (1997) Secure Computing with Java: Now and the Future, at
http://java.sun.com/marketing/collateral/security.html

[Sun, 1997b] The Java Virtual Machine Specification, (1997) available in the Web at
http://java.sun.com/docs/books/vmspec/

[Sun, 1997c] Sun Microsystems, (1997) Frequently Asked Questions - Applet Security, at
http://java.sun.com/sfaq/

[Wallach, 1997] D.S.Wallach, D.Balfanz, D.Dean, E.W.Felten, (1997) "Extensible Security Architectures for Java", *Proceedings of the 16th Symposium on Operating Systems Principles.*

[Zhang, 1997] X.N.Zhang, "Secure Code Distribution", (1997) IEEE Computer.

Model and Implementation of a Secure SW-Development Process for Mission Critical Software

Ferdinand J. Dafelmair

TÜV Energie- und Systemtechnik, Westend Street 199, 80686 Munich, Germany
fdaf@tuev.spacenet.de

Abstract. With the growing dependency of many technical, commercial, administrative and even social processes from computer software, the number of mission critical software projects rapidly increases. The rapid integration of formerly stand-alone systems into global networks subjects these systems to yet unknown threats. Even mission critical systems may be deliberately manipulated to let malicious attackers access vital system functions or to take over the entire system. Though such systems feature protection mechanism during operation, they are rather vulnerable during their software design and development process. This paper defines a secure software development process to reduce the risk of manipulation and enhance the trustworthiness of critical software produced by renowned manufaturers according to high quality standards. It also explained how this process may be implemented cost efficiently.

Introduction

Whenever software is mission critical, e.g. when it controls processes with a high potential of danger, designers need to be very careful to avoid design faults in both the software and its associated computer system hardware and they have to cope with random failures caused by different physical effects. A lot of research has been carried out addressing these topics. The widespread use of data communication technologies with globally networked systems used both in software development environments as well as in situ installations including mission critical systems, introduces a quite knew kind of risk - the deliberate modification of systems either to let them fail in critical situations or to get in control of the mission, e.g. the dangerous process, through undetected backdoors.

The intention of this behavior may have whatever reason - the fact is that the anonymity of the modern communication society supports such kind of dangerous activities. Furthermore developers of mission critical systems need to design countermeasures against such threats right into their systems. And not only the system itself needs to be protected but its whole design process, especially for the software, because once a malicious part of code found its way into the system, it could be very difficult to prevent it from jeopardizing important and critical functions. Besides clearly structured design processes with unambiguously assigned responsibilities, careful configuration management (CM) plays a key role in preventing such hacking because configuration management integrates important quality assurance activities, e.g. identification, inspection, verification, and validation into the development flow and handles corrective actions as well as later adaptations. This paper shows how configuration management may be easily enhanced to achieve full traceability of the whole design process and easy detection of any manipulations, either within the mission critical software itself or its development process.

Cryptographic Basics

A secure software development process heavily depends on the application of cryptography. Therefore it's a prerequisite for the following discussion to introduce some basic functions, algorithms and protocols used in cryptography.

One -Way Hash Functions

This functions are central to cryptography and used in many protocols. Hash functions h=H(M) transform a variable length input data string M called pre-image into an output value of fixed length, named hash value h. The hash value is typically much shorter (typically 100 to 200 bits) than the input data string. Hash values fingerprint the pre-image. Changes in the pre-image lead to changes in the hash value, too. One way hash functions let one easily compute the hash value from the pre-image, but it's very hard to generate a pre-image that hashes into a given hash value. Hash functions useful for cryptography are also collision free, meaning that it is very difficult to create two pre-images with the same hash value [1].

Asymmetric Encryption Algorithms

Asymmetric encryption algorithms use two different keys (K1, K2) for encryption E and decryption D and both operations are complementary as follows:

$$D_{K2}(E_{K1} (M)) = M \qquad (1)$$

In contrast, symmetric encryption algorithms use the same key for encryption and decryption (see Fig. 1).

Asymmetric encryption algorithms are also called public key algorithms because one of the keys (e.g. the encryption key) can be made public such that only the owner of the corresponding decryption key can decrypt a message encrypted with his „public" key. That algorithm works because it's very hard to calculate one key from knowing the other one. Asymmetric encryption algorithms play a key role for implementing digital signatures [1].

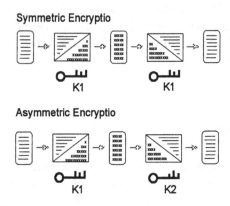

Fig. 1. Encryption Algorithms

Digital Signatures

Digital signatures on electronic documents shall fulfill some important requirements derived from handwritten signatures. They shall convince the recipient that the sender really signed the document and the signature is authentic, the signature shall be unforgeable, not reusable and it shall not be repudiated and last but not least the signed documents shall not be alterable [4]. There are many algorithms to implement digital signatures. All of them are public-key algorithms with secret keys to sign the documents and public keys to verify them. An example of such an algorithm is given below.

Signing a digital document

To sign a document M the signer named Alice calculates the hash value H(M) to reduce the amount of data for further processing. This may be done since H(M) fully represents M to fulfill the above stated requirements for signatures. Alice then encrypts the hash value of M with her private key and appends the resulting signature

$$Sig_A = (E_{As}(H (M)))$$ (2)

to the message M to form a signed document SM.

$$SM = (M, Sig_A). \tag{3}$$

SM also carries basic information about the sender Alice, e.g. the name and the server where to obtain the public key of Alice from.

A document may also carry more than one signature.

$$SM = (M, (Sig_A, Sig_B \ldots Sig_n)) \tag{4}$$

The secret key A_S is usually stored in a tamper-resistant module (e.g. a smartcard) which needs to be enabled through additional information (keycode) or biometric identification. To avoid the encryption operation be jeopardized, a crypto-chip is included in the module.

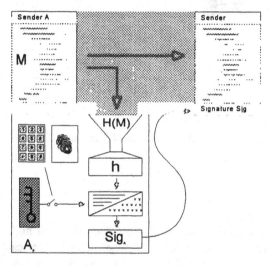

Fig. 2. Signing a digital document

Verification of Signatures

To verify a signature on a signed document SM, the recipient Bob needs to decrypt the Signature on the document Sig_i, which he supposes to belong to Alice, with Alice's public key A_P. It is very important that a recipient of a signed document has an authentic public key of the sender to avoid cheating with signatures. Because it's not feasible to verify all public keys of one's communication partners oneself, a Trust Center takes over the role of a provider for authentic public keys. Bob requests Alice's public key A_P from a trust center. He gets it with a proof of authenticity and decrypts the signature Sig_i with it. If the result of this operation equals H(M) which he recalculates from the signed document, he verified Alice's signature and can be sure that she signed the document if the following equation is true:

$$D_{Ap}(Sig_i) = D_{AP}(E_{AS}(H(M))) = H(M) \tag{5}$$

In practice, timestamps need to be added to ensure some of the above mentioned requirements.

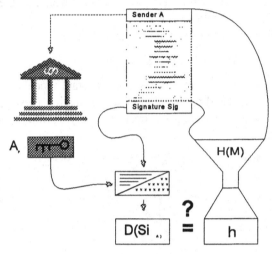

Fig. 3. Verification of Signatures

Trust Center

Trust Centers are trusted third parties that provide users with high quality key pairs for public key algorithms. Furthermore the trust center authenticates new users and assigns them a unique key pair. The trust center certifies this assignment according to a trusted and secure procedure and generates public key certificates for the users, e.g. C_A for user Alice, which are stored in a publicly accessible database [2]. The secret key is transmitted authentically and secretly to his owner, usually embedded in a tamper-resistant chipcard. The trust center ensures that certificates are always up to date and authentic. When it delivers public key certificates for signature verification, it certifies the authenticity of the delivered certificates by its own signature. Trust centers often provide additional services e.g. arbitrator services, timestamp services, and directory services with additional certified information. This data then is guaranteed to be as authentic than the public key (see Figure 4).

Timestamps

Timestamps are required to certify that something happened or existed at a certain time. With electronic documents time-stamping is critical since these documents may be altered easily without any signs of tampering. A feasible solution to this problem is the introduction of arbitrators. Often trust centers act as arbitrators. To get a timestamp TS for a document M the user sends H(M) to the arbitrator, who adds the time to the hash value, signs both and returns the result back to the user.

$$TS(M) = S_{TC} (H(M),T) \tag{6}$$

where S_{TC} is the signature of the trusted arbitrator and T is the time of reception of H(M).

This basic cryptographic functions and algorithms are now used to model a secure and traceable software generation process (see Figure 5).

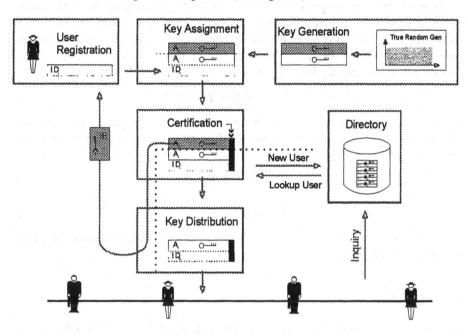

Fig. 4. Trust Center

The traceable SW Generation Process

In the sense of this document, a software generation process basically consists of the implementation and verification phases of astate-of-the-art software development processes as indicated in the various software life-cycle models. Specification and refinement of the design is not considered within the scope of this paper, despite the methods of achieving traceability by the help of coding theory and cryptography, may as well be applied to this early development phases.

Coding

Starting from an approved detailed functional specification for the software, a Development Engineer (DVE) starts coding using a high level language thereby generating atomic source code items, in the following referred to as Terminal Software Modules (TSM). The further discussion makes no assumptions on language type or other language properties. Every TSM consists of source code (TSC) and an identification string TSMID = (TSM Name, TSM Version Nr.). In addition to this traditionally well-known parts of a TSM each TSM gets assigned an Authenticity Certificate (TSMAC). This certificate contains TSMID and the timestamp of the source-code TSC which is the hash value of the source code H(TSC) as it existed at the time given in the timestamp. The TSMAC is appended to the Source Code and ID data and is considered part of the "certified" TSM.

$$TSMAC = S'_{DVE} (TSMID, TS (TSC)) \tag{7}$$

S_A' (M) designates a modified signature function that requires a Certificate verification Key (CVK) for reading and verification of the signature in contrast to the open Signature $S_A(M)$.

$$S_A'(M) = (M, E_{CVK}(A, Sig_A)) \tag{8}$$

$$S_A(M) = (M, A, Sig_A) \tag{9}$$

with M being the signed message, A the signer's name and Sig_A the actual signature code (see Section on Signatures).

Code Inspection

According to good practice of software quality management the TSM is subjected to code inspection carried out by the Code Inspection Engineer (CIE). He states the correct inspection of the TSM by adding an Inspection Certificate (TSMIC). With his signature the CIE not only states exactly what code he inspected when, but also indicates that he inspected authentic code primarily signed by the DVE.

$$TSMIC = S'_{DVE} (TSMID, TS(TSC), H(TSMAC)) \tag{10}$$

By this way each TSM receives a coding and a code inspection certificate.

Code Transformation

Next step in software generation is to transform the TSM into binary modules, called Terminal Binary Modules (TBM) through a Code Transformation Tool (CTT). This may be either classically a compiler or - as today also common practice - a code generation tool as it is for instance used in special process computer software development environments (e.g. for PLCs etc.).

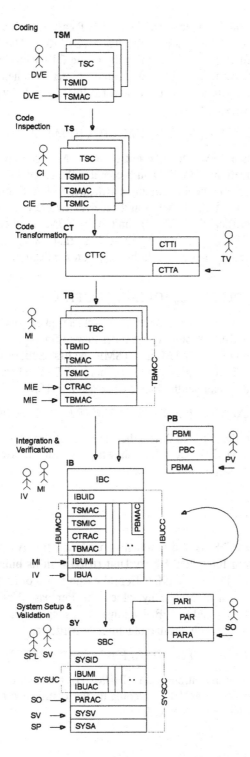

Fig. 5. Secure SW Develiopment Process Modell

To identify this transformation exactly, the CTT carries besides an identification string (CCTID) also an authenticity certificate (CTTAC). The Tool Verification Engineer (TVE) confirms correct functionality of the CTT which he checked during Tool Testing and confirms optional Manufacturers' Authenticity Certificates (MFGAC) he could verify to be genuine and trustworthy, e.g. by assessment of the manufacturers' quality systems.

$$CTTAC = S'_{TVE} \ (CTTID, TS(CTTC), [H(MFGAC)]) \tag{11}$$

The CTT transforms a TSM into a Terminal Binary Module (TBM). It is identified by the TBM identification (TBMID) and it contains the target specific machine code (TBC). The TBM inherits the authenticity certificates from the corresponding source code module TSM (TSMAC, TSMIC) and receives two new certificates, the Code Transformation Certificate (CTRAC) and the TBM Authenticity Certificate (TBMAC). The CTRAC identifies all CTTs that were involved in code transformation, since this process could be based on application of n different tools, each with its own CTTAC.

$$CTRAC = S'_{MIE} \ (CTTAC_1, ..., CTTAC_n) \tag{12}$$

With the TBMAC the Module Integration Engineer (MIE) confirms the correct transformation of the Code by signing the timestamped fingerprint of the binary code TBC and by inclusion of the CTRAC and TSMIC he first certifies that he applied the tools identified in CTRAC to generate the particular TBM and second he states that he used an inspected and authentic Source Code Module TSM.

$$TBMAC = S'_{MIE} \ (TBMID, TS(TBC), H(CTRAC), H(TSMIC)) \tag{13}$$

The Certificates of the TBM all together are referred to as the Configuration Certificate of the TBM (TBMCC). It is shown later how the user may verify code integrity using this configuration certificate.

Integration

At integration several TBMs and optionally Purchased Binary Modules (PBM) are put together to form a Integrated Binary Unit (IBU) with its binary code IBC. The PBMs are treated like TBMs, but differ from those in terms of certificates applied to them. A PBM carries a certificate by which the Purchase Verification Engineer (PVE) confirms that he tested the PBM against his test speci fications for third party software and optionally it includes manufacturers' certificates.

$$PBMAC = S'_{PVE} \ (PBMID, TS(PBC), [H(MFGAC)...]) \tag{14}$$

The IBU Module Configuration Data (IBUMCD) forms the main part of the certificates associated with an IBU. It contains the certificates of n TBMs and m PBMs contained in the IBU as follows[1]:

---

[1] & is the concatenation operator

$$IBUMCD = \begin{pmatrix} \overset{n}{\underset{i=1}{\&}}(TSMAC_i, TSMIC_i, CTRAC_i, TBMAC_i), \\ \overset{m}{\underset{j=1}{\&}}(PBMAC_j) \end{pmatrix} \qquad (15)$$

The Module Integration Certificate of the IBU (IBUMIC) associates the fingerprint of the IBU's binary code IBC with the time and the module certificates in IBUMCD. Thus the MIE confirms which modules he integrated at what time.

$$IBUMIC = S'_{MIE} (IBUID, TS(IBC), H(IBUMCD)) \qquad (16)$$

Verification

The final certificate stating the authenticity of the IBU (IBUAC) indicates exactly, what the IVE verified during verification tests and when he carried out these tests. Furthermore the certificate includes with the timestamp of the Test Report Tag (IBUTRT) - the fingerprints of all test reports - an exact and provable bi-directional reference between the IBU and the test reports for the IBU (IBUTR). Undetected alterations of neither of both are not possible under this scheme.

$$IBUAC = S_{IVE} (IBUID, TS(IBUMIC), TS(IBUTRT)) \qquad (17)$$

with

$$IBUTRT = \overset{k}{\underset{i=1}{\&}} H(IBUTR_i) \qquad (18)$$

Again, the certificates of the IBU all together are referred to as IBU Configuration Data IBUCC - another basic element of configuration management.

Dependent on the complexity of the system, this integration process may take place on different levels. To keep this example clear and understandable, only one level of integration is indicated. Nevertheless integration on more levels may be easily accomplished by applying the same scheme recursively.

System Validation

At the last step of the software generation process the System Operating Engineer (SOE) sets up the system parameters and the System Validation Engineer (SVE) evaluates the system under final operation conditions.

The first section of system level certificates, the System Unit Configuration Data (SYSUCD) describes the IBUs the system is built from stating the code fingerprints and the configuration data fingerprint of each IBU in the system (IBUMIC) and indicating the integrity of the IBUs providing their IBUAC.

Because many modern software systems are highly configurable, the correct setting of system parameters is a prerequisite for correct operation. The Parameter

Authenticity Certificate (PARAC) indicates, that all parameters have been approved by the SOE.

$$PARAC = S'_{SOE} (PARID, TS(PAR)) \qquad (19)$$

The result of system validation is documented in System Validation Reports (SYSVR). The SVE signs the System Validation Certificate (SYSVC) consisting of the SYSVR's fingerprint tag SYSVT and the fingerprints[2] of the system binary code SBC and the System Unit Configuration Data (SYSUCD) to state correct validation of an unambiguous system configuration.

$$SYSVC = \quad S'_{SVE} (SYSID, TS(SBC), TS(SYSUCD), TS(SYSVT)) \qquad (20)$$

$$SYSUCD = \underset{i=1}{\overset{p}{\&}} (IBUMIC_i, IBUAC_i \qquad (21)$$

$$SYSVT = \underset{i=1}{\overset{l}{\&}} H(SYSVR_i \qquad (22)$$

Software Release

The final top level certificate of the Software generation process is the System Authenticity Certificate (SYSAC) signed by the System Project Leader (SPL).

$$SYSAC = S_{SPL} (SYSID, H(SBC), H(PAR), TS(SYSVC, PARAAC)) \qquad (23)$$

This certificate is signed not before the successful completion of the software generation process. Notice that this certificate carries an open signature that is readable and verifiable by anyone and that it carries the official release date of the System within the time-stamp and the approval of the system Validation and Configuration. This master certificate represents all the other certificates of the software generation process and stands for all software quality measures undertaken throughout the software generation process.

The Verification of correct SW Generation

In contrast to standard software development processes this secure development process allows the customer, who ordered the software from the manufacturer, to easily verify that the code he is using is the same than that one the manufacturer released and it further allows him to trace back the generation process and verify that every step of the software generation process has been carried out by trusted persons. The customer accomplishes this in the following way:

---

[2] precisely: timestamped fingerprints

Detection of Modifications

The basic authenticity certificate is SYSAC which the customer gets together with the software delivery. He may verify the signature of the System project leader (see section about verifying digital signatures) since the signature is open available. From the verified SYSAC he retrieves the Hash values of the system code and its parameters (H(SBC) and H(PAR)) and may check them against the actual hashes he calculates from the system instance he runs. This check can either be done manually or it can be integrated into the system startup or into periodic internal system self-checks such that this verification is done automatically. Unauthorized modification of the software is detected also automatically this way.

Tracing Software Generation

For a more in depth verification of the software generation process, the customer needs to check the certificates created during the development process. The software manufacturer stores all the certificates mentioned above in a certificates database (CDB) within configuration management (CM). Note that the certificates may be kept separated from the associated code because all of them carry authentic references to the software modules they belong to. Furthermore the certificate database does not carry any internals about the software and thus is not needed to be kept confidential in order to protect intellectual property. In fact the certificate database is handed over to the customer together with the code.

He may use this database to extract fingerprint signatures (hashes) for every module or unit to verify the integrity of his code down to code-part level. He also may trace back the Quality Management Measures (QMM) and identify when a QMM has been carried out with the help of the timestamps. With this information the customer is able to pinpoint exactly where his software instance differs from the manufacturers master copy without having access to this master copy. This is especially useful if the system goes trough several loops of changes. To verify the signatures of the detailed certificates in the CDB the customer needs to verify signatures of type S'.

$$S'_A(M)=(M,E_{CVK}(A, Sig_A)) \tag{24}$$

Without the Certificate Verification Key CVK this signatures may not be verified. Without this key it is not possible to identify the real persons behind their roles in the software generation process because neither their name nor their signature is readable. Thus the manufacturer may control who is able to trace his software generation process back to the responsible people by providing only those people, e.g. third party assessors or certification bodies with the CVK key.

Through the timestamps it is possible to verify that QMM were carried out in their correct sequence and that no QMM was left out. The construction of certificates guarantees, that for any single part of code in the final system instance it may be prooved who designed it, who changed it, who tested it, what the result from testing was and even what tools (compilers etc.) were used to generate it. Especially for tools they allow to determine the tool by name, version and code such that one could detect, whether non authorized and possibly manipulated tools were applied. The discussion of all information that could be derived from the certificates must be left to a more in depth discussion of the model.

Deterrence by Transparency

Despite the model offers a high degree of transparency and authenticity of software generation process it cannot solve the problem of detecting sabotage by staff members. However two factors limit the danger of sabotage. First of all sabotage may no longer be carried out anonymously and secondly the sabotage must either be applied so concealed that the code inspector does not detect it or the code inspector must collaborate with the saboteur. It needs a far higher degree of commitment to pursue sabotage if, once the sabotage is detected, the saboteur may be unambiguously identified through the signature on the certificate he signed. [3]

Certified Software Repository

One aspect that was not discussed yet is that code modules or test result that were subject to evaluation by a third party assessment (e.g. with type tested systems) could also receive a certificate similar to those of the manufacturer. Because this certificate is inextricably linked with the code it's an easy and very efficient way to enhance the level of confidence in a pre-developed and probably reused code module. Repositories of such certified software would efficiently reduce qualification costs of new software designs and increase the trustworthiness of a software with every certificate it receives. Thus manufacturers could enhance the reputation of high quality mission critical software component repositories through accumulation of provable certificates.

Implementation of the Scheme

The complexity of the model for secure software generation might give the impression that implementation of this scheme is complex and costly. The required basic technology however is completely developed and widely available in commercial products and because the increasing utilization of public networks demands comparable security solutions, this high volume market offers a variety of low cost solutions.

---

[3] The German Signature Law IuKDG §3 specifies, under what conditions electronic signatures are considered to be secure.

Cryptography Software

Because the whole scheme is based on digital signatures, implementation of it requires software to digitally sign documents and verify signatures. Besides commercial solutions the very well-known pgp-software package (Pretty good privacy) is available including source code at very moderate costs [3]. PGP also allows encryption and is available on many system platforms. The source code for different hash algorithms is also available in source code and binaries for all major platforms.[4]

Database software

The certificates are signed accumulations of data items, which could again be certificates. The certificates as well as the signatures are encoded in ASCII and are standard text items. For the terminal source code modules TSM the certificates could be directly appended to the source code as lines for comment. Thus the certificates could even be handled by any standard source code management systems.

For a better solution including the management of all certificates in the process and for development environments without ASCII source code like PLC software specification systems and binary codes (TBM, IBU, SYS), certificates are kept in a database. Because all certificates are standard text items the requirements for the database, that should be relational, are low and the handling of certificates and their components is easy.

The entire scheme may be realized for test purposes taking note [4] into account using a standard database on a PC and freeware or public domain software.

Conclusion

The application of proposed model for a secure software generation process is a very effective measure to counteract against the threats of viruses, Trojan horses or any kind of software sabotage during the software generation process. It is also very cost

---

[4] The aspect of source-code availability is crucial to ensure that cryptographic software itself is correct and doesn't include malicious code or faked algorithms. It also needs to be mentioned, that the selection of software used for cryptography is critical since the use cryptography is restricted by law in some countries or cryptographic products include functions for key escrow, meaning that there exists a way to decrypt encrypted messages without the original keys using a "master key" which is under control of usually the state authorities. Another problem is that export versions of some software products featuring strong cryptography are restricted to a low maximum key length which makes it much easier to crack them. To avoid such flaws in cryptographic software it's highly recommended to select the software vendor carefully and to avoid dependencies from foreign industry and legislation as far as possible.

effective, especially when software items are designed to be used in several mission critical applications because it drastically reduces evaluation costs. Technology for the implementation is fully available at quite moderate costs and the infrastructure necessary to achieve legal acceptance for the scheme - accredited trust centers - is just built.[5]

The enhanced traceability of the process furthermore leads towards a higher commitment of staff members to high quality work, since everyone signs with his name for the quality of the work he carries out.

The fact, that the scheme supports automatic code authentication even reduces operating costs by reducing security auditing costs.

Especially in mission critical applications protecting software with such a secure generation process will drastically reduce the risk of software sabotage and increase the reputation of high quality software manufacturers.

References

[1] Bruce Schneier, „Applied Cryptography", John Wiley & Sons, New York 1996
[2] CCITT/ITU, Recommendation X.509, „The Directory - Authentication Framework", Consultation Committee International Telephone and Telegraph, International Telecommuniactions Union, Geneva, 1989.
[3] P.R. Zimmermann, „The Official PGP User's Guide, MIT Press, Boston, 1995
[4] Bundesgesetzblatt der Bundesrepublik Deutschland, Jahrgang 1997 Teil 1 Nr. 52, ausgegeben zu Bonn am 28. Juli 1997, „Gesetz zur Regelung der Rahmenbedingungen für Informations- und Kommunikationsdiesnte (Informations-Kommunikationsdienste-Gesetz-IuKDG)", Artikel 3, „Gesetz zur Digitalen Signatur (Signaturgesetz - SigG)"

---

[5] According to German legislation.

Impact of Object-Oriented Software Engineering Applied to the Development of Security Systems

Silvije Jovalekic[1] and Bernd Rist[2]

[1] Fachhochschule Albstadt-Sigmaringen - University of Applied Sciences, Professor for Software-Construction and Real-Time Systems, Jakobstraße 6, 72458 Albstadt, Germany
[2] Eff-Eff company, Software Engineer in the Security Systems Division, Joh.-Mauthe-Str. 14, 72458 Albstadt, Germany

Abstract. In the development of security systems the need for reuse, maintenance, adaptability and reduction of development time are becoming highly important in addition to the classical requirements such as concurrency, schedulability, high reliability and safety. This paper proposes a system development model based on object-oriented methods, schedulability analysis and validation of software requirements. The application of these methods to a remote receiver unit DEZ-9000 demonstrated improvements in software reliability, significant reduction of time-to-market and development and maintenance efforts.

1 Introduction

The purpose of security systems is to protect property and life from unexpected events like burglary, fire. In security systems defects and failures are dangerous. These may be due to wrongly computed control signals or non-functioning automatic supervision. Hard real-time requirements have to be fulfilled to avoid unacceptable loss of material or even life.

Security systems are often built from non-standard hardware- and software components. At the supervisory system level the main effort consists in the software construction. The need for the software to respond to a rapidly changing environment imposes requirements on reliability and ease of modification. These together with the need to conform to stringent safety guidelines impose severe constraints on the software development process.

An effective strategy to fulfil safety-critical requirements consists in systematic defect avoidance. System developers attempt to discover and repair the defects early, before the system is put into operation. Fault-tolerance using redundancy, e.g. diverse programs, is seldom used because of high costs [1].

The object-oriented approach includes concepts to ensure the reliability and ease of maintenance of the designed software components. During the design process, the structure of requirements can be transformed naturally into software structure. The principles of data abstraction, inheritance and polymorphism through dynamic binding, supports consistent development throughout the phases.

2 Remote Receiver Unit DEZ-9000

The remote receiver unit DEZ-9000 is designed for universal reception of indications, registration and operation of alarms, troubles and tests from danger detection and fault indication systems. It should serve as pre-operator and service concentrator for connected monitoring and remote control stations. If no monitoring station is present, the unit operates as a universal receiving computer in stand-alone mode. The DEZ-9000 has to analyse and interpret the received digital messages, assign them to previously stored objects and show a corresponding uncoded text message on the display [2].

2.1 System Overview

The System Context Diagram of the remote receiver unit in Figure 1 describes the structural overview of the environment. It shows the actors and their relation to the system by small arrows [4]. The unit is connected to danger report devices over the public telecommunication network or other connections. It has to receive messages in the form of many different protocols, store them in history-storage, print them out and pass them on to the monitoring and remote control station.

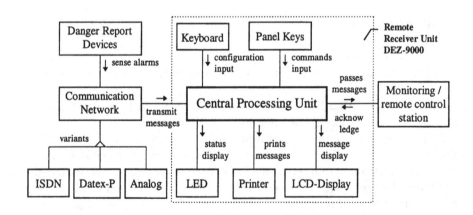

Fig. 1. System Context Diagram of the remote receiver unit

The target-hardware of the remote receiver unit consists of a microprocessor, some serial and parallel communication ports, I/O-Ports, a keyboard interface, a watchdog-subsystem, 2-4 MB static RAM and 2 MB EPROM. This hardware is used in other security systems and represents a stable and reliable product platform.

2.2 System Requirements

To carry out an effective development, the user needs and requirements have to be defined as exactly as possible. The requirements listed in the Requirements Specification Document are expressed as simple, verifiable and quantifiable items. The requirements list for DEZ-9000 includes functional requirements regarding monitoring, communication, memory and user-interface:

- a menu-driven user-interface
- status display and command input over front panel
- several connections to communication networks
- message output on display and thermo printer
- integrated monitoring function
- operation in combination with a monitoring and remote control station or as a stand-alone device
- various interface standards for connected monitoring units
- configuration by monitoring unit or the directly connected keyboard
- automatic remote request to danger report devices
- event tracking for danger report devices
- possibility to deposit user-defined text macros
- various statistics collection and diagnostic functions

Major security requirements for the Remote Receiver Unit are:

- permanent supervision of all system components and reporting of found errors
- ability to connect danger report devices over various networks with scalable control functions to secure the transport media
- contionous checking of connected monitoring stations for correct function
- extensive functions to react on failures and errors of the system through exception handling

The system design has to meet the requirements of the standards by VDE 0833 and by VdS (Verband deutscher Sachversicherer). The integrated emergency power supply and the permanent function and system control have to fulfil the system reliability requirements of the remote monitoring unit. DEZ-9000 was designed to meet the Environment Class II of VdS guidelines (VdS-Approval-Nr. G 196 801), the protection class IP 30 of DIN 40 050. It has to be CE conformant and has got the BZT approval (Nr. A 115 202 E). The communication protocols are implementations of the DIN 66 019 and DIN 19 244 (VdS 24 65) standards [3].

3 System Development Model

During the system development, risks regarding feasibility, costs and schedules can be reduced by means of incremental phase-oriented project management. As

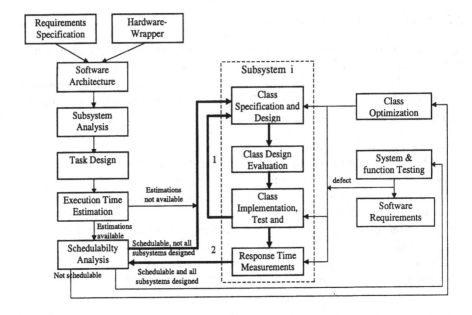

Fig. 2. System Development Model

shown in Figure 2 the whole development is structured into following phases: requirements analysis, incremental design and implementation, integration, testing and validation of requirements.

In the requirements analysis the requirements from user's viewpoint are described. Requirements specification and validation are supported by several means. A project independent outline is used to structure the specification. It can be adapted to special project needs. System Context Diagram gives a precise overview of the system environment and the actors and their interaction through inheritance, association and aggregation. The list of traceable requirements describes required properties and capabilities of the product. It is used for requirements verification and validation. A glossary of the application area supports the understandability of the specification [4][5].

Hardware-dependent requirements should be handled separately. They are encapsulated by a software layer subsystem called the hardware wrapper, which should be analysed, designed and implemented early for several reasons. The hardware wrapper simplifies the design of application subsystems. It may capture the timing requirements of the hardware interface. It relieves the application subsystems by implementing synchronisation requirements. Early testing in real situations reveals constraints of the application subsystems. It minimises the risk of transforming software design into programs for the given hardware.

The software architecture represents the decomposition of the whole system into subsystems and definition of subsystem interfaces. The decomposition process can be improved by the use of architecture patterns, e.g. Layers, Broker, for given problems [6]. The decomposition supports parallel development, simple and flexible assignment of packages to team members and reuse at a higher level than classes.

Further development is performed incrementally. Each increment consists of specification and design of subsystem classes, design evaluation, implementation and testing of the subsystems. In systems with real-time requirements additional estimation and/or measurement of task execution times, schedulability analysis and class code optimisation is performed. Loop 1 is run through frequently. Significant changes in time behaviour of the task system require additional activities according to loop 2. After completing the system and functional testing the model considers the validation of system requirements as well.

A vital part of the model is estimation and measurement of task's execution times. Early determination of execution times is important for the calculation of the processor utilisation and worst case response times of the tasks. These values reveal the needs for optimisation of code and structure of the task system [7].

4 Task Components Design

After the specification of application subsystems and their interfaces, the task system is designed. One or more tasks realise each subsystem. The task system is designed graphically by means of task diagrams. Besides the scheduling information it contains synchronisation and communication between tasks. Task details are described in tabular form and contain task activities, resources used, periods, activity execution times, deadlines, atomicity of activities and priorities. In Table 1 several tasks for the remote receiver unit DEZ-9000 are given with their details. Interrupt handlers have the highest priority, asynchronous services triggered by interrupt handlers come next. Periodic and aperiodic application tasks have normal priority and background tasks are assigned low priority.

Table 1. Example of task details

Taskname	Activity	UsedResources	Period T_i[ms]	Execution time ΔT_i[ms]	Deadline D_i[ms]	Atom-icity	Prio-rity
p_ibus	A1.1	CPU, Interface	2	0,05	2,5	j	1
	A1.2	CPU		0,13	hard	n	
	A1.3	CPU, Message-Queue		0,1		j	
	A1.4	CPU		0,1		n	
p_display	A2.1	CPU, Shared Memory	100	0,3	150	j	2
	A2.2	CPU		0,1	weak - hard	n	
	A2.3	CPU, LCD-Display		12,6		j	
tkibus	A3.1	CPU, Message-Queue	70	0,1	200	j	3
	A3.2	CPU		0,1	weak	n	

4.1 Schedulability Analysis

In security systems with hard real-time requirements like the remote receiver unit keeping to deadlines is very important. For that reason it is advisable to determine the time behaviour before detailed task design. It is necessary to prove that each task fulfils its timing requirements and the processor utilisation is within 30-50% to be able to react to unexpected events.

Each task is assigned a certain amount of processor utilisation, which should not be exceeded. From the estimated task execution times ΔT_i and maximal allowed periods T_i the total processor utilisation $U = \sum \Delta T_i / T_i$ is calculated. Aperiodic tasks are treated as equivalent periodic tasks with minimal period. Execution times can be estimated from similar projects or by measurements of partly coded tasks. If given utilisation bounds are reached or even exceeded task code and structure optimisation have to be performed. A simple rule to decrease processor utilisation is to increase task periods but still staying below the maximum values allowed. A practical set of code optimisation rules can be used very effectively to reduce the processor utilisation [8]. During the development of the remote receiver unit DEZ-9000 the optimisation gains totalled 15%.

5 Object-Oriented Design

After defining tasks the analysis of the object-oriented aspects is performed. It consists of task transformation into classes, working out inheritance relationships between similar classes and client-server relationships between the dependent classes. Inheritance relationship means that a subclass inherits from the superclass all methods responsible for object behaviour and data representing the state. Client-server relationship exists when server object offers services to the client objects. To model the structure of the subsystems Object Modelling Technique (OMT) [9] is used. The relations between the classes can be planned in advance, so that the implementation of the class referring to the total system is easy to understand. This approach reveals any design errors at an early development stage.

5.1 Class Relationship Design

After analysing the objects and classes of the application, the relationships between the classes are defined. Major aims are to maximise code reusability and the reliability of the software.

The inheritance relationship, which is defined at compiling-time is used if (1) the classes are in is-relation, e.g. an object of a subclass is as an object of its super-class, (2) classes have the same data elements, (3) classes share the same algorithm, (4) classes are special cases of a general concept. The common things are abstracted in a super-class. Inheritance eliminates code redundancy without reducing efficiency . If objects of the subclasses have to behave like objects of the super-class, class specification has to be inherited. If the code of the super-class should be reused, its implementation has to be inherited.

The client-server relationship can either be defined at translation-time or at runtime. By delegating the function-call to an object at runtime, the above-mentioned advantages of inheritance and the flexibility of dynamic linking can be combined.

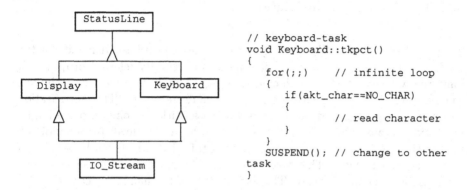

```
// keyboard-task
void Keyboard::tkpct()
{
    for(;;)      // infinite loop
    {
        if(akt_char==NO_CHAR)
        {
                     // read character
        }
    }
    SUSPEND(); // change to other task
}
```

Fig. 3. Classes and task of user interface subsystem

Figure 3 shows the classes of a subsystem and their correlation with the tasks. The interface to the user among others consists out of a LCD-Display and a Keyboard, which are abstracted by the classes `Display` and `Keyboard`. The subclass `IO_Stream` realises the C++-Stream. An object of this class can be used to output data on the display and to read data from the keyboard. The output of the display is made by the task `p_display`, the reading from the keyboard is done by the task `tk_pct`. These tasks are coded in the form of private member-functions of the accompanying class.

5.2 Class Design

The access levels of data elements and methods of a class have to be defined. Restricted access is recommended. Data elements should usually be private because of the advantages of data encapsulation. Besides, the maintenance of access on private data over public functions is easier than the direct access to public data elements. A change of the data structure can often be accommodated by modifying the access functions.

The necessary class methods have to be identified. Basically they can be divided into administrative, access and implementation methods. Administrative methods consist of constructors to create and initialise objects and a destructor to delete the class objects. Further classes contain the copy-constructor and the assignment operator. These will be generated automatically by the compiler, if they are not specified by the developer. This often leads to problems when data elements point to objects. The unintentional use of these should be prevented by specifying them as private methods, without implementing them. This will

150

prevent the object-assignment. Access methods to return the state of an object should be specified as constant functions. This makes the declaration more comprehensible and faulty implementations are recognised at compile-time.

5.3 Developer's Documentation

Because of the strict quality requirements for the software, the demands for the quality of documentation are higher than in non security relevant projects. To limit the work of developer's documentation, a simple but effective technique can be used. A class specification is done before its design. This specification describes the abilities and functions of the class, without going into the implementation details. This description is made in form of a developer's handbook for the class. All characteristics of objects of this class which can be seen from outside are documented. This developer's handbook substantially contributes to the reusability of the software. The formal style of the handbook can be based on the UNIX-Manuals.

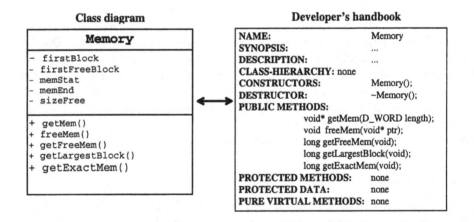

Fig. 4. Forms of class-specification

Besides the developer's handbook, the class can be specified through a class diagram according to OMT [9]. This represents a general view of the class structure. Graphical symbols show explicitly, if the described class is an abstract or concrete one. In the class diagram a distinction has to be made between the data elements to describing the object state and those defining relations to other classes. The methods should be sorted by the level of access. Public methods, so-called services, ought to be grouped according to their meaning for the class. Figure 4 shows class diagram and developer's handbook for the class Memory.

5.4 Class Optimisation for Real-Time Situations

In real time systems, dynamic but foreseeable creation and destroying of objects is required. Even with a constant number of objects, they have to be reorganised or regrouped. Efficient memory management becomes very important. Using the operators `new` and `delete`, an own efficient memory management can be implemented. Normally it doesn't provide an automatic reorganisation of the object-memory.

Storing and releasing free objects into a pool can increase the efficiency of the memory management. When needing objects at runtime, the object management chooses already created objects from the pool and initialises them with the passed parameters. If the user program does not need an object any more, it will be put back in the pool of free objects. The number of free pool-objects at starting-time should be defined by the user of the class.

6 Pattern-Oriented Design

Elegant solutions to general problems during software design have been described recently by software patterns. Object-oriented methods and languages, e.g. OMT, C++ are increasingly used to describe patterns in development of real-time and security systems.

The use of patterns during software design offers several benefits in enabling the developer to: (1) document existing well proven design experience, (2) identify and specify abstractions above the level of single classes and instances, (3) provide a common vocabulary and understanding of design principles, (4) document software architectures, (5) support the construction of software with defined properties, (6) help to build complex and heterogeneous software architectures and (7) help to manage software complexity [6].

Software patterns support the reuse of software designs and components at high level and reduce repeated discovery of solutions to known problems. Reported patterns contain the knowledge of many developers and therefore represent optimal solutions. Existing patterns cover various range of abstraction. Some patterns help to structure software systems into subsystems. Other patterns support the refinement of subsystems and components. Yet others help in implementing some design aspects in a specific programming language.

Architecture patterns are templates for concrete software architectures and describe the fundamental structure of software systems. They provide a set of predefined subsystems with their responsibilities and include rules to organise the relationships between them. Patterns become increasingly important for systems with real-time requirements. Pattern Task describes concurrent activities and their scheduling [10].

Design patterns are used to refine subsystems or components of software systems. They describe commonly recurring structures for communication between components. They are medium-scale patterns and smaller than architecture patterns. They are language independent. To describe the communication between the tasks of a software system, design pattern Communicator can be used [11]. Design pattern Observer is the solution for the state consistency problems of co-operating components. This is achieved by notification of changes of independent components to their dependent components. This pattern supports loose coupling of components, which increases the reuse of each component. Design pattern Singleton is used when only one instance of a class may exist. It increases the reliability of a system [12].

Idioms are low-level patterns specific to a programming language. They describe how to implement some aspects of components and relationships between them using the features of a given language. The coding idiom describes how to specify a class in C++ to ensure that user-defined types behave in the same way as fundamental data types. The handle/body idiom is used to increase software reliability, memory and time efficiency [13].

7 Software Quality Assurance

To verify the subsystems, identifiable requirements in the requirements specification are used. The traceability matrix assigns identifiable requirements to software components classes, tasks and functions and provides means for project management. It gives a quick and exact overview of the status of the project. This helps to validate the product and simplifies estimating the cost of changes and adjustments.

7.1 Assessment of Real-Time Requirements

In real time systems it has to be proved that the system will fulfil the hard real time demands and that the processor utilisation will lie between 30% and 50%. For this, an exact measurement of the processor utilisation of every task is required. By this method one can confidently assert that the system will fulfil the expected demands even under extreme loads. To do this, every task gets assigned a maximum processor utilisation in the planing of the project. This value must not be exceeded by the later system. If the system reaches the limit, steps have to be taken to reduce the execution time of this task.

7.2 System and Function Testing

After completing the last development increment, a final function test is carried out. In this phase of the project, the software product is tested against the Requirements Specification. Additionally user-friendliness, system-reliability, etc. are also tested. In the system load tests, long term tests and general reliability tests are made.

When possible, tests should be carried out by independent testers, to cover a broad range of test cases and practical situations.

7.3 Defect Recording

To record the problems at testing, summary forms are used, which form the basis of weekly statistics. In these forms, the term of testing, the main emphasis, the person and the number and kind of the found defects are noted. Before starting the tests, criteria for completion are defined, which can easily be controlled by these statistics.

An example for such finishing criteria could be: The test will be finished if less than 0.2 defects per hour of testing-time were found or the number of heavy defects does not exceed 50% of the expected value of 2 errors per 8 hours testing-time.

Every problem found should be documented in a specific form. This form describes the defect in detail. To guarantee backward traceability of defects, the exact name of the device, the device number and the version of the software have to be noted. Besides the description of the defect, things like suppositions, suggestions and defect valence are written down by the tester. The defect valence is divided up into the following categories: heavy defect, slight defect, question / lack of clarity, information / request for modification. Another point is how to react to defects. Possible reactions are: `noted` (developer has noted the problem), `corrected` (the problem is eliminated), `will not be corrected` (the problem will not be eliminated).

By evaluating the forms which were completed while testing, a chart was constructed of the frequency of defects found in relation to the duration of the project was made. Figure 5 summarises testing results.

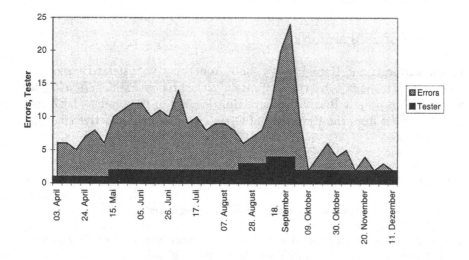

Fig. 5. Testing statistics

8 Experience and Recommendations

The system development model described above, was used for the development of a remote receiver unit DEZ-9000. The software consists of 16 subsystems: service functions, user interface, printer controller, clock, communication to other systems, history-storage administration, exception and error handling, integrated bus-systems, etc. These subsystems are realised in more than 10 tasks and are structured through more than 100 classes. The software development for the remote receiver unit up to the first release took less then 15 months - much less than similar development projects without object oriented methods. Based on the experience gained during the implementation, the following practical recommendations can be made:

1. Requirements Specification from the viewpoint of the user should be the basis for software design. Usually it is not complete because many requirements are identified during the actual use of the product.
2. The design of the classes and their relationships is the foundation for the object oriented software design. It is an important factor for the success of the project.
3. Early and repeated verification of the hard-time requirements and of processor utilisation minimises the project risk. Estimation based on inaccurate or wrong measurements will not provide the basis for a successful project plan and software design.
4. The effectiveness of function and system testing can be optimised a lot through a formalised procedure and the simultaneous work of several test persons.
5. The system development model, and the methods used to increase quality and productivity have to take into consideration the training of the developer and special demands on the product.

9 Acknowledgements

Ulrich Schwieger and Harald Sauter, both from Security Systems Division, Effeff company, made possible the verification of the proposed system development model within project Remote Receive Unit leading to the product DEZ-9000. Sati McKenzie from the University of Greenwich made constructive comments on this paper.

References

1. Lauber, R.: Prozeßautomatisierung, Band 1; Springer Verlag 1989; ISBN 3-540-50195-9
2. Automatic Dialling & Transmission Systems; Remote Receiver Unit DEZ-9000; effeff Fritz Fuss GmbH&Co. KG a.A. 1997; P20701-01-0G0-01
3. VdS e.V. Köln; Richtlinien f. Gefahrenmeldeanlagen, Übertragungsprotokoll für Gefahrenmeldeanlagen; Verband der Sachversicherer e.V. Köln; 1994

4. Awad, M.; Ziegler, J.; Kuusela, J.: Object-Oriented Technology for Real-Time Systems: A Practical Approach using OMT und Fusion, Prentice Hall International 1996, ISBN 0-13-227943-6

5. Jovalekic, S.: Rechnerunterstützte Spezifikation von Anforderungen für Automatisierungssysteme; Dissertation Universität Stuttgart 1985

6. Buschmann, F.; Meunier, R.; Rohnert, H.; Sommerlad, P; Stal, M.: Pattern-Oriented Software Architecture - A System of Patterns, John Wiley & Sons 1996, ISBN 0-471-95869-7

7. Klein, M.H.; Rayla, T.; Pollak, B.; Obenza, R.; Harbour, M.G.: A Practitioner's Handbook for Real-Time Analysis: Guide to Rate Monotonic Analysis for Real-Time Systems, Kluwer Academic Publishing, 1993

8. Laplante, P.A.: Real-Time Systems Design and Analysis: An Engineer's Handbook, IEEE Press, 1993, ISBN 0-7803-0402-0

9. Rumbaugh, J.: OMT: The Object Model; Journal of Object-Oriented Programming; January 1995; S. 21-27

10. Conrad, M; Jovalekic, S.: Einsatz und Bewertung von objektorientierten Entwurfsmustern bei der Auswahluntersuchung eines Echtzeitbetriebssystems; Kongreß Echtzeit'97, Wiesbaden 9.-11. September 1997; veranstaltet von Elektronik, S. 68-73.

11. Dietrich, D.; Jovalekic, S.: Konstruktion wiederverwendbarer objektorientierter Echtzeitsoftware unter Verwendung von Entwurfsmustern; Kongreß Echtzeit'96, Karlsruhe 18-20. Juni 1996; Franzis Verlag, ISBN 3-7723-2502-5, S. 73-79.

12. Gamma, E.; Helm, R.; Johnson, R.; Vlissides, J.: Design Patterns, Elements of Reusable Object-Oriented Software, Addison Wesley 1995, ISBN 0-201-63361-2

13. Coplien, J.O.: Advanced C++ Programmming Styles and Idioms, Addison Wesley Publishing Company 1992, ISBN 0-201-54855-0

Medical Informatics

"Profit by Safety" or Quackery in Biomedical Information Technology?

Bas A. de Mol[1], and Floor Koornneef[2]

[1] Academic Medical Center, Dept. Cardiopulmonary Surgery,
Meibergdreef 9, 1105 AZ Amsterdam Zuidoost, The Netherlands
B.A.deMol@amc.uva.nl
[2] Delft University of Technology, Safety Science Group,
Kanaalweg 2b, 2628 EB Delft, The Netherlands
F.Koornneef@et.tudelft.nl

Abstract. A Dutch painting "The Quack" helps to clarify from different user perspectives the risks involved in the application of today's medical systems in a major hospital. The liability due to unsafe medical equipment and implants not only represents the application risks for patients, but also viability threats to health care providers and manufacturers of medical devices. Safety and credibility of equipment contribute largely to the credibility of modern medicine. Legislation and government actions are not sufficient to make drugs, medical devices and medical procedures adequately safe. Lessons from device failure constitute the challenge to users and creators of dependable systems to combine forces and make things better, or keep the quack alive.

1 Introduction

It is not unlikely that we are presently experiencing the Golden Age of our health care. Everybody has still access to it, all advanced facilities are available whenever necessary, waiting rooms are crowded, and waiting lists are mostly still acceptable. Nevertheless, this Golden Age has its dull/shady sides too: damage to patients cannot be covered anymore by the usual liability insurance, fraud in medical research has become a reality, and who cannot mention some failed implants [1, 2, 3]? Anxiety among the general public is a stronger impulse to improve the safety in health care than the number of accidents per year, per kilometer, or per number of medical treatments. Talking about safety includes talking about the acceptance of risks, the reliability of safety measures, and the assistance to victims [4, 5, 6]. For quite some time, safety in hospitals or e.g. at airports is not determined anymore by just a single surgeon or pilot [7, 8]. The demand for safety is socially and culturally determined, as is the transformation of the well-organized solitary medical practice into the practice of a multidisciplinary team.

2   Medicine as an Industrial Activity

While medical practice developed into an industrial activity, the warnings of dangerous medical treatments evolved slowly. From an historic perspective, I will discuss Gerrit Dou's painting "The Quack" (1652), which is a masterpiece of art of the economic Golden Age.

"The Quack" can be found in the Boymans van Beuningen Museum in Rotterdam. In the painting of Gerrit Dou, the decor is formed by the city of Leyden where the oldest university of our country is located. A number of similarities with our hospital the Academic Medical Center Amsterdam (AMC), the biggest and most quoted university hospital of The Netherlands, is obvious. The solitary healer has nestled himself at the crossroad of social activities, the equivalent of today's Amsterdam Southeast business quarter. The scenes in the painting by Dou can be experienced in today's lobby of the AMC. In Dou's painting, the painter participates by surveying the scene with his palette in his hand. A colorful public that is served by a wide variety of commercial activities surrounds the healer. Oil dumplings are sold, a baking tray and the ingredients for sausage rolls are present, fruit and vegetables are available, and a baby has its diapers changed, just like in a day-care center.

In short, not much is changed over the time in health care. The mischiefs are included also: a woman, seemingly quite impressed by the healer, is robbed of her wallet. Today, this is common event in any hospital. Even the primate that has become the object of many a laboratory activity, in terms of animal experimentation for the purpose of improving health care, is present in Dou's painting. It is chained up, but its condition seems fairly good. The utensils that can be seen as the precursors of an advanced medical laboratory are placed within reach of the healer and are clearly visible for the public.

When we look at the big and small carafes, Dou's painting already reflects the "illusion" as a management policy for health care, although this is just speculation. Therefore, scientism and high-tech medicine as means to convince people are not bound to time. They are part of the placebo effect of healing, both in a positive sense and in a negative sense, as can be concluded from the contents of an unparalleled series of recent publications in the influential medical magazine The Lancet [9]. Faith and trust in invisible manipulations are still the basis of recovery.

The paradox of today's progress is that the future medical successes will take place in the cell molecular field, information technology and imaging manipulation, which is as close to fantasy to the patients as the medical progress of the middle ages. High expectations among patients and doctors lead to major disappointments and a sense of unsafety when recovery does not take place or when complications arise. Because medical success and failure can be invisible and inexplicable, health care demands that safety in medicine is at least visible, which comes in addition to the basic principle of medicine "first do not harm".

3   Criticism on the Practicing of Medicine

The quality of medical practice can always be better. In the 17th century, the subject of "the quack amidst a fascinated public" was a major theme in drama and comedy plays and provided ample opportunity to display joy, sorrow, and deception, and also sound reasons to moralize. At the present time, television programs have taken the place of paintings. Last year, major public TV networks showed series such as "The Hospital", "Medical Failures", and "Medical Mistakes". These programs were televised on Saturday night, at times that are actually reserved for maximal entertainment. Meanwhile, we were not spared reruns either. Despite the public's high expectations in regard to the doctor's fight against diseases, the critical perception of health care has not changed very much.

Today, we know that improved life expectancy is achieved by raising the standard of living and by preventive medicine. The efforts to guarantee quality norms for drugs, prosthetic material, and the provision of health care by means of government interference or self-regulation, are not new either. Evaluation procedures, which are now called "accreditation" or "certification", were already common in the 17th century. Dou already shows this. An excerpt of the register of the "College of Physicians and Surgeons" of those days is placed on the healer's table such that it catches the eye: it is a real certificate including an impressive seal. The rationale of this depiction of the 17th century is that the general public must guard against fake by healers and certificates. Also in those days, it was necessary to point out that injudicious "healing" is damaging. The scene of baby's diapers being changed refers to a similar picture entitled "This body - what else is it but stench and manure?". At that time, it was quite popular, putting the care for the human body in the basic perspective.

4   The Liability due to Unsafe Medical Equipment and Implants

The damaging effects of the sleeping drug Thalidomide or the Softenon represent one of the biggest dramas in modern health care. The potential dangers of drugs made governments take on the task of strict supervision, starting with drugs.

However, legislation and government action are not sufficient to make drugs, medical devices and medical procedures adequately safe, in spite of an appeal for more regulation after each new failed device affair [10].

For quite some time, the US Food and Drug Administration (FDA) is charged with monitoring the quality of medical devices, such as pacemakers, mechanical heart valves, and silicon breast prostheses. The FDA's functioning strongly influences the process of quality assurance of medical devices in The Netherlands. The FDA's organizational structure and responsibilities are held up as shining examples.

However, dominant government supervision does not guarantee safety. It can even be counterproductive. By attempting to conceal the lack of supervision of it's part the FDA merely facilitated the drama that can be considered the equivalent of the Softenon-drama for medical devices, i.e. the case of the fractured Björk-Shiley convexo-concave heart valve, the FDA, if anything, contributed to this problem.

The BScc heart valve had been implanted in approximately 80,000 patients all over the world. In more than 500 patients, however, it fractured, in most cases causing death or serious disability. The real number of victims is thought to be considerably higher [11]. In 1990, the US Congress held a hearing on this developing problem. Also the role of the FDA was critically reviewed. The findings were summarized in the report "Earn as you learn. Shiley Inc.'s breach of the honor system and FDA's failure in medical device regulation" [14]. Thanks to the relentless efforts of the American lawyer John T. Johnson from Houston, Texas, the general public became aware of the misconduct of the multinational Pfizer Inc., although this was not until November of 1991 [13]. A Dutch publication in The Lancet in January of 1994, concluded that flaws in the welding technique were to be kept responsible for strut fractures of the BScc valves.

The threat of criminal prosecution became ominous. As is customary in the US, however, the manufacturer managed to reach a settlement with the Department of Justice, which made the consumer organization "Public Health Citizen" speak of a "travesty of justice". Such developments contribute to an undermining and devastating prejudice among the general public: in health care, one sticks to the slogan "earn as you learn", even if this is at the expense of the patient's safety. Meanwhile, the US Congress reacted adequately by introducing the Safe Medical Device Act, while the FDA now demands test procedures that are even stricter than before. Because of the numerous new products and the extensive bureaucracy of the FDA, more and more US manufacturers of medical devices take refuge to Europe and Asia to carry out their experiments. There, pioneers and entrepreneurs find co-operative governments and co-operative medical professionals.

Another current example of counterproductive distant regulation involves the silicon breast prostheses. After more than 25 years of breast implantations, the FDA stated that proper research on the interaction of silicon and the human body was never performed and that adequate postmarketing surveillance had not been carried out either. The implantation of silicon prostheses was subsequently prohibited [14].

The US Law on Product Liability stipulates that also the suppliers of raw materials and components can be held responsible for the damage suffered by the end-user, in this case the patient. As a consequence, enormous insurance claims were submitted to the supplier of the raw material for the silicon breast prosthesis, who subsequently withdrew from the market. Today, hardly any silicon breast implant is manufactured in the USA. As a result of the enormous financial consequences that were brought on by producing a simple material such as silicon, suppliers of other basic materials, such as micro-electronics and ceramic materials, followed this example and withdrew from the market as well [15]. In contrast to the large quantities of raw materials supplied for use in the industry, the quantities supplied for medical use were only small. Nevertheless, due to the insurance claims following the simple use of silicon in breast prostheses, product liability represents too big a risk, even tens of years later.

An article in the Dutch newspaper "De Volkskrant" of November 12, 1993, with the appealing heading "Du Pont does not dare to continue the manufacturing of artificial legs", informed us about this problem [16]. On further reading, it became clear that the US-based company Du Pont de Nemours had supplied polytetrafluorethene to another company, which had used it to manufacture a (not very successful) jaw implant. This transaction had only the value of a few Dollar-cent pieces, whereas the legal costs to neutralize the insurance claims amounted to tens of millions of US dollars.

5   About Electronic Devices and Information Technology

These examples demonstrate that disregarding obvious safety requirements can lead to a victim crisis (the Shiley case), a compensation crisis (the breast prostheses), and a biomaterials crisis, which can severely damage an entire branch of industry. There is no reason to believe that risks of liability differ from other industries. In contrast, health care is used to failures as the phenomenon is unstable and adverse outcome often is seen as a complication or bad luck additional to the disease.

Smart devices such as pacemakers may give problems. For instance, the FDA's Medical Device Reporting System contains examples of an implantable pacemaker that was designed switch functional modes from 'monitor + therapy' to 'monitor only' and visa versa by exposure to a magnetic field. In the 'monitor only' mode, the pacemaker will not generate pulses to activate that heart when needed. Thus, the patient may carry a device that functions correctly according to design specifications. The neat feature of the functional mode switch activated by a magnetic field, though, may become killing when the pacemaker is switched to 'monitoring only' mode unnoticed. The reports show that system failure can occur while passing through an airport metal detector, while playing with an electrical toy at home, or while carrying a magnet to pick up nails. The physician's manual does not guide the patient after he leaves the doctor's office. It states that an active pulse generator is deactivated when place in a magnet field for 30 seconds... and that patients should avoid equipment or situations where their device would be exposed to strong (>10 gauss) magnetic fields.

This example demonstrates again that the context of the operational phase of this medical device was not taken into account adequately during the design and development of the dependable system. However, failure awareness amongst patients and cardiologists is not high. Sudden death is a consequence of the disease, and a post-mortem examination rarely takes place. Removal of the device for a check-up is even more rare. Serial accidents with radiation equipment have been documented. Bugs in software determining intensity of the radiation or the location were found to be the cause of serious radiation damage. Anecdotal reports of data representation on anesthesia monitors may be found on Internet. However, no big cases so far in terms of numerous victims or stupidities. Medical equipment and smart devices seem to do pretty well, and failure is either well accepted or acceptably dealt with.

Nevertheless, public outrage should never be underestimated as a cause for a hard business interruption. According to Sandman, public outrage will increase when accidents are associated with a) a poor physical outcome such as death or serious disability; b) a large scale-occurrence; c) the fact that the risk was not self-chosen (like in sports or traffic), but imposed by a doctor who used his equipment; d) the observation that the risk affects the poor and weak, or just women and may be experienced as unfair [17].

6   Medical Technology in the Hospital

Safety measures reduce the fear of risks and are effective as such when they are logic and clear to the public. However, when this is not the case while the risk can be seen or heard, as is caused in the Amsterdam district "Bijlmermeer" by low-flying planes approaching Amsterdam airport, a lot of energy has to be invested in credibility. Without credibility, safety measures do not improve the risk acceptance. When undergoing a risky procedure, the patient is usually anaesthetized, whereas the risk of a heart valve that may fracture was imperceptible until the first media reports. It also applies to health care that risk acceptance is enhanced by the credibility of the safety measures and correct claim settlement in case of damage.

Hospitals have the habit to show just their hardware during guided tours or in TV programs. When visiting a "safe" plant, like a nuclear or chemical process industry, the visitor first of all notices the special clothing, helmets, the flashing lights on the control panels and the safety instructions. The doctor's white coat, which has lost its sacred aura by now, cannot stand the comparison. Safety in hospitals will therefore have to be demonstrated to patients in a different manner.

This is especially important when a new technique is introduced. An example of such a technical improvement was the use of minimally invasive surgery or "key hole surgery". Although the number of complications is not much higher than in conventional surgery, or, which is more likely, may even be lower, very serious complications can occur, leading to disability and death, which could have been avoided in case of a better control of the technique. The profession has recognized this safety problem, but at that time this had become overdue. This gave cause for discussions on the learning curve, the distribution of new technology and training programs [18]. Of course, it will always remain a shame that there were unnecessary victims.

Some knowledge of safety principles within the companies that had pushed the devices on the market, among the doctors, and in the hospitals where this technology was so rapidly and passionately embraced, could have prevented the damage to patients. The most difficult aspect is controlled distribution, well-trained doctors, and a minimal number of victims during the learning period. The principle "profit by safety for everybody" should be the guideline when treating patients with new technologies.

7   Doctors and Engineers: Let's Make Things Safer

Safety and reliability of equipment and implants contribute largely to the credibility of modern medicine. The exposure of failures may result in outrage, blame and claims. So, one has to encourage reporting on unsafe practices for the sake of a higher principle than business: damage control and improvement. This process asks for protection, which ought to be given by regulations and trust with the profession and patients. Learning from failures and improving shortfalls becomes even more difficult, when it is not even clear that an equipment flaw causes an adverse event. Too often users blame equipment for personal and/or organisational failure. In contrast, this same attitude prevents early detection of precursors of equipment failure. Therefore, equipment failure only becomes apparent in case of unexpected outcome, huge damage or a complete breakdown. The latter is the "safest way" of device failure, as for that situation back-up scenario's or replacement are available. The millennium-bug threat is creating awareness for large-scale one-time failure. But what about these slowly progressive deviations of what are believed to be a true representation of reality?

Therefore, in order to make things safer, users have to be educated to look for potential failures and to remain critical towards what is considered acceptable and safe output. As Leveson and Turner [19] conclude from the Therac-25 case study, "it is clear that users need to be involved". Users found the problem with the Therac-25, forced the manufacturer to respond, and organised the Therac-25 user group meetings that were important to the resolution of the problem.

A second approach relates to increased awareness where software is vital to processes and what such a dependency means. This attitude prevents surprises, learns users to accept failures, and stimulates to maintain back-up scenarios. In all health care systems doctors are responsible and liable for equipment and implant failure occurring during the course of treatment. Of course, they may transfer this burden to another party such as the manufacturer or the maintenance service provider. Therefore, depending on the complexity and vital status of equipment or infrastructure the practitioner is a key role player as buyer, operator and controller. This implicates that medical professions will change from more gently touching (which is called minimal invasive) to smarter and more distant sensing (which is called intelligent monitoring). The efficacy and safety of this approach depends largely on engineers with a touch of medicine and doctors with a touch of information technology.

Epilogue

Will programmable electrical or electronic medical devices ever be safe and reliable enough? The metaphor of the butcher's, doctor's and murderer's knife comes into mind. It depends on the user. However, equipment is more complex and often more powerful. Information technology is considered feasible and controllable. It therefore, generates high expectations of performance. The comparison of software with the genetic control of life processes emerges. Embedded software flaws determine, similar to embedded errors of genetics primary success, early failure (cancer), and durability (ageing). Putting software reliability in the perspective of other life cycles, we may conclude that - fortunately - it well never be safe enough.

In contrast to this philosophical approach we must be aware of the fact that information technology is business, ruled by the laws of profit making, cost effectiveness, minimal standards of expected performance and risks of litigation. Within that framework we must observe that commercial interests are dominant and that health care is a business world like others. Users are relying heavily on what them is promised, although their good faith is betrayed so now and then. Therefore, the ultimate consequence of software transfer to doctors and patients is to make it even softer. This means that products must be experienced as reliable enough, useful enough and as an enrichment of daily medical practice. At that stage, Quackery is not that bad in the ongoing battle to prolong a happy life.

References

1. Newspaper De Telegraaf, Sept 12, 1994.
2. Overbeke AP. Wangedrag in Medisch-Wetenschappelijk Publiceren. Ned. Tijdschr. Geneeskd. (1994) 1822-6.
3. Fielder JH. Getting the bad News about your Artificial Heart Valve. Hastings Center Report 1993; 23(2): 22-8.
4. Pochin EE. The Acceptance of Risk. Br Med Bull (1975); 31: 184-90.
5. Sandman PM. Emerging Communication Responsibilities of Epidemiologists. J. Clin. Epidemiol. (1991) 44 (suppl. I): 41S-45S.
6. Kroes de J. Slachtoffers. Farewell Address as Professor of Transportation Safety, Delft University of Technology (1994).
7. Perrow Ch. Normal accidents. Living with high-risk Technologies. New York: Basic Book Publishers, Inc. Wiley and Sons (1987).
8. Bignell V, Fortune J. Understanding System Failure. Manchester: Manchester Univ. Press (1984) 79-116.
9. Johnson AG. Surgery as a Placebo. Lancet (1994) 344: 1140-2.
10. Dyer C. Faulty Heart Valves: Need for Regulations. Br. Med. J. (1990) 301: 139-40.
11. Graaf van der Y, Waard de F, Herwerden van LA, Defauw JJ. Risk of Strut Fracture of Björk-Shiley Valves. Lancet (1992) 339: 257-61.
12. Committee on Energy and Commerce. U.S. House of Representatives. The Björk-Shiley Heart Valve: "Earn as You Learn". Shiley Inc.'s Breach of the Honor System and FDA's Failure in Medical Device Regulation. U.S. GPO 26-766, Washington, Feb (1990).
13. Carley WM. Pfizer Unit's faulty Artificial Heart Valves are tied to Falsified Manufacturing Records. Wall Street Journal, Nov 9 (1991).
14. Kessler DA. The Basis of the FDA's Decision on Breast Implants. N. Engl. J. Med. (1992) 326: 1713-5.
15. Galletti PM. Embargo on Biomaterials. Science, May 20 (1994).
16. Newspaper De Volkskrant, Nov 13 (1994).
17. Sandman PM. Emerging Communication Responsibilities of Epidemiologists. J. Clin. Epid. (1991) 44 (suppl. 1): 41S-45S.
18. Society of American Gastrointestinal Endoscopic Surgeons. Guidelines for Granting of Privileges for Laparoscopic (Peritoneoscopic) General Surgery. Surg. Endosc. (1993) 7: 67-8.
19. Leveson NG, Turner CS. An Investigation of the Therac-25 Accidents. IEEE Computer. July (1993) 18-41.

Formal Methods II

Languages and Verification

Towards Automated Proof of Fail-Safe Behavior

Peter Liggesmeyer, Martin Rothfelder

Siemens AG, Corporate Technology, Otto-Hahn-Ring 6, 81730 Munich, Germany

Abstract. Formal risk analysis (FRA) is a means for automatic generation of fault trees for failures of sensors, actuators, and other input and output devices. FRA can be used to automate significant parts of the manual fault tree analysis work, and hence automate the proof of fail-safe behavior. Because FRA is based on information that is already used for formal verification, no additional effort is necessary for the automatic generation of fault trees with FRA. While formal verification focuses on the functional aspects, in particular safety functions, the fault tree analysis with FRA focuses on the system integrity. FRA significantly reduces the effort for the generation of fault trees. This paper describes Formal Risk Analysis and its application for the proof of fail-safe behavior.

1 Introduction

One of the most laborious tasks related to safety-related control systems such as controllers for chemical or nuclear plants, interlocking systems, or – increasingly – in the automotive industry is the prove of the fail-safe behavior of a system. One of the methods used for this proof is fault tree analysis (FTA).

By means of Boolean logic, fault trees represent the relationship between causes and undesired or hazardous events. Fault trees are usually generated manually. Highly skilled, experienced engineers analyze the system based on existing documents that describe the system. Considerable knowledge, system insight, and overview are necessary to consider many failure modes and their consequences at a time. This manual work is error-prone, costly, and usually incomplete. FTA can be started early in the design process. Typical questions are: Does the chosen design meet the reliability and safety requirements? What are the most critical components? Design options can be judged reasonably. Expensive design errors can be detected early. FTA is proven and accepted in reliability and safety engineering.

In safety-related systems, both the safety function and the safety integrity of the system have to be demonstrated.

Functional safety can be proven using formal verification techniques. One of these techniques is the model checking approach. Our approach extends this process of formal verification by the analysis of the effect of failures. Formal models used for verification are reused for FRA.

This paper describes a possible application of Formal Risk Analysis (FRA), namely its use for the proof of fail-safe behavior. First we describe principles and an implementation of FRA. This also includes important underlying concepts like finite state machines, symbolic model checking and ordered binary decision diagrams. Then we discuss a case study: An elevating rotary table of a production cell for which a complete fault tree for sensor failures has been generated automatically. We conclude with a description of how FRA can be used in the proof of fail-safe behavior.

2 Formal Risk Analysis

Formal risk analysis is a particular way to automate FTA. Some approaches for the automated generation of fault trees already exist. For example, Allen's approach ([2], pp. 22) requires a second description that is sufficiently formalized for the generation of fault trees. This description is generated manually which causes additional effort and is error-prone itself.

Besides information on the system's behavior during normal operation, design documents also comprise implicit information on the system's behavior in case of failures. With the FRA approach, we make use of such existing documents and specifications. No additional, manual modeling is necessary.

The system comprises a controller and the controlled process. Controller and process communicate via sensors and actuators. Both, controller and process are represented formally. The formal specifications consist of the *Technical Process Description*, the *Controller Specification*, the *Failure Model*, and the *Safety and Liveness Requirements* (Figure 1). The controller specification is used both to generate the executable code for the controller and for the verification. In FRA, the technical process description is used for the formal verification of safety and liveness requirements of the system. The failure model specifies which types of failures of actuators or sensors shall be assumed:

- Intermittent or persistent
- Single failures or multiple failures

A failure of an actuator or sensor means that the respective device may show any value that the controller recognizes or is able to generate, namely all declared values for the device. The above-mentioned specifications are now used to automatically generate a set of *all* failures of sensors and actuators of a system that might lead to an undesired event.

Relationships between possible causes (failures) and the undesired event are generated in form of a fault tree. This fault tree is *complete*, i.e. *all* simulated failures of sensors and actuators that might cause a violation of the safety and liveness requirements are identified and shown in the fault tree.

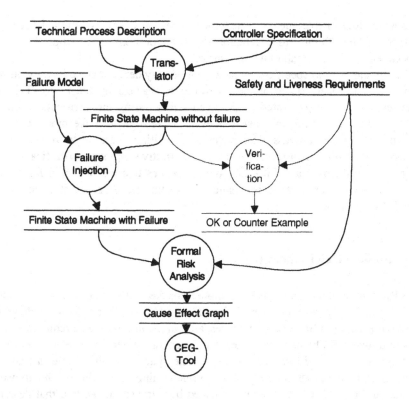

Fig. 1. Generation of cause effect graphs based on formal specifications

3 Finite State Machines as System Models

To represent the system comprising controller and the technical process, finite state machines are used. They are often used to specify systems with a discrete state space. Finite state machines are appropriate representations in, for instance, digital circuit design or telecommunication appli cations.

Finite state machines represent the controller and the environment in an intermediate for mat called FSM (short for finite state machine).

The controller is represented by a deterministic state machine. The model is written in CSL (Control Specification Language). Together with the process model, this is translated into the intermediate FSM format which in turn is used for both verification (by model checking) and generation of executable code.

In general, the process is non-deterministic, and so is the corresponding model. Initially, the verification assumes that the process may produce any arbitrary input for the controller (that is, the process specification is empty). This will in most cases yield unreasonable inputs to the controller. By means of assumptions in the process specification, transitions of the process are restricted to those that are physically reasonable. Reasonable means: The process observes certain physical laws. For instance, if the (failure-free) actuator for a motor commands stop, the related physical entity (e.g., the table) will not move.

Usually the process specification needs not be very detailed since its only purpose is to restrict the state space of the controller to reasonable transitions. Typically these restrictions are generated as the need arises during the verification process. From a verification point of view it is even desired not to make more restricting assumptions on the process than necessary. Writing these restrictions, i.e. the process specification, is a critical task: Too restrictive a process specification may cause both verification and FRA to prove properties that are not valid for the real system. However, once there is a suitable system specification, it is reused for formal risk analysis.

4 Symbolic Model Checking

For FRA we use the same symbolic model checker [10] as it is used for system verification. The model checker is based on ordered binary decision diagrams. These represent both finite state machines, and safety and functional requirements.

Deterministic finite state machines can be characterized by a set of recognized input symbols, a set of output symbols, a state space, an initial state, a transition function, and an output function. For non-deterministic machines, the transition *function* and the output *function* are replaced by a transition *relation* that describes transitions together with related outputs.

Both, functions like the transition and output function, as well as the transition relation can be represented by characteristic functions. Ordered binary decision diagrams are used to efficiently represent the characteristic function. Ordered binary decision diagrams (BDDs) were introduced by Bryant [6] based on binary decision diagrams ([11], [1]). BDDs can be analyzed and manipulated easily. For Boolean functions and the systems they represent, many operations are available. For example, tests (e.g., for functional equivalence, or satisfiability), application of algebraic operations, composition, and logic operations ($\wedge$, $\vee$, $\neg$, $\exists$, $\forall$).

Functional requirements for a system including those for safety functions can be expressed using temporal logic [8]. Conditions or changes in time can be expressed. It can be expressed, that there will never be a deadlock (liveness requirements) or that an unsafe state of the system will never be reached. The following temporal operators can be used to express these requirements:

Xf is true in the present iff (short for *if and only if*) f will hold in the next state.
Ff is true iff f will hold for some state in the future.
Gf is true iff f will hold at any moment in the future.
EFf is true iff f is possible in the future.

A safety function requirement may be that a state *unsafe* is never reached, in temporal logic: *NOT (EF unsafe)*.

Symbolic model checking is used to check temporal logic specifications for a given finite state machine. Basically, a reachability analysis is performed on the finite state machine starting from the initial state.

5 Fault Tree Generation

For fault tree generation, we have to consider two aspects which are discussed below:

* Which kinds of faults are to be modeled?
* How shall we model them?

5.1 Types of Faults

Single Faults. Only one fault is considered. In many applications, particularly in fail-safe systems, it is the goal to prove that any single fault is dealt with appropriately (e.g., shut-down in sufficiently short time). If this can be proven it is not required to consider multiple faults.

Multiple Faults. It is considered possible that the system exhibits more than one fault at a time. Even faults that are not critical as single faults might, in combination with others, be critical now.

There is another distinction: A fault can be intermittent or permanent. Intermittent means: During model checking we follow both paths, the path(s) for the correct sensor value and the path(s) for the faulty sensor value. Permanent means that we follow the path for the faulty value only.

The choice of the appropriate fault model is not trivial. The worst case fault model, namely the model that identifies all critical paths, is to be chosen. In our case study, the intermittent fault is worst case with respect to the given safety requirement. For liveness requirements this modeling approach may not yield all deadlocks, i.e. the intermittent fault is not worst case. However, the permanent fault is not worst case either. In case of intermittent faults, the system may follow transitions that are possible due to the fault only but avoid a deadlock. For instance, one could imagine systems with *intermittent* faults leading to potential deadlock situations. Once the system is in that area of potential deadlock situations, it would not get out of deadlocks in the presence of *permanent* faults. Violation of liveness requirements may also impact safety functions. For example, the emergency shutdown of a system might be prevented by a deadlock. Essentially, the maximum number of steps between two states is of interest here. Approaches like [9] are applicable. In general, how to appropriately model faults for the verification of liveness is an area for future work.

5.2 Fault Injection

There are different ways to model the effect of failures: explicit modification of sensor and actuator images, or the implicit behavioral failure modeling. In the following, these alternatives are described for intermittent sensor faults (Figure 2). This is similar for permanent faults. The principle is the same for actuators.

Figure 2a shows a simple example that contains a controller's finite state machine and a finite state description of the controlled process, both without failure. It is assumed that these finite state machines asynchronously trigger state changes. The sensor X and the actuator Y are the interface. Sensor X provides values x_i as inputs to the controller. Actuator Y transforms software outputs into process inputs. The initial state of the system is (x_0, y_0). This is the combination of the initial states of the controller and the process. Due to the logic of the system, only a few combinations of controller states and process states are reachable.

Assume there is an intermittent failure of a sensor X such that sensor X sometimes signals x_i instead of x_0. The following may happen:

- The system performs all correct state changes, if the sensor works correctly, or
- the system may perform state changes that are associated with the value x_i of state variable X in those situations where X is x_0.

5.3 Modeling with Explicit Sensor Images

Figure 2b shows an explicit failure model of the failure *Sensor X sometimes signals x_i instead of x_0*. The explicit modification of the model makes use of an image of the sensor and actuator values (primed state variables in Figure 2b). This image represents what the controller „thinks" to be the status of the process as opposed to the real status. Explicit modeling injects the failure into the controller's image of inputs. If necessary, the image has to be generated. Since all sensors are known, this generation is automatic.

5.4 Implicit Behavioral Sensor Failure Modeling

As an alternative, failures can be represented by appropriate modifications of the software's finite state machine. The above mentioned failure can be represented by adding the bold, dashed transition (Figure 2c).

Formally speaking: If R is the characteristic function of the system's finite state machine then R' is the characteristic function of the system with the above mentioned intermittent failure: $R' = R \vee (R|_{x=x1} \wedge X=x0)$.

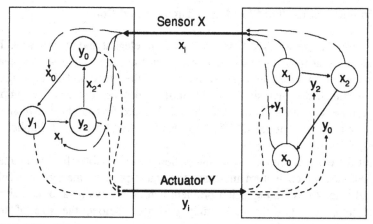

(a) System without failure

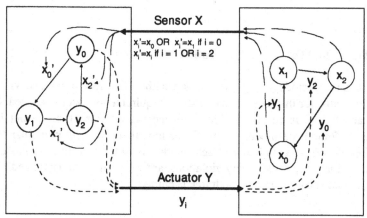

(b) Explicit model of the system with failure

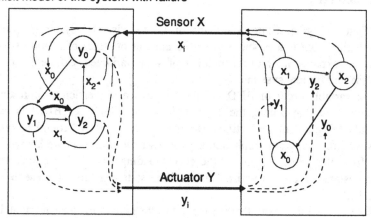

(c) Implicit model of the system with failure

Fig. 2. Failure modeling

5.5 Implicit vs. Explicit Modeling – The Pros and Cons

The explicit approach is at first sight the more elegant and clearer way. This is due to the fact that it distinguishes between what the state of the process really is and what the controller assumes to be the state of the process. This clear distinction is very useful in the analysis of critical failures because it eases the comprehension. The counter examples for the violation of the specified safety or liveness condition generated by the model checker are hard to read with the implicit modeling approach.

But the explicit approach introduces new state variables for the image of inputs and outputs, which in turn increases the state space of the system. This may be critical since the state explosion problem cannot always be avoided with an BDD-based approach. For the case study described below, the size of the models increased by about 30%. The increase for other systems will be a concern of future work.

5.6 The Actual Fault Tree Generation

The generated model is used to check whether and how states that violate system requirements, for instance, safety function requirements, can be reached. One model for each failure is generated. Since all necessary information is contained in the system's finite state model, the modifications that represent particular failures can be introduced automatically. Each model is subjected to the model checker. Failures, that may cause safety violations, are reported in the generated fault tree. If there are no such failures the fault tree is empty.

5.7 Complexity

When applying finite state machines to discrete systems, computational complexity often is a problem since the number of states of a finite state machine increases exponentially in the number of state variables. Efficient representations are essential for real systems.

The variable order of BDD variables is critical for efficient representation [7]. For some variable orders, the computational complexity of BDDs is exponential. The identification of an optimal variable order is an NP-complete problem [4]. However, for many real applications good variable orderings are known, and BDDs are efficient representations for the corresponding Boolean functions. Large hardware designs have been verified using finite state machines represented by BDDs ([8], e.g.).

Besides the complexity that is inherent to the system models and model checking, FRA has its own complexity. That is, for m sensors where the ith sensor may indicate n_i values, the current FRA approach requires the generation of N models:

$$N = \sum_{i=1}^{m} n_i^2 - n_i \qquad (1)$$

For a more detailed description of the FRA algorithm see [13]. The can be reduced by using failure catalogues that represent only those failure modes that are really possible for a device. For fail-safe components, for instance, this would considerably reduce the number of models since fail-safe components typically exhibit only one failure mode.

6 A Case Study: Elevating Rotary Table of a Production Cell

The example (Figure 3) is taken from [12] to illustrate FRA: *The production cell processes metal blanks which are conveyed to a press by a feed belt. A robot takes each blank from the feed belt and places it into the press. (..) The task of the elevating rotary table is to rotate the blanks (..) and to lift them to a level where they can be picked up by the first robot arm.*

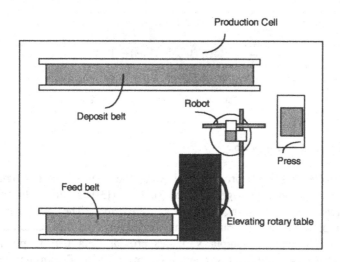

Fig. 3. The production cell

The actuators and sensors of the rotary table are:

Actuator	Name	Values
Vertical Movement	vmov	plus, minus, stop
Horizontal Movement	hmov	plus, minus, stop
Sensor	**Name**	**Values**
Vertical Position	vpos	y0, y1, y2
Horizontal Position	hpos	x0, x1, x2
Part on Table	part_on_table	yes, no

The initial position (Figure 4) is *hpos=x0, vpos=y0*, there is no movement (*hmov=stop, vmov=stop*). The vertical movement (*vmov=plus*) of the rotary table commences as soon as there is a part on the table (*part_on_table=yes*). When *vpos=y1* is reached the table starts to turn (*hmov=plus*). After a while the table arrives at the target position (*hpos=x2, vpos=y2*) so that the robot can take the blank from the table (*part_on_table=no*). Then the table begins to return to the start position: First it rotates horizontally only (*hmov=minus*). When it reaches the position *hpos=x0*, the vertical movement begins (*vmov=minus*) and the horizontal movement is stopped (*hmov=stop*). As soon as *vpos=y0*, the vertical movement stops, too (*vmov=stop*).

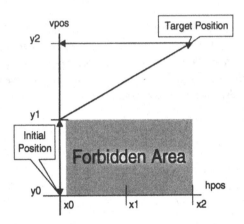

Fig. 4. Movement of the rotary table

The controller has been programmed using the state-machine language CSL (Control Specification Language) (Figure 5). CSL ([3]) is similar to commercial programmable controller languages, e.g., *HiGraph*. The software contains declarations of variables and transition rules. Variables that are declared as inputs are connected to sensors. Output variables provide data that is propagated to actuators. These type declarations are used by FRA to determine the sensors connected to the controller and their possible values. The variables' default values define the system's initial state. The transitions are specified as rules. Their left hand side define preconditions. If these are fulfilled, the transition rule causes modifications of variable values in the next state. This is denoted by the next state operator ** in the right hand side of the rule. Rules use logical operators (e.g., /\,\/).

```
..
StateVariables
      input   vpos: [y0, y1, y2] default y0;
      input   hpos: [x0, x1, x2] default x0;
      input   part_on_table: [no, yes] default no;
      output  vmov: [stop, plus, minus] default stop;
      output  hmov: [stop, plus, minus] default stop;
```

```
Transitions
    start_up:= (part_on_table = yes /\ vpos = y0)
           ==> (** vmov = plus);
    rotate:=   (part_on_table = yes
               /\ vpos = y1 /\ hpos < x2)
           ==> (** hmov = plus);
    stophigh:= (part_on_table = yes /\ vpos = y2)
           ==> (** vmov = stop);
    stop_rot:= (part_on_table = yes /\ hpos = x2)
           ==> (** hmov = stop);
    rot_back:= (part_on_table = no
               /\ vpos = y2 /\ hpos = x2)
           ==> (** hmov = minus);
    start_down:= (part_on_table = no
               /\ hpos = x0 /\ vpos = y2)
           ==> (** hmov = stop /\ ** vmov = minus);
    stoplow:=  (part_on_table = no /\ vpos = y0)
           ==> (** vmov = stop);
    ..
```

Fig. 5. The controller specification

In Figure 1, this software is depicted as *Controller Specification*. The behavior of the process (*Technical Process Description* in Figure 1) as well as the *Safety and Liveness Requirements* have been described using a temporal logic language that is used in the model checker environment.

There is a safety condition for the rotary table: The table must not move to the *Forbidden Area* (Figure 4). Figure 6 shows the safety part of the safety and liveness requirements: There should never (~(ef(...))) be a *collision*, which will occur if the table is not elevated but moves to a horizontal position different from *hpos=x0*.

```
...
collision := vpos=y0/\(hpos=x1\/hpos=x2).
safety    := ~(ef(collision)).
...
```

Fig. 6. Safety specification

FRA for the elevating rotary table is performed as described above. The table uses three sensors. Two of them distinguish three values. The third sensor signals Boolean data. This causes 14 possible failure situations that translate into 14 different finite state machines.

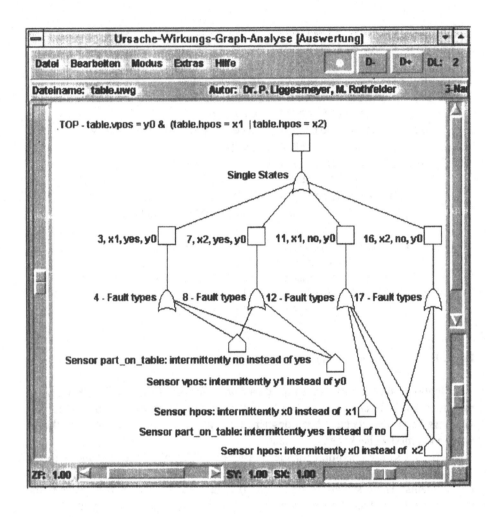

Fig. 7. The fault tree generated for sensor failures

FRA produces the fault tree in Figure 7. The predicate of the top event describes the violation of the safety requirement. The analysis reveals four states that fulfill this predicate, i.e., violate the safety requirement. These states are reachable if the sensor failures associated with the leafs of the fault tree occur. Some of the failures can obviously cause the effect. These are failures of the sensors that indicate positions. When the sensor for the vertical position signals $y1$ at position $y0$, the control software starts the horizontal movement. This may lead to a violation of the safety requirement. A similar situation is caused by failures of the sensor for the horizontal position if the table is moving back to its initial position. On the one hand, these effects are obvious. Formal analysis is probably not necessary to demonstrate them. On the other hand, the formal analysis revealed failures of the sensor *part_on_table* as potential causes of safety requirement violations. These are not obvious. A manual analysis of the software robustness would probably not reveal them.

The fault tree is shown in our *CEG-Tool*. The *CEG-Tool* can be used to modify fault trees: Probabilities for initiating events can be provided. This tool can also be used to attach component cause effect graphs, a special type of fault trees, in order to model component failure events.

7 Proving Fail-safe Behavior

Besides other applications such as reliability analysis or cost-optimized designs, FRA can be used to automate important parts of the proof of fail-safe behavior. A system like the one shown in Figure 8 is susceptible to failures in different areas. The human operator is prone to errors and mistakes. Besides that, the input and output devices that the operator uses to control the system may exhibit failures. The controller itself and the sensors and actuators are subject to failures. The process may show a behavior that is unknown or unexpected.

The model used for FRA covers failures of input devices, output devices, actuators, and sensors since input and output devices are similar to sensors and actuators.

Typically failures of the controller are too complicated to be modeled with FRA. Here design approaches such as dual- or three-channel architectures or vital mono-processors may be reasonable.

Assumptions on the process or human operator can be represented in the so-called process description of FRA (see Figure 1). If there are no such assumptions on the behavior of the human operator in the process description, even the operator's errors are taken into account. Similarly, if the system model has no assumptions on the technical process, all possible reactions of the technical process are taken into account during FRA. In this case unexpected behavior of the technical process is covered by FRA.

If assumptions on the process or the human operator have to be made, these should be regarded safety-critical and validated with appropriate care. But, as opposed to other approaches, FRA clearly states which assumptions are critical for the proof.

8 The Design Process for Fail-safe Systems

While formal verification (the *Verification* bubble in Figure 1) focuses on the functional aspects, in particular safety functions, the fault tree analysis with FRA focuses on the system integrity. Below we discuss the application of FRA for a fail-safe design. Many systems are required to be fail-safe, i.e. in case of a failure the system remains in a safe state. But it is unacceptable if the system would be unavailable due to frequent failures. The design process for a reliable fail-safe system may look like this with FRA (Figure 9):

First, the system (without failures) is verified against operational requirements and safety requirements. The assessment of results may show that the system satisfies both operational and safety requirements. If it is not, the system design is changed accordingly and re-verified.

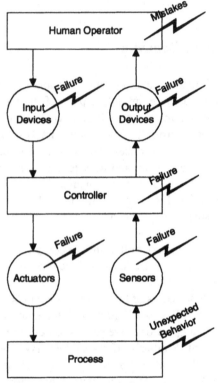

Fig. 8. A system susceptible to faults and failures

Next FRA is used to show that the system is safe even in the presence of failures. This takes into account safety requirements and all failure modes modeled with FRA. If FRA produces an empty safety fault tree, we have a functionally correct fail-safe system design. If not, appropriate re design is initiated.

The fail-safe system design is then analyzed regarding functional and liveness requirements in the presence of failures. FRA will produce a fault tree that represents the relationship between failures and possible violations of the functional and liveness requirements. Failure rates of sensors and actuators are taken into account to calculate the system's failure rate. If acceptable, the system design is reliable and fail-safe; if not, appropriate redesign starts.

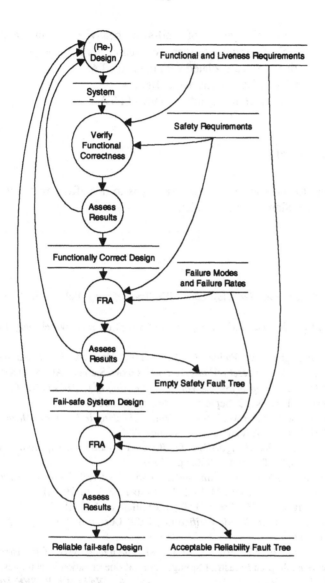

Fig. 9. Design of reliable fail-safe systems

9 Summary

FRA automatically generates complete fault trees for sensor and actuator failures. There is almost no additional effort to generate the fault trees because this generation makes use of existing documents. FRA is a means to automate

significant parts of the proof of fail-safe behavior. Fault modeling and computational complexity require further investigations. FRA is expected to
- significantly reduce costs associated with manual FTA,
- provide dependable reliability and safety figures,
- and enhance the completeness, and accuracy of FTA.

Acknowledgments

We would like to acknowledge the contributions to this effort made by W. Büttner and P. Warkentin (Siemens AG, Munich).

References

1. Akers S. B. *Binary Decision Diagrams*, IEEE Trans. Comp. Vol. C-27, No. 6, June 1978, pp. 509–516
2. Allen D. J. *Digraphs and Fault Trees*, Hazard Prevention January/February 1983, pp. 22–25
3. Bader P., Päppinghaus P., Pichler C., Schmid R., Umbreit G., Winkelmann K. *CSL Referenzmanual – Sprachbeschreibung*, Internal Report, Siemens AG, München, 1996
4. Bollig B., Wegener I. *Improving the Variable Ordering of OBDDs is NP-Complete*, IEEE Trans. Comp., Vol. 45, No. 9, September 1996, pp. 993-1001
5. Bormann J., Lohse J., Payer M., Venzl G. *Model Checking in Industrial Hardware Design*, 32nd ACM/IEEE Design Automation Conference 1995
6. Bryant R. E. *Graph-Based Algorithms for Boolean Function Manipulation*, IEEE Trans. Comp., Vol. C-35, No.8, August 1986, pp. 667-691
7. Bryant R. E. *Symbolic Boolean Manipulation with Ordered Binary-Decision Diagrams*, ACM Computing Surveys, Vol. 24, No.3, September 1992, pp. 293-318
8. Burch J. R., Clarke E. M., Long D. E., McMillan K. L., Dill D. L. *Symbolic Model Checking for Sequential Circuit Verification*, IEEE Design & Test, Vol. 13 No. 4, April 1994, pp. 401–424
9. Campos S., Clarke E., Marrero W., Minea M. *Timing analysis of industrial real-time systems*, In: Workshop on Industrial Strength Formal Specification Techniques, 1995.
10. Filkorn T., Schneider H.-A., Scholz A., Strasser A., Warkentin P. *SVE Users' Guide*, Internal Report, Siemens AG, München, 1996
11. Lee C. Y. *Representation of Switching Circuits by Binary-Decision Programs*, The Bell System Technical Journal 38, July 1959, pp. 985–999
12. Lewerentz C., Lindner T. *Formal Development of Reactive Systems: Case Study Production Cell*, LNCS 891, Springer-Verlag, January 1995
13. Liggesmeyer P., Rothfelder M. *Improving System Reliability with Automatic Fault Tree Generation*, Proc. FTCS-28, Munich, Germany, 1998, pp. 90-99

Verifying a Time-Triggered Protocol in a Multi-language Environment

Agathe Merceron[1], Monika Müllerburg[2], and G. Michele Pinna[3]

[1] Basser Department of Computer Science, University of Sydney
Madsen Building F09, NSW 2006, Australia
agathe@staff.cs.su.oz.au
[2] GMD - German National Research Center for Information Technology
Schloss Birlinghoven, D-53754 Sankt Augustin, Germany
muellerburg@gmd.de
[3] Dipartimento di Matematica, Università degli Studi di Siena
Via del Capitano 15, I-53100 Siena, Italy
pinna@miele.mat.unisi.it

Abstract. The multi-language environment SYNCHRONIE supports the design and formal verification of synchronous reactive systems. Presently, SYNCHRONIE integrates three synchronous languages, ESTEREL, LUSTRE, and ARGOS. In the synchronous approach, not only the system but also its properties can be specified using a synchronous language. In SYNCHRONIE properties can be formalised textually as ESTEREL or LUSTRE programs, or graphically as ARGOS programs. Moreover, properties may also be specified as temporal logic formulas with past or future operators. It is shown how to specify and automatically prove properties of a time-triggered protocol taking advantage of this environment.

1 Introduction

This paper demonstrates how the multi-language environment SYNCHRONIE [13] can ease the formal verification of reactive systems. Reactive systems continously react to stimuli from their environment. They are often embedded in electronic products, mass transportation systems, and industrial plants. Since malfunction of such systems may well impose economic penalties or introduce unacceptable risks of personal or environmental damage, rigorous validation is important.

The synchronous paradigm is considered as particulary well suited for developing such systems, since properties such as reactivity (i.e. the system *always* reacts to an input and the *unique* reaction terminates within a fixed amount of time) and satisfaction of timing constraints can be guaranteed. The synchronous paradigm views a system run as a sequence of events which individually consist of a computation step and the exchange of signals (possibly with data) between system and environment. Synchronous languages are based on the synchrony hypothesis [1] which stipulates that calculations are carried quickly enough so that, for the environment, output signals appear to be synchronous with the inputs. Thus, time is divided into non-overlapping instants where reactions take place. Note, that a synchronous system is deterministic, in spite of the fact that it can be made of several parallel components.

Several synchronous languages have been developed [5]. They look quite different: ARGOS, for instance, a Statechart variant, is graphical in style, ESTEREL is imperative, and LUSTRE is data flow oriented. Integrating these languages, SYNCHRONIE enables multi-style design: the designer is free to adopt the language most appropriate for different aspects of the same design. The integration of the languages is achieved via a common semantic model, called *Synchronous Components* [8]. A *Synchronous Component* consists of a control and a data part. The control part, called *Boolean Automaton*, is basically a kind of finite state machine encoded by a set of Boolean equations. It is used to represent the control part of a synchronous program which calculates the instantenous reaction: given a set of input signals provided by the environment, the set of output signals to be fed back to the environment is calculated. The data part, triggered by the control part, calculates the values, if any, of the emitted signals. This paper concentrates on the verification of the control part, since the properties one is interested in mainly concern the emission of the right signals at the right instant.

It turns out that *Boolean Automata* can easily be tranformèd into the input format of the existing model checkers SMV [10] and VIS [4]. Hence, properties to be checked can be formalized in CTL (Computation Tree Logic) [3], the specification language used by the tools, and a logic widely accepted in the hardware community. However, specifying properties in CTL may be awkward. The synchronous approach provides a simpler way of specification: the same language which is used for modeling the system may also be used to formally specify safety properties. In addition, SYNCHRONIE supports PTL, a logic with past temporal operators [9, 2]. Hence, in SYNCHRONIE properties to be checked may be specified in either logic or in any of the synchronous languages. This multi-language aspect is a unique feature of SYNCHRONIE.

The flexibility of such an environment for formal verification is demonstrated using the example of the time-triggered communication protocol PROSA (Protocol for Safety-Critical Applications) [14].

The paper is structured as follows. The next section, Section 2, introduces the multi-language environment provided by SYNCHRONIE and its use for formal verification. Sections 3 and 4 present a simplified model of the protocol, explaining those parts which are needed for understanding the verification. Section 5 is devoted to the formal specification and verification of protocol properties. Finally, Section 6 concludes the paper.

2   The multi-language environment SYNCHRONIE

The multi-language environment is provided by SYNCHRONIE, a (prototype) workbench for constructing and validating reactive systems. The workbench supports synchronous and object-oriented design from the system's specification to the generation of efficient software or hardware. In addition to the synchronous languages ARGOS, ESTEREL, and LUSTRE, an inhouse object-oriented synchronous language called synchronousEIFEL is provided which integrates synchronous languages (currently ESTEREL and ARGOS) with the object-oriented language EIFFEL. The workbench provides tools for editing, compilation, simulation, test, verification, debugging, and code generation.

A unique feature of SYNCHRONIE is the *semantical* integration of the supported synchronous languages. The rational for this integration is that the different styles of the synchronous languages reflect different application areas: while a declarative dataflow language like LUSTRE is well suited for signal oriented applications (continuous behaviour) as in navigation systems (sampling with different related frequencies), ESTEREL and ARGOS are adequate for modelling control oriented spontaneous behaviour with interrupts. Since complex reactive systems often consist of components with different characteristics, it is desirable to formulate each component in the most appropriate style.

2.1 Language integration: the role of *Boolean Automata*

Within SYNCHRONIE, language integration is understood at a much deeper level than if it were limited to some external call mechanism. The workbench is founded on a common semantical model of synchronous programs called *Synchronous Components*. All the synchronous languages can be (and the supported ones in SYNCHRONIE are) compiled into this format. All other tools, for instance, linker, reactivity checker, verifiers and code generators, are working on this format and therefore source code independent. The control part of a *Synchronous Component*, being a *Boolean Automaton* (*BA* for short), may be translated into any programming language and also into hardware (netlists). Since Boolean expressions are part of any language, their translation is simple.

A *BA* contains two kinds of objects: signals and registers. If the Boolean equation of a signal evaluates to `true`, then the signal is emitted. A state of the *BA* is characterised by all the registers whose Boolean equations evaluate to `true`. The signals appearing on the right hand side of an equation refer to the present instant while the registers refer to the values in the previous instant. For registers, the Boolean equations are to be solved in parallel. For signals, the Boolean equations must be solved in an order that has to be found. If such an order cannot be found, there is a causality problem [1].

2.2 Verification in SYNCHRONIE

Automatic verification in SYNCHRONIE is based on *BA*. They allow various ways to specify and verify properties.

Since a *BA* can easily be transformed into the input formats of the model checkers SMV and VIS, those model checkers can be tied to SYNCHRONIE allowing to use CTL for specifying properties. CTL is a branching time temporal logic with future operators. The model checker automatically checks whether the property is verified by the program. This is a well-known way to specify and verify (temporal) properties.

On the other hand, a *BA* is an automaton, and an automaton is a language generator as well as a language acceptor. Taking this second interpretation of an automaton, a *BA* can be used to represent the property working as an acceptor for the computations of the program. For any instant, if the property is true for the computation, the associated *BA* emits the special signal ok. To check that the program verifies the property, it is sufficient to compose in parallel the *BA* of the program with the *BA* associated to the property and to feed the resulting *BA* to some model checker. The model checker can check whether ok is in the label of every state of the reachability space, i.e. it is emitted constantly. If yes, the program verifies the property expressed in the *BA*. This approach has been taken in [15] and specialised to the synchronous context in [6] where a property written as a synchronous program is called an *observer*.

Presently there are two ways to specify *BA* acceptors in SYNCHRONIE: a property may be specified either as a formula in the logic PTL which can be translated into a *BA* [2], or as a program in a synchronous language which is translated into a *BA* by the same compilers that translate programs.

To sum up, SYNCHRONIE supports three main ways to specify and automatically verify properties: using the logic with future operators CTL, using the logic with past operators PTL, and using any of the synchronous languages. Note that in any case, the original programs themselves, via their compilation into *BA*, are proved, hence no extra models need to be drawn for verification purposes.

3 Informal description of the protocol

The protocol for automotive applications presented in [14] is a time-triggered protocol [7] which allows a fixed number of stations to communicate via a shared bus. Messages are broadcasted to all stations via the bus. Each station that participates in the communication sends a message when it is the *right* time to do so. Therefore, access to the bus is determined by a time division multiple access (TDMA) schema controlled by the global time generated by the protocol. A TDMA cycle is divided into *time slices*. The stations are ordered and time slices are allocated to the stations according to their order. During its time slice, a station has exclusive message sending rights. Focusing on control, we consider a time slice as being composed of two parts: a *frame*, which includes the identification of the station, and an *acknowledgement window*. A TDMA cycle for three stations looks like in Figure 1.

The protocol is fault-tolerant. If a message is not properly received, the station(s) that notice(s) the transmission error send(s) a veto in the acknowledgement window and all the stations change from normal mode to error mode. If the faulty sending station is not able to recover it will be excluded. For the fault-tolerance algorithm to work properly, each station maintains a *membership service*, which indicates which stations are in normal mode.

To participate in the communication, a station starts in the initialization mode. It enters the normal mode as soon as it succeeds synchronizing with other stations.

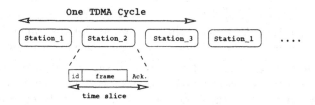

Fig. 1. A TDMA cycle for 3 stations.

Suppose $station_i$ wants to participate in the communication. It has to find out when it is its time to access the bus. Therefore, it goes first in the initialization mode. Upon entering the initialization mode, it sets its timer to a time T1. During this time, it listens to the traffic on the bus. As soon as it recognizes a valid frame, i.e., a frame whose acknowledgement window does not have any veto, it knows which station is sending. Consequently, it can deduce when it will have to send, since time slices are statically allocated. It synchronizes and enters the normal mode, updating its membership service for any valid frame.

If $station_i$ is the first to require a communication, it won't hear any valid frame during T1. When time T1 elapses, it sends a frame and sets its timer to $T2_i$, a time proper to $station_i$ and different from any $T2_j$ for any $station_j$ with $i \neq j$. Communication needs at least two partners, therefore $station_i$ will continue listening to the traffic during time $T2_i$, sending a message when $T2_i$ elapses and resetting its timer to $T2_i$. If a second station, say $station_j$, needs also to communicate, it enters the initialization mode too. Because $T2_i$ and $T2_j$ are different, eventually one of the two stations will recognize a valid frame and synchronize, thus switching to the normal mode. It sends a message in its own time slice, allowing the second station to synchronize as well. Notice that during the set up of the protocol, collisions may occur, for instance if two stations start in the same instant, since T1 is the same for everybody.

Besides its time-triggered aspect, a relevant feature of the protocol is to allow a quick change of mode and a membership service with minimal overhead both in message length and in the number of messages.

4 Formal description of the protocol

We illustrate briefly the overall structure and some parts of the realization of the protocol. Using the synchronous approach to formally specify the time-triggered protocol gives the global clock for free. A time unit for the protocol is the reaction time of its synchronous realization.

The protocol is modeled by a number of stations running in parallel, presently three. The bus is modeled implicitly as the set of global messages, i.e. those messages that are not local to any station. A frame (sent by $station_i$) is modeled by two signals, bframe_i and eframe_i: the first signal represents that the station begins to send a frame, and the second one represents the end of this operation. In the actual implementation they come in two consecutive instants (this can be easily extended to cope with larger frame windows). A time slice has a length of three time units: the first two are for the frame (bframe_i and eframe_i) and the third one is for the acknowledgement window.

Taking advantage of the graphical style of ARGOS and of its refinement operator for states, the current top level of the protocol consists of four parallel single state automata: three for the three stations and one for the collisions controller. All four states are further refined.

The controller of collisions checks whether signals on the bus collide. It emits the signal rframe_i every time the frame sent by *station*$_i$ does not collide with any other frame and does not have veto in its acknowledgement window. This state is refined by a Lustre program.

A station is refined by an ARGOS automaton which essential parts are shown in Figure 2 for *station*$_1$. It consists of three parallel components: application, engine and timer. Each component is again an ARGOS automaton. Their initial states are marked by bold frames. The components share some local signals which are listed at the bottom of the rectangle representing the station: start_i, off_i, ...

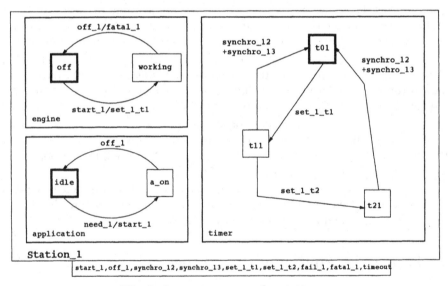

Fig. 2. ARGOS automaton for *station*$_1$

The automaton application models the status of the station which is either idle or a_on. The automaton engine represents the station's protocol engine, which is either off or working. The state working is refined by the ARGOS automaton shown partly in Figure 3. The automaton timer is responsible for counting the instants in the initialization mode. It has three states, an initial one, t01, and two others, t11 to count time T1 and t21 to count time T2. They are refined by the same LUSTRE program realizing a counter.

Starting an automaton with parallel components, all parallel initial states are entered, hence starting the automaton in Figure 2, the three parallel initial states idle, off, t01 are entered. Further, because of the synchrony hypothesis and broadcasting of signals, the following happens when $station_i$ needs its protocol engine. Upon a request from the environment (issued via the input signal need_i), the automaton application emits the signal start_i and enters the state a_on. Signal start_i is immediately received by engine which changes to state working, emitting set_i_t1 which is in turn received by the timer causing it to change to state t11 for counting the first time. As soon as timer receives synchro_ij (representing the success in synchronization), it goes back in its initial state. If the station does not succeed in synchronization within time T1 the counter issues the signal timeout_i at the end of the counting. This causes the sending of the frame in the initialization mode and the resetting of the counter to T2. The timer changes to state t21 where it stays until it receives signal synchro_ij. The counter is periodically reset to T2.

The working state of engine is refined by three automata running in parallel: StationIsOn, StateVector, and SliceDistributor (see Fig. 3). We present briefly StationIsOn and StateVector.

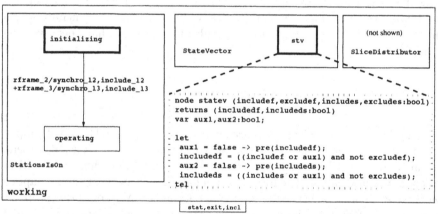

Fig. 3. ARGOS automaton for protocol engine (detail)

The automaton StationIsOn models the status of the protocol engine: it is either in the initialization mode or in the operating mode, where operating mode covers normal and error mode. Hence the automaton StationIsOn consists of the two states, initializing and operating. Both states are further refined by ARGOS automata, not explained here. The automaton switches from initializing to operating when it receives rframe_j. Changing the state, the signals synchro_ij and include_ij are emitted.

The automaton StateVector models the membership service. It consists of just one node which is refined by the LUSTRE program shown in Figure 3. The body (between let and tel) is a set of equations which are evaluated in parallel. There is one equation for each output parameter and each local variable.

An equation defines the value of a signal by the expression on the right hand side of the symbol '='. The expressions use two special LUSTRE operators, ->, for initialization, and `pre` for giving access to a signal's value in the previous instant. Variable `aux1`, for instance, has the value `false` in the first instant, and in all further instants it has the value that `includedf` had in the previous instant. The state vector represents the state of the system as it is perceived by the station: each station knows which stations are participating to the game, i.e. which are *included*. This is important for the error mode. For a station which is not included, the acknowledgement window should be ignored. For an included station, if the acknowledgement window contains `veto`, the station may need to be excluded (depending on the signal `exclude` emitted by the `sliceDistributor`).

5 Specification and verification of protocol properties

As stated in Section 2, SYNCHRONIE supports three main ways to formally specify and automatically prove properties: using any of the synchronous languages, using the logic with future operators CTL or using the logic with past operators PTL. The most important properties we proved regarded synchronisation and collision avoidance. To cut down complexity, properties have been verified modularly [11].

5.1 Properties as CTL formulae

The property *a station will synchronize* refers to something good that will happen in the future (liveness property). A station will synchronize if (1) it is able to send a frame and (2) if there is another station that wants to synchonize as well or has already synchronized. The formalisation has to describe what should happen sometime in the future, hence the use of CTL formulae. We proved this property in two parts. If $station_1$ is in the state `idle` and `need_1` is present, then it will always send its frame. For the second part, it will synchronize, `rframe_2` (or `rframe_3`) must be emitted sufficiently often. This will be the case if $station_2$ and $station_3$ are not both `idle`. For both parts it is assumed that `off_1` remains absent, which is safe, as `off_1` is emitted only in the error mode, not in the initialization. The CTL formulae are:

$$AG((\text{idle } and \text{ need\_1}) \Rightarrow AF \text{ bframe\_1})$$

$$AG((\text{idle } and \text{ need\_1}) \Rightarrow AF (\text{synchro\_12 } or \text{ synchro\_13}))$$

The temporal operator AF stands for always in the future. The first formula, for instance, says that `bframe_1` will always be emitted some instants after `idle` and `need_1`.

Putting these properties together, we conclude that $station_1$ will synchronise.

5.2 Properties as synchronous automata

There is no collision if two stations never send a frame in the same instant, i.e., if their slice distributors do not emit state_slice in the same instant. This is quite easy to formalise as a LUSTRE observer, for instance, for $station_1$ and $station_2$:

$$ok = not\ (\texttt{state\_1\_slice}\ and\ \texttt{state\_2\_slice}).$$

The property AG ok was proved as true. To carry up the proof for more than three stations, we had to use some reasoning. This involved checking that the collisions controller never emits rframe_i and rframe_j at the same time. This is also formalised as a LUSTRE observer and checked as true:

$$ok = not\ (\texttt{rframe\_}i\ and\ \texttt{rframe\_}j).$$

These properties, because they are simple exclusion, would have been equally easy to formalise either with CTL or PTL. However, many properties, particularly if they involve intricate sequences of signals, are much easier to formalise using automata rather than temporal formulae. An example is the property start_1 *and* off_1 *alternate and* start_1 *begins*. To formulate it in CTL requires to reformulate the property saying that if start_1 occurs, then, at the next instant, it does not occur anymore until off_1 occurs. And the symmetrical has to be formulated as well, if off_1 occurs, then it does not occur anymore until start_1 occurs. Moreover, in CTL, the until is strong, i.e., off_1 has to occur after start_1, and start_1 has to occur after off_1, which is not required by the simple *alternate*. To formulate that start_1 begins brings even more complications. By contrast, such a property is easely formulated as an ARGOS automaton as shown in Figure 4 where – means *not* and & means *and*.

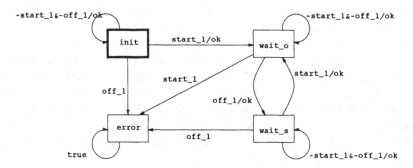

Fig. 4. The automaton for start_1 and off_1 alternate.

5.3 Properties as PTL formulae

Additional properties have been proved. In particular it was shown that the LUSTRE node for StateVector maintains the membership service correctly. First, if $station_j$ is included in the state vector of $station_i$, then it has always been included since the signal include_ij has been emitted. The property is best formalised using a logic with past operators. For $station_2$ included in the membership service of $station_1$ this is written as follows:

$$AG \ (\texttt{included\_12} \ \Rightarrow \ (\texttt{included\_12} \ Since \ \texttt{include\_12}))$$

Further, if a station is not included, then either it has never been included or it has not been included since an exclude has been emitted. Again, it is best formalised by a PTL formula:

AG (*not* included_12 $\Rightarrow$

    (P *not* include_12) *or* (*not* included_12 *Since* exclude_12))

where P should be red as *always in the Past*. Proving this last property led to discover an erroneous initial reaction in the original LUSTRE program.

These properties for the membership service could have been formulated with LUSTRE. However it would have been lenghty to do so as **pre**, the past operator of LUSTRE, refers to the previous instant solely. It would have been necessary to define several variables to remember whether some signal has always occured in the past or always occured since the occurrence of some other signal.

6 Conclusions

The development of the time-triggered protocol takes advantage of the multi-language facilities of SYNCHRONIE. The multi-language aspect is used both to describe formally the system and to specify properties concerning the protocol's reactive behaviour. Properties have been proved automatically. Automatic verification is achieved through a simple analysis of the state space. For better efficiency or to handle bigger systems, verification can be done modularly [11]. Focusing on control, this paper emphasizes automatic verification of properties. However, particularly when data are involved, automatic verification is not always possible and a deductive approach has to be used in addition.

The fact that the same languages used for modeling the system may also be used for specifying properties, at least safety properties, is very advantageous from an engineer's point of view: no additional specification language is needed. Further, critical system properties often are safety properties. The graphical language ARGOS takes a particular place, since it allows to specify properties as automata, as demonstrated by the automaton for start_1 *and* off_1 *alternate* in section 5. Further, automata can formalize safety properties that cannot be formalized with PTL or CTL [16].

The relevance of temporal logics for verifying concurrent systems is well established. SYNCHRONIE provides support to specify and automatically verify properties written as temporal logic formulae. Though it would be possible to write any safety formula with past temporal operators using a LUSTRE program, the use of the logic PTL is quite valuable in practice as illustrated in Section 5. In principle many properties can be formalized by a CTL formula: not only safety properties but also liveness properties. The support of CTL has been necessary to prove that a station will synchronize. However, verification based on this logic has a disadvantage from an engineer's point of view: the specification may be difficult if the property is somewhat intricate and does not refer naturally to future operators as illustrated with the property start_1 *and* off_1 *alternate*. When liveness properties are not critical, a practical approach to effective and efficient validation could be to test liveness properties and formally verify safety properties [12].

References

1. A. Benveniste and G. Berry. The synchronous approach to reactive and real-time systems. *Proceedings of the IEEE*, 79(9), 1991.
2. R. Budde and A. Merceron. A generator of boolean acceptors for safety properties. In A.L. Wendelborn, editor, *The 5th Annual Australasian Conference on Parallel and Real-Time Systems, PART'98*, to appear. Springer-Verlag, 1998.
3. E. M. Clarke, E. A. Emerson, and A. P. Sistla. Automatic verification of finite-state concurrent sytems using temporal logic specifications. *ACM Transactions on Programming Languages and Systems*, 8(2):244–263, 1986.
4. The VIS Group. VIS: A system for verification and synthesis. In *8th International Conference on Computer Aided Verification*, volume 1102 of *Lecture Notes in Computer Science*, pages 428–432, July 1996.
5. N. Halbwachs. *Synchronous Programming of Reactive Systems*. Kluwer Academic Publishers, 1993.
6. N. Halbwachs, F. Lagnier, and P. Raymond. Synchronous observers and the verification of reactive systems. In *Third Int. Conf. on Algebraic Methodology and Software Technology, AMAST'93*, Workshops in Computing. Springer-Verlag, 1993.
7. H. Kopetz and G. Grünsteidl. A time triggered protocol for automotive applications. Research report 16/92, Institut für Technische Informatik, Technische Universität Wien, Vienna, Austria, 1992.
8. O. Maffeïs and A. Poigné. Synchronous automata for reactive, real-time and embedded systems. Arbeitspapiere der GMD 967, Forschungszentrum Informationstechnik GmbH, January 1996.
9. Z. Manna and A. Pnueli. *The Temporal Logic of Reactive Systems*. Springer Verlag, 1992.
10. K. L. McMillan. *Symbolic Model Checking*. Kluwer Academic Publishers, 1993.
11. A. Merceron and G. M. Pinna. Refinement and modular verification. Proceedings, First International Workshop on Constraint Programming for Time Critical Applications, Schloß Hagenberg, Austria, Oct. 27-28, 1997.
12. M. Müllerburg, L. Holenderski, O. Maffeïs, A. Merceron, and M. Morley. Systematic testing and formal verification to validate reactive systems. *Software Quality Journal*, 4(4):287–307, 1995.
13. A. Poigné, M. Morley, O. Maffeïs, L. Holenderski, and R. Budde. The synchronous approach to designing reactive systems. *Formal Methods in System Design*, 12:163–187, 1998.
14. R. v. Hanxleden, J. Bohne, L. Lavagno, and A. Sangiovanni-Vincentelli. Hardware/software co-design of a fault-tolerant communication protocol. In *Proc. of the IEEE Intern. Workshop on Embedded Fault-Tolerant Systems*, 1996.
15. M.Y. Vardi and P. Wolper. An automata theoretic approach to automatic program verification. In *Proceedings of the First Annual Symposium on Logic in Computer Science*, pages 332–344. IEEE Computer Society Press, 1986.
16. P. Wolper. Temporal logic can be more expressive. *Information and Control*, 56:72–99, 1983.

Methods and Languages for Safety Related Real Time Programming

Wolfgang A. Halang[1]* and Alceu Heinke Frigeri[2]

[1] Faculty of Electrical Engineering · FernUniversität Hagen
Wolfgang.Halang@FernUni-Hagen.de
[2] Faculty of Electrical Engineering · FernUniversität Hagen
on leave from: Federal University of Rio Grande do Sul
Dept. of Electrical Engg. · Porto Alegre · Brazil
Alceu.Frigeri@FernUni-Hagen.de

Abstract. Programs employed for purposes of safety critical control must be verified rigorously, i.e., subjected to formal safety licensing, which constitutes a very difficult and hitherto not satisfactorily solved problem. The essential issues and fundamental principles of safety related programs and computer applications are elaborated, and the importance of the human element in their development process is pointed out. At any time, utmost simplicity should be strived for, and self-discipline should be exercised. To each of the four safety integrity levels as defined by IEC SC 65A is assigned, respectively, a set of static and inherently safe language constructs, as well as a typical programming language or method, whose syntax enforces observation of the prevailing restrictions and rules. This is done in accordance with simplicity and comprehensibility of the verification methods available for the selected programming paradigms to meet the requirements of the individual safety integrity levels and, thus, the trustworthiness of the corresponding results. The programming methods cause/effect tables and function block diagrams on the basis of verified libraries assigned to the two upper safety integrity levels SIL 4 and SIL 3 are the only ones so far allowing, at the present state of the art, to verify automation software, which has to meet high safety requirements, in easy and economic ways. For the lower safety integrity levels, textual languages are introduced, viz., for SIL 2 a partial language enabling formal program verification, and for SIL 1 a static language with safe constructs for asynchronous multitasking. To formulate sequential function charts, an inherently safe language is defined.
Keywords: Safety controllers, Real time systems, Programming languages, Safe language subsets, Cause/effect tables, Function block diagrams, Safety integrity levels.

1 Introduction

The significance of programmable electronic systems with safety related applications in daily life is increasing rapidly. The wide spectrum covered by these sys-

---

* This paper summarises the results of research project F 1636 funded by Bundesanstalt für Arbeitsschutz und Arbeitsmedizin, Dortmund

tems is to be characterised here by some examples: control units of anti-blocking systems, computer tomographs, structurally unstable aircrafts, magnetic railways, power stations and power distribution systems, air traffic monitoring, as well as satellites and space stations. In the interest of human well-being substantial efforts are necessary to master them safely. With just a few facts the following citation points out the importance of the problem:

"We are now faced with a society in which the amount of software is doubling about every 18 months in consumer electronic devices, and in which software defect density is more or less unchanged in the last 20 years." [4].

Highly dependable programmable electronic systems for safety critical control and regulation applications form a completely new field, that stands at the very beginning of its scientific treatment. Its significance arises from the growing awareness for safety in our society on the one hand, and from the technological trend towards more flexible, i.e., program controlled, automation devices on the other hand. It is the aim to reach the state that computer based systems can be constructed with a sufficient degree of confidence in their dependability that enables their licensing for safety critical control and regulation tasks by the pertaining authorities on the basis of formal approvals.

More and more, also the general public realises the intrinsic safety problems associated with computer software. Although there is already a number of established methods and guidelines for software development and licensing, according to the current state of the art, however, these measures cannot guarantee the correctness of larger programs with mathematical rigour. Therefore, the licensing authorities are still very reluctant to approve safety related automation systems, whose behaviour is exclusively program controlled. However, since it appears unrealistic to relinquish the utilisation of computers in safety related automation applications — quite on the contrary, there is no doubt that for economical reasons their employment will increase rapidly and significantly —, the problem of software dependability will exacerbate severely.

Since the programming practice prevailing in developing process control systems is characterised by the use of inadequate means, in this paper for each of the four safety integrity levels language constructs really necessary to formulate all relevant control problems will be identified giving rise to corresponding, inherently safe language subsets. Thereby the expressive power is restricted in order to make computer based automation systems more manageable and, thus, take a step forward towards enabling their formal safety licensing. To this end, particularly methods oriented at the engineers, i.e., graphical programming paradigms, are emphasised.

The safety aspect is the central subject of our considerations. A safe control system has to fulfill its specified automation functionality, as long as no hazard is provoked or tolerated, respectively. Otherwise, a safety reaction has to be initiated, which may consist of transferring the controlled system into a safe state or taking any other appropriate provisions.

This paper summarises the results of a research project on programming language subsets for safety related control applications. Owing to severe size restrictions, many of the results obtained can only be reported here. For the complete arguments leading to them, we refer to the project report which was published as a book [3].

2 Fundamental Considerations

Software has an entirely different quality than hardware. Thus, it is not subject to wear but, on the other hand, it is inherently error-prone and contains only systematic errors, i.e., design errors, which are always being present. Furthermore, software is *not continuous*, i.e., the effect of small errors is not necessarily small as well, and may not even be bounded. For safety related applications, in principle software must be valid and correct. This necessitates two verification steps, which constitute serious problems:

1. Demonstrating that a software fulfills its problem specification, establishes its correctness. Such proofs need to be carried through with mathematical rigour, since tests cannot prove the absence of errors due to the too large a number of cases to be taken into consideration. It is well known that with tests only the presence of errors can be detected.
2. Actually, it also needed to be shown that given specifications indeed meet the specifier's more or less vaguely formulated requests, or even his or her unexpressed thoughts or ideas.

Although there is still no satisfactory solution to the first one of the two above mentioned problems, in principle it appears to be solvable by scientific and technical means, whereas the second one will never be completely solved, because human factors are involved.

Safety related computer based automation systems operate in the real time mode, i.e., the processing of programs must be temporally synchronised with events occurring in external technical processes, and must keep pace with these processes. Thereby, not processing speed is the decisive factor, but the timeliness of reactions within predefined time bounds oriented at worst case load requirements. All system reactions must be precisely planned and predictable. Only fully deterministic system behaviour will ultimately enable the safety licensing of programmable electronic systems for safety critical applications. In principle, the problem of temporal overloads of real time systems can be solved by adequate planning, dimensioning, restriction and operation. Overloading of computer systems is only caused by exaggerated and unrealistic requirements, one does not dare to impose on other — better understood — technical systems.

To prove the correctness of software with a maximum of trustworthiness and a minimum of effort, the utilisation of programming concepts and architectural features appears to be mandatory, which support the process of verification as far as possible. Verification, and thus the assertion that a program is apparently error free, is indeed the main pre-condition for granting a safety certificate.

The requirements and objectives to be fulfilled by safety related automation systems can only be achieved if *simplicity* is selected as the fundamental design principle, and if the (mainly artificial) complexity is fought. At the present state of the art, simplicity is a key pre-requisite to enable the licensing authorities to formally approve the utilisation of computer based systems for purposes of safety related control, since a simple system is easy to understand and its behaviour is easy follow up. This is the essential step towards the verification of its correct behaviour in the sense of Descartes: [1]:

> "verum est quod valde clare et distincte percipio".

Descartes' notion of clear and distinct comprehension is also the key to understand the nature of verification, which is neither a scientific nor a technical, but a *social process*. This holds for mathematical proofs as well, whose correctness is based on consensus of members of the mathematical community that certain chains of reasoning lead to given conclusions. Applied to safety related computerised systems, and considering their importance to human lives and health, but also to the environment and capital investments, this consensus ought to be as wide as possible. Hence, systems must be simple, and appropriate software verification methods must also be easily understandable for non-experts — however without compromising rigour.

3 Programming Language Constructs Appropriate at the Different Safety Integrity Levels

The development of techniques for the safety licensing of computer programs is still in a very early stage, and the state reached so far is still totally insufficient. Hitherto, formal correctness proofs are feasible for relatively small programs only — fortunately covering a large amount of safety critical functions. Additional methods often employed in this area and having comparable rigour are symbolic program execution or even complete tests. To verify that a large program fulfills all requirements of a safety related control system, until now only the technique of diverse back translation [8] is available.

In Table 1 a set of language constructs, and in Table 2 a corresponding typical programming language or method, respectively, is assigned to each of the four safety integrity levels as defined in IEC SC 65A [6] according to the simplicity and understandability of the verification methods — and, thus, the trustworthiness of the results achieved — available for the different programming paradigms.

Based on a comparison of the sets of language constructs given in Table 1 with a variety of programming languages, Table 3 contains an evaluation of their suitability for use in the different safety integrity levels according to IEC SC 65A. The selection of the programming languages is based on Table D-5 of the Draft International Standard IEC SC 65A, but was slightly modified with respect to the versions considered for reasons of actuality.

Table 1. Assignment of language constructs and verification methods to the safety integrity levels according to IEC SC 65A

Safety Integrity Level	Verification Methods	Language Constructs
SIL 4	Social consensus	Marking table entries
SIL 3	Diverse back translation	Procedure call
SIL 2	Symbolic execution Formal correctness proofs	Procedure call Assignment Case selection Repetition restricted loop
SIL 1	All	Inherently safe ones Application oriented ones

Table 2. Association of typical programming methods or languages with the safety integrity levels according to IEC SC 65A

Safety Integrity Level	Typical Programming method
SIL 4	Cause/effect tables
SIL 3	Function block diagrams with verified libraries
SIL 2	Language subset enabling formal verification
SIL 1	Static language with safe constructs

4 Cause/Effect Tables

A programming paradigm that is already well established for a long time as a means for the construction of protection systems and which appears to be appropriate to meet the highest safety requirements is constituted by cause/effect tables. Despite its exact and unambiguous nature, software formulated in form of cause/effect tables is simple, clear, and straight-forward to such an extent, that this concept leads to programs most easily verifiable by widest possible social consensus. Software for protection systems is represented in form of filled-in decision tables called cause/effect tables (cp. Figure 1), whose rows are associated with events, the occurrence of which gives rise to Boolean pre-conditions. By marking fields that belong to certain columns in such a table, and which are associated with specific actions, respectively, the user selects pre-conditions and specifies, that these actions shall be performed, if all corresponding pre-conditions become true in the sense of logical conjunctions.

The contents of cause/effect tables does not yield programs executable on the classical von Neumann computer architecture, but instead, is to be understood as a parameterisation configuring a multipurpose controller to perform a specific function. Since specifications are formulated in a commonly understandable, but nevertheless formal manner, which can be easily checked and verified by (social) consensus, and since specified operations can be directly interpreted and executed by machines without requiring complicated transformations and corresponding verification of correct implementation, cause/effect tables are the

Table 3. Evaluation of the suitability of programming languages for safety related programming according to the requirements of the safety integrity levels defined in IEC SC 65A

Programming Language	SIL 1	SIL 2	SIL 3	SIL 4
Ada 95	—	—	—	—
Ada 95 subset	*	*	—	—
Modula 2/3	—	—	—	—
Modula 2/3 subset	*	*	—	—
Pascal	—	—	—	—
Pascal subset	*	*	—	—
FORTRAN 77	—	—	—	—
FORTRAN 77 subset	*	—	—	—
C	—	—	—	—
C subset	—	—	—	—
C++ without C	*	—	—	—
PLM	—	—	—	—
PLM subset	—	—	—	—
Assembly languages	—	—	—	—
Assembly language subsets	—	—	—	—
Ladder Diagram (LD)	—	—	—	—
Ladder Diagram subset	*	—	—	—
Function Block Diagram (FBD)	—	—	—	—
Function Block Diagram subset	*	*	*	—
Structured Text (ST)	—	—	—	—
Structured Text subset	*	*	*	—
Instruction List (IL)	—	—	—	—
Instruction List subset	—	—	—	—
Sequential Function Chart (SFC)	—	—	—	—
Sequential Function Chart subset	*	*	*	—
BASIC	—	—	—	—
BASIC subset	—	—	—	—

— not recommendable, * recommendable with reservations

ideal form to program computer based control systems meeting highest safety requirements.

5 Function Block Diagrams with Verified Libraries

A programming paradigm allowing for software to be easy to grasp and to verify with respect to both source and object code is available in form of the graphical language Function Block Diagram (FBD) defined within the standard IEC 1131-3 [5]. With its long tradition in control engineering, graphical programming in form of function block diagrams as depicted in Figure 2 is already well established in automation technology.

The function block diagram language consists of four different structural elements, only:

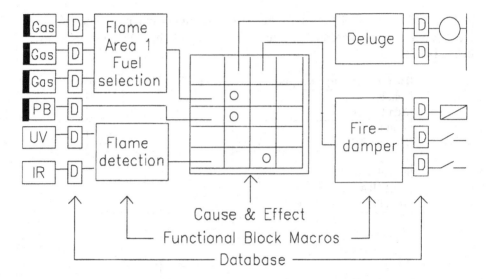

Fig. 1. A typical cause/effect table

1. instances of functions and function blocks, i.e., rectangular symbols,
2. dataflow lines, i.e., connection lines,
3. names, i.e., identifiers, and
4. (external) connection points.

Functions and function blocks are highly application dependent and re-usable elementary units of application programming on a higher abstraction level. In principle, they are subroutines having inputs and outputs of arbitrary data types, and are able to perform arbitrary processing functions. Functions do not have any internal states. After being executed they yield exactly one data element as a result, which may be multivalued. Multiple named instances, i.e., copies, can be created of function blocks. Each instance possesses an associated designator and a data structure, which contains its output and internal variables as well as possibly its input variables. All values of the output variables and the internal variables in such a data structure persist from one execution of a function block instance to the next. Therefore, invocation of a function block with the same arguments does not necessarily yield the same output values. This is necessary to be able to express feedback and internal storage behaviour. Only the input and output values are accessible outside a function block instance, i.e., a function block's internal variables are hidden from the outside and are, thus, strictly protected. By the connection lines within a function block diagram a data flow is represented.

Graphical, system independent program development in form of function block diagrams is very easy, and takes place in two steps:

1. *only once* building a library of functions and function blocks, and
2. *application specific* interconnection of functions and function block instances.

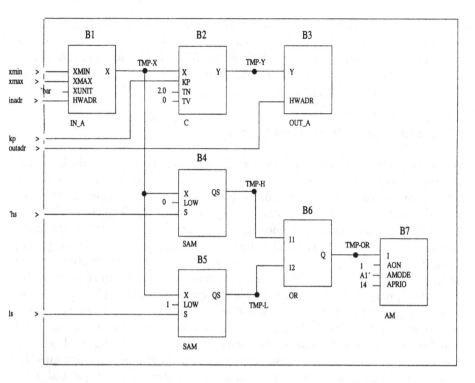

Fig. 2. Function block diagram of a program for pressure regulation and supervision

Corresponding to this development procedure, likewise the verification of programs constructed in the form of function block diagrams is carried out in two steps:

1. Before being released, first all functions and function blocks contained in a library are verified employing appropriate, usually formal methods. Such a rather expensive safety licensing needs to be carried through only once for a certain application area after a suitable set of function blocks has been identified. The licensing costs justified by the safety requirements can therefore be spread over many implementations, leading to relatively low costs for each single automation project. In general, rather few library elements are sufficient to formulate all programs in a particular area of process automation.

2. Then, for any given application program, only the correct implementation of the corresponding interconnection pattern of invoked functions and function block instances (i.e., a certain dataflow) needs to be verified. For this purpose the commonly understandable method of diverse back translation introduced in [8] can be employed in an easy and economical manner by automation engineers and official licensors on the interconnection level of programs composed of already verified function blocks, and having the quality and abstraction level of application oriented specifications. Owing to the

nature of this development method, the verification effort always remains small. In order to keep object code mapping function block diagrams as simple as possible, this programming paradigm may be supported by a corresponding architecture, which could be implemented in software, firmware, or directly in hardware, respectively.

6 Sequential Function Charts

A special class of control applications are sequence controls, in which control algorithms are defined as sequences of steps, to be elaborated in a sequential manner or — sometimes — concurrently. To describe such sequence controls, the standard IEC 1131-3 [5] defines the special language Sequential Function Chart (SFC), which is unique among programming languages. Its functionality can be characterised as partitioning of program organisation units into steps and transitions, which are linked by directed connections. With each step a set of actions, and with each transition a Boolean transition condition is associated.

The language Sequential Function Chart according to IEC 1131-3 [5] is, however, inadequate for safety related control applications, since its syntax permits the programming of deadlocks and to violate a number of safety rules sequential function charts are subjected to. To overcome these shortcomings with a minimum of additional language constructs, every sequential function chart must be enclosed in syntactical brackets in its entirety. The structure of sequential function charts is reflected by nesting special, new language elements, and becomes evident by explicit use of some constructs for the selection of control flow alternatives and the formulation of concurrency, respectively. Actions are expressed in form of sequential code and procedure calls directly within the bodies of steps and are, thus, associated with them. Hence, action qualifiers become superfluous. Finally, only one single form of branching into alternatively selectable sequences is provided.

To avoid inconsistent behaviour it can be syntactically enforced, that sequence controls always end with a step, and that the single branches of a parallel construct always commence and terminate with a step each. Within the branches of an alternative construct, however, besides steps even parallel constructs are permitted after the initial transition and before the terminating one. Owing to safety reasons and since the semantics of sequential function charts provide for the cyclic execution of the single steps, anyway, the possibility to program cycles in the control flow is deliberately relinquished. Actually, sequence controls are, however, frequently processed repeatedly in their entirety. This can be easily realised by embedding a sequential function chart into a loop construct.

7 A Language Subset Enabling Formal Verification

Only in very rare cases all features of high level programming languages are necessary to formulate the functionalities of the functions and function blocks required in control engineering. Therefore, we define an inherently safe language subset restricted to those constructs which are really necessary and, thus, indispensable. The correctness of programs formulated with this subset can be proven with adequate tool support by higher order logic (HOL), a typified variant of Church's higher predicate logic [7]. For the formal definition of the subset given in Table 4 we use an extension of the classical Backus Naur form (EBNF), and brackets [ ] to denote optional syntactical expressions as well as the symbols * and + to denote repetition of the corresponding marked expression at least zero times or once, respectively. By the attribute READ within the declaration of an interface variable it is ensured, that other modules are only permitted to read the declared variable, but not to write it. Variables, procedures and types are just names within this language. Expressions contain the usual Boolean and arithmetical operations.

Table 4. Formal syntax of a verifiable language subset

⟨module⟩ ::=	MODULE [(⟨name⟩)] [⟨mod-ext⟩]; [⟨intf-spec⟩]* [⟨decls⟩]+ MODEND;
⟨mod-ext⟩ ::=	EXTEND (⟨name⟩ [,⟨name⟩]+)
⟨intf-spec⟩ ::=	INTERFACE (⟨name⟩) ⟨intf-decl⟩* ;
⟨intf-decl⟩ ::=	⟨intf-var-decl⟩	⟨intf-proc-decl⟩
⟨intf-var-decl⟩ ::=	SPC ⟨name⟩ : ⟨type⟩ READ;
⟨intf-proc-decl⟩ ::=	SPC ⟨name⟩ : PROC ⟨lst-of-par⟩ ⟨return-type⟩;
⟨decls⟩ ::=	⟨var-decl⟩	⟨proc-decl⟩
⟨var-decl⟩ ::=	DCL ⟨name⟩ : ⟨type⟩;
⟨proc-decl⟩ ::=	⟨name⟩ : PROC ⟨lst-of-par⟩ ⟨return-type⟩; ⟨body⟩ END;
⟨lst-of-par⟩ ::=	(⟨par-decl⟩ [, ⟨par-decl⟩]*)
⟨par-decl⟩ ::=	⟨name⟩ : ⟨type⟩
⟨body⟩ ::=	[⟨var-decl⟩]+ [⟨stmt-seq⟩]
⟨stmt-seq⟩ ::=	[⟨stmt⟩;]*
⟨stmt⟩ ::=	(⟨stmt-seq⟩)	⟨assign-stmt⟩	⟨cond-stmt⟩	⟨while-stmt⟩
⟨assign-stmt⟩ ::=	⟨variable⟩ := ⟨expr⟩
⟨cond-stmt⟩ ::=	IF ⟨Bool-expr⟩ THEN ⟨stmt-seq⟩ [ELSE ⟨stmt-seq⟩] FIN
⟨while-stmt⟩ ::=	WHILE ⟨Bool-expr⟩ REPEAT ⟨stmt-seq⟩ END

8 Safety Related Real Time Programming Languages

Comparing the requirements for real time languages and systems with the capabilities of available languages, it becomes obvious, that the latter still do not, or only in rather rudimentary form, provide various elements being especially important for the development of dependable software. Without any doubt the language PEARL [2] can be considered as the most powerful high level programming language for the formulation of real time and process automation applications. With its clear concepts and its unmatched, application adequate expressive means it clearly stands out among all other real time programming languages, which is the reason why it is so well suited for industrial applications and is increasingly being used for teaching purposes. On the other hand, the language was not specially developed with safety related control applications in mind. To fulfill the requirements of safety related real time programming on the safety integrity level SIL 1, in addition to the functionalities already provided by the present version of PEARL the language constructs, operating system and runtime system services as well as the verification tools as mentioned in Table 5 are needed.

Table 5. Real time functionalities enhancing safety

Additional language constructs enhancing safety
— Application oriented synchronisation constructs
— Supervision of the occurrence of events within time windows
— Supervision of sequences of event occurrences
— Temporal supervision of synchronisation operations
— Temporal supervision of resource claims
— Ability to bound the execution times of all statements
— Structured handling of exceptional situations
— Availability of current states of tasks and resources
— Restriction to static features, if necessary
Operating system services enhancing safety
— Inherent prevention of deadlocks
— Guaranteeing system schedulability
— Feasible scheduling algorithms
— Early detection and handling of transient overload situations
— Determination of overall and residual task execution times
— Predictable run time behaviour – also and particularly in exceptional situations
— Precise time information
— Precise timing of operations
— Dynamic reconfiguration of distributed systems upon error occurrence
— Support of software diversity
Tools for program verification
— Extension of every program unit with semiformal pre/post-conditions and invariants
— Application oriented simulation accounting for the operating system overhead
— Interrupt simulation
— Interrupt and event monitoring
— State tracing

Complexity and costs of the realisation of larger projects in the area of real time application programming require to design systems very systematically and with continuous consideration for their further development. Employing a parallel object model resembles the development process of larger real time systems and, hence, constitutes a very promising approach to overcome the problems of software safety by introducing inherently safely applicable and, thus, safety related statements. Building on PEARL and the functionalities mentioned in Table 5, to use the paradigm of object orientation essentially the concept of multiple access interfaces to a module is required, only. This allows to improve the readability and maintainability of the resulting code, since a module implementation structure can be defined without special regard to the possible applications of a module, and the module's interfaces can be individually designed for a specific use each, thus completely documenting the module's intended purpose. This way, a module is no longer just a simple conglomerate of data, its state, and its methods, but a processing unit with documented purpose.

9 Safety Related Real Time Programming

Safety related process automation must guarantee, that the occurrence of arbitrary failures does not lead to inadmissable and hazardous states of the devices controlled. The safety relevant part of an application is to be reduced to a minimum, with the safety critical functions to be clearly separated from all other ones, and from each other as well. Constructive exclusion of faults is the most effective provision to meet safety requirements. With respect to software, fault prevention by perfection should be aimed for and, additionally, for safety related control applications at least two diverse channels are required. According to the principle

"Keep It Small and Simple"

one has to restrict oneself to the really necessary and discipline one's wishes. In any case utmost simplicity is to be strived for. Since the definition of the tolerable maximum risk determining the safety of an application also depends on socio-cultural considerations, software safety licensing should always be based on methods allowing to be applied with widest possible social consensus. Indeed, verification methods have to be rigorous, but not necessarily formal: the more commonly understandable a method is, the more suitable it is. The more safety critical a system is, the more restrictive design guidelines are to be set and observed, and the more restrictive methods must be employed. Always the human cognitive capabilities have to be accounted for.

10 Outlook

This paper addresses a serious and pressing problem. It does not present solutions to all questions still open in software safety licensing, but a beginning is made which is practically feasible and applicable to a wide class of safety related control problems. We especially pointed out the influence of human aspects on the process of program development. Actually, these human factors are so far being neglected in many — or virtually all? — programming concepts. The majority of these methods refer to formalised approaches and computer support, with the mathematical and technical aspects of tools always playing the main rôle. In contrast to this, our approach is particularly oriented at ergonomic criteria. It is a step forward towards a software engineering paradigm featuring simple, inherently safe programming — and as a consequence, better specification — and design integrated verification, not only having the quality of mathematical rigour but also being oriented at *non-experts' capabilities of comprehension*. This paradigm should replace empirical a posteriori validation (testing), and facilitate safety licensing. Regarded as a social process of reaching a consensus, program verification is facilitated by features such as graphical programming, re-use of pre-engineered and already certified components, specification level programming by filling in decision tables and, generally, by striving for utmost simplicity in all relevant aspects. To keep everything as small and simple as possible, one should always discipline one's wishes.

Further work should focus on the facilitation of re-using software components once they have been proven correct, and on the correctness proof of program packages constructed on the basis of such components employing as simple and easily understandable methods as possible. Future developments must aim to create system environments which, in the framework of distributed process control systems and programmable logic controllers, are suitable to carry out safety related functions, and whose architectures inherently support ergonomic software verification based of mathematically founded proving techniques. This requirement is *radically* new: whereas the development of computers during the last half century was solely dominated by aspects such as processing speed, capacity, and performance, it is now the time to address the increasingly pressing problem of software safety, and to orient computer architectures at the human needs as well as to optimise them with respect to human capabilities.

References

1. **DESCARTES, R.**: *Medidationes de prima philosophia, in quibus Dei existentia et animae humanae a corpore distinctio demonstrantur*. Paris, 1641.
2. **DIN 66 253-2**: *Programmiersprache PEARL 90*. Berlin-Cologne: Beuth Verlag, 1998.
3. **HALANG, W.A., FRIGERI, A.H., LICHTENECKER, R., STEINMANN, U. and WENDLAND, K.**: *Methodenlehre sicherheitsgerichteter Echtzeitprogrammierung*. Schriftenreihe der Bundesanstalt für Arbeitsschutz und Arbeitsmedizin. Bremerhaven: Verlag für neue Wissenschaft, 1998.
4. **HATTON, L.**: *Safer C: Developing for High-Integrity and Safety-Critical Systems*. McGraw-Hill, 1995.
5. **IEC 1131-3**: *Programmable Controllers, Part 3: Programming Languages*. Geneva: International Electrotechnical Commission, 1992.
6. **IEC SC65A(Secretariat)123**: *Functional Safety of Electrical/Electronic/Programmable Electronic Systems: Generic Aspects — Part 1: General Requirements*. Geneva: International Electrotechnical Commission, 1992.
7. **JOYCE, J.J. and SEGER, C.-J.H.** (Eds.): *Higher Order Logic Theorem Proving and Its Applications*. Lecture Notes in Computer Science, Vol. 780. Berlin-Heidelberg-New York: Springer-Verlag, 1993.
8. **KREBS, H. and HASPEL, U.**: Ein Verfahren zur Software-Verifikation. *Regelungstechnische Praxis rtp* 26, 73 – 78, 1984.

ANSI-C in Safety Critical Applications
Lessons-Learned from Software Evaluation

Arndt Lindner

Institut für Sicherheitstechnologie (ISTec) GmbH
Forschungsgelände
D-85748 Garching bei München
Germany
lia@istecmuc.grs.de

Abstract. The Institute for Safety Technology (ISTec) has been involved in software reliability research and assessment for more than 25 years. The emphasis has been placed on applications in nuclear power plants, especially on software based instrumentation and control (I&C) systems important to safety. In this context potential sources of weakness in ANSI C programs, which may be error prone have been investigated from a practical point of view. The paper describes essential results of this study; it gives not a complete list of weakness points, but essential examples are shown. From the potential sources of weakness recommendations are derived to improve the C code also in view of software modification and maintenance, which is important because of the long life-time of I&C systems in nuclear power plants.

1 INTRODUCTION

The Institute for Safety Technology (ISTec), formerly part of the Gesellschaft für Anlagen- und Reaktorsicherheit (GRS) has been involved in software reliability research and assessment for more then 25 years. ISTec has gained extensive experience in this field /2/ - /5/. Besides general tasks of software reliability the interest has been focused on applications in nuclear power plants, especially on software based instrumentation and control (I&C) systems important to safety. However, also applications in other fields like transportation, aviation, etc. have been dealt with.

The paper describes the experience that ISTec gathered in the evaluation of safety critical software in the nuclear field manually written by programmers in ANSI-C. From this experience and additional knowledge about the use of C in other fields of industry recommendations for the use of ANSI-C in safety critical applications will be outlined.

2 Programming guidelines

The programming language C is frequently used in non-safety industrial applications. Compilers, linkers and locators for C code are available and often used during several years. Therefore, it is certainly true that many well educated C programmers with long-term experience are available. Both facts are important in view of design and implementation of high quality software. For that reason vendors of software based I&C systems use C also in safety critical applications.

To avoid a wide spread of different idioms the American National Standards Institute set up a standard for C (ANSI-C) in the years 1983 to 1989. The ANSI-C standard became a de-facto international standard. The standard should support many kinds of applications and should not be restricted the programming language C. For this reason a set of features is included in the ANSI-C that must be kept apart from safety critical applications or which require special evaluation. The vendors of safety critical software therefore design special programming guidelines for safety critical C programs.

In the field of I&C systems important to safety in nuclear power plants the software will be in operation for about 10 to 20 years. Therefore the aspects of software modification and maintenance must be considered very carefully. Program constructions which can be error prone in the case of software modification must be avoided.

Programming guidelines are necessary to reduce the degrees of freedom in the language C. In the nuclear field there is an explicit requirement in IEC 880 /1/ to use detailed programming guidelines for each programming language, but also in other fields like transport such guidelines are used /7/. Comparing several programming guidelines one can find different even contrasting requirements. The following table gives an example.

Table 1. Example of different requirements of programming guidelines

programming guidelines "A"	programming guidelines "B"
Substitution of reserved words, operators, and special characters is not allowed.	Some operator characters (e.g., "&&", "&", "|", "¦", etc.) must be substituted by macros (e.g., "&&" by "AND", "&" by "BITAND", "¦" by "NOT", "|" by "BITOR", etc.)

Both recommendations are well founded. The substitution of operators will enhance readability of the source code (e.g., "NOT" and "BITOR" can be distinguished easier as "!" and "|"). Non substitution of operators will maintain clear C syntax. It is important to strictly fulfill this requirement in a project.

In programming guidelines only the degrees of freedom of the programming language are reduced by forbidding several programming constructs. In the case of C it is necessary also to extend the language by several requirements.

It is an obvious fact that some features of the language C as dynamic memory allocation or pointer arithmetic's are banned from safety critical applications. Therefore, such features are not dealt with.

3 DATA TYPE TEST

3.1 Problem

An ANSI-C compiler does not check the types of unstructured data. The following construction will be compiled without any remark, warning or error message and transformed to computable machine code.

```
unsigned char a;
float         b;
   .
   .
   .
a = b;
   .
```

An implicit type transformation is performed. This type transformation may be associated with loss of accuracy or loss of data. Therefore the programmer must use unstructured data types very carefully. This must be observed especially using logical variables, which will be dealt with later on.

In contrast to the fact mentioned above at the highest diagnosis level some compilers generate for function calls with constant parameters (declared with #define pre-processor statements) remarks like

```
... AT LINE n OF xxxx.c: argument #1 does not match
with prototype
```

The consequence is, that for practical reasons programmers choose a lower diagnosis level which suppress remarks. The result is that also important and helpful remarks are suppressed like remarks that give hints to errors in the use of comments.

3.2 Recommendations

1. Carefully use of data types.
2. Type transformations should be done explicit and should be commented in detail.
3. Source code check with compiler switches or external code checkers that support type test also for unstructured data types.

4 LOGICAL VARIABLES AND LOGICAL EXPRESSIONS

4.1 Problem

The ANSI-C standard bears inconsequences regarding logical variables and logical expressions. On the one hand it defines logical operators (&&, ||, !), on the other hand there is no data type defined for logical data. In addition, there are operators (&, |, ~) defined for bit by bit logical operations which work in a totally different way.

For both kinds of logical operators the same standard data types are used. This circumstance gives potential for severe programming errors, which are hard to identify.

The main differences between the bit by bit logical operators and the Boolean logical operators are shown in the following table.

Table 2. Differences between bit by bit logical operators and Boolean logical operators

	bit by bit "logical" operators	logical operators
result	bit by bit combination examples: 4 & 5 result in 4 4 | 5 result in 5 ~4 result in -5	"0" or "1" examples: 4 && 5 result in 1 4 || 5 result in 1 !4 result in 0

computation	complete computation
	
	example:
	a = 0;
	b = 1;
	c = (a & b) & ++a;
	result: a and c are 1 (the result of ++a, It must be considered, that at first the expression ++a is carried out. Therefore the "a" left in the whole expression is really a+1!)
		computation is done strictly from left expressions to right ones; if the result is non-ambiguous, the computation of the expressions is stopped (incomplete computation)
		example:
		a = 0;
		b = 1;
		c = (a && b) && ++a;
		result: a and c are 0, ++a will not be carried out

Because of the possible incomplete computation of logical expressions programming guidelines often ban the use of increment and decrement operators on the right hand side of the logical operators "&&" and "||".

The ANSI-C standard defines the value which is interpreted as "false" by 0 and the value which is interpreted as "true" by 1. Nevertheless each value unequal to 0 is interpreted as true. Therefore a comparison of two logical variables where each is interpreted as true can yield the value false. The following example shows the problem

```
      .
      .
      .
  #define true 0xff;

  typedef unsigned char BOOL;

  BOOL function do_anyting()
  {
      .
    a = b + 1;
      .
    return a > b;
  }
      .
    if ( do_anything() == true)
      statement_1;
    else
        statement_2;
    if ( do_anything() )
      statement_1;
    else
      statement_2;
      .
      .
```

In the first "if-statement" the "statement_2" is carried out. In the second "if-statement" the "statement_1" is carried out.

4.2 Recommendations

1. Define a unique data type for logical data.
2. Use additional tools to check the source code (strong data type check)
3. Use logical operators (&&, ||, !) only with logical data.
4. Do not compare logical data with "==". (That means, if someone needs an equivalence relation for "a" and "b" he should implement "(a && b) || (!a && !b)" not "a == b").

5 if-statements

5.1 Problem

This problem must be seen close to the problem of logical expressions. Especially in the implementation of software which is close to the hardware (e.g., operation systems, device drivers, interrupt handlers, etc.) the feature that an if-statement can be controlled by any unstructured data type is often used to compact the code and/or to increase computation speed. This may lead to errors in the case of code modification, even if the original code is working correctly.

Another problem is also close to the above chapter. Lets assume "true" and "false" are defined as values for the logical variables. Often one can find expressions like

```
if ( a == true ) ...
```

where a is a logical variable, even in programming tutorials. Nobody will write code like

```
if ( a && true ) ... or if ( a || false ) ..
```

because everybody knows "a && true" and "a || false" are equivalent to "a". But in the same way "a == true" is equivalent to "a" (assuming "==" is intended to be the equivalence relation for the logical variables).

5.2 Recommendations

1. The control expression of an if-statement should always be a logical variable or a logical expression.
2. Avoid over-engineering by implementing unnecessary expressions like "a == true" for a logical variable "a".

6 Increment and decrement operators

6.1 Problem

Increment and decrement operators are often forbidden on the right hand side of logical expressions. That is why the expression may be calculated incompletely.

From the example in chapter 4.1 it can be seen, that increment and decrement operators may be a source of errors in any expression and not only in logical expressions. The variable "a" in the sub-expression "(a & b)" is already incremented by "++a". That means "(a & b) & ++a" is equivalent to "((a + 1) & b) & (a+1)" but if the increment operator is used in the postfix notation "a++" than the expression "(a + & b) & a++)" is equivalent to "(a & b) & (a+1)".

The use of increment and decrement can be very error prone especially in view of code modification and maintenance.

6.2 Recommendations

1. Increment and decrement operators should not be used in any expression. They should be allowed only as single statement.

7 Integral promotions

7.1 Problem

The problems resulting from Integral Promotion are clearly described in /6/. The following example from /6/ should illustrate the problem

```
#define START_OPERATION   0x5A

unsigned char c;

void test(void)
{
  if (c == ~START_OPERATION)
    anything_to_do();
}
```

The function anything_to_do() will not be executed at any time. That means, with all possible values for the variable "c" the comparison

```
(c == ~START_OPERATION)
```

will result to false. The operator "~" (bit by bit negation) requires integral promotion. Therefore the value of START_OPERATION will be extended to two bytes. ~START_OPERATION results in ~0x005A, that is 0xFFA5. Since the variable "c" can only reach a value of 0x00FF the high byte of the extended variable "c" is always zero, because of the type of "c". The comparison is than

```
if (0x005A == ~0x005A)
```

equivalent to

```
if (0x005A == 0xFFA5) .
```

This is never true.

The problem can only be solved by explicit casting.

```
if (c == (unsigned char) ~START_OPERATION)
```

The same error will occur in the statement

```
if (c == ~d)
```

where "c" and "d" are of the same type "unsigned char". Even in this case explicit casting is necessary. That means, the type of "d" will be changed although "d" is of the same type like "c" and it is combined only with "c".

Similar effects can occur in arithmetic expressions /6/. In /6/ it is recommended to check the particular compiler with examples.

7.2 Recommendations

1. The recommendation of /6/ ("...check your compiler with ... examples.") is not a good recommendation, because code is generated that depends on the compiler.
2. Use variables and constants very carefully, especially if they are one-byte types. Use explicit casting if necessary.
3. If it is not completely clear in which way the compiler works explicit casting should be used.

8 Summary

The paper describes from a practical point of view potential sources of weakness in C programs, which may be errors or can lead to errors during software modification and maintenance. It is not a complete list, but essential examples are shown. From the potential sources of weakness recommendations are derived to improve the C code bearing in mind also the software modification and maintenance necessities, which are of particular interest due to the long life-time of I&C systems in nuclear power plants.

9 Literature

1. IEC 880, Software for computers in safety systems of nuclear power stations, CEI (1986)
2. Bastl, W., Bock, H.-W.: German qualification and assessment of Digital I&C systems important to safety. Reliability Engineering and System Safety 59 (1998) 163-170
3. Brummer, J., Kersken, M., Lindner, A., Miedl, H.: Validation of Transformation Tools. In Licensing of Computer-Based Systems Important to Safety, OECD/GD(97)91 Paris (1997) 400-411
4. Lindner, A., Miedl. H.: Methodology and Tools for Independent Verification and Validation of Computerized I&C Systems important to Safety. In Proc. of IAEA Spec. Meeting on Computerized Reactor Protection and Safety Related Systems in Nuclear Power Plants, IAEA-IWG-NPPCI-98/1, IAEA, Vienna (1998) 127-138
5. Miedl. H.: Reverse Transformation of Normed Source Code. In Cacciabue, C., C., Papazoglu, I., A. (eds.): Probabilistic Safety Assessment and Management, ESREL'96-PSAM-III. Springer-Verlag, London (1996) 1139-1144
6. Rohner, A.: C-Compiler und Sicherheitsaspekte. Design & Elektronik-EmbeddedControl, (06.03.1996) 71-77
7. Edwards, P., D., Rivett, R., S.: Towards an Automotiv 'Safer Subset' of C. In: Daniel, P. (ed.): Safecomp 97. Springer-Verlag, London (1997) 185-196

Applications

A Structured Approach to the Formal Certification of Safety of Computer Aided Development Tools[*]

Piergiorgio Bertoli[1], Alessandro Cimatti[1], Fausto Giunchiglia[1], Paolo Traverso[1]

Mechanized Reasoning Group
IRST - Institute for Scientific and Technological Research
38050 - Povo - Trento, Italy
Phone: + 39 461 314438, Fax: + 39 461 314591
{bertoli,cimatti,fausto,leaf}@irst.itc.it

Abstract. Safety-critical systems are often designed using development support tools which perform translations of high-level specifications into lower-level counterparts. The correctness of the translation is critical to the safety of the resulting systems. However, using non failure-safe components to implement translators is desirable because of the extremely high cost of certified components. In order to ensure the correct behavior of development tools, we adopt a solution based on the idea of verifying each of their executions. In order to perform the verification in an automatic and efficient way, we follow an innovative approach, by distinguishing an off-line and an on-line verification phases. Each proof in the two phases is guaranteed correct by designing the certifying tools according to a logging-and-checking architecture. We describe the off-line and on-line logging-and-checking methodology, its application in the frame of an industrial project, and the ongoing logging-and-checking redesign of a state-of-the-art prover which we intend to use in future applications.

1 Introduction

Safety critical software is often developed using support which allow users to write specifications or to implement programs at a suitable high level of abstraction, and to generate automatically the concrete system which runs on hardware platforms. For instance, machine loadable software implementing on-board Automatic Train Protection functions might be implemented through a tool providing a high level special purpose visual programming language. We call the tools which support the development and implementation of safety critical systems, *(safety-critical) computer aided development* tools. Such development tools are indeed critical themselves. If they introduce errors, the final system is not guaranteed to behave safely, regardless of its design.

---
[*] Financial support for part of the work described in this paper was provided by an ANSALDO - IRST project, Contract Number 158/242140 (NA). Paolo Pecchiari has provided unvaluable contribution to this project. We thank all the people of ANSALDO and UNION SWITCH & SIGNAL we have been working with in the project: Bruno Pietra, Joe Profeta, Dario Romano and Bing Yu.

Several computer aided development tools are equipped with components which translate the designer input – e.g. high level specifications, programs in high level languages – into data suitable for the actual run-time system – e.g. actual machine loadable code (see figure 1). Such translations are often complex, and their safety is sometimes harder to be guaranteed than the safety of the user-provided input. Consider for instance, the compilation of a program written in a high level programming language into binary code.

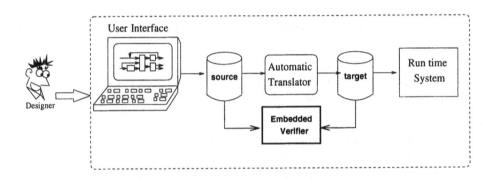

Fig. 1. Computer Aided Development Tools

The goal of our work is to provide a structured approach to the problem of guaranteeing the safety of the translation steps performed by computer aided development tools. Our approach bases on the design of a verifier embedded into the computer aided development tool, called *Embedded Verifier* (see figure 1). For each run of the translator, the Embedded Verifier takes as input the source and the target of the translation and verifies formally (by generating a formal proof) that the translation has been performed correctly. Thus we formally verify the correctness of the result of each translation, rather than proving the correctness of the translation algorithm or code; this is a shift w.r.t. standard practice in formal verification. There are some main motivations for this choice. First, given the input and the output of the translation, it is often simpler and faster to verify whether the output is a correct translation of the input than verifying the translator itself. Second, most computer aided development tools are implemented on top of commercial, off-the-shelf hardware/software platforms (COTS), which are not guaranteed to be fail-safe. For instance, the tool might run on a Pentium, with Windows-NT as operating system. This allows companies to enlarge the usability of such tools and to contain their cost, by avoiding the use of expensive certified hardware and software platforms [12]. In these cases, the formal verification of the translation algorithm or even of its code is not sufficient, because of the possible occurrence of platform-induced runtime errors. It is instead still possible for the Embedded Verifier to detect a wrong result of the translation due to some of the possible run time errors.

Since the Embedded Verifier is part of the safety critical computer aided development tool, it has to satisfy the following requirements.

Requirement 1. Since development tools are operated by users which are not experts in formal verification, the Embedded Verifier must perform the proof automatically. Moreover, the proof must be easily understood and validated by end-users. Finally, since in most cases users need to interact with the development tool, the verification process is subject to time constraints.

Requirement 2. In order to guarantee that the verification is performed correctly, any tool used to achieve it must be itself certified, i.e. there must be a way to guarantee that the Embedded Verifier is itself correct.

In order to achieve such requirements, our approach is based on two main steps:

Step 1. The full formal verification of the correctness of each translation is in general a difficult theorem proving problem. An Embedded Verifier which performs this task automatically and efficiently (Requirement 1) appears to be unfeasible. We decompose this task in two parts: the task of the Embedded Verifier is to prove that the result of each translation satisfies some simple conditions, which are designed to be sufficient to guarantee the correctness of the translation. The task of the Embedded Verifier can be performed automatically and efficiently. The second task is to actually prove that the simplified conditions guarantee the correctness of the translation. This task is performed off-line and once for all, using a prover which is different from the Embedded Verifier and can be operated interactively by experts in formal verification. This decomposition of the proof of correctness of the translation into an on-line and an off-line proof allows us to achieve Requirement 1.

Step 2. According to Requirement 2, both tools used to perform the formal verification (the Embedded Verifier for the on-line proof, and a different prover for the off-line proof) must be certified. We decompose both provers into two independent programs, a Logger and a Checker. The (complex) Logger performs the hard task of finding a proof; the (simple) Checker the easy task of checking that the proof is correct. If the Logger generates a wrong proof, and the Checker is correct, the Checker will not accept it. Thus only the Checker is critical; but its correctness can be trusted, since it is extremely simple. This allows us to achieve Requirement 2 in practice: the correct execution of verification tools (which might be very complex, e.g. megabytes of code) is guaranteed by that of a very small and simple kernel, e.g. few lines of code.

The paper is structured as follows. Section 2 and 3 describe step 1 and 2, respectively. Section 4 describes a successful application of the approach in the framework an industrial project. The final sections of the papers describe related work and draw some conclusions.

2 Step 1: Off-Line/On-Line Verification Decomposition

Intuitively, verifying a translation means to verify that a given notion of equivalence holds between the source and the target of the translation. Given a formal semantics to the source and the target, it is possible to define a formal notion of semantic equivalence which corresponds to the intuitive one of "equivalent behavior". In general, we address the problem of proving the correctness of a translation from an expression of a language $\mathcal{L}$ to an expression of another language $\mathcal{L}'$; we will refer to it as the *translation verification problem*:

Let T be a translator from a source language $\mathcal{L}$ to a target language $\mathcal{L}'$. Let "$\equiv_{sem}$" be a formally defined notion of semantic equivalence. Let $\overline{P}$ be an expression in $\mathcal{L}$. Let $\overline{P'}$ be the expression produced by the execution of T on $\overline{P}$. Prove the correctness of the execution of T by showing the semantic equivalence between $\overline{P}$ and $\overline{P'}$:

$$\overline{P} \equiv_{sem} \overline{P'} \tag{1}$$

In general, proving the semantic equivalence of two expressions of two different languages is too difficult to be dealt with in an automatic and efficient way by the Embedded Verifier. Our divide-and-conquer style solution consists in decomposing the problem of verifying the correctness of the translation (by proving (1)) into two problems. We identify some "simplified" verification conditions "$\equiv_{simp}$", which both imply the semantic equivalence, *and* are amenable to an automatic and efficient on-line verification. The proof of semantic equivalence can therefore be split in a proof of the "simplified" verification conditions (2), and a proof of the fact that they imply semantic equivalence (3):

$$\overline{P} \equiv_{simp} \overline{P'} \tag{2}$$

$$\forall P, P' : (P \equiv_{simp} P') \supset (P \equiv_{sem} P') \tag{3}$$

(2) and (3) are a correct refinement of the formal specification of the translation verification problem, since they imply (1). The proof of (2) is simple "by design", both because it involves concrete expressions (the particular input $\overline{P}$ and output $\overline{P'}$ of one translation), and because of the way "$\equiv_{simp}$" has been defined. This allows for the development of the Embedded Verifier as a custom, automatic and efficient on-line prover, "tailored" over the particular equivalence theorem to be proved. The proof of (3) guarantees that the simplified notion of equivalence (2) entails the given notion of semantic equivalence (1), i.e. that the design of the Embedded Verifier is correct. This proof can be performed off-line, once-for-all, *a priori*. In general, this proof is rather complex, both because of the universal quantification (it is done for all possible inputs and outputs of the translation), and because of the gap between the arbitrarily complex "$\equiv_{sem}$" definition and the "easy to check" alternative "$\equiv_{simp}$". Therefore, it is practically necessary to use a generic, full blown state-of-the art prover to perform the proof. This will be operated interactively by theorem proving experts, and the resulting proof is delivered as a part of the system. Notice that it is not required that the (once-for-all) proof is performed efficiently or automatically.

To resume: our approach envisages two provers: the Embedded Verifier which is delivered as part of the computer aided development tool and runs automatically after each translation, proving the one theorem it hardcodes; and a generic prover which is used only once, to guarantee that the design of the Embedded Verifier is correct.

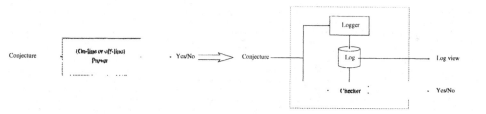

Fig. 2. The logging-and-checking approach.

3 Step 2: Tool Certification via Logging-and-Checking

According with Requirement 2, each of the two provers used for the on-line and off-line proofs must be certified. We adopt the logging-and-checking architecture, shown in Figure 2, as a solution to this problem for both provers. In the logging-and-checking architecture, a proving component is specified in terms of two independent programs, a Logger and a Checker. Intuitively, the approach relies on decoupling a small, compact and trustable critical section (the Checker) from the overall system, making the remaining part (the Logger) non critical. This is achieved as follows. The Logger generates a Log, containing (a description of) the proof of the conjecture. The Checker certifies the correctness of the proof by checking that the Log actually represents a proof of the conjecture. Since the Checker only needs to check that the Log is compliant to a set of given rules (the rules of the logic used by the prover, e.g. first order logic), its implementation is in general much simpler than that of the Logger, and its validation is often feasible by simple code inspection. Thus, the Checker can be assumed to be correct. The representation in the figure is conceptual; when instantiating the logging-and-checking architecture to the on-line prover, the input theorem is represented, in the concrete, by the two expressions $\overline{P}$ and $\overline{P'}$. Critical software components are shadowed in the figure. The Logger is *not* critical, since every error it introduces is caught by the Checker, which causes the Logger's execution to be rejected.

Of course, in case the Checker is run on a hardware/software platform which is not guaranteed to be fail-safe (e.g. a platform composed of COTS), an incorrect execution of the Checker is possible due to a platform-induced runtime failure, leading to an unsafe behavior of the overall system: no absolute guarantee of safety can ever be achieved. Our achievement is nevertheless very significant, even in the case of unsafe platforms: by making the correctness of the overall system dependent only on a selected, trusted section of code, we improve its safety. Intuitively, the probability of an error occurring in the execution of the (independent and trusted) Checker such that it annihilates a correspondent error occurred in the corresponding execution of the Logger is much lower than that of an error occurring in the (untrusted) Logger itself, or in the untrusted Translator.

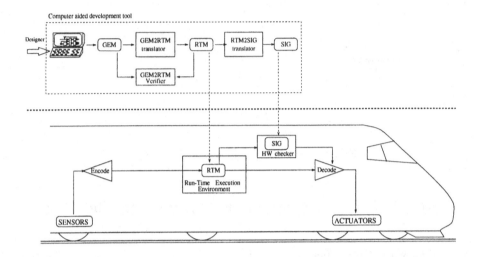

Fig. 3. The computer aided development tool for the reactive run-time system

4 An industrial case study

The methodology presented so far was applied in a technology transfer project [2], aiming at the on-line certification of a translator of a safety critical computer aided development tool which is part of one of UNION SWITCH & SIGNAL's next-generation products [12]. The tool is used to develop safety critical reactive systems, such as Automatic Train Protection systems (ATPs), which cyclically read the train speed and position from sensors, checks whether the speed is consistent with a "safety speed curve", and drives the train breaking devices accordingly.

Figure 3 depicts the architecture instantiated on a safety critical railways application. Two subsystems can be identified: the on-board subsystem (below the dotted line), and the Computer Aided Development tool (above). On board, the "Run-Time Execution Environment" is a platform for the execution of reactive programs in RTM format (which is a binary, loadable machine language). The "Run-Time Execution Environment" is based on COTS technology. The correctness of the run-time execution is guaranteed by a fail-safe, very simple (and thus cheap) Hardware Checker. This Checker compares information on the status of each RTM execution with a set of criteria which must be satisfied for the execution to be correct (SIG in figure).[2] Data from sensors and to actuators are encoded/decoded (with Cyclic Redundant Checksums and Residue Number Systems) to protect from data corruption by means of simple, fail-safe components.

---

[2] The details of the HW Checker cannot be disclosed in this paper since they involve proprietary information. However, the details are not necessary to the goal of this paper.

At development time, the user interacts with the Computer Aided Development tool, by specifying an application program on the graphical interface. The program is stored in GEM (Generic Entity Model) format, a simple high level language. The Computer Aided Development Tool is responsible for the translation of the application program into RTM format, which can then be safely executed. The Computer Aided Development tool is also based on COTS technology. It is a complex software package, written in a high level language, including graphical libraries, compiled on a conventional compiler, running on a portable PC, and intended to be operated on the field by design engineers. The project addressed the on-line verification of the (safety critical) GEM2RTM Translator (in figure 3), generating RTM programs from GEM programs.

The resulting on-line prover (GEM2RTM Embedded Verifier in figure 3) was developed according to the methodology described in this paper.

GEM and RTM programs can be thought of as cyclically acquiring data from sensors, executing the corresponding instructions, and delivering outputs to actuators. GEM and RTM programs are given semantics as functions mapping finite sequences of inputs into sequences of outputs. Intuitively, a GEM program G and an RTM program R are semantically equivalent if they feature the same input/output behavior for all possible sequences of inputs. The formal definition of this notion relies over a state-based semantics definition of GEM and RTM instructions, and can be found in [2].

The definition of the simplified equivalence "$\equiv_{simp}$", exploited in the on-line proof phase, relies on the definition of a mapping T between GEM instructions and (sequences of) RTM instructions, and on the existence of a mapping M between the variables of G and those of R. The T mapping must be semantically preserving: corresponding instructions exhibit corresponding state transformations. A sequence $\mathcal{R}_M$ of instances of translation rules, representing the translator's behavior, is used to witness this property. The simplified conditions are described as a set of structural conditions over G, R, M, $\mathcal{R}_M$ and T; they are formally defined in [2]. If two particular programs $\overline{R}$ and $\overline{G}$ are such that $\overline{G} \equiv_{simp} \overline{R}$, we say that they satisfy the Syntactic Verification Conditions. The reduction given by the off-line/on-line decomposition is that the Syntactic Verification Conditions are much simpler to prove than semantic equivalence.

The correctness of the off-line/on-line decomposition is guaranteed by proving Theorem 3:

$$\forall G, R : (G \equiv_{simp} R \supset G \equiv_{sem} R) \tag{4}$$

where the corresponding definitions for "$\equiv_{simp}$" and "$\equiv_{sem}$" are used. The proof is performed by induction on the length of input sequences and on the structure of programs. The off-line verification was carried out manually. Nevertheless, a bug was found in the design of the translator during the off-line phase. In particular, one of the translation rules $\mathcal{R}_M$ was not semantics preserving. Since $\mathcal{R}_M$ is derived from the informal specification of the translator, it turned out that the translator itself implemented a non semantically preserving transformation. In the future we plan to mechanically verify the off-line proofs.

The Logging and Checking approach to the certification problem for the on-line phase was very valuable in this particular problem. Indeed, proving the Syntactic Verification Conditions requires to identify witnesses for the mappings (namely M, T and $\mathcal{R}_M$), and may require a lot of search. Since the Logger is not critical, it was possible to exploit the custom nature of the problem and use the data structure provided by the translator (e.g. the symbol table) in order to drive the search (e.g. the correspondence M from GEM to RTM variables).

The project required the design of an efficient Checker which could be understood and validated by the user. This deeply influenced its design, resulting in a custom program, containing a number of special purpose decision procedures, whose code can be directly mapped to the formal specifications of the Syntactic Verification Conditions. The developed Checker is a few hundred lines of C code, with an extremely simple control structure. The developed Verifier is extremely efficient. It is able to verify the translation of thousands of instructions in a few seconds.

In parallel to this application, we have undertaken a project whose goal is that of obtaining a general purpose prover adhering to the logging-and-checking architecture. We chose to undergo a redesign of ACL2 [6], one of the existing state-of-the-art provers according to the logging-and-checking architecture, already successfully used in several large scale verification projects (see [7] for a comprehensive review). ACL2 is especially suited to formalize software systems such as those we consider, and verify their properties. Unfortunately, ACL2's proof reports solely consist of an informal commentary which describes the proof construction. Therefore, in order to fulfill our requirements, ACL2 needs to be reconfigured as a Logger, and a Checker must be built for it[3]. In order to achieve our aim, we adopted the Open Mechanized Reasoning Systems (OMRS) technology [3] as the methodology to proceed to the ACL2 logging-and-checking redesign.

Relevantly to our purposes, as a result of a proof of a conjecture, an OMRS produces a structured proof account called a Reasoning Structure. A Reasoning Structure is basically a graph describing the proof construction, and from which a proof Log can automatically be extracted.

Currently, OMRS has been used to specify, and reimplement, the top-level proof search algorithm of ACL2. As a result, the OMRS-revised prototype is able to build proof logs which describe the proof by considering ACL2's high-level heuristics as basic inference steps. More details can be found in [1].

5   Related Work

As far as we know, no previous work has proposed the idea of decomposing the verification task into two distinct phases, the off-line proof done "once for all" and the on-line proof for each individual translation.

---

[3] Actually, a limited Emacs-based proof tree facility is available, together with a companion checker named Acl2-Pc. Neither tools are satisfactory w.r.t. our aims, both because of the Checker's size, and because it is strictly integrated with the Logger, rather than being an independent piece of code.

In the off-line phase, we adopt a logging-and-checking mechanism to address the problem of the certification of the ACL2 proof. To this extent, the closest work to ours is that on the EVES prover [8]. Even if similar in spirit, our work is in practice rather different: we aim at logging and checking a complex and powerful prover such as ACL2 in a principled way by using the OMRS technique. According to the OMRS approach, the theorem proving strategies are expressed as tactics. This resembles the idea underlying tactic-based theorem provers (e.g. HOL [4]). In fact, an alternative approach to the certification of the off-line proof is the use of a tactic-based theorem prover. Indeed, in principle, proofs generated by means of tactics are guaranteed to be sound given the correctness of primitive tactics. Nevertheless, state-of-the-art tactic based provers, when used to verify complex systems, e.g. in hardware verification, have required a rather onerous development of several special purpose tactics which would be hardly applicable in our application domain.

The idea of coupling a translator with an on-line prover which compares for individual translator runs inputs and outputs is a major shift w.r.t. standard practice in formal verification. This idea has been independently promoted by Pnueli, Siegel, and Singerman [11], where a syntactic simulation-based proof method is used to verify automatically the correctness of a compilation from the language SIGNAL to C-code. In their approach, no off-line proof is devised.

To this extent, some similarities exist with the work on Proof Carrying Code (PCC) [10, 9]. The PCC technology has been devised for application domains which are very different from ours, namely the problem for a fail-safe host platform to execute code provided by an untrusted code producer. The producer must couple each program with a proof which is then proof checked by the host. The checker must check the proof against the actual untrusted code. This idea is similar to our idea of an on-line logging-and-checking of the proof log against the actual inputs and outputs of the translator (see Section 4 for a discussion about this problem in the industrial case study). In PCC, the checker is general, for instance based on simple extensions of Natural Deduction encoded in LF. Our on-line checker is based on special purpose decision procedures in order to check efficiently the proof log, to keep the log size reasonable, and to have both the checker and the log which can be understood and validated by end-users with no experience in logic. Finally, the current PCC framework does not seem to address the problem of the generation, the logging and the checking of complex proofs, even if some extensions in this sense are currently planned.

6 Conclusions and future work

In this paper, we have described a methodology for the automatic verification of safety-critical translators, run on top of non-failure-safe platforms. The methodology involves the reduction of the on-line verification phase through an off-line phase, and the design of proving tools following the logging-and-checking approach. We have showed the application of the methodology in the frame of an industrial project; in such case, off-line proofs were conducted by hand rather than exploiting an automated tool. In order to be able to fully exploit the technology in other projects, we pursue the aim of obtaining a logging-and-checking version of a state-of-the-art prover, ACL2, by re-engineering it through OMRS. We have already designed a coarse ACL2 specification, and obtained an ACL2 Logger prototype. This was performed in few man-months of work, inclusive of a startup time needed to design a number of re-engineering support tools.

As a part of our ongoing ACL2 redesign project, we intend to refine the OMRS specification, in order to build a finer grained Logger; to design and implement the correspondent Checker, and to test them in proving conjectures such as that defined in the off-line phase of the project shown in section 4. Moreover, we intend to test our methodology by verifying other translators, possibly more complex than the GEM2RTM we showed, where identifying automatizable verification conditions is likely to become a major issue.

References

1. P.G. Bertoli. *Using OMRS in practice: a case study with* ACL2. PhD thesis, Computer Science Dept., University Rome 3, Rome, 1998. Forthcoming.
2. A. Cimatti, F. Giunchiglia, P. Pecchiari, B. Pietra, J. Profeta, D. Romano, and P. Traverso. A Provably Correct Embedded Verifier for the Certification of Safety Critical Software. In *Proc. Computer-Aided Verification (CAV'97)*, Haifa, Israel, June 1997.
3. F. Giunchiglia, P. Pecchiari, and C. Talcott. Reasoning Theories: Towards an Architecture for Open Mechanized Reasoning Systems. Technical Report 9409-15, IRST, Trento, Italy, 1994. Short version published in Proc. of the First International Workshop on Frontiers of Combining Systems (FroCoS'96), Munich, Germany, March 1996.
4. M.J. Gordon. A Proof Generating System for Higher-Order Logic. In G. Birtwistle and P.A. Subrahmanyam, editors, *VLSI Specification and Synthesis.* Kluwer, 1987.
5. D. Guaspari, C. Barbash, and D. Hoover. Checking critical code. Tech. Report ORA TM-95-0081, Odyssey Research Associates, Ithaca, USA, September 1995.
6. M. Kaufmann and J. S. Moore. ACL2 Version 1.8 User's Manual. Available on line at http://www.cs.utexas.edu/users/moore/acl2/index.html.
7. M. Kaufmann and J S. Moore. Design Goals for ACL2. Technical Report 101, Computational Logic Inc., Austin, Texas, 1994.
8. S. Kromodimoeljo, B. Pase, M. Saaltink, D. Craigen, and I. Meisels. The EVES system. In *Proc. of the Int. Lecture Series on "Functional Programming, Concurrency, Simulation and Automated Reasoning".* McMaster University, 1992.
9. G. Necula. Proof-carrying code. In *24th Annual ACM-SIGPLAN-SIGACT Symposium on Principles of Programming Languages (POPL'97)*, 1997.
10. G. Necula and P. Lee. Safe kernel extensions without run-time checking. In *Second Symposium on Operating Systems Design and Implementation (OSDI'96)*, 1996.
11. Amir Pnueli, Michael Siegel, and Eli Singerman. Translation validation. In *Proceedings of TACAS'98. To appear.*, 1998.
12. J. Profeta, N. Andrianos, B. Yu, B. Jonson, T. DeLong, D. Guaspari, and D. Jamsek. Safety Critical Systems Built with COTS. *Computer*, 29(11):54–60, November 1996.

Applying Formal Methods in Industry
The UseGat Project

Sandro BOLOGNA[1], Rocco BOVE[1], Giovanni DIPOPPA[1],
Giorgio MONGARDI[2], Gino BIONDI[2], Carmen PORZIA[2],
Benny Graft MORTENSEN[3], and Niels KIRKEGAARD[3]

[1] ENEA C.R. CASACCIA Via Anguillarese, 301, I-00060 ROMA, Italy
{bologna | rocco.bove | giovanni.dipoppa}@casaccia.enea.it
[2] ANSALDO Segnalamento Ferroviario Via dei pescatori, 35, I-16129 GENOVA, Italy
{gmongard | cporzia | gbiondi}@asf.atr.ansaldo.it
[3] IFAD Forskerparken 10, DK-5230 ODENSE, Denmark
{benny | niels}@ifad.dk

Abstract. The use of formal methods in real project is still a challenge. The paper reports the results of a Trial Project, partially funded by the European Communities, with the goal to measure difficulties and benefits associated with the use of integrated graphical and textual formal specification languages. The reference application used for the trial project was the development of a *platform door control* function of a more complex system in the field of railway applications.

Introduction

The purpose of UseGat[1] (Use of Integrated Graphical & Textual Formal Specification Languages in Industry) project was to demonstrate the suitability and viability of combining structured and formal methods to develop real large-scale applications. UseGat focused on measuring the initial investment needed to incorporate such a technology in an industrial environment and its effect on the product quality and costs, especially in the development and validation of safety critical systems.

The baseline project used within the project was a component of an interlocking system of a driverless metropolitan light railway that has been installed on the test track ring in Ansaldo Trasporti, Naples.

This paper describes the results of the project in the light of the original objectives.

1 Project Objectives

The use of Formal Methods in Industry is controversial in several aspects:

---

[1] *UseGat* is partially funded by the European Communities under the ESPRIT programme, project no. EP20237.

- Difficulty to use.
- Impact on the production process.
- Impact on the product quality.

The original UseGat project objectives were to investigate all three aspects throughout a well-defined experiment, suitable for the working environment and the application domain of Ansaldo Segnalamento Ferroviario (ASF). In particular:

- To complement the technology already in use (StP)[1] with a formal notation (VDM-SL)[2] to support the software development life cycle, in particular specification analysis through animation, limiting as much as possible the necessary effort to move from StP technology to UseGat.
- To investigate the possibilities to customize the notations to the application domain, in order to provide a notation as user friendly as possible.
- To assess the impact of the UseGat technology and method on the production process and the product quality, throughout a well-defined and realistic experiment incorporating typical functional and safety requirements, as well as time constraints, of the application domain.

The UseGat Experiment

Identification of Trial Application

The baseline project adopted as the reference application for the project, was the development of the *platform door control* function of the Automatic Train Control System (ATCM) for the Automatic Metropolitan Light Railway Project (called the ML1 project). In the ML1 project a fully automated driverless train system is developed. The model of the platform door control function developed with the UseGat technology focused on describing the logical behavior of the function. Some real-time constraints have also been addressed, as the Metropolitan Light Railway System has to interact with the real world. A functional real-time requirement is that the doors must be opened and closed while a train is positioned in the right position on the rail-track at a platform; a safety real-time requirement is that the doors must be re-opened immediately if an obstruction is detected. To match such real-time requirements, synchronization and control of different tasks composing the function have been specified in a way that deadlocking will be avoided and the service given by this module more dependable.

The UseGat Technology

The UseGat environment is made of:

- A methodology combining structured analysis (the SA/RT notation proposed by Hatley&Pirbhai [3]) and formal methods (the formal specification language VDM-SL).

- A methodology that can be customized such that it satisfies specific requirement of particular users.
- Tools supporting the methodology (StP/SE, the IFAD VDM Toolbox, and the Specification Animator).

The UseGat technology aims at improving the software development by putting emphasis on the early development phases. The idea is to build abstract executable models. Building abstract models has the advantages that one can focus on the essential properties, abstract away details that are not relevant, and raising early queries to the requirements. Building executable models has the advantage that validation can be performed also in the early development phases. In the combined notation the process specifications of the SA/RT data flow diagrams are written in VDM-SL. Furthermore VDM-SL values are flowing on data and control flows, and are stored in stores. The combination has defined an unambiguous semantics for all elements of graphical notation and their combinations, and the well-defined semantics of VDM-SL provides a precise semantics of the process specifications. The combined notation hereby provides a graphical formal method. The customisability enables adaptation of combined graphical and textual notation to comply with development processes and requirements of individual companies. For example the scheduling of the execution process order, when more than one process is ready for execution, can be customized according individual requirements. Examples of different scheduling are depth-first and breath-first scheduling.
In the UseGat environment three tools support the combined notation:

- StP/SE, giving support to editing and static checks of graphical models.
- The VDM-SL Toolbox, giving support to static checks, interpretation and debugging of VDM- SL specifications.

These two tools have been combined to provide execution and graphical animation of combined graphical and textual models. The two tools in combination is called the Specification Animator.

Rationale for choosing the UseGat Technology

The CENELEC EN 50128 [4] standard for railway prescribes the use of formal methods as Highly Recommended for safety related software. The UseGat technology aims at overcoming a number of barriers to the introduction of formal methods in industry:

- The combination of a graphical and a textual notation provides a graphical approach to formal methods. StP was already used within ASF before the UseGat project and therefore the introduction of the combined graphical and textual formal methods was regarded as more easy to learn, as it only required minor changes of the existing development process.
- Formal methods are often regarded as very academic and difficult to master, and in particular performing formal proofs is very time consuming and requires special skills. The UseGat technology allows gradual introduction of

formal methods by building abstract models and performing testing which is a well-known engineering validation technique. Later more advanced aspects of formal method can be introduced.

The Reference Process Model

The end-user reference development process, based on ISO/IEC 1207 [5], contains the following phases (Figure 1):

1. Requirement Specification
2. Design Analysis
3. Functional Analysis
4. Detailed Design
5. Coding
6. System Integration

To each phase a verification and validation (V&V) activity is associated.
The UseGat technology was introduced into the development process in the following three phases:

– Analyzing the design from the requirements specification.
– Analyzing the functionality of the design.
– Producing the detailed design.

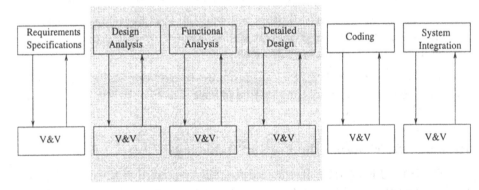

Fig. 1. The end-user development life-cycle. The shadowed area illustrates the phases, where the usegat technology was introduced.

The introduction of the UseGat technology was performed such that to disturb the existing process as little as possible, but at the same time to provide the advanced analysis features of the technology. The end-user development process includes tools for generating test cases and code and for simulating specific installations [6,7]. The UseGat technology was incorporated such that it extended the development process by interoperating with the existing tools, not replacing them. The V&V activities follow the development plan, that is they do not entail a posterior intervention, but rather a more composite activity, wherein to each stage in the product development corresponds an appropriate verification and validation activity (something like a step by step verification), but which can come back to processes in previous phases if it needs. The V&V activities during the UseGat project regarded the definition of functional test-cases on the basis of the requirement specification using proprietary tools (Decision Table Tool and Test-case Specification Tool) [6, 7], the production of refined test-cases translated into a formalism compatible with the UseGat technology, the execution of the test-cases on the detailed specification with the VDM-SL Toolbox and with the Specification Animator and the comparison of the obtained results with the expected ones. Even if the duration of analysis phase was longer than the standard one (without the UseGat methodology) the results obtained permitted to check the model before the coding activity, that is in a earlier phase of the development process.

Size of Experiment

In the development of the platform door control function and in the evaluation of the new technology, three persons were directly involved for development and evaluation, simultaneously one person was involved in preparation of the *assessment framework*. Moreover the Quality Department participated in defining of *quality plan*. And along the project a variable number of persons within the end-user assisted the UseGat staff with their expertise. This was in order to better define the technology and methodology requirements, to assess the risks of introducing the UseGat technology, and to solve the technical problems on the platform.

The size of the model developed was:

- 7 StP data flow diagrams on three levels of hierarchy, and
- 2500 lines of VDM-SL specification.

The project had a duration of 18 months, and the collaboration between the three partners (ASF, ENEA, IFAD) permitted to work in the different sites, but the most part of the activities was at the final user in order to better integrate the technology results.

Prior to this experiment the project team involved in the development of UseGat model had some experience in formal methods, but none in the formal method VDM-SL. Previous experiences with formal methods where gained from attending seminars and conference only. At the beginning of the project one other department within ASF had a deep knowledge of the StP tools, whereas the project team had only theoretical knowledge but no practical experiences.

Modeling the Application

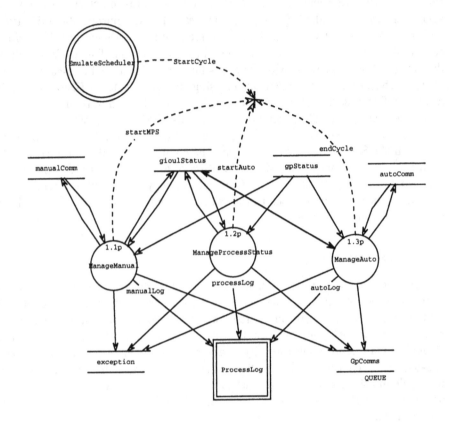

Fig. 2. Flow Diagram Example

In the example of figure 2 the scheduling mechanism model is depicted with a control specification enabling the different processes (*ManageManual, Manage-ProcvessStatus and ManageAuto*) in a specified order and avoiding the multiple access to the shared data (*gioulStatus data store*). VDM-SL specifications are associated to each single process. In the specification example below, the process *ManageManual* manages the manual commands received. Such messages are sent in cases where problems are arisen, e.g. to force a door to open. The process *ManageProcessStatus* manages the switching the states that the control of the platform door can be in. The process *ManageAuto* manages automatic commands received, e.g. automatic opening of doors. The order of execution of the three processes is important such that *ManageManual* is executed before *ManageProcessStatus*, which again is executed before *ManageAuto*. This is controlled by the control specification of the diagram.

Data Dictionary Example

types

```
PresentAbsent = <Present>|<Absent>;
FreeBusy = <Free>|<Busy>;
EnableDisable = <Enable>|<Disable>;
AutoManual = <Auto>|<Manual>;
RemoteLocal = <Remote>|<Local>;
OpeningPredispositionStatus = <DoorA>|<DoorB>|<DoorAB>|<Absent>;
ProcessStatus =  <OpeningPredispositionRequest>|<PredisposedOpening>|
                 <OpeningEnablingRequest>|<EnabledOpening>| ...;
GioulStatus :: -- READ / WRITE
  processStatus: ProcessStatus     autoOpeningStatus: PresentAbsent
  autoClosingStatus: PresentAbsent doorStatus: FreeBusy   ...;
GpStatus :: -- Read only
  doorAOpeningControl: bool doorBOpeningControl: bool
  obstructionDetected: bool doorAlarm: bool   ...;
ManualComm =
  <Open>|<Close>|<EnableA>|<EnableB>|<DisableA>|<DisableB>|..;
```

Minispec Example

```
ManageManual(manualComm: ManualComm, gioulStatus:GioulStatus,
   gpStatus:GpStatus) gioulStatus':GioulStatus, gpComms:GpComms,
   manualComm':ManualComms, exception: [Exception], startMPS: int,
   manualLog: [ManualLog]==

if manualComm = [] then return mk_(gioulStatus,[],[],nil,1,nil)
else
cases (hd manualComm)
 <Open> -> RequestManualOpening(gioulStatus,gpStatus,manualComm),
 <Close> -> RequestManualClosing(gioulStatus,gpStatus,manualComm),
 <EnableA> -> RequestEnableOpeningA(gioulStatus,gpStatus,manualComm),
 <EnableB> -> RequestEnableOpeningB(gioulStatus,gpStatus,manualComm),
 <DisableA> -> RequestDisableOpeningA(gioulStatus,gpStatus,manualComm),
 <DisableB> -> RequestDisableOpeningB(gioulStatus,gpStatus,manualComm),
  others -> return mk_(gioulStatus,[],tl manualComm,nil,0,nil)
end;

RequestManualOpening(manualComm: ManualComm, gioulStatus:GioulStatus,
 gpStatus:GpStatus) gioulStatus':GioulStatus,  gpComms:GpComms,
manualComm':ManualComms, exception: [Exception], startMPS: int,
manualLog: [ManualLog]== ...

VerifiedRMO(gpStatus:GpStatus,gioulStatus:GioulStatus)
  exceptionT:ExceptionT == ...
```

Evaluation and Results

The main goal of the project was to evaluate how and under which terms it could be possible to introduce the UseGat technology into the ASF development process, and how it could be adapted to existing practices and standards used at ASF.

Evaluation

The evaluation was divided into two parts. The first part was performed after the *specification and design phases* (referring to the phases in Figure 1 these are the Design Analysis, the Functional Analysis and the Detailed Design boxes) and was called the *specification and design assessment*. The second part was performed after the *implementation phase* and was called the *implementation assessment*. The specification and design assessment evaluate the "Methodology and Language" and the "Software and Toolset". It assessed the graphical notation annotated with textual VDM-SL process specifications, the VDM-SL textual notation stand-alone, and the supporting tools. Questionnaires based on the ISO/IEC 9126 standard [8] and adapted for the ASF's development model were used for the development in term of consistency analysis. This assessment was performed comparing the development results to a process having similar complexity , as well as considering the evaluation of the testing activity and the production of documentation.

Results

The future international standard for developing high integrity software CEN-ELEC EN 50128 [4] describe the use of formal methods as "Highly Recommended". The principles in applying this are:

1. top-down design methods
2. modularity
3. verification of each phase of the development life cycle
4. verified modules and module libraries
5. clear documentation
6. auditing documents
7. validation testing

It was shown how the use of StP data flow diagrams in the UseGat technology offered support for a top-down design method and for modularity (items 1. and 2.) The concepts of incremental prototyping and dynamic execution of models improved the verification at each phase of the development life cycle (items 3. and 4.) The technology improved the quality of the documentation (item 5.) Testing could start at an earlier stage of the development life cycle (item 7.) This led to an overall positive result within the assessment. The conclusion was also based on the detailed assessment of the methodology and language and on the impact of the standard development life cycle.

The results were not likewise good for what concerns the maturity of the tools, since too many problems related to user-friendliness of the interface and performance were found. At the end of the assessment it was possible though to affirm that the UseGat technology has good potentialities that could increase the efficiency of the development life cycle, but at the moment the depicted problems do not permit its complete introduction in the production process. More details are given below.

The introduction of the UseGat validation activities in the design phases helped and guided the parallel verification and validation activities. The combination of structured and formal notations offered a more complete definition and design of the life cycle activities, from the analysis to the detailed design.

Evaluation of the combination of the graphical and textual notations was positive, although some problems were faced in the expressiveness of the graphical parts. The evaluation of the toolset reached a fair level. A number of improvements that would increase the level of the toolset are listed in the next section.

Analysis regarding changes and improvements linked to the introduction of the UseGat technology into the ASF product life cycle showed that the technology could easily be integrated into the existing development cycle. Furthermore, the introduction added more value to the detailed analysis and corresponding verification activity:

- It was possible to test the abstract model.
- Increased test coverage was obtained.

The technology is not directly suitable for real-time logic analysis. However it was shown that it could support analysis of hierarchies of processes, regarding issues as concurrent activation and priorities.

The V&V task was complemented by the animation of data flow diagrams, testing at the analysis level, and the combination of topological coverage information with functional coverage.

The application chosen for the trial project analyzed a process that interacts with a complete system, integrating the functionality of the platform door control. The technology also gave sufficient support for documentation of this aspect.

Tools and Technology Improvements

In order to improve the Specification Animator's debugging facilities it is recommended to add a facility for adding and modifying values during a debugging session. This would in particular facilitate analysis of particular subparts of a model.

The error messages should be clarified and the on-line help should be improved to better impact the reliability, the usability and the analysability. This would further increase the fault tolerance and the recoverability of the animation part of the technology.

Constraints on the graphical notation imposed both by the tool supporting it and by the integration with the formal textual notation have to be considered if the technology should offer efficient support to the design process. The installation procedure could benefit from being refined.

Moreover, it should be studied whether and how the introduction of a temporal variable and a dynamic delay in the methodology could increase the efficiency and the capability of the UseGat technology to deal with the real-time constraints.

Key Lessons Learnt

Technical issues

The UseGat technology supports execution of abstract models, i.e. validation of designs using early testing. This eases the introduction of the technology because testing is a well-known software engineering technique.

The combination of structured and formal notations (SA/RT and VDM-SL) is really powerful and offers a more complete definition and design in all phases from analysis to detailed design. In addition the coding activity becomes clearer and better documented.

Having reached a sufficiently detailed design interpretation of models becomes fundamental. As a first step the testing activity can work on the detailed design, identifying the problems of the specification at an earlier stage. For this reason, even though currently the final code can only be produced manually from the UseGat specifications, the UseGat technology can also affect the testing of the code. Many analysis and design errors can be detected in the early development phases, and thereby their propagation through to the code is avoided.

Future automatic translation from the UseGat specifications to the final code would be very beneficial. In this sense the quality of the whole development process can be increased with the introduction of the UseGat technology for design of safety critical systems.

Test coverage of the functional behavior is important for testing a system, but the topological test coverage also offered by the UseGat technology is very beneficial to increase the confidence in the model developed. The general architecture, which was defined for the design of the platform door control process, can be easily re-used for the modeling of another logic process. The validation and verification activities in the project are related to the design of a specific railway logic process, but it can be generalized to any other logic process, not necessarily restricted to the railway field.

Technology Transfer

The UseGat technology was new to the ASF team: the VDM-SL notation was completely new, only a limited knowledge of StP was present, and no experience at all of the combination of StP with VDM-SL was present. This is a typical situation within a trial project. A tight coordination and intensive consultancy was essential to ensure that the end-user could reach a high level of mastering the technology, otherwise the real benefits and restrictions of the technology could not be fully understood. That was reached through a number of seminars.

Business point of view

A very important aspect of this experiment of using formal methods was its use in a real project. A clear function was isolated to be developed and inserted into a well-known system and on clear conditions, demonstrating the possibility of integrating the conventional and the new technologies. So a clear and realistic picture of the potentialities and the weaknesses of the new technology was drawn. It was also a good starting point for studying the risks of introducing the new technology into a real development environment. However, the new methodology was not applied to an entire large-scale system within this project. This would have been too high as goal to reach and there would have been too many risks. The UseGat experience has paved the way for new projects and activities of this type.

Another result of this experiment is that new skills on a formal method have been introduced into ASF. The ATCM application is a good starting point for future applications using the UseGat technology. Furthermore, ASF could supports the technology provider with input about the strengths and the weaknesses of the technology.

Conclusions

The introduction of formal languages into the existing ASF development process was one of the objectives that the UseGat project fulfilled, since the new technology was integrated into the traditional ASF procedures.

The other objective of the UseGat project was to study the suitability and viability of combining structured and formal methods to develop real applications. The new methodology was applied in the modeling of functional and safety requirements, and was efficiently integrated into the developed context with the standard methodology. This limited perhaps the complete evaluation of the methodology, but gave an overview of its potentialities.

Moreover the work done for the notation customization to met the application domain produced a technology which could be integrated into the StP environment.

The assessment analyzed the impact of the technology on the internal life cycle in terms of the final quality of the product. The UseGat project offered to ASF the possibility of identifying the potentialities of a formal method, but the supporting tools are considered immature at the moment for a complete introduction into the product life cycle.

References

1. Software through Picture:*Core: Fundamental of StP*,Release 2, IDE, February 1996
2. The IFAD VDM-SL Documentation, March 1996.
3. D.J.HATLEY, I.A.PIRBHAI: *Strategy for Real-Time System Specification* Dorset House Publishing New York - 1997, ISBN: 0-932633-11-0
4. CENELEC European Committee for Electro-technical Standardization: *Railway Applications: Software for Railway Control and Protection Systems*, Draft prEN50128, August 1996
5. ISO/IEC 1207 International Standard: *Information technology Software lifecycle processes*
6. A. Traverso: *A tool for Specification Analysis: Complete Decision Table*, SAFECOMP'85
7. C.Abbaneo, G.Biondi, M.Ferrando, G.Mongardi: *Testing of Computer Based Interlocking Software: Methodology and Environment*, SAFECOMP'92
8. ISO/IEC 9126
   Information technology - Safety product evaluation - Quality characteristics and guidelines for their use, 1991

Increasing System Safety for By-Wire Applications in Vehicles by Using a Time Triggered Architecture

Th. Ringler*, J. Steiner*, R. Belschner* and B. Hedenetz*

* University of Stuttgart, Institute for Industrial Automation and Software Engineering
Pfaffenwaldring 47
D-70569 Stuttgart, Germany,
Tel.: +49 - (0)711 - 685 - 7296, Fax: - 7302
email: {ringler, steiner}@ias.uni-stuttgart.de

* Daimler Benz AG
FT2/EA, HPC T721
D-70546 Stuttgart, Germany,
Tel.: +49 - (0)711 - 17 - 41930 / - 41341, Fax: - 47058
email: {belschner, hedenetz}@dbag.stg.daimlerbenz.com

Abstract. *By-wire* systems have been established for several years in the area of aircraft construction and there are now approaches to utilize this technology in vehicles. The required electronic systems must evidently be available and safe. In the same time the requirements of mass production have to be reached (long life time, long maintainability intervals, low costs, fulfillment of standards). This paper addresses a new automotive architecture approach - based on a time triggered architecture - and a framework for the application design of future by-wire systems in vehicles.

Introduction

The driving forces transforming our world towards the information society are also dramatically changing the mechanical engineering market domains. There is a clear trend to substitute mechanical, hydraulic, or pneumatic systems by computerized by-wire components in automotive systems. The aircraft domain has been the technology driver till today. A well-known example is the flight control system of the Airbus A320. However, it is estimated that the automotive industry with its huge market for components will take this role in future. It is estimated that in 2006, 25% of the total cost of a passenger car will be accounted for electronic parts. This also includes electronic brake and steering systems, which are supposed to offer a better functionality than conventional systems and therefore have the potential to increase overall traffic safety significantly. Further advantages but not less important are reduced costs for assembly during line production (reduction of packaging problems, no brake fluid, no bleeding, simple maintenance) and easier adapting of assistance systems like anti braking system (ABS), electronic stability program (ESP), etc., since they could be realized only by software and sensors without additional mechanical or hydraulic components. To be affordable for mass production, the electronic systems have to offer the same availability and simultaneously safety of their mechanical/hydraulic counterparts, so that no mechanical/hydraulic backup solutions are needed. This means in the last consequence that the safety critical system must provide an electronic backup system which is realized by electronic redundancy.

The Time-Triggered Approach

A system architecture that suits best for the described application domain is based on the Time-Triggered (TT) approach. In a TT architecture all system activities are initiated by the progression of a globally synchronized time. It is assumed that all clocks are synchronized and every observation of the controlled object is timestamped with the synchronized time.

This paper addresses a new automotive architecture approach using the fault-tolerant Time-Triggered Protocol TTP [Kope97] that has been designed due to the class C SAE classification [SAE93a] for safety critical control applications, like brake-by-wire or steer-by-wire. Time-triggered systems based on TTP can provide the required high level of dependability, which has been clearly demonstrated in the ongoing EC-funded projects X-By-Wire [Dilg97a, Dilg97b] and TTA [HeTh98, Sche97]. The intention of the TTP architecture is to tolerate one arbitrary fault within electronic systems without any effects to the system behavior.

Time-Triggered Protocol (TTP)

For the realization of a distributed time-triggered architecture a communication network is necessary that provides the features mentioned above. None of the commonly used in-vehicles communication systems (CAN, A-BUS, VAN, J1850-DLC, J1850-HBCC[SAE93b]) meets the requirements for safety related by-wire systems since they were not designed for this case [KrSc97]. They are all lacking in being deterministic, in synchronization and fault tolerance characteristics. These missing properties are the motivation for developing new approaches for in-vehicle communication systems. As a new start we examine the Time-Triggered Protocol developed by the University of Vienna and Daimler-Benz Research. TTP is especially designed for safety related applications and fulfills these requirements. TTP is an integrated time-triggered protocol that provides:

- a membership service, i.e., every single node knows about the actual state of any other node of the distributed system

- a fault-tolerant clock synchronization service (global time-base),
- mode change support,
- error detection with short latency,
- distributed redundancy management.

All these issues are supported implicitly by the protocol itself. A comprehensive description of the TTP protocol is given in [KoGr94, Kope97a, Kope97b]. The TTP protocol has been designed to tolerate any single physical fault in any one of its constituent parts (node, bus) without an impact on the operation of a properly configured cluster [KoGr94].

The overall TTP hardware architecture is characterized by both the TTP system architecture and the TTP node architecture as shown in Fig. 1. A TTP real-time system consists of a host subsystem, which executes the real-time application and the communication subsystem providing reliable real-time message transmission. The interface between these subsystems is realized by a dual ported RAM (DPRAM) called *Communication Network Interface (CNI)* [KrKo95, Krüg97]. The assembly of host and TTP-controller is called *Fail Silent Unit (FSU)*. Two FSUs form a single redundant *Fault-Tolerant Unit (FTU)*. The physical layer consists of two independent transmission channels.

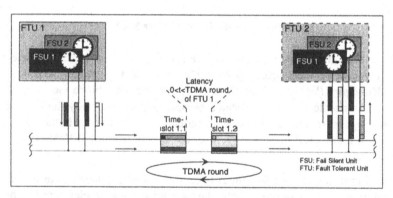

Fig. 1.: Architecture of a TTP-Based Fault-Tolerant Real-Time System

The communication network topology is a broadcast bus. Bus access is granted to the nodes under the control of a static TDMA scheme. In accordance to the time-triggered concept, the timeslots in which a node may send and receive frames on the bus are pre-allocated at the design time of the system. This TDMA message schedule is stored locally within each node. To achieve an orderly access to the bus, the nodes maintain a globally synchronized time base. This operation is an integral part of TTP. For fault-tolerance reasons a dual channel system has to be used.

Brake-by-Wire Case Study

As an example we are currently evaluating this approach within a brake-by-wire research car [HeBe98] (case study) without mechanical backup (see Fig. 2). The intention of this architecture is to tolerate one arbitrary fault without any effects of the system's performance. For this purpose, we use hot redundancy in hardware (electronic computing units - ECU) as well as redundancy in communication (TTP). Nevertheless the electric components like sensors, actuators and power supply are also designed redundantly.

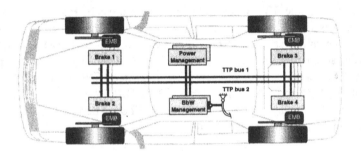

Fig. 2.: Brake-by-Wire Case Study

Our fault tolerant architecture consists of a set of two redundant ECU's (electronic control unit) for both the *Brake-by-Wire-Manager (BBW-Manager, BBWM)* and the *Power-Manager (PM)*, and 4 single ECU's, one for each brake (see Fig. 2). The ECU's are connected by two replicated busses. In this case study the brake ECU's are not designed redundant, in order to reduce costs, since the failure of a single brake is not considered to be as severe as the failure of the BBW-Manager, or the Power-Manager.

The function of the BBW-Manager is to read the sensor values of the brake pedal, the revolution counters of the wheels, the yaw-sensor, the acceleration sensors, and to calculate from these signals the brake force set points for the four brake actuators. The BBW-Manager should also manage higher assistance functions like ABS, traction and driving dynamic control. The Power-Manager controls the charge of the batteries, proceeds active power management and monitors the status of the power supply. If the generator or one of the redundant power circuits fails or the charge of the batteries is going low the Power-Manager generates a warning signal. Each of the four brake actuators have one brake electronic to control the electric motor of the brake actuator. The brake electronics get the brake force set points from the BBW-Manager.

In contrast to event triggered systems a TTP system is built up by defining first the static message schedule. Fig. 3 depicts the result of this phase, namely the communication matrix of the above example on a brake-by-wire network. The Fig.

3 shows the static synchronous TDMA schedule and its constraint that each subsystem has to send exactly once in a TDMA cycle. The messages marked with 'I' are called I-Frames, used for reintegration of lost members and do not transmit information for the application layer.

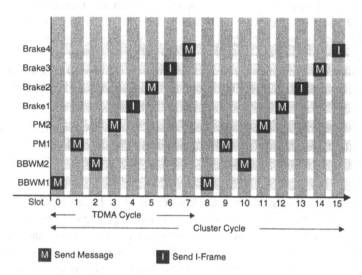

Fig. 3: Communication Matrix of the Brake-by-wire Case Study

The FSU's of the BBWM and the PM send their messages in vice versa time slots. In this way short burst errors can be recovered. A FSU slot has a length of about 1.2 msec. New brake force set points could be sent every 10 msec, which is needed for an ABS control loop. The brake control ECU's send their status and the current brake force. These messages are not as time critical as the transmission of the brake force set points. The brake ECU's send their messages only once in a cluster cycle, each 16 FSU slots. In the leaving FSU slots the brake ECU's send I-Frames for the network management.

Application Design Approach

In our brake-by-wire case study, a software fault, the exact same software running on redundant ECU, will lead to the same faulty reaction. This could be prevented by diverse software design, possibly developed by different teams. It would take more than double the effort and studies show that diverse software design does not automatically increase the reliability of the system [Bril90]. We think a more useful approach is to invest in the additional expenditure of reusable software components.

Software Components

Unlike the development of todays software, which is generally directly based on command lines, a comparable procedure in hardware development is inconceivable. In an analogous manner, no-one would think to achieve the functionality of an integrated circuit (IC) by using individual diodes, resistors and transistors. With the introduction of integrated hardware components the work of hardware engineers has changed from dealing with the detailed problems of circuit development to the integration of standard hardware components (e.g., IC). To achieve a corresponding method for software development, software components are needed in order to build an application from a design level. Therefore, the application designer does not need to deal with details at the code level.

The advantages for utilizing software components within the whole application system are simple maintainability and expandability, system quality improvement and increasing system safety with the use of sufficiently tested components. There are also predictable time and cost factors for project planning.

The development of software components requires an initial large investment, which is only worthwhile if the components are reusable to a high degree. The problem of specific software components is that their functionality is pre-defined and fixed. If the available components do not fulfill the desired requirements, a new component must be found or developed in order to fulfill these special requirements. This inflexibility reduces the reusability of software components. A promising solution for solving the problem of specific software components is to use *generic components*. We define a generic component as a reusable system element which has a closed functional unit that represents a specific problem area. However, unlike a specific software component, a generic component has flexible characteristics. By configuring certain system characteristics and setting certain parameters, a generic component can be adapted to the specific requirements of an application to be developed.

Operating Systems

We are convinced that deterministic system behavior is basically needed for safety critical applications. Determinism can only be reached, if the application software is also time triggered. In the case of TTP, the application software system is strongly interconnected with the time division multiple access (TDMA) bus access scheme. In contrast to event-triggered networks, the global time triggered network rules over the application. The TTP communication subsystem has predefined, static binding points in time, when the host subsystem has to interact with the communication subsystem and, therefore, the operating system has to take care that the static time bounds are guaranteed. If the host subsystem does not interact as defined, the communication subsystem assumes a host error and becomes passive, due to the claimed fail-silent behavior. This cannot be managed by tasks themselves, sometimes developed by different subcontractors. A fail tolerant operating system (FTOS) is necessary.

Prime-Level Scheduler (PLS)

As a prototype, an operating system called Prime-Level Scheduler (PLS) has been developed [Krug98]. The PLS is a time driven scheduler, which is based on an off-line task schedule. Tasks, which are scheduled by the PLS, are called fault-tolerant tasks (FT-tasks). The FT-tasks are only activated by the progression of time, they are non-preemptive and repeated periodically. The PLS is responsible that the time constraints of the FT-tasks are met. This concept was extended by features and services especially relating to the synchronization with TTP. In the following list the main characteristics of the PLS are summarized:

- The FT-tasks are executed cyclically by a given start time. The cycle time is based on the duration of one TTP-cluster-cycle. If the task exceeds the deadline, the task will be suspended (see Fig. 4).
- The time management is synchronized with the global time of TTP.
- The reintegration of a suspended task for the next cycle is optional.
- The PLS terminates itself in a predefined way if certain tasks are suspended.
- In the case of a failure of the communication network (reset, short-circuit, interruption), the PLS detects this and goes into an exception mode. In this mode, the FT-tasks are still executed in accordance with the tasks timetable.
- During run time, the PLS sends additional messages for diagnosis via CAN (Controller Area Network).

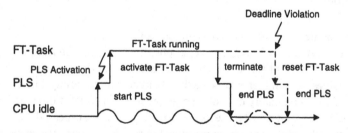

Fig. 4: PLS call (the dotted lines illustrate the faulty case)

For the deadline value of a task, its worst-case execution time has to be known. Since the execution time varies, the available CPU time isn't completely used. For that reason, a Multi-Level Scheduler has been developed.

Multi Level Scheduler (MLS)

In order to use the CPU time in a more efficient way, a second task level for non fault-tolerant tasks (NFT-tasks) was introduced with the MLS [Fisc98]. This results in a two level system consisting of a primary and secondary level. The primary level has the functionality of the described PLS. In contrast to the primary level, the secondary level is to perform non safety related tasks without time constraints. The non safety related tasks are only executed, if the MLS detects enough free time at the primary level.

Examples of task classification:

Primary Level
- tasks dependent on the TTP communication
- tasks operating with quantitative variables (e.g., the loss of these variables would lead to a damage of vehicle and person)

Secondary Level
- tasks delivering diagnostic information (e.g., diagnostic information for automobile workshop)

More than two task levels are not practical, because the more levels exist, the more time has to be invested by the CPU for organizing the task levels.

Generally, to generate the required predefined schedule, the worst-case execution times of all tasks has to be known. Possible methods are described in the following chapter.

Worst-Case Execution Time (WCET) Analysis

The above mentioned PLS and MLS have to be supplied with the worst-case execution times which have to fulfill two requirements, they have to be safe, means they must not under-estimate the worst case and they have to be tight, to avoid the waste of resources.

Real-Time Software in Automotive Applications

The software structure of automotive applications is characterized by a cyclic execution: Reading in physical values, execution of algorithms and giving out the computed values. Assembler has been the standard programming language, which has been optimized manually due to the high pressure on costs of the used hardware. But there is a visible trend to use higher level languages especially C and code, generated by tools, which have been improved in respect to code efficiency.

There have only used processor with simple architecture and flat memory in automobiles. But the increasing functionality, which will be realized in future by software, leads to usage of hardware platforms with higher performance. The decision, if platforms with caches and pipelines will be used in time triggered architectures depends on the powerfulness of WCET-analysis and the possibilities in making them deterministic enough by deterministic cacheing strategies for example.

Known Approaches

The estimation of the worst-case execution time of a real-time software is a complex task. The influences of all participating parts - application software, compiler and used hardware platforms have to be taken into consideration. There are described two general approaches for estimating the worst-case execution time in literature [Kope97c]: The pragmatic approach by on-line measurement and the analytical approach by modeling all participating parts. Their characteristics are discussed below:

Analytical Approach - Modeling
An analytical model has to be built for each part (software, compiler and hardware platform). Because of the strong influence of the underlying hardware and used the compiler, the analysis has to be done at source code and machine code level. By this model-based method, it is generally possible to compute safe worst-case times, and there could be reached successes for simple hardware architectures [PuSc97], but it is still a big challenge for modern hardware architectures with parallel units and hierarchical memory organization. There are known many approaches focusing sub-problems, but there is still a lack of a general method. And because of the complexity there is no professional tool available [Pusch97].

Pragmatic Approach - Measurement
This approach is based on measuring the execution times on-line during runtime without costly modeling, only with few additional lines of code and external equipment like logic analyzer or oscilloscope. But there is no guarantee to find the path through the code with the maximum execution time.

We are convinced, that for practical usage of the WCET-analysis a mixture between the presented approaches is required, which allows fast configuration for other hardware platforms and gives a maximum of safe bounds of predicted WCET (but no guarantee). So we have focused our researches to a method, based on intelligent measurement including model-based components: The source-code is included with additional functions, which are recording timing information during runtime, in an early state of system evaluation. After runtime, timing information is analyzed by a timing tool, computing the worst-case path.

Developing Tools

Every part of the developing process should be supported by tools in order to handle the complexity of the system, accelerate the design process and increase the reliability. A tool environment for realizing time triggered architectures has to support the design of the task and message schedule, the realization of the application, the system integration and the test of the availability and safety requirements. We need several kinds of tools:
- For definition of the static message and task schedule a tool has to be available. This tool has to allow a graphical definition of the time and message constraints and generates a valid message and task schedule. A first prototype realization was developed by the University of Vienna [Noss97].

- For realization of applications in the automotive environment typically tools like Matlab/Simulink and Statemate are used, to develop control loops and simulate the system behavior. These tools have to adapted to the constraints of time triggered architectures. Also the possibilities to integrate software components and worst-case execution times have to be supported.
- For system integration a tool for monitoring the messages on the communication channels and for simulation of non-available nodes is required. During development the complete system is usually not available or subsystems are developed by other departments or outhouse partners. For testing and evaluating issues the simulation of the non-available nodes are required [Flei97].
- For testing the availability and safety requirements we need the possibilities for fault injection in software and hardware and reliability modeling. For fault injection on the communication bus a fault injection device called TTP-stress is available [HeSc98].

Conclusion

In this paper we present a new architecture approach for future automotive by-wire systems without mechanical or hydraulic backup based on a time triggered architecture. In the first part of the paper we introduce the time triggered architecture and the time triggered protocol. We showed that time triggered architectures are well suited for safety critical by-wire applications. In the second part we describe demands for the application design. This part contains demands for reusable software components, for the operating systems and tools for the developing process.

References

[Bril90]   S. Brilliant, J. C. Knight, N. Leveson: „Analysis of faults in an N-version software experiment," IEEE Transactions on Software Engineering, SE-16(2), February 1990.

[Dilg97a] E. Dilger et al.: „Towards an Architecture for Safety Related Fault Tolerant Systems in Vehicles", Proceedings of the ESREL´97 International Conference, June 1997.

[Dilg97b] E. Dilger, T. Führer, B. Müller, S. Poledna, T. Thurner: „X-By-Wire: Design von verteilten, fehlertoleranten und sicherheitskritischen Anwendungen in modernen Kraft-fahrzeugen", Tagungsband der 17. VDI/VW-Gemeinschaftstagung Systemengineering in der Kfz-Entwicklung, Wolfsburg, 3.12. - 5.12.97

[Fisc98] M. Fischer, „Entwicklung eines fehlertoleranten TTP-basierten Multi-Level-Schedulers für den 80C167", master thesis, Institute for Industrial Automation and Software Engineering, University of Stuttgart, Stuttgart, June 1998

[Flei97]   W. Fleisch, Th. Ringler, R. Belschner: „Simulation of application software for a TTP real-time subsystem", European Simulation Multi Conference, May 1997.

[HeBe98] B. Hedenetz, R. Belschner, „Brake-by-wire without Mechanical Backup by Using a TTP-Communication Network", SAE International Congress 1998, SAE 981109.

[HeSc98] B. Hedenetz, A. V. Schedl: „Fault Injection and Fault Modeling for a Safety Critical Automotive Communication System", ESREL 98, Trondheim, Norway, June 1998.

[HeTh98] G. Heiner, T. Thurner, „Time-Triggered Architecture for Safety-Related Distributed Real-Time Systems in Transportation Systems", FTCS-28, June 1998.

[Karl95] J. Karlsson, P. Folkesson, J. Arlat, Y. Crouzet, G. Leber, „Integration and Comparison of Three Physical Fault Injection Techniques", Predictably Dependable Computing Systems, Springer Verlag 309-329, 1995.

[KrKo95] A. Krüger, H. Kopetz, „A Network Controller Interface for a Time-Triggered Protocol", SAE Symposium on Future Transportation Electronics: Multiplexing and In-Vehicle Networking, SAE, 1995.

[Kope94] H. Kopetz, G. Grünsteidl, „TTP - A Protocol for Fault-Tolerant Real-Time Systems", IEEE Computer, pages 14-23, January 1994.

[Kope97a] Kopetz et al.: „A Prototype Implementation of a TTP/C Controller. Proc. SAE Congress '97", Detroit, Michigan, 1997.

[Kope97b] H. Kopetz, „Real-Time Systems - Design Principles for Distributed Real-Time Systems", Kluwers Academic Publishers, 1997.

[Kope97c] H. Kopetz, „The Systematic Design of Embedded Real-Time Systems", Three day intensive Seminar, Munich, 1996

[KrSc97] Markus Krug and Anton V. Schedl: „New Demands for Invehicle Networks", Proceedings of the 23rd Euromicro Conference", pp. 601-606, Budapest, Hungary, September 1997.

[Krüg97] A. Krüger, „Interface design for Time-Triggered Real-Time System Architectures", doctor thesis, Institut für Technische Informatik, Vienna University of Technology, 1997.

[Krug98] M. Krug: „Concept and Implementation of a Dependable Automotive Operating System", doctor thesis, Institut für Technische Informatik, Universität Tübingen, 1998.

[Krüg97] A. Krüger, „Interface design for Time-Triggered Real-Time System Architectures", doctor thesis, Institut für Technische Informatik, Vienna University of Technology, 1997.

[Noss97] Roman Nossal, „An Application-Oriented Methodology for the Development of Real-Time Applications", doctor thesis, Institut für Technische Informatik, Vienna University of Technology, 1997.

[PuSc97] P. Puschner and A. Schedl. „Computing maximum task execution times - a graph-based approach", Real-time Systems, 13(1):67-91, July 1997

[PuVr97] P. Puschner and Alexander Vrchoticky „Problems in Static Worst-Case Execution Time Analysis", Research Report No. 6/96, Institut für Technische Informatik, Vienna University of Technology, 1996.

[SAE93a] SAE, „Class C Application Requirement Considerations", SAE Recommended Practice J2056/1, SAE, June 1993.

[SAE93b] SAE, „Survey of Known Protocols", SAE Information Report J2056/2, SAE, April 1993.

[Sche98] Scheidler, G. Heiner, R. Sasse, E. Fuchs, H. Kopetz, C. Temple, „Time-Triggered Architecture - (TTA)", Advances in Information Technologies: The Business Challenge, J.-Y. Roger et al. (Eds.), IOS Press, 1997, pages 758-765.

Fault-Tolerant Communication in Large-Scale Manipulators

H.-D. Kochs[1], W. Geisselhardt[2], H. Hilmer[1], and M. Lenord

[1] Gerhard-Mercator-University Duisburg, Germany
Faculty of Mechanical Engineering, Department of Information Processing
{kochs, hilmer, lenord}@mti.uni-duisburg.de
http://www.mti.uni-duisburg.de
[2] Gerhard-Mercator-University Duisburg, Germany
Faculty of Electrical Engineering, Department of Dataprocessing
gd@uni-duisburg.de
http://www.fb9dv.uni-duisburg.de/dve.html

Abstract. In this paper concepts for fault-tolerant communication systems in large-scale manipulators for heavy weights are introduced. This class of robots makes high demands on safety and real-time behaviour of data transmission, which cannot be fulfilled by conventional communication systems. According to different types of data the communication system has to cope with, two fault-tolerant architectures, based on the CAN-protocol and on the ATM system, are exposed.

1 Introduction

Large-scale manipulators build a special class in the area of big robots. They cover a wide range of applications. Examples are the employment in the building industry, the cleaning and restauration of buildings, the inspection of freeway bridges, the employment in the mining industry and as evacuation equipment in disaster control operations.

As an example, Fig. 1 demonstrates a scenario of the mining industry. It shows a tunnel drilling robot like it is applicated nowadays. A specialist handles the robot locally. In the future the operator will work over-meet and remotely observe and control the robot. A head-mounted-display, a data-cage or a data-glove can be employed. All versions of heavy load handling systems have a very complex data processing system, which is clarified on the basis of a further configuration in Fig. 2. It covers a multiplicity of sensors, on the one hand for environment recording, on the other hand for the positioning of the joints with consideration of the elasticity. Further units fulfill those functions: drive, trajectory planning, collision avoidance, man-machine interface (MMI) and monitoring. As a result, various data flow between the components, which require a suitable communication system. Due to the multiplicity of the components, the spatial expansion and the safety and reliability requirements a distributed system structure on the basis of serial bus systems is aimed at. The communication system does not only have to meet high temporal requirements for the fulfilment of the control

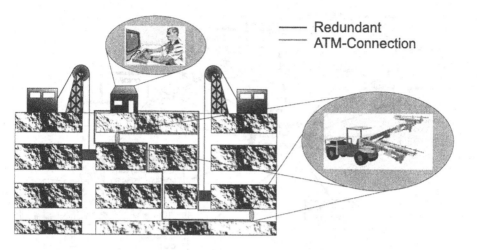

Fig. 1. Application from the mining industry

functions, but is also subject to very high safety and reliability request. These result from the dynamics and size of the device as well as the possible stay of humans in the work area. Data flows cover data with different characteristics. Therefore different communication protocols and architectures are to use. In the following two fault-tolerant architectures are introduced, which can be used for the data communication in different levels of the data processing hierarchy of a large-scale manipulator.

2 Data Processing in Large-Scale Manipulators

In order to specify the requirements in detail a view of the most important processes is necessary, which run on a distributed computer system and are linked together. The operator only moves the endeffector of the robot arm, all further arm segments align themselves independently. Since the manipulator arm has several degrees of freedom in the motion, it can move in such a way around obstacles. This requires a complex calculation of all joint angles [8]. Besides, mechanical components must be held on the debit position by an intelligent controller. On the basis of a layer model the necessary processes are structured from the point of view of the communication system.

2.1 Hierarchial Model of Data Processing

In the automation engineering communication units are roughly classified [3] by a hierarchial model. Fig. 3 shows the model of the data processing in large-scale manipulator systems, which makes a classification according to the control tasks of a layer and the data processing components.

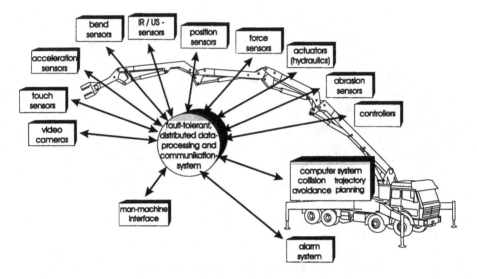

Fig. 2. Prototype of a large-scale manipulator

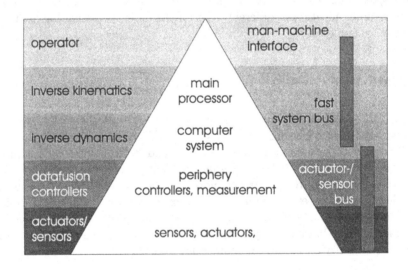

Fig. 3. Hierarchial model of the data processing

– Operator's layer

The operator controls and observes the working process of the large-scale manipulator. The core function is the movement of the endeffector. If the control station is far away, it is called telerobotics. A possible scenario was already described in chapter one. The user needs a very large quantity of data to control the system (video, sound, sensor and control data).

– Inverse kinematics

Processes of this layer receive the coordinates of the endeffector and determine the appropriate joint angles of all arm segments. Also information of the sensor layer is transfered to this point. Major task is the on-line trajectory planning including the collision avoidance.

– Inverse dynamics

This layer executes processes, which have been invoked by the inverse kinematics. Major tasks are calculations for the inverse dynamics. The torque is calculated in order to transfer the joint into the desired angle position. Therefore data of all layers are necessary.

– Datafusion, controllers

In this layer the controlling of hardware components takes place. Joints are driven into certain positions by force control. The control processes obtain their reference input from the inverse dynamics and are linked over field busses.

– Sensor/actuator layer

Here, the collection and preprocessing of sensor information as well as the controlling of the actuators takes place.

2.2 Communication Requirements

Regarding the data processing requirements, the communication system has to provide:

– Real-time behaviour (sufficient bandwidth, determinism of data transfer, i.e. worst case delays have to be guaranteed);
– High safety (fail-safe behaviour);
– High reliability.

According to the different layers of data processing there is a great number of data types, distinguishing from the following characteristics:

– Data length;
– Frequency of data occurence;
– Kind of data occurence: event-driven (spontanous) time-driven (cyclic, periodic); Performance requirements;
– Determinism requirements (e.g. maximum jitter);
– Safety-related;
– Kind of addressing: uni-, multi- or broadcast.

Regarding data lengths and real-time requirements, there are two major categories of data:

1. Large Quantities of data, comprising large message lengths, to be transfered under medium real-time constraints. These kind of data arise in high layers of data processing (e.g. telerobotics).
2. Short messages occurring with high frequency, to be transfered with high determinism. Data of the sensor/actuator layer belong to this category.

In general, communication systems like Ethernet (TCP/IP), FDDI and ATM are utilized for the transfer of data of the first category. But, regarding the high safety and reliability requirements of large-scale manipulators, these protocols are not suitable without fault tolerance enhancements. Standardized communication systems belonging to the fieldbus or sensor/actuator domain may meet the real-time constraints of the low level data transfer of the second category, but suffer from limited fault tolerance capabilities, too. In the following, fault-tolerant communication architectures, on one hand suitable for sensor/actuator communication and on the other hand adapted for telerobotics, are introduced. As far as possible, standardized protocols and components are used, enhanced by software (protocol) and hardware features in order to improve the safety and reliability of data transfer.

3 Sensor/Actuator Communication

On the lowest level of the control hierarchy, the sensor/actuator level, data is characterized by information occuring predominantly cyclically. The transfer of these periodic values, controlling the process, are subject to high real-time constraints i.e. defaulted time limits must be kept with high accuracy. By the predetermination of cyclical data occurence, both the communication protocol and the application software can use fixed processing schedules which guarantee a high determinism. In addition to information occuring periodically, a bus system must provide transmission capacity for acyclic event-oriented data. These messages, such as emergency signals of the process, error messages concerning the communication system components or acyclic control instructions, are subject to high temporal constraints, too. For example, an error message has to be transmitted very rapidly in order to start fault tolerance measures without effecting the process seriously. Overcoming both periodic and event-oriented data transfer under high realtime, safety and reliability constraints, depends on the kind of the chosen communication protocol, in particular the bus access strategy. Cyclical bus access mechanisms like token-, polling- or time slice mechanisms are tailored to the deterministic transfer of cyclically occurring data. The transfer of event-oriented data requires reserving bus capacity which remains unused in the case of not occurring events. As a result, the bus load increases leading to an increase in the medium bus access delay, especially regarding networks, which comprise a high number of nodes. In contrast, event-oriented (multi master, CSMA) strategies provide a high efficiency, i.e. low bus access delays, transfering event-driven data. Using a multi master protocol, each node is allowed to start the transmission of a message at any point of time, unless the bus is occupied by another transmission activated before. Due to collisions, i.e. the concurrent bus access of two or more nodes, determinism of data transfer is worse compared to time-driven mechanisms. The complex nature of data in a large-scale manipulator, comprising event-triggered as well as time driven data, requires the combination of different protocol strategies.

In order to achieve high safety and reliability, it has to be guaranteed that data transfer continues even in the case of a component fault. Mainly, there are two types of faults:

- Global faults lead to a breakdown of the system-wide communication. This causes the crash of the overall system function. Sample global faults are: short failures of the transmission line, open failures of the transmission line (interruption of a bus wire), short failures at a bus-side output of a network node, bubbling idiot failures, i.e. a deadlock of the bus due to a permanently transmitting node.
- Local faults are limited to malfunctions of node components, leading
- to a separation of the erroneous node, but do not influence overall
- system communication seriously.

Moreover, faults can be classified as

- temporary faults, which disturb the system operation for a limited amount of time;
- permanent faults, which are not reversible.

Global faults such as a total breakdown of a transmission line only can be tolerated by the use of hardware redundancy, for example the duplication of bus lines. Redundancy has to be managed in an efficient way, comprising several stages:

1. Fault detection
2. Fault separation (to avoid impairment of the system operation by an erroneous component)
3. Fault notification (to all of the network nodes)
4. Redundancy switch-over (i.e. replacement of an erroneous component by an operational replica)
5. Recovery of a consistent system state

The primary goal of fault-tolerant system design is that in case of a fault redundancy handling takes place without any loss, corruption, and duplication of messages. In other words, data consistency has to be maintained even in the case of component faults without exceeding the timing constraints. With respect to real-time requirements, the delays of the fault handling stages have to be minimized. A very important aspect of fault-tolerant system design is fault detection. Faults have to be detected with a high probability, i.e. with a high error coverage, and within a minimal amount of time, i.e. with a minimal error latency. In the following, a concept for a fault-tolerant system is introduced, comprising enhanced fault tolerance features and redundant system structures. The system is based on the event-triggered standardized communication protocol CAN.

3.1 A Fault-Tolerant System Concept based on CAN

The Fault-tolerant System Architecture

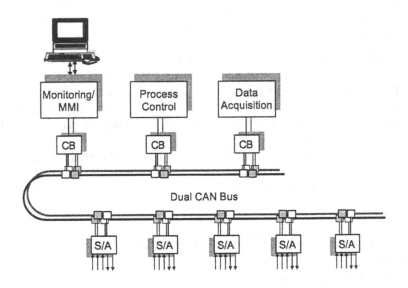

Fig. 4. Sample sensor/actuator communication system

As to be seen in Fig. 4, a distributed communication system of a manipulator using the proposed fault tolerance concept [5] includes several functional units such as process control, MMI (Man Machine Interface), monitoring and data acquisition, as well as sensor and actuator components. Each unit is attached to a dual CAN bus by the use of a communication board or a sensor/actuator board, respectively. A board, also known as node, provides two fully redundant bus links, each link comprising a micro-controller, a CAN communication controller, and a transceiver, as is illustrated in Fig. 5. The micro-controller initiates transmissions of data, selects received messages and passes them on for processing. In addition, the enhanced mechanisms for redundancy management and fault control are executed by the micro-controller. The CAN controller controls all of the mechanisms specified in the CAN protocol [1]. Finally, the transceiver carries out the physical connection of the node to the transmission medium.

Basics of the CAN Protocol. CAN, which was originally developed for use as a sensor/actuator bus in a motor vehicle, is suitable for wide areas of automation technology. Above all, the realization of a highly reliable and effective atomic multicast transmission principle and the mechanisms for fault detection

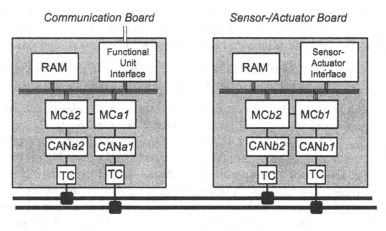

Fig. 5. Redundant communication nodes

make CAN a basis for highly reliable real-time systems. CAN networks are multi-master systems, i.e. bus access for every node is allowed if the bus is idle, also referred to as CSMA/CR or Carrier Sense, Multiple Access, with Collision Resolution. In the case of a collision, the message of highest priority prevails and may continue transmission. Therefore, a priority is assigned to every message.

Thus, worst case access times for all messages can be calculated during system design. The maximum data rate for a CAN system is specified at 1 Mbit/s. The transfer of data in a CAN network takes place as follows. A node broadcasts a message to all other nodes. If any node discovers a transmission fault, it destroys the message while the transmission is still taking place by overwriting the bus level with an error frame. As a result, all of the nodes discard the erroneous message and the transmitter starts a new transmission. This corresponds to the principle of atomic multicast. A negative confirmation mechanism is realized, i.e. in a fault-free case, a transaction requires the transmission of only one message. CAN has built-in mechanisms for error detection and localization. Defective nodes are switched off the bus, implementing a fail-safe behavior. For this purpose, each node maintains an internal error counter, which is incremented after a transmission fault has been detected and decremented after each fault-free transmission. If an error counter reaches the value 127, the node automatically goes from the error active into the error passive state, i.e. it may continue to transmit and receive messages but cannot destroy any faulty message by transmitting an error frame. A CAN controller having an error counter which reaches the value 256 switches into the bus off state, i.e. it no longer participates in the bus traffic in any way. That means, a faulty node disrupts the bus traffic by transmitting error frames until it goes into the passive state.

Enhanced Fault Tolerance Management. Since CAN is designed for use in single bus systems it has a number of disadvantages with respect to the requirements explained relating to fault tolerance. The limitations of CAN are:

- The management of redundancy is not provided for in the CAN protocol.
- Concerning node component faults, high error latencies may occur.

The redundant realization of system components, in particular of the bus line, requires additional mechanisms for the consistent switch-over to the replicated components in the case of a fault without exceeding real-time constraints. In addition, the negative confirmation mechanism of CAN causes high error latencies: the transmitter of a message does not detect the failure of another network node but rather assumes that if error frames do not occur all of the receivers have received its message without faults. Thus, node losses cannot be detected, especially in a sufficient period of time. The proposed protocol enhancements eliminate this through the use of a fault-active mechanism comprising system monitoring and error notification methods. The fault-active mechanism allows each communication link to be monitored by the other link of its node. For this purpose each micro-controller serves as a watchdog processor for the other link. In addition, in case of a component fault a node is able to become active autonomously, i.e. it informs all network nodes about the failure by transmitting an error notification message through the operational link and communication channel. Thus, the second bus system fulfills the function of a watchdog bus. During normal operation the entire process data traffic is executed through one communication channel. A sample fault reaction process started after the occurence of a failure of CAN controller a1 (Fig. 5), takes place as follows: CAN controller a1 disrupts all network traffic on bus 1 until its error counter reaches 128; reaching the error counter value 96 CAN controller a1 transmits an error interrupt to micro-controller a1; micro-controller a1 informs micro-controller a2 of the loss of the CAN controller; micro-controller a2 starts the transmission of an error notification message through bus 2; all of the network nodes receive the error message through the links 2; all nodes switch off bus 1 and continue the transmission of process data through bus 2. The advantage of this method lies in the fact that the fault tolerance process is executed while the faulty CAN controller is in the active error state (error counter 127). This controller therefore continuously destroys the message which is detected as being faulty up to the switch-over process. As a result, no message is lost and no faulty message is processed until the bus switch-over has finished. Concerning the recovery of a consistent system state after the occurence of faults, an important aspect is the maximum number of messages, which are lost while the fault tolerance measures take place. Message losses may occur because the faulty node is not able to receive any message until it is replaced by its redundant component. Lost messages have to be retransmitted through the use of time-consuming recovery processes. Regarding the proposed concept, in case of a CAN controller fault no message loss occurs. Regarding specific malfunctions of a micro-controller, it may not be possible to entirely exclude a message loss. This situation can occur, for example, if the fault latency is greater than the duration of the transmission of a message. Nevertheless, only a few messages are to be retransmitted causing a minimal recovery effort. Thus, the preconditions of maintaining the consistency of data in the case of a fault are fulfilled.

4 Fault-Tolerant Data Transmission in the Telerobotics

For a better understanding the following exposition is based on the mining scenario introduced in chapter two. Main topic is the communication link between the control station over-meet and the large-scale manipulator working down in the tunnel. To fulfil the requirements for safety and reliability a redundant realisation is necessary. The communication links don't only have to be implemented dual, but they must also run on spatial separate paths. Otherwise a collapse in a single part of the tunnel could lead to a complete damage of both links. A possibility to communicate via an ATM network enhanced concerning safety is presented.

4.1 The Model of an ATM Communication

ATM connects the following components:

- the man-machine-interface,
- the video cameras,
- the sensors for the acquisition of environment data e.g. ultra-sonic sensors and
- the distributed computer system. Parallel bus systems like VME or
- PCI are not appropriate because such a tight coupling does not avoid
- error propagation.

4.2 Reasons for the Implementation of ATM

ATM is known to be a high performance communication system for telecommunication and multi-media. The following reasons show why ATM is suggestive in this case.

- In the telerobotics mainly multi-media information is present. Most important sensors are the video cameras, which have to transfer a realistic picture of the robot environment in real-time.
- ATM is not only implemented in wide area networks (WAN). The employment as a computer-computer communication system has been proved. The Washington University in St. Louis has formed the term DAN (desk area network) and has developed a micro chip which supports the communication in the local computer environment (APIC, ATM Port Interconnect Controller)[2].
- ATM is a real-time system. The quality-of-service-protocols guaranty properties of the transmission (maximum cell transfer delay - CTD, cell delay variation - CDV).

Yet ATM cannot fulfil the high safety requirements. Therfore enhancements for redundant communication paths are introduced.

4.3 Safety Enhancements

Figure 6 shows two ATM nodes which are linked via an ATM network. The layer model of ATM is not derived from the ISO/OSI model ([4], [6], [7]). The ATM network consists of many ATM switches. As an example the figure shows the functional structure of one. Which enhancements have to be made to improve ATM concerning safety requirements?

- The signaling protocol has to be extended. On demand two redundant, disjunctive routes have to be found. The maximum difference of the transmission delay has to be transfered to the ATM layer.
- The ATM layer has to evaluate two streams of data. It has to buffer the incoming cells until the redundant cells have been received in order to compare them. The sender also has to handle a buffer in order to enable a backward recovery.

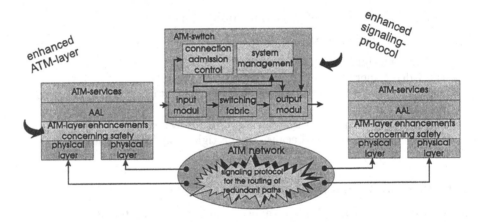

Fig. 6. Enhancements of ATM concerning the safety

4.4 Fault Detection and Handling

The process of error handling is roughly shown in Fig. 7. The upper boxes present four important possibilties of faults. The lower ones show four ways to handle the faulty state.

If two incoming ATM cells are different, the error handling depends on the priority of the information they carry. For this reason the cell loss priority flag (CLP) in the ATM-header is used. If CLP equals 1 the information has low priority e.g. video or audio data. The faulty information can be interpolated by the system (forward recovery). In the case of high priority data a backward recovery has to be made. The receiver rejects all incoming cells beginning from this point of time and demands a repetition. Therefore the sender copies all

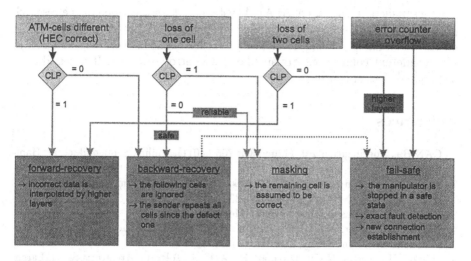

Fig. 7. Fault detection and handling in the ATM layer

outgoing cells into a ringbuffer. If the backward recovery fails, the operation has to be stopped and the system must be transfered into a safe state. If a running cell exceeds the maximum difference of the transmission delay, it is lost. Again the priority determines the way to handle this error. In the case of low priority information the system assumes the remaining cell to be correct (masking). Even if the data is faulty, it has no negative effect on the operation. If the cell has high priority, the way to handle this state depends on the consideration whether safety or reliability dominates. If on the one hand reliability is more important, you can mask the fault because the occurance of two faulty cells is very improbable. On the other hand a safe system has to invoke the backward recovery to avoid any risk of a faulty state. The case of two lost cells is very unlikely, but has the most dangerous effects. It is very difficult to detect this kind of fault. If the cells have high priority only higher layers can avoid catastrophic consequences. It has to be analysed, if a single-error assumption is maintainable or if employments have to be implemented to detect it. In all error cases a counter is incremented. If this counter exceeds a defined number in a period of time, the system has to be transfered into a safe state. It must run an exact diagnostic programm.

5 Conclusion and Future Work

Conventional communication systems do not meet the high requirements concerning safety/reliability and real-time of large-scale redundant manipulators. Therefore standardized protocols have been enhanced by extensive fault tolerance measures. The proposed CAN-based system is suitable for data transfer in the sensor/actuator layer. The requirements of higher communication layers can be satisfied by the extended ATM system. Within the scope of the research project SFB 291 these concepts will be applicated to real prototypes. In addition an ATM simulator is being developed. A virtual ATM network can be built, in which different connections are simulated and errors injected. It is based on a distributed system concept.

References

1. CAN Bus Specification 2.0. (12nc 9398 706 64011). Philips Semiconductors, Hamburg (1994)
2. Dittia Z.-D., Zubin D., Cox, J.-R., Parulkar, G.-M.: Washington University's Gigabit ATM Desk Area Network. (1994) 315–333
3. Eilmes, C.: Feldbus ja, aber welcher? Messtech (1996)
4. Händel, R., Huber, M.-N., Schröder, S.: ATM Networks Concepts, Protocols, Applications. Addison-Wesley, Cambridge (1994)
5. Hilmer, H., Kochs, H.-D., Dittmar, E.: A Fault-Tolerant Architecture for Large-Scale Distributed Control Systems. In: Proceedings of the 14th IFAC Workshop of Distributed Computer Control Systems (DCCS'97), Seoul (1997)
6. Onvural, R.-O.: Asynchronous Transfer Mode Networks. Artech House, Norwood (1995)
7. De Prycker, M.: Asynchronous Transfer Mode. Prentice Hall International, Hemel Hempstead (1995)
8. Schneider, M., Hiller, M.: Nonlinear Motion Control of Hydraulically Driven Large Redundant Manipulators. In: Proceedings of the IFAC-Workshop Motion Control, Munich (1995)

Distributed Fault Tolerant and Safety Critical Applications in Vehicles – A Time-Triggered Approach

E. Dilger, T. Führer, B. Müller

Robert Bosch GmbH
Postfach 106050, 70049 Stuttgart
{dilger, fuehrer, mueller}@fli.sh.bosch.de

Abstract. For various reasons complex safety related functions in future automotive systems will be based on electronics without relying on mechanical or hydraulic back-up. Benefits of these so-called „X-By-Wire"-systems are simplified packaging, an increase of active and passive safety, the easy integration of driver assistance systems and the absence of hydraulic fluids. The objective of the Brite EuRam III Project „Safety Related Fault Tolerant Systems in Vehicles (X-By-Wire)" is to develop a framework for an electric/electronic architecture for X-By-Wire systems. For safety reasons these systems must be distributed, fault-tolerant and connected by a fault-tolerant real time communication medium. The time triggered protocol TTP/C satisfies the communication requirements. This protocol operates on a duplicated bus, it sends actively replicated messages and provides error detection in the domains of time and value as well as a globally synchronized time base. Within the X-By-Wire project a prototype of a steer-by-wire system is assembled. This prototype will demonstrate the application of the general ideas, the principles, and the mechanisms developed by the X-By-Wire partners.

1. INTRODUCTION

Complex safety related functions in future automotive systems will be more and more based on electronic components. They will no longer rely on mechanical or hydraulic back-up. The general tendency towards dry systems, the constructive advantages resulting from the simplified packaging of non-mechanical components, the big potential of increasing passive and active safety and the easy integration of driver assistance systems are some of the benefits of these so-called „X-By-Wire"-systems. Thus, to be competitive the European automotive and supplier industry has to realize these systems.

Automotive systems are embedded systems and figure 1 shows a possible scenario of an in-vehicle network today (resp. tomorrow).

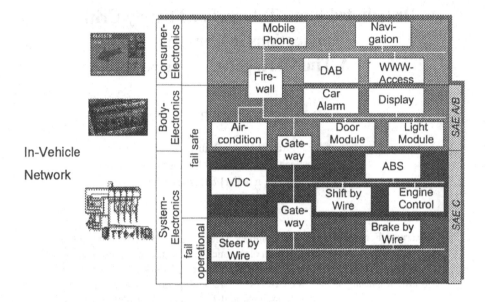

Fig. 1. **In-Vehicle Network**

The requirements for this network are quite various. In the field of consumer electronics (mobile phone, navigation, digital audio broadcast, access to world wide web, ...) we need high bandwidth and availability. Body electronics (alarm, door, light, air condition, ...) has to meet soft real time communication requirements, system electronics (antilock braking system, vehicle dynamics control, engine control, ...) needs (very fast) hard real time communication and steer and brake by wire systems without mechanical/hydraulic back-up must be highly dependable and fault-tolerant.

Clearly no single in-vehicle network will fulfill these requirements, therefore, two, three, or four networks connected by gateways, separated by firewalls will exist.

It is the objective of the Brite-EuRam III-project "Safety Related Fault Tolerant Systems in Vehicles" to define a framework for the introduction of safety related fault tolerant electronic systems without mechanical back-up in vehicles (so-called "X-By-Wire systems"). The "X" in "X-By-Wire" represents any safety related application such as steering, braking, powertrain or suspension control. These applications will greatly increase overall vehicle safety by liberating the driver from routine tasks and assisting the driver to cope with critical situations.

Due to the required level of safety an X-By-Wire system must be distributed and consisting of fault tolerant units connected by a reliable real time communication medium. Therefore, for the communication system, the time-triggered TTP/C real-time communication protocol was selected. TTP/C provides fault-tolerance message transfer, state synchronization, reliable detection of node failures, a global time base, and a distributed membership service.

The consortium of the Brite-Euram III Project "Safety Related Fault Tolerant Systems in Vehicles" consists of the following partners: Daimler-Benz Research, Fiat

Research Center, Ford Europe, Volvo, Bosch, Magneti Marelli, Mecel, University of Chalmers, and the Vienna University of Technology.

The objective of this project is the development of an architecture for future X-By-Wire systems in vehicles which allows to avoid conventional mechanical or hydraulic back-up solutions. This architecture should be archetypical for future standardization activities. It comprises

- Overall design (e.g. time triggered design)
- Fault tolerance strategy
- Layout of electronics and electric energy supply
- Communication protocol (e.g. time triggered communication)
- Software concept
- Selection and coupling of actuators and sensors
- Development process.

Motivation

Due to enormous development and research costs no vehicle manufacturer has until now brought to market fault-tolerant safety-relevant X-By-Wire systems without conventional back-up. Today's systems must detect failures and switch off reliably; the available back-up level is sufficient in order to achieve a safe state. X-By-Wire systems must fulfill however even in the case of an otherwise fatal failure their specified functionality in any case. From the point of view of vehicle electronics new concepts are necessary.

For the European industry an efficient and coordinated basic development must be activated. In addition a prerequisite for economical mass production is a uniform specification, and in order to come to a European standard, the course must be set by the automotive industry. A common first beginning as in the project X-By-Wire can prevent expensive and unnecessary parallel developments and divergent methodologies in the area of X-By-Wire.

2. SUBSTANTIAL ITEMS OF THE X-BY-WIRE ARCHITEC-TURE

In principle an X-By-Wire system is designed as a distributed fault-tolerant system. It must be assumed that it consists of components which have been developed at different companies and which are integrated in varying configurations. However it must be possible to guarantee the reliability of the required total functionality at any time in any stage of the development of the system.

This target can only be achieved by a methodology, which consistently and systematically considers this demand for reliability in each development step from the design phase to the implementation. This means that during design of these X-By-Wire systems nothing should be left to chance. Hereunder applies the rule that complex relations must generally be reduced to simple and visible mechanisms as far as possible. Parallel to this at no point in time ambiguity should be given to the system, i.e. the system has maximum pre-knowledge on the possible system states and their causal order. An architecture must contain these rules implicitly.

In the following some substantial features of the X-By-Wire architecture are described. The emphasis is on the safety-relevant communication system connecting the parts of the distributed systems.

Timing

An electronic system is called a real time system, if it does not only calculate a correct output value from defined input values, but does this also at the correct (given) point in time. A correct result at a wrong point in time is just as worthless in a real time system as a falsely calculated value at the correct point in time.

Therefore, the reliable delivery of a correct result at the correct point in time is of vital importance for safety-relevant X-By-Wire (real time -) systems. The safety demand for simple and visible concepts in the time domain can most easily be fulfilled by a systematically time-controlled architecture. This means that all processes for reading in, processing and outputting values only are permitted at given points in time and thus run under a strict temporal control. Thus as the maximum bandwidth necessary for the dynamic processes within the system is a priori known, with correct and careful sizing the system can never be overloaded.

Fail Silent Principle

The demand for the correct result at the correct point in time is valid only for the error free operational case. What however, if errors intrude and either values are calculated falsely or are delivered at the wrong point in time? In this case the following "fail silent strategy" applies: All components or subsystems check continuously their timing and results themselves. If deviations from the given operational sequence are detected, the component or the subsystem must behave immediately quiet, i.e. it must switch into a state regarded as uncritical for the external world. This can be realized for example via spontaneous self-disconnection of the component or the subsystem. A prerequisite for this is that power-off shifts the attached peripheral device into a non-safety-critical passive state.

This concept has the advantage that all errors which can occur within a component are converted into only one visible error, i.e. into power-off of the component. This single "error case" is however well-known system-wide and can be intercepted if necessary by active replication (e.g. hot redundancy) of the component. Thus any error is localized and encapsulated at the place of origin. The propagation of an error via several components is not possible any longer. Originally complex error handling strategies on the global system level can be simplified drastically. In the following a fail-silent unit (FSU) is a computing node exhibiting fail-silence behavior. A fault-tolerant unit (FTU) can be a combination of FSUs.

Distributed System

The design of an X-By-Wire system as a distributed fault-tolerant system allows an ideal vehicle-module-oriented adjustment of the system to the vehicle. On the other hand the availability of the total system can be increased by local fault encapsulation of the components due to the "fail silent" principle. If active redundancies are involved, the system itself is a distributed system per se.

3. COMMUNICATION SUBSYSTEM

In a distributed system the information flow plays a key role. If the applied communication protocol and -medium offers reliable access, all members of the distributed system benefit from the advantages of a multicast communication connection. This has already been discovered by the SAE Vehicle Network for Multiplexing and Data Communications Standard Committee, where prerequisites and requirements for distributed systems are analyzed. In [10] requirements for safety sensitive control loops in motor vehicles are created. There in particular vehicle communication protocols applicable for distributed real time systems are dealt with. In this document topics are treated such as temporal performance, dependability and implementation constraints of safety sensitive networks and a typical benchmark problem is pointed out. In [11] the result of the benchmark test was published: none of the tested typical vehicle communication protocols (J1850, CAN, VAN, AUTOLAN, etc..) complies with the requirements of distributed, safety critical applications in motor vehicles.

Requirements

Regular communication: In most safety critical applications processes read periodically data or sensor values, process these and finally forward the calculated values to other processes or appropriate actuators. This periodic data exchange (repetitive data elements) differs from unexpectedly occurring events (chance events) by its calculable bandwidth requirement. If for example an error occurs, which cannot be treated within the sphere of influence of a normal process cycle, this error can result in an unexpected communication expenditure for proclamation and handling.

If there is a minimum repeating period between two similar, successive chance events, then this event can be regarded as a quasi-periodic event and thus regular communication can be guaranteed [6].

Minimum message latency: The latency of a message is defined as the interval between the point in time of the production of the data element at the sender and the earliest point in time of the complete receipt. The maximum latency is always determined by the requirements from the application and can be in the ms area.

The obtained latency of a communication system essentially depends on the following factors: Bandwidth of the communication medium, protocol logic and the access method to the medium. From the user point of view the communication system should always keep the latency jitter, the difference between maximum and minimum message latency, minimal.

Error detection: In a distributed system, where actively replicated nodes are combined into a functional unit, besides local error detection the recognition of an incorrect partner is particularly important. This information (membership information) should be integrated in the protocol services of the communication system.

Fault tolerance: Pure error detection in sensitive applications is not sufficient in order to maintain the required functionality, but the recognition of errors and the uniform and correct handling of them in real time (fail operational behavior). Fault tolerance must be achieved up to a specified number of failures.

Replica Determinism: In most cases the fault-tolerance requirements can only be fulfilled by active redundancy. However, redundant systems require replica determinism to synchronize the internal states of the partners [7]. The replicas must make the same decisions at the same point in time. The communication protocol must support this process with reliable communication and minimum latency jitter.

Robustness: In the automotive area in particular the wiring is exposed to different disturbances. Therefore, when applying a communication system in vehicles, the used types of cable, of connectors and the EMV robustness of these parts are essential. The communication controller itself should show minimum latency to reintegrate a component into the running system after a transient failure.

Acknowledgment and atomic transfer: In many applications the information about the status of the transmission of messages must be available. An acknowledgment of the transmitted message by the recipient may cause additional communication, thus under peak load the system can become unstable (trashing under peak load). The situation is still more critical, if in multicast operation an atomic message transfer is required.

Testability: A real time system should grant constructive testing, where each subsystem is tested independently. After the integration into the global system, the additional communication must not induce unforeseen interactions and must not require repeated testing of local functionality.

4. CONSEQUENCES FROM THE X-BY-WIRE ARCHITECTURE

In addition to the substantial items of the X-By-Wire architecture, like fault tolerance, distribution aspects and appropriate selection of the communication system, real time ability, reliability and composability play an important role.

Real time ability is fulfilled to a large extent by the requirement of regular communication and the demand for minimum message latency. Also the aspect of reliability is essentially covered by the demands for error detection, fault tolerance (by active redundancy), and in addition, by the demand for robustness. In the following the requirements concerning composability in X-By-Wire systems have to be examined in more detail.

Composability: In many engineering disciplines complex systems are structured by assembling well-specified and validated subsystems. In fact it is substantial that the characteristics validated on subsystem level are not violated by system integration. This constructive concept of the system design is called composability.

Accordingly an architecture is composable with respect to a characteristic which was validated on subsystem level already if the characteristic does not become invalid by system integration.

Typical examples of such a characteristic are correct behavior in time or testability. So the temporal correctness of the total system can be derived from the temporal correctness of the subsystems in a composable system. This integration to a distributed global system can be obtained only by the use of a communication system.

In real time systems, as they are considered in X-By-Wire, composability must be achieved both in the domain of time, and in the domain of value.

Special interests of the automotive industry: From the roles and responsibilities within the automobile industry in the case of product development there results a clear demand for composability. The car manufacturer has the job of the system integrator and is responsible for the entire system. The suppliers have the roles of the subsystem manufacturers and are responsible for the subsystems created by them.

In co-operation between the partners involved composability plays an important role. If it is given, clear interfaces and responsibilities can be defined. If composability is not given, a smearing of the responsibilities as well as interface problems result: The subsystem supplier has validated his subsystem and supplies it to the system manufacturer, but the complete system does not operate properly, since the individual subsystem in interaction shows an incorrect behavior, which is not manifested in isolation. Thus the interfaces of the subsystems are specified de-facto incompletely and hidden mutual influences result, which cause incorrect behavior. This influence mechanism is often called hidden interface.

Composability in central computer systems: The mutual influence via hidden interfaces is within a central network architecture much more present than within a distributed network architecture. Because all resources are centrally administered, the individual subsystems are in competition for these resources, e.g. CPU time or storage space. If the number or the behavior of the competitors for common resources changes, this effects availability of resources for the individual subsystems. In a distributed computer system it is possible to minimize hidden inter-faces i.e. commonly used resources. The only common resource, which still exists in a distributed system corresponding to the demands shown, is the communication system.

Composability and temporal encapsulation: In order to guarantee composability in a distributed real time system, it must be ensured that the individual subsystems are temporally decoupled and cannot mutually influence each other via a hidden

interface. This requirement for an interface can be implemented by the concept of the temporal firewall, a mechanism for the achievement of temporal encapsulation [4]:
The temporal firewall is a
- unidirectional data interface with state semantics,
- where at least one subsystem exclusively accesses the interface at a priori admitted points in time
- and for which at each point in time it holds that all available information within the temporal firewall is valid at least for a determined interval of time in the future.

5. THE TIME TRIGGERED PROTOCOL TTP/C

Communication protocols can be divided into event-triggered and time-triggered protocols. The difference is mainly based on how the transmission of a message is initiated. An event-triggered protocol transmits a message as soon as the data which shall be transmitted is available and the send routine of the communication protocol is activated. Considering the global system the problem arises that using this methodology the local control flow influences the control flow of the other communication users via the communication medium, e.g. as a result of the collision of two transmissions at the same time. Thus there is a mutual influence in the temporal performance of the subsystems [2]. A procedure for the access regulation on the communication medium becomes necessary and the associated expenditure of time directly influences the latency jitter of the messages.

Despite usual procedures for the access regulation the demand for temporal encapsulation cannot be fulfilled in a distributed event-triggered real time system. Even with periodic processing the control flow can be shifted temporally due to collisions on the bus. This can lead even to missing deadlines or disturbing the order of events. Even by writing and reading of the messages in the controller network interface (CNI) of a communication controller, thus by data buffering, this problem can not be solved in sensitive real time applications.

Time division multiple access (TDMA): This access method is based on the idea that within a period one time interval in which a bus user possesses exclusive broadcasting rights is given to each member of the distributed system. Each user knows the intervals of the other bus users, so a collision is impossible. The big advantage consists of the fact that each user possesses the same priority, the message latency is calculable and almost constant and the required temporal encapsulation is guaranteed.

The disadvantage of this access procedure is that shifts of the individual access intervals must be avoided. Therefore, a globally synchronized time base (global time) is necessary. Each user of a communication network with TDMA must refer its activities to this global time and a procedure for clock synchronization without additional protocol overhead must be available.

For safety critical applications, the communication network interface (CNI) between a node and the bus must have an additional feature preventing a faulty node or bus controller from sending messages on the bus at the wrong time. This can be done by a bus guardian, an independent component which gives the node access to the bus only at legal times. This bus guardian ensures fail silence in the time domain.

A communication protocol, which offers these possibilities, is the Time Triggered Protocol for Class C applications (TTP/C), which has been developed at the Technical University of Vienna, Institute for Technical Computer Science [1, 3, 5]. It offers among other things the following services:

- temporal encapsulation
- error detection at sender and receiver
- implicit message acknowledgment
- support for fault tolerance
- clock synchronization.

6. SYSTEM SOFTWARE

There are various requirements to the system software. Besides doing its job and being economic in the use of hardware resources, it should provide systematic mechanisms for error detection, robustness, and fault tolerance and support comparability, reusability and testability.

Bosch's DFR model [8, 9] which has been chosen for detailed design of the prototype software is a meta object model and comprises three separate, orthogonal domains: the value domain, the time domain, and the distribution domain. The value domain is concerned with the functional behavior of objects only, without any consideration of synchronization, temporal aspects, or distribution issues. The time domain is concerned with the temporal behavior of the objects of a concurrent software system located on a single processor node like the dynamic interaction of objects and the events triggering changes in the system state. Finally, the distribution domain looks at the assignment of software components to processor nodes and the temporal pattern of communication between the nodes

As objects in different domains are independent from each other (as far as possible) the application developer can design and test for instance objects of the value domain without considering the specific temporal and distributional setting.

Systematic Mechanisms for Error-Detection and Fault-Tolerance

The DFR model supports systematic mechanisms for node-level error detection and system-level fault-tolerance allowing to decouple the application software as far as possible from the fault-tolerance considerations [8, 9]. For instance, the implementation of a process should not be concerned with the degree of replication. The node-level error detection strategies (double execution, double execution with reference check, validity checks, and signature checks) were designed to provide high coverage for the fail-silence assumption. In the DFR model, software components are replicated at the granularity level of subsystems (for a more detailed discussion of DFR object types, see [8]).

Thus, replicated and non-replicated subsystems may reside on the same FSU. This allows the application designer to select the necessary level of redundancy.

If replicated subsystems are present, they must show identical - replica deterministic [7] - behavior in the value domain as well as in the time domain. Non-determinism in the value domain arises for instance due to slightly different sensor readings while non-determinism in the time domain can arise due to slight variations in the processing speed of nodes. As this may have severe consequences agreement on the diverging values resp. times must be supported by a fault tolerance layer in the system software. The DFR model supports enforcement of replica determinism in both domains.

The DFR meta object model was the basis for the development of the xERCOS [8] operating system for embedded real-time control applications and the accompanying off-line tool xOLT. This operating system has been chosen for the prototype. In addition, the OLT generates the complete code for the interface between the processor node and the TTP communication controller.

Generally it can be said, that the combination of the TTP/C protocol and xERCOS/xOLT satisfies the above requirements concerning system software and communication subsystem and thus provides a suitable framework for the prototype implementation.

7. PROTOTYPE

The partners of the X-By-Wire project agreed upon building a non-mobile prototype, intended to demonstrate the general ideas for a steering system.

Fault-Tolerance Characteristics

The table below summarizes the required fault tolerance characteristics of the most important subsystems and gives an example of a prototypical realization of them. These requirements have been derived from the system requirements specification, a document which has been constructed as a part of the X-By-Wire project. Although not all of these requirements necessarily will be those of a future series steering system (this certainly will depend on the manufacturer) the table represents the fault tolerance requirements agreed on by the X-By-Wire partners.

Failure sources	Situation	Functional Degradation	Prototypical Realisation
Permanent failures (not recoverable within 100 ms)			
Power supply (alternator)	all	FrS	1 alternator
Power supply (battery)	engine running	FO/FrS	2 batteries
	engine not running	FrS	
Road wheel steering actuators	all	FO/FrS	3 actuators
Road wheel steering angle sensors	all	FO/FrS	3 sensors
Tactile feedback actuators	all	FO/FrS	2 actuators
Steering wheel angle sensors	all	FO/FrS	3 sensors
FTU	all	FoS	2 FSU
Communication	all	FO/FrS	2 busses
Transient failures			
Transient failures	all	no functional degradation (recovery within 100 ms)	

In this theoretical framework, „actuators" are devices able to independently generate force or torque. Moreover, actuators and sensors are considered fail-silent. Here „O" means fully operational, „o" means fully operational for a predefined time interval, „R" means operational, but functionally reduced, „r" means operational, but functionally reduced for a predefined time interval and „S" means „Safe State", i.e. vehicle stands. Note, that for the tactile feedback, only two actuators are needed to give a two-level fault-tolerance characteristic because it is possible to drive without feedback. Additionally, tactile feedback may not be necessary everywhere (for instance the American market). For the communication only two busses are needed to give the FO/FrS characteristic because each bus itself is intrinsically fault-tolerant.

General Architecture of the Prototype

Fig. 2 is a scheme of the steering-prototype without mechanical backup. The TTP/C communication bus is the backbone of the demonstrator as it connects the three electronic main parts: steering-wheel actuator, steering control unit and steering actuator. Details can be found in [12].

Two replicated nodes form the fault-tolerant steering-wheel actuator. They get the commands from the driver by angle and torque measurement and send these values to the bus. Additionally, they receive the feedback commands from the steering control unit, which gets the appropriate values from the road wheel unit.

The steering control unit also consists of two nodes. They receive the commands from the driver (provided by the steering-wheel actuator) and the feedback from the road-wheels. Furthermore, the steering control unit performs the overall control- and comfort functionality. This function is intended to assist the driver in critical situations, e.g., the car is starting to drift and it also helps the driver during parking maneuvers. Additional information from other systems, e.g., ABS can be taken into account as well. The output is sent by means of the TTP/C-bus to the steering actuator as well as to the steering-wheel actuator.

At the front of the prototype, three micro-controllers form the steering actuator. They are performing a simple control-loop by driving the electro-motors to reach the desired angle of the road wheels. They also control current, angle, and torque by reading their angle and torque sensors. The angle and the torque are communicated to the rest of the system to give the driver a feedback from the road-wheels.

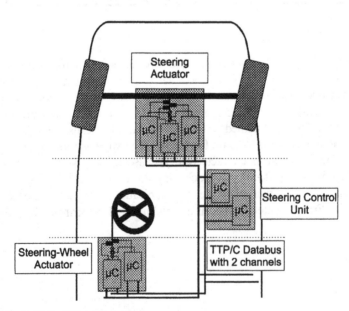

Fig. 2. X-By-Wire Prototype

8. DETAILED DESCRIPTION OF THE STEERING ACTUATOR

We now concentrate on the Bosch part of the prototype which is the steering actuator. As it was not the goal of this project to develop a steering actuator from scratch but to show that it is possible to construct a fault-tolerant steering actuator out of off the shelf components, we used Bosch ABS-motors/power electronics as actuating components. In the present context to fulfill the FO/FrS requirement at least three motors are necessary, because an actuator consisting of two motors will not leave the system operational if both motors have failed. Although one might think that triple redundancy is wasteful in an automotive application, this triple redundancy can have economic and constructive advantages. In a triplicated system each motor has to provide 50% of the necessary torque in order to fulfill the FO/FrS-requirement. In a duplicated system where at least one failure is to be tolerated fully operational, each motor has to provide 100% of the necessary torque. In practice, as a rule of thumb, doubling the power of a motor means triplicating its volume, weight and price. Thus the three motor solution probably can even be more economic than the duplicated system.

In principle it is possible to connect three motors with two FSUs, using intelligent motor interfaces and a bus solution. However, in this project this has not been an option as the necessary off the shelf components have not been available. Thus the complete system is triplicated.

There are different reasons for adding a current sensor into the system. First of all the torque provided by one motor is roughly proportional to its current. Thus the current measurement allows a torque estimation, and the torque is available for tactile feedback. A second reason is to guarantee the fail silent assumption of the motors.

A motor can be assumed fail silent if none of its failure modes results in a blocking of the system or in a reversing of direction. Any failure mode which only implies, that the motor does not supply actively torque any more but does not need (significant) torque to be driven, is a fail silent failure mode. If the motor itself blocks, a non-fail-silent failure mode is present. And if the gear to which the motor is coupled is blocking, when the motor does not actively drive it, again a non-fail-silent failure mode is present. Reversing of direction can be made improbable by design and off-line testing, and can be detected on line by a current measurement. The design of the gear (and the motors) should be done in such a way that a blocking of the system is avoided for instance if a motor is cut off from power. This is indeed possible and has been done in the prototype. Finally most of the motor failures that result in a blocking (for instance melting or loosening of parts by strong magnetic fields) can be avoided if too high currents can be avoided. Thus by adding a current sensor the coverage of the fail silence assumption can strongly be improved.

The general layout of the prototype steering actuator is detailed in the subsequent figure.

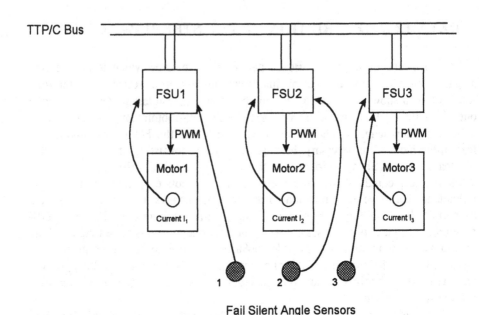

Fail Silent Angle Sensors

Fig. 3. **General layout of steering actuator**

Three FSUs are connected to the TTP/C bus. Each FSU controls one motor via a PWM signal and gets the current signal of the motor. Moreover each FSU is connected to an angle sensor.

If each FSU independently tries to move the controlled object into a certain position it cannot be avoided, that, at least in some positions, one motor works against another one. This is due to slight differences in the angle sensor readings, which always is possible when converting an analogue value into a digital one. This typical replica determinism problem can only be solved, if it is ensured, that all the three FSUs use the same angle value. Thus agreement of the FSUs has to be done via the TTP/C bus and the fault tolerance layer of the system software. It has to provide an agreed value even in the presence of faults. An „inner control loop" using the non-agreed position value must be avoided.

A more detailed look on the sphere of control of one FSU gives the following picture.

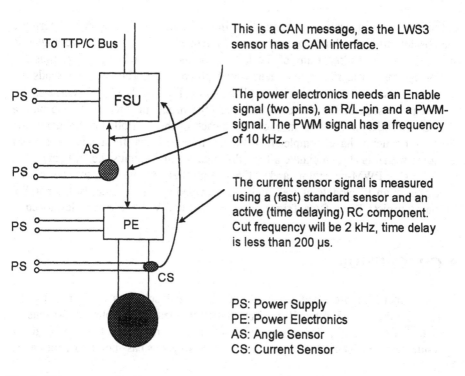

To TTP/C Bus

This is a CAN message, as the LWS3 sensor has a CAN interface.

The power electronics needs an Enable signal (two pins), an R/L-pin and a PWM-signal. The PWM signal has a frequency of 10 kHz.

The current sensor signal is measured using a (fast) standard sensor and an active (time delaying) RC component. Cut frequency will be 2 kHz, time delay is less than 200 µs.

PS: Power Supply
PE: Power Electronics
AS: Angle Sensor
CS: Current Sensor

Fig. 4. **Objects controlled by one FSU**

Description of the Components

The motor is an ABS motor, the Bosch motor ABS 5.3 L. This motor has all the advantages of a series product including availability and low cost. The maximum torque it can supply at 12 V is about 200 Ncm which is well enough for the demonstration (a transmission ratio of 160 is given by the mechanical construction). In this case the motor will need a current of about 80 A.

The power electronics originally has been developed to be part of an intelligent actuation component of a truck clutch, thus is a series part as well. It has been chosen because it is able to handle the high currents needed by the motor. To control it the FSU must send a PWM signal (at 10 kHz), to enabling bits and a left/right signal.

The current sensor is a combination of a standard fast sensor (LEM) and an active RC component. The time resolution of the LEM sensor is so small that the output of the sensor still has the PWM signal form. As for current and torque measurement the smoothed value is relevant, an active, time-delaying RC-component with cut frequency 2kHz was added. The time delay in this case is less than 200 ms, thus will not significantly decrease the performance.

The angle sensor is the fail silent LWS 3.1 sensor. The fail silence property is derived from the fact, that internally two magnetic sensor elements are present. Each of them produces a relative angle and both informations together allow to determine the absolute angle within a certain range. Moreover, each of the relative angles is sufficient to detect almost any of the failures of the other relative angle, thus the sensor can be considered as fail silent with high coverage. The LWS 3.1 sends the angle value as CAN message which implies that the FSU needs a CAN interface.

As can be seen in the above picture, the FSU needs an interface to the bus (a TTP/C controller) as well as an interface to each of the controlled components. As these components have completely different interfaces an IP module has been designed which is able to handle all the different in- and outputs, i.e. A/D and D/A converters, a PWM-generator, and a CAN controller. At the moment the TTP/C controller is an IP module as well and was provided by TU Vienna. In the parallel European project TTA (Time-Triggered Architecture) a VLSI version is developed.

9. CONCLUSION

This paper has presented some of the ideas and solutions developed by the partners of the Brite-EuRam III-project "Safety Related Fault Tolerant Systems in Vehicles" (X-By-Wire) for future automotive systems without mechanical or hydraulic back-up. The solution presented as a prototype is based on four paradigms: These are

- distributed composable architecture,
- time triggered communication,
- replica determinism,
- fail-silent property.

By the construction of the prototype it has been shown that these theoretical concepts can be realized in practice. We feel that using such an approach results in „simple" system architectures with

- predictable and
- reproducible behavior.

These are well suited for dependable applications where there is a high demand for trust-worthiness of a system such that reliance can justifiably be placed on the service it delivers.

ACKNOWLEDGEMENT

We are very obliged to the members of the X-By-Wire project, as well as to the colleagues with Robert Bosch GmbH for the outstanding co-operation. Moreover special thanks to Professor Kopetz, TU Vienna, his co-workers, and the project partners at Daimler-Benz are expressed.

REFERENCES

[1] H. Kopetz., G. Gruensteidl: TTP - A Time-Triggered Protocol for Fault-Tolerant Real-Time Systems, Proc. 23rd IEEE International Symposium on Fault-Tolerant Computing (FTCS-23), Toulouse, France, IEEE Press, 1993, (pp. 524-532), appeared also in a revised version in IEEE Computer. Vol. 24 (1). (pp. 22-26)

[2] H. Kopetz: Should Responsive Systems be Event-Triggered or Time-Triggered? IEICE Trans. on Information and Systems Japan (Special Issue on Responsive Computer Systems), Vol. E76-D(11), 1993, (pp. 1325-1332).

[3] H. Kopetz: Real-Time Systems: Design Principles for Distributed Embedded Applications, Kluwer Academic Publishers, 1997.

[4] H. Kopetz: Component-Based Design of large Distributed Real-Time Systems, to appear in Control Engineering Practice.

[5] M. Krug: A Prototype Implementation of a TTP/C Controller, SAE Technical Paper Series, 970296, February 1997.

[6] A.K. Mok: Fundamental Design Problems of Distributed Systems for the Hard Realtime Environment, Ph.D. dissertation, MIT, 1983.

[7] S. Poledna: Fault-Tolerant Real-Time Systems: The Problem of Replica Determinism, Kluwer Academic Publishers, 1996.

[8] S. Poledna, C. Tanzer: DFR Objects: A Meta Object Model for Distributed Fault-Tolerant Hard Real-Time Systems. Submitted to IEEE International Symposium on Object-Oriented Real-Time Distributed Computing. 1998.

[9] S. Poledna, C. Tanzer: Software Support for Fault-Tolerance. Submitted to International Symposium on Fault-Tolerant Computing. 1998.

[10] J2056 I.R. Class C Multiplexing, Part 1 JUN93 Applications Requirements, Society of Automotive Engineers, Warrendale, PA, 1994

[11] J2056 I.R. Class C Multiplexing, Part 2 APR93 Survey of Known Protocols, Society of Automotive Engineers, Warrendale, PA, 1994.

[12] E. Dilger, T. Führer, B. Müller, S. Poledna: The X-By-Wire Concept: Time-Triggered Information Exchange and Fail Silence Support by new System Services, SAE Technical Paper Series, 980555, February 1998.

Model Checking Safety Critical Software with SPIN: An Application to a Railway Interlocking System

Alessandro Cimatti[1], Fausto Giunchiglia[1], Giorgio Mongardi[2], Dario Romano[3], Fernando Torielli[2], Paolo Traverso[1]

[1] Istituto per la Ricerca Scientifica e Tecnologica (IRST) 38050 - Povo, Trento, Italy
[2] Ansaldo Segnalamento Ferroviario (ASF), Via dei Pescatori 35, 16129, Genova, Italy

Abstract. This paper describes an industrial application in formal verification. The analyzed system is the Safety Logic of an interlocking system for the control of railway stations developed by Ansaldo. The Safety Logic is a process-based software architecture, which can be configured to implement different functions and control stations of different topology.

The applied technique, model checking, allows for the representation of the analyzed system as a finite state machines. Specialized algorithms allow for the automatic and efficient verification of requirements by means of an exhaustive exploration of the state space.

In this paper we describe how a formal model of the Safety Logic has been develped in the language of the SPIN model checker. This model retains the configurability features of the Safety Logic. Furthermore, we discuss how the automated verification of several significant process configurations was carried out without incurring into the state explosion problem.

1 Introduction

This paper describes a joint project between Ansaldo and IRST. The goal of the project was the evaluation of the possibility to integrate formal methods technology within the development cycle of a safety critical application. Particularly relevant was the assessment of formal methods techniques as an advanced debugging tool for the design.

The project focuses on a complex real-world safety critical application developed by Ansaldo, called ACC ("Apparato Centrale a Calcolatore"), a highly programmable and scalable computer interlocking system for the control of railway stations, implemented as a vital architecture based on redundancy [4]. The system is composed of a central nucleus connected to peripheral posts for the control of physical devices (e.g. level crossings, track circuits, signals and switches). The nucleus of the system is based on three independent computers, connected in parallel to create a "2-out-of-3" majority logic. Each of these sections runs (independently developed versions of) the same application program. When one of the sections disagrees, it is automatically excluded by vital hardware. The peripheral posts are also based on a redundancy architecture, with a "2-out-of-2" configuration of processors.

The "Safety Logic" of the ACC implements the logical functions requested by an external operator (e.g. preparing a path for moving a train from track to track). The distinguishing feature of the Safety Logic is that it is highly programmable and scalable. First, it is possible to program the modalities under which the commanded logical functions are performed. Furthermore, it is possible to program different configurations of physical devices, i.e. control for different stations. This is achieved by means of a logical architecture composed of a Scheduler controlling the activation of application-dependent processes. The Safety Logic is designed by specifying the processes controlled by the scheduler, which are then converted into executable code.

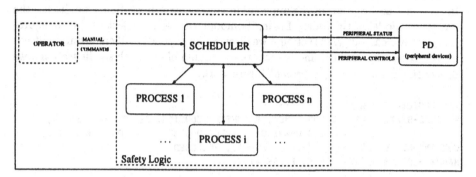

Fig. 1. The architecture of the SL and its environment

Specifying processes for this architecture is not a trivial task, due to two intrinsic sources of complexity. The first is the size of the controlled physical plants. Railway stations can contain a high number of physical devices, and processes of many different kinds can be required, to take into account the relations and interconnections among physical devices. The second source of complexity is nondeterminism, although the software is completely deterministic, and the possible external events (e.g. task requests, response and even faults of peripheral devices) have been exhaustively classified. The system can not know if and when external events will happen. For instance, tasks can be requested at any time. Furthermore, the peripheral devices will typically react to controls with (unpredictable) delays, and may even manifest (classified forms of) faulty behaviours.

Currently, the specification is validated by means of traditional techniques, such as simulation. The project aimed at the assessment of the possibility to integrate formal methods as a powerful debugging technique for the development cycle of the Safety Logic. Different formal methods techniques and tools, including theorem provers, CASE tools based on formal methods, and model checkers, have been preliminarly evaluated with respect to the particular features of the problem. Model Checking was preferred to other techniques, being completely automatic and therefore easier to integrate within the development cycle. Among different model checkers, SPIN [3] was selected for its robustness and quality as a software product, the adequacy of its input language PROMELA for the specification of the Safety Logic, and the graphical interface which greatly eases the interaction with the user.

The structure of the Safety Logic imposed several precise requirements on the solution. First, it should be possible for the project engineers to manipulate the formal model, and understand its relations with the Safety Logic. Second, it should be possible to obtain a large part of the model in a mechanical (and therefore automatizable) way from the specification. Finally, the model should retain the property of the Safety Logic that different configurations share the same Scheduler. From the computational side, the problem to be avoided, at least for significant configurations of the Safety Logic, is the so-called "state explosion problem", i.e. the fact that large amounts of memory can be needed to complete the exhaustive exploration of the model.

In the rest of this paper we show how these goals have been achieved using SPIN. In section 2 an overview of the application is presented. In section 3 we discuss the PROMELA model of the Safety Logic, its modularity with respect to the configuration, and its scalability. In section 4 we discuss how several significant configurations were successfully verified, and we report the results of the analysis. In section 5 we draw some conclusions and present future work.

```
*** LOGICAL STATE VARIABLES ***
PROCESS-STATE: WAITING-FOR-TIMER, REQUESTED-CLOSING, REQUESTED-OPENING,
               ACTIVATED-OPENING, COMPLETED-OPENING, RESTING (I.V.)
COMMAND-STATE: AUTOMATIC (I.V.), MANUAL, RECLOSED
MANUAL-OPENING-STATE: TRUE, FALSE (I.V.)

*** CONTROL STATE VARIABLES ***
P-COMBINATOR-STATE:  NORMAL, REVERSE, UNDEFINED (I.V.)
A-COMBINATOR-STATE:  RESTING, WORKING, UNDEFINED (I.V.)
CONTROL-POSITION-STATE: CLOSED, OPEN, UNDEFINED (I.V.)

*** PD CONTROLS ***
P-COMBINATOR-NORMAL, P-COMBINATOR-REVERSE, A-COMBINATOR-WORKING

*** MANUAL COMMANDS ***
CLOSE, OPEN, RESTORE-AUTOMATIC-MODE

*** AUTOMATIC COMMANDS ***
CLOSE, OPEN (from process SHUNT)

*** ACTIVATION TABLE ***
* MANUAL COMMAND        -> MANUAL OPERATION
CLOSE                   -> LC-MAN-OP-CLOSE
OPEN                    -> LC-MAN-OP-OPEN
RESTORE-AUTOMATIC-MODE -> LC-MAN-OP-RESTORE-AUTOMATIC-MODE

* STATE             -> STATE OPERATION
WAITING-FOR-TIMER -> LC-STATE-OP-ACTIVATE-CLOSING
REQUESTED-CLOSING -> LC-STATE-OP-CHECK-CLOSING
REQUESTED-OPENING -> LC-STATE-OP-ACTIVATE-OPENING
ACTIVATED-OPENING -> LC-STATE-OP-COMPLETE-OPENING
COMPLETED-OPENING -> LC-STATE-OP-FINISH-OPENING

* AUTOMATIC COMMAND -> AUTOMATIC OPERATION
CLOSE               -> LC-AUTO-OP-REQUEST-CLOSING
OPEN                -> LC-AUTO-OP-REQUEST-OPENING
```

Fig. 2. The Specification for the signature of Level Crossing Process

2 The Safety Logic

A high level picture of the Safety Logic of the ACC, together with its environment, is reported in figure 1. The Safety Logic (SL) is connected to the Peripheral Devices (PD) of the station and to the external operator (OP). The SL can be thought of as a deterministic reactive controller embedded in a nondeterministic environment. The SL repeats a cycle which consists of reading its inputs and determining the corresponding outputs according to its internal state. The SL takes as input the commands issued by OP (also called *Manual Commands*) and the status of PD. Manual Commands specify the tasks to be performed by the SL. Some examples are "Set route from track 2 to track 5", and "Open level crossing 3". The status of the peripheral devices (also called PD Status) represents information as conveyed from connected sensors. Examples might be "Position of Switch 12 is normal" and "Level crossing 3 is open". The output of the SL are *Peripheral Controls*, i.e. the controls (also called PD Controls) issued to PD. Examples of PD controls are "Move Switch 12 to normal position", and "Close level crossing 3".

```
3.3.4 LC-STATE-OP-COMPLETE-OPENING
(Activated when PROCESS-STATE has value ACTIVATED-OPENING).
I - VERIFY:
a.      P-COMBINATOR-STATE with value REVERSE;
b.      MANUAL-OPENING-STATE with value FALSE.
II - SEND:
a.      to PD the control A-COMBINATOR-WORKING;
if:
1. A-COMBINATOR-STATE has value other than WORKING.
III - ASSIGN:
a. to PROCESS-STATE the value
COMPLETED-OPENING.
IV - AFTER THE OPERATION THE PROCESS
a.      does not terminate;
b.      does not continue.


EXCEPTIONS
[a]
WAIT
ACTIONS : ---

[b]
ERROR
ACTIONS:
I - ASSIGN:
a. to MANUAL-OPENING-STATE the value FALSE.
```

Fig. 3. Specification of an Operation for the LC process

The architecture of the SL is based on a general Scheduler controlling a number of Processes. Intuitively, the Scheduler can be thought of as an operating system's scheduler, i.e. a general program controlling the activation, suspension and termination of Processes according to their execution status and activities. (Further details on the behaviour of the Scheduler are proprietary information and can not be disclosed in this paper.) The processes controlled by the Scheduler can have different functionalities. For example, a process can be devoted to the control of a PD (e.g. a level crossing, a switch), or be responsible for a logical function (e.g. shunting, that is setting a route through the station). Processes are (often) organized in a hierarchical way, so that a "routing" process can control the activities of a "device" process. Therefore, Processes are able to issue commands, called *Automatic Commands*, to each other. During its activation, a process can issue PD controls and automatic commands, and can terminate its computation with different modalities. Processes implement the functionalities to be guaranteed by SL. Intuitively, a process can be thought of as a procedure with a persistent state. It is associated with a set of (state) variables, defining its configurations, and with certain operations, defining its behaviour.

Processes are designed by means of structured specifications written in a structured semi-natural language. The specifications define the signature and the behaviour of processes. Figure 2 shows the specification[3] defining the signature for the Level Crossing (LC) process. State variables are distinguished in Logical Variables and Control Variables. Logical Variables represent the status of the process computation. Each process is associated with a special variable called PROCESS-STATE, which, in this case, can assume the six specified values. The value RESTING is tagged as initial (I.V.), and is assigned to the variable at the system startup. The other variables are specified similarly. A process can modify the values of its logical variables during the execution of the operations associated with it. Control Variables represent the status of the peripheral devices of interest to the process (as perceived by the sensors). The values of control variables can not be modified by the process. They are set at the begin of the cycle of the SL by the sensing operation, and do not change until the next cycle. Then, the controls that the process can send to PD are specified. An Activation Table is specified which associates an operation to each event determining the activation of the process. For instance, the LC process will execute the operation LC-STATE-OP-COMPLETE-OPENING when its execution is resumed and the value of its state variable PROCESS-STATE is ACTIVATED-OPENING.

Each operation referenced in the activation table is fully defined by a specification. Operations are described in a semi-natural language, and follow a fixed pattern. Figure 3 shows the specification for the operation LC-STATE-OP-COMPLETE-OPENING. Operations are collections of basic actions to be performed by the process. Basic actions include testing the value of variables, assigning values to logical (state) variables, sending PD controls to peripherals and automatic commands to other processes. These actions can be conditioned to tests.

Statements in operations are interpreted sequentially. The VERIFY tests are executed first. If one of the tests is not satisfied (e.g. test b.), then the corresponding

---

[3] In this paper they have been translated from italian and slightly edited for sake of readability.

```
proctype lc (chan from_sched, to_sched)
{
/* Initialization */
lc_prc = resting; lc_cmd = automatic; lc_man_open = false;

do
:: from_sched?transition ->  /* Read the activation event */
   if
   :: (transition == lc_manual_open) -> goto manual_open
   ...

   :: (transition == lc_state) -> goto state

   :: (transition == lc_auto_close) -> goto auto_close
   ...
   fi;

   /* Manual Operations */
   manual_open: <operation_body> goto test_end_transition
   manual_close: <operation_body> goto test_end_transition
   restore_automatic_mode: <operation_body> goto test_end_transition

   /* Automatic Operations */
   auto_close: <operation_body> goto test_end_transition
   auto_open:  <operation_body> goto test_end_transition

   /* State Operations */
   state:
   if :: (lc_prc == waiting_for_timer) ->
         <operation_body> goto test_end_transition
      :: (lc_prc == requested_closing) ->
         <operation_body> goto test_end_transition
      :: ...
      :: else -> assert(0)
   fi;

   /* Check termination of transition */
   test_end_transition:
   if
   :: (terminates) -> goto lc_return
   :: (!terminates && !continues) -> add_next_cycle_processes(lc_name);
                                     goto lc_return
   :: (!terminates && continues) -> goto state
   fi;

   /* Return control to Scheduler */
   lc_return: to_sched!lc_done
od
}
```

Fig. 4. The PROMELA model for Process Structure

EXCEPTION action (e.g. exception [b]) is executed and the execution of the operation ends. If the preliminary tests are satisfied, then commands may be issued during the SEND part, and then variables may be set during the ASSIGN part. After the execution of an operation, a process can act under different modalities according to what specified in part IV.

3 A scalable model of the Safety Logic

We discuss now how the SL described in previous section was formalized in PROMELA, the input language of the SPIN model checker. PROMELA (Process Meta Language) is a non-deterministic language, loosely based on Dijkstra's guarded command language notation and Hoare's language CSP, extended with some powerful new constructs. It contains the primitives for specifying asynchronous (buffered) message passing via channels, with arbitrary numbers of message parameters. It also allows for the specification of synchronous message passing systems (rendez-vous). Mixed systems, using both synchronous and asynchronous communications, are also supported. Concurrent entities can be modelled as different PROMELA processes and communicating through channels.

The formalization of the Safety Logic in PROMELA is depicted in figure 1 (the figure describing the SL itself). Boxes are interpreted as PROMELA processes, and arrows are interpreted as PROMELA channels. Each process of the Safety Logic is modeled as a PROMELA process with a fixed structure, taking two channels in input, and implementing the general activation table described in previous section. This structure is presented in figure 4 for the case of the LC process. The definition and initialization of logical variables can be determined according to the specification (control variables are set by the Scheduler upon the receipt of sensed data). Then, a loop begins where the process waits for the Scheduler to pass control. Waiting is represented by means of handshacking on the synchronous channel from_sched. Reading from a channel is specified with the operator ?. The activation event, which is specified by the scheduler through a message sent on the channel from_sched, is stored in the variable transition, which is then tested to devise the operation to be executed. The activation table is implemented as a set of conditioned jumps. <operation_body> stands for the set of PROMELA statements which model each operation. After each operation there is a jump to the test_end_transition location, where the boolean variables terminates and continues are tested to check whether control can be returned to the Scheduler (for instance, requesting a further activation at next cycle), or another operation must be executed. lc_return returns the control to the Scheduler by sending a lc_done message on the synchronous channel to_sched. Notice that the information exchanged between modeled SL process (e.g. LC) and the Scheduler can be determined direclty from the process signature, and does not depend on the actual functionality of the operations.

Given this general structure, the PROMELA model for a process can be completed by filling the slots corresponding to the local variables and the operations. The model of the operations of the process can be obtained directly and mechanically from the specifications described in previous section. The fully automatization of this translation, upon which the integration of the model checker as a debugging tool in the process of designing the specifications is based, in under investigation.

```
...
:: (lc_prc == activated_opening) ->
   if
   :: (lc_p_cmb == reverse) ->              /* Verify a. */
      if
      :: (lc_man_open == false) ->          /* Verify b. */
         if
         :: (lc_a_cmb != working) ->        /* Send PD controls */
            cur_pd_ctrl.a_cmb_working = true
         :: else -> skip
         fi;
         lc_prc = completed_opening;        /* Assign */
         terminates = false;                /* After the operation */
         continues = false
         :: else ->                         /* Exception b. */
         lc_man_open = false;
         terminates = false;
         continues = false
      fi
   :: else ->                               /* Exception a. */
      terminates = false;
      continues = false
   fi
...
```

Fig. 5. The PROMELA model of the operation specified in figure 3

In figure 5 we report the PROMELA model for the operation specified in figure 3 (i.e. one instance of <operation_body> in figure 4). It is easy to see that for each action specified there is a corresponding PROMELA statement. Exceptions are modeled depending on the kind of operations. An exception during a state operation is modeled as "Does not terminate and does not continue", which usually amounts to waiting for the conditions to become ready and trying again next cycle. An exception during a manual or automatic operation is interpreted as "Terminates", as the process should reject a command if the preconditions for executing it are not satisfied. This similarity made it possible for the development engineers to understand and validate the PROMELA model of operations.

Modeling the Scheduler required a strict integration between IRST and Ansaldo, in order to clarify and understand the relevant features of the SL. Although the details can not be disclosed in this paper, the final PROMELA model of the Scheduler represents in detail the different computation phases of the cycle of the Safety Logic. Furthermore, just like the Safety Logic, the model of the Scheduler is largely independent of the structure and number of processes of the configuration. Therefore, it retains the reusability and scalability properties of the Safety Logic.

4 Experimental Results

In this section we discuss the exhaustive analysis with SPIN of models of the SL discussed in previous section. Given a PROMELA model, SPIN can be used as a simulator, allowing for rapid prototyping with a random, guided, or interactive simulations to gain confidence in the behaviour of the model with respect to the modelled system. SPIN can be used as an exhaustive state space analyzer, in which case it is capable of rigorously proving the validity of user specified correctness requirements. The idea is that the initial configurations of the model are recursively generated and stored, until states can no longer be expanded (i.e. exploration is completed), or a violation of some form (e.g. a deadlock, a behaviour which does not obeys the specified requirements) is detected. SPIN tackles the state explosion problem with different techniques (e.g. state space compression, partial order reduction) to optimize the search (see [3]).

The first configuration of the SL to be validated, which was specified in [2], was composed of a physical level crossing, together with two processes in the Safety Logic, namely a Shunting and a Level Crossing. This configuration was considered to be of rather complex nature. Previous attempts by other research teams to the verification of such a configuration had lead to the state explosion problem, and had not been completed. The performance obtained analyzing this configuration were very good. It was possible to complete a full verification of state properties in less than ten seconds on a SUN-SPARCSTATION 10. Rather than being a sign of simplicity of the problem, we believe that this shows that the model was carefully designed to exploit all the constraints.

Other more complex configurations were attempted. In the following we discuss the results of the analysis of a more complex configuration, modeling the control of a physical railway track divided in three parts and containing a level crossing. The SL contains four processes, and was obtained by extending the model for the first configuration (Shunting-Level Crossing) by adding the model of two additional processes of different type (Liberation). Intuitively, the Shunting process is in charge of preparing the conditions for the train to pass, for instance book the parts of railway track and command the level crossings to close. When the conditions are ready, it signals the free way to the train. When the train has passed, the Liberation processes are activated to free the track components which had been booked and open the level crossing.

Several requirements were modelled on this model. The first requirement is "the process Shunt does not signal free way to the train if the Level Crossing is not closed". This is an obvious safety requirement, which was represented as an assertion (i.e. a predicate which must be verified of the states corresponding to a given control point) relating the controls to be delivered to PD and the status of peripheral devices. Other requirements such as "the SL never issues contradictory PD controls during a cycle" were represented in a similar way.

The formalization of the following requirement was more complex: "if the free way was signaled to the train, and the Level Crossing was closed with a manual command, then the manual command RESTORE-AUTOMATIC-MODE must leave the Level Crossing closed". This criterion is a liveness property. It relates a generic state in which the premises must hold, a following state in which the manual command RESTORE-AUTOMATIC-MODE is issued, and then a sequence of future states where

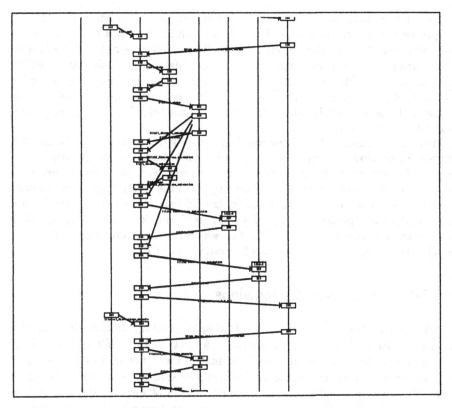

Fig. 6. Trace of the activation of the resting liberation.

no further manual commands are issued to the SL. This criterion was modeled by means of a temporal logic formula, in order to express the relation between the previous and future behaviours of the system. Such temporal logic formulae can be analyzed by SPIN by extending the model of the SL with a translation into observing automata.

Another relevant issue was testing for the termination of the cycle of the SL (a nontermination in the model would result in a deadlock in the actual SL). Non termination can in principle occur in two different situations. First, a process can have a non terminating transition, depending on the termination value returned by the operations. Second, the automatic phase may not terminate, depending on the nature of the command flow among processes (e.g. if two processes keep to send automatic commands to each other). This was expressed requiring that the beginning of cycle of the SL to be a point of progress (this property can be automatically analyzed by a particular modality of the exhaustive analysis).

These properties, together with a number of assertions to make sure that the data flow was correctly modeled, were all analyzed with SPIN. Analyses were performed checking state properties, acceptance cycles and non-progress cycles. Again, the resource required to analyze such a complex configuration were rather limited. The complete analysis of the liveness property discussed above took less than two minutes, while the non-progress cycles check required less than 6 minutes.

During the analysis, SPIN was able to detect an anomalous behaviour. One of the processes was activated while being in a resting state, i.e. a state having no associated operations in the activation table. The significance of this behaviour is that it was present in a prototype version of the Safety Logic. This was solved by associating by default every resting state with a fictitious operation which simply returns control to the Scheduler. Pinning out this behaviour was very valuable to highlight the power of exhaustive verification. Such a behaviour is extremely hard to point out via testing.

After the anomalous behaviour was found, the SPIN mechanism for finding the shortest counterexample was very useful to reduce the length of the trace. The "shortest" trace we could come up with is generated by a particular sequence of four manual commands issued during seven cycles of the Safety Logic, and amounts to several hundred steps of simulation. In figure 6 part of the trace shown by the SPIN interface is reported, in form of a Message Sequence Chart, covering just a little more than one cycle of the SL. The vertical traces represent (from left to right), OP, Sched, LC, Shunt, the two Liberations and PD.

5 Future Work and Conclusions

In this paper we have described an industrial application of formal methods, model checking in particular, to the verification of a safety critical railway interlocking system. The system has been modeled and analyzed with the SPIN tool, which uses efficient algorithms for the verification of complex systems. SPIN uses a language especially designed to allow a natural representation of software systems. It also combines model checking and reduction techniques to determine system correctness and to provide useful information about its behavior.

This project has been a successful experience in formal methods applied to the design of safety-critical systems. Although the configurations analyzed in this project are simpler than the ones needed to control a large-size railway station, it is possible to deal with configurations of significant size and complexity, which can help the designer to gain confidence in the system being specified. This is a great advantage with respect to traditional methods such as testing, as very often the exhaustive analysis of a scaled down configuration can reveal problems which are present also in larger configurations.

Future activity will try to scale up the size of configurations which can be exhaustively and automatically analyzed. Preliminary experiments show that there is room for improvement by using different representations of the system, and different (e.g. symbolic) model checking techniques [1].

References

1. A. Cimatti, E. Clarke, F. Giunchiglia, and M. Roveri. NuSmv: a reimplementation of smv. In *Proceeding of the International Workshop on Software Tools for Technology Transfer (STTT-98)*, pages 25–31, Aalborg, Denmark, 1998. BRICS Notes Series, NS-98-4. Also IRST-Technical Report 9801-06, Trento, Italy.
2. A. Cimatti, F. Giunchiglia, G. Mongardi, B. Pietra, D. Romano, F. Torielli, and P. Traverso. Formal Validation of an Interlocking System for Large Railway Stations: A Case Study. Confidential IRST Technical Report, 1996.
3. G.J. Holzmann. *Design and Validation of Computer Protocols*. Prentice Hall, 1991.
4. G. Mongardi. Dependable Computing for Railway Control Systems. In *Proceedings of the Working Conference on Dependable Computing for Critical Applications*, pages 255–273. IFIP Working Group, 1992.

EURIS, a Specification Method for Distributed Interlockings

Fokko van Dijk[1], Wan Fokkink[2], Gea Kolk[1],
Paul van de Ven[1], and Bas van Vlijmen[3]

[1] Holland Railconsult, PO Box 2855, 3500 GW Utrecht, The Netherlands,
fjvandijk@hr.nl, gpkolk@hr.nl, phjvandeven@hr.nl
[2] University of Wales Swansea, Singleton Park, Swansea SA2 8PP, Wales,
w.j.fokkink@swan.ac.uk
[3] Utrecht University, Heidelberglaan 8, 3584 CS Utrecht, The Netherlands,
vlijmen@phil.uu.nl

Abstract. Safety systems for railways have shifted from electronic relays to more computer-oriented approaches. This article highlights the language EURIS from NS Railinfrabeheer, which champions an object-oriented method for the specification of interlocking logics.

1 Introduction

The control and management of a railway system consists of three separate tasks. First, control instructions for the railway yard have to be devised in the logistic layer. Second, control instructions have to be passed on to the infrastructure, which consists of points, signals, sections, level crossings, et cetera. This task is almost always fully automated. Third, it has to be guaranteed that the execution of control instructions does not jeopardise safety; that is, collisions and derailments have to be avoided. This is done by means of an interlocking, which is a medium between the infrastructure and the logistic layer together with its interfaces. An interlocking logic is the embodiment of safety principles and basic rules, according to which a train moves through a railway yard.

Traditionally, an interlocking logic served as a local solution for a specific railway yard, whereby the logic could be designed to cope with the peculiarities of the railway yard. Modern computer-based railway systems demand a uniform specification method which can be used to formulate interlocking logics for all railway yards. The safety restrictions that are imposed on different railway yards are reasonably consistent, depending mostly on the parameters of autonomous elements such as signals and points. Based on this observation, Middelraad *cum suis* from NS Railinfrabeheer evolved a modular specification method EURIS (EUropean Railway Interlocking Specification) [3], to describe fully automated interlocking logics. EURIS assumes an object-oriented architecture, which consists of a collection of generic building blocks, representing the elements in the infrastructure such as signals and points, and of two clearly separated entities in the outside world, representing the logistic layer and the infrastructure.

The building blocks, which together make up the interlocking logic, communicate with each other by means of data-structures called telegrams. The building blocks can also exchange telegrams with the logistic layer and the infrastructure.

EURIS not only denotes a specification method, it is also the name for a graphically oriented imperative specification language that is based on this method. A Logic and Sequence Chart (LSC) specifies a building block. Each LSC consists of the graphical representation of procedures, which can adapt and test the values of variables, and which can ultimately trigger the transmission of a telegram. Such telegrams can be received by neighbouring building blocks, by the logistic layer, and by the infrastructure. Reversely, each building block can also receive telegrams from neighbouring building blocks, from the logistic layer, and from the infrastructure. The graphical format for LSCs evolved as a compact notation when the Nassi Schneidermann diagrams, which were originally used to express EURIS specifications, became unclear due to deep nestings of if-then-else statements.

A strong advantage of an object-oriented architecture is the possibility to reuse components of a specification. In EURIS, the heart of a specification defines the way that building blocks handle incoming telegrams. When all types of building blocks have been specified in full detail, the specification of a particular railway yard is constructed by simply connecting its separate building blocks in the appropriate manner. A second advantage of the distributed approach is that if the behaviour of say a signal is changed, then this can be taken into account on the level of EURIS by adapting the specification of the corresponding building block. A disadvantage can be that in EURIS applications a procedure such as claiming a route is specified implicitly in the designs of several building blocks, so that adapting such a procedure can become non-trivial.

UniSpec [3, 11] is a particular instance of the EURIS method, which has been developed by NS Railinfrabeheer as a complete set of generic elements to compose interlocking logics for the Dutch railway system. Holland Railconsult has implemented a simulator for UniSpec [9, 10], which enables to animate the behaviour of a UniSpec specification. The simulator is part of a toolset named GUIDE, which is currently used by NS Railinfrabeheer to support both the design and validation of UniSpec specifications. After designing a set of LSCs, the user can join instantiations of these LSCs according to the topology of a railway yard. The result is checked for design rule errors and compiled, after which situations at the railway yard can be simulated via a graphical interface. The simulator enables to locate flaws in an interlocking specification at an early stage of the system engineering process. Furthermore, a simulation session gives a detailed insight of the behaviour of the specification, which can be useful in the communication with customers.

This article presents a description of the the EURIS method and its specification language. We describe the features that are present in [3, 7, 9–11], and which have been singled out as being essential by railway experts. There are several interpretations of the semantics of EURIS around, such as the founding article [3], and the implementation of the simulator. We formulate a semantics for

EURIS that, following the simulator, is based on a discrete time model. Bergstra, Fokkink, Mennen, and van Vlijmen [4] presented a more detailed semantics for EURIS in discrete time process algebra [1].

Acknowledgements This research was funded by Holland Railconsult. Daan van der Meij and Peter Middelraad from NS Railinfrabeheer, and Jan Bergstra, Jan Friso Groote, Marco Hollenberg and Wendi Mennen from Utrecht University, are thanked for their support.

2 Overview of EURIS

EURIS is a graphically oriented, parallel, event-driven, weakly typed, imperative specification language. A EURIS specification consists of the graphical description of elements in the form of *LSCs* (see Section 2.3), which are connected by *ports* (see Section 2.2). Each element consists of procedures with an imperative character, called *flows* (see Section 2.1). Elements can send data-structures called *telegrams* (see Section 2.2) to each other via their ports. Reception of a telegram by a element causes the execution of a flow, which is determined by the telegram and the channel via which the element received the telegram. Changing the value of a variable can also cause the execution of a flow (see Section 2.2).

EURIS assumes the two standard data types of Booleans and integers. The Booleans consist of 1, representing *true*, and 0, representing *false*. Three standard functions are defined on the integers: addition, subtraction, and multiplication.

2.1 Flows

We consider a certain element, with a unique element name. A *flow* for this element is a procedure that is built from the following five basic constructs:

- An *execution condition* formulates under which circumstances the flow is executed. There are two possibilities.
  If the execution condition is of the form T ▶ p, then the flow is executed if telegram T is received at port p of the element; see Section 2.2.
  If the execution condition consists of a variable name X, then the flow is executed depending on the (change of) value of X; see Section 2.2.
- A *case* tests the value of a variable; the returned value influences the subsequent execution of the flow.
- An *assignment* adapts the value of a variable.
- A *termination* statement marks the end of the execution of the flow.
- A *send* action p ▶ T instructs that telegram T is sent out via port p of the element. A send action is always followed by termination of the flow.

An element is specified by its flows, where the execution conditions of the flows cover all telegrams that can be received by the ports of the element.

Flows are represented graphically, whereby the tests and assignments of the flow are connected with each other by continuous lines. A test whether variable X equals value v is denoted either by placing v in the flow below variable X, or by placing the expression $(X = v)$ in the flow. An assignment of value v to variable X is denoted either by placing $>v$ in the flow below variable X, or by placing the expression $(X : v)$ in the flow. The graphical layout of flows is important for the interpretation of tests and assignments; see the picture below.

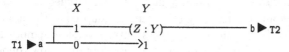

The execution condition at the left of this flow expresses that it is executed if telegram T1 is received via port a. First, the flow tests the value of the variable X. If this value is 0, then the flow assigns the value 1 to variable Y, after which it terminates. If the value of X is 1, then the flow assigns the value of Y to Z, after which it sends out telegram T2 via port b. Z is a telegram field; if this field does not yet exist then it is created, and otherwise its value is changed.

2.2 Ports, Telegrams, and Variables

A EURIS specification assumes a logistic layer and an infrastructure, and specifies the behaviour of a number of elements. In particular, it is described how these separate entities send messages called telegrams to each other, and how the elements react when they receive a certain telegram from a certain entity. The elements and the logistic layer and the infrastructure can send telegrams to each other via communication channels, which are constructed by the combination of *ports*. EURIS recognises the following two kinds of ports.

- An element has one or more *route* ports. Each route port p of an element e is linked with exactly one route port p' of another element e', establishing a communication channel between e and e'. If element e sends a telegram into port p, then this is received by element e' through port p', and vice versa.
- An element may have a port that connects it with the logistic layer, and a port that connects it with the infrastructure. Telegrams can travel from the element to the logistic layer and to the infrastructure via these ports. Vice versa, for each element, the logistic layer and the infrastructure may have a port via which they can send telegrams to this element.

A *telegram* has a unique name and carries a *telegram table*, which assigns Boolean and integer values to telegram variables. A telegram may be passed on between a number of elements, which all update the information in the table of the telegram. If a flow terminates by sending out a telegram, then it attaches the telegram table that was created, or adapted, during the execution of the flow. Telegram variables are only meaningful for an element as long as the flow that belongs to the telegram in the element is being executed.

A *route* telegram is sent from one entity to another entity, whereby entities can be elements, the logistic layer, or the infrastructure. It consists of a telegram name, a telegram table, and a port name from which it is sent out. An *internal* telegram is generated inside an element by special types of variables, depending on the (change of) value of such a variable. An internal telegram consists of a telegram name together with the name of the variable that produced this telegram, and of an empty telegram table.

EURIS distinguishes several types of internal variables. The initial values of *input* variables, which carry the version symbol '!', are latched. The values of internal variables without a version symbol can be adapted without giving rise to the execution of a flow. Finally, variables with a version symbol from $\{@, \&, \$, \#, ?\#, >>\#\}$ may trigger the execution of a corresponding flow, depending on the (change of) value of such a variable. A detailed description of the behaviour of these variables is given in the full version of this article [6].

Time plays an important role in the specification of an interlocking logic. It enables to model delays; for example, if a train has passed a section, then for safety reasons this section has to be unoccupied for a certain period of time. We assume a discrete time model, in which time progresses in distinct steps called time steps. Methods such as VPI [5, 8] from the General Railway Signal Company and EBS [2] from Siemens, which are used for the implementation of real-life interlockings, and the simulator of EURIS, are based on a discrete time domain. Furthermore, it has been shown in practice that it is technically feasible to synchronise the parallel processes of a EURIS specification on time slices.

2.3 Logic and Sequence Charts

An LSC consists of a number of graphical representations of flows. An LSC takes as basis a list of internal variables, whereby variables carry their version symbols. Figure 1 presents an example of an LSC. X_1, X_2 and X_3 are internal variables. X_1 is an input variable, which is denoted by the version symbol '!'. X_2 is a one-shot variable, which is denoted by the version symbol '&'. X_3 does not carry a version symbol. The graphical representations of the flows that make up the LSC are drawn below this list. Thus, we obtain the picture that is displayed in Figure 1. Below each variable name we have drawn an imaginary vertical dashed line. Each test and assignment in a flow is placed on such a dashed line, in order

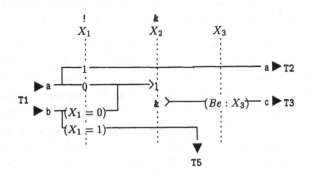

Fig. 1. An LSC Example.

to relate it to the variable of which the value is tested or adapted. Some of the flows share the same tail, which means that from some point onwards they have the same functionality. However, flows are independent entities. We explain the meaning of each flow.

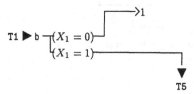

The flow above is executed if the telegram with name T1 is received via port a. If the input variable X_1 is 0, then this flow assigns the value 1 to the one-shot variable X_2, after which it terminates. If X_1 is 1, then this flow sends out the telegram with name T2, and with the unaltered telegram table, via port a.

The flow above is executed if the telegram with name T1 is received via port b. If the input variable X_1 is 0, then this flow assigns the value 1 to the one-shot variable X_2, after which it terminates. If X_1 is 1, then this flow sends out the telegram with name T5 to the infrastructure.

The flow above, generated by one-shot variable X_2, assigns the value of variable X_3 to variable Be. Next, the telegram with name T3 is sent out via port c.

3 UniSpec

UniSpec [3, 11] is a particular instance of the EURIS method that is under development, with the aim to obtain a complete set of generic elements to compose interlocking logics for the Dutch railway system. It transforms the layout of a railway yard into LSCs in three subsequent steps. The topology of the railway yard, and the types of its elements, such as signals and points, are described in a track layout. The elements are provided with ports, which are combined to obtain communication channels between the elements, based on the topology of the track layout. Thus, we obtain the element connection layout. Elements are provided with ports to and from the logistic layer and the infrastructure, and the parameters of the elements and the communication channels are refined, to obtain the logical element connection layout. Finally, this representation is used to obtain the LSCs of the separate elements. These transformation steps have been automated in the simulator [9, 10].

3.1 Track Layout

A track layout of a railway yard is constructed from its separate elements; we distinguish signals, sections, points, crosses, level crossings, and approach monitoring devices for level crossings. Each element in the track layout has a unique name, based on standard (Dutch) railway conventions. We proceed to present the graphical representations of the elements.

1. A section with name N is represented by

2. A signal with name N is represented by

3. Points and crosses with name N are represented by

4. A level crossing with name N on a section with name N' is represented by

Each path in a railway yard that leads to a level crossing should encounter an approach monitoring device, which is represented by $\overset{N''}{\blacktriangleright}$. The name N'' always starts with AS, which abbreviates Approach Starting point. An approach monitoring device serves for only one direction, which is determined by the orientation of its graphical representation.

Figure 2 presents an example of a track layout, which is constructed by linking instances of the elements mentioned above.

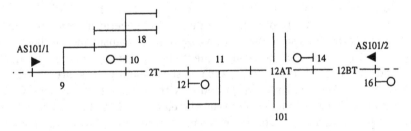

Fig. 2. Example of a Track Layout.

3.2 Element Connection Layout

For each element in a given track layout we generate a graphical element, with a unique name, and with a maximum of four ports called a, b, c en d. We discuss these graphical elements.

1. A signal *N* that is directed from left to right is represented by

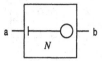

2. Sections, points, and crosses of name *N* are represented by

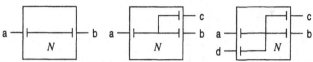

3. A level crossings is captured implicitly by its monitoring devices: AS (Approach Starting) signals that a train is approaching, while SCD (Signal Clearance Delay) signals that a train has passed the level crossing. AS as well as SCD pass on their information to an element AM (Approach Monitoring). These elements can monitor trains in only one direction, so a level crossing needs two AM elements to monitor approaching trains from opposite directions. The information of the two AM elements is passed on to a central element AMC. Element AMC is represented by a box without ports. Elements AM and AS and SCD of name *N* are represented by

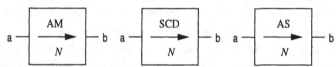

In order to transform a track layout into an element connection layout, all elements are replaced by their boxes. The ports of these boxes are connected to each other, based on the topology of the track layout. Figure 3 depicts how the track layout in Figure 2 is transformed into an element connection layout.

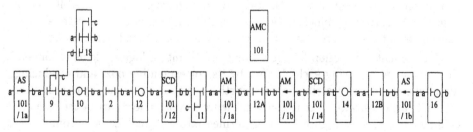

Fig. 3. Example of an Element Connection Layout.

3.3 Logical Element Connection Layout

An element connection layout is transformed into a logical element connection layout as follows. Each pair of linked ports produces one or two directed channels

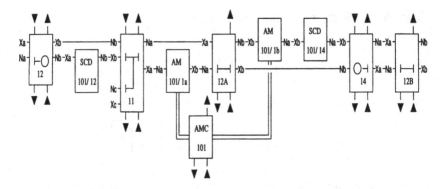

Fig. 4. Example of a Logical Element Connection Layout.

between the elements of the ports. The entry and exit side of a channel are marked 'N' and 'X', respectively. If both ports belong to a bi-directional element (signal, section, points, cross), then two channels are produced, one for each direction. If a port belongs to a uni-directional element (AM, SCD, AS), then one channel is produced in the same direction as this element. An AMC element is connected to each of its AM elements by two channels, one for each direction.

Every element is provided with channels to and from the logistic layer and the infrastructure. Boxes for signals and points are provided with all four channels. Channels from logistic layer to element and from element to infrastructure carry instructions to the signal or points. Channels in the opposite direction carry information on the status of the signal or points. Boxes for sections and crosses are provided with three channels; the channel from logistic layer to element is missing. The channel from element to infrastructure serves to carry instructions on automatic train protection, which automatically halts trains that do not respect the speed limit. AS, SCD, and AM boxes have no channels. AMC boxes have the same three channels as boxes for sections and crosses. The channel from element to infrastructure serves to carry instructions to the level crossing.

An element connection layout is transformed into a logical element connection layout by replacing each element by its corresponding box, and producing directed channels as described above. Furthermore, each box has a private set of internal variables, which are initialised. Figure 4 depicts how part of the element connection layout in Figure 3 is transformed into a logical element connection layout. The initialisation of internal variables is omitted from the picture. Finally, the logical element connection layout is used to produce an EURIS specification. Each type of box is specified by an LSC, which contains the flows that are produced by the box when it receives telegrams. Such specifications are far from trivial; see [3]. Information on channels and the initialisation of variables is not taken into account in LSCs. If a box can be presented in two symmetric ways (as is the case for the box of a signal), then two symmetric LSCs are specified, whereby each flow from left to right in the one LSC occurs as a flow from right to left in the other LSC, and vice versa.

4 Conclusion

EURIS is a specification method for interlocking logics. The object-oriented approach of EURIS is a strong point in its favour, and its graphical format allows for compact specifications. However, this compactness can obstruct the clarity of EURIS specifications, especially because in practice EURIS is often treated more like a programming language than as a specification language. LARIS [7], a symbolic variant of EURIS, is a first attempt to remedy this imperfection.

UniSpec exemplifies the practical use of EURIS for the specification of interlocking logics. Currently, UniSpec contains special operators to cope with specific situations in Dutch railway yards, which hampers the clarity of its semantics. In future, UniSpec should be polished and reduced to a core set of essential operators with sufficient expressive power, and ideally it should be shown to be a correct implementation of the desired interlocking logic. It is yet unclear how functional requirements such as "if points are occupied then their position should be fixed" can be verified for UniSpec. In future interlocking systems, the topology of railway yards may become more dynamic; e.g., positions of signals may become variable. It remains to be seen whether EURIS can cope with such a shift; the specification of elements in UniSpec is based on a fixed topology of railway yards.

References

1. J.C.M. Baeten en J.A. Bergstra. Discrete time process algebra. *Formal Aspects of Computing*, 8(2):188–208, 1996.
2. J.W.F.M. Beljaars. Prozeß Ablauf Pläne: introduction to a specification method. Report 1992/JBe/3, IB ETS-T&K, 1992. In Dutch.
3. J. Berger, P. Middelraad, and A.J. Smith. EURIS, European railway interlocking specification. UIC, Commission 7A/16, May 1992.
4. J.A. Bergstra, W.J. Fokkink, W.M.T. Mennen, and S.F.M. van Vlijmen. *Railway Logic via EURIS*. Quaestiones Infinitae XXII, Zeno Institute of Philosophy, 1997.
5. W.J. Fokkink. Safety criteria for the vital processor interlocking at Hoorn-Kersenboogerd. In *Proceedings 5th Conference on Computers in Railways (COMPRAIL'96)*, Berlin, pp. 101–110. Computational Mechanics Publications, 1996.
6. F.J. van Dijk, W.J. Fokkink, G.P. Kolk, P.H.J. van de Ven, and S.F.M. van Vlijmen. EURIS, a specification method for distributed interlockings. Technical Report, Department of Computer Science, University of Wales Swansea, 1998.
7. J.F. Groote, M. Hollenberg, and S.F.M. van Vlijmen. LARIS 1.0: language for railway interlocking specification. Report, CWI, Amsterdam, 1998, To appear.
8. J.F. Groote, J.W.C. Koorn, and S.F.M. van Vlijmen. The safety guaranteeing system at station Hoorn-Kersenboogerd. In *Proceedings 10th IEEE Conference on Computer Assurance (COMPASS'95)*, Gaithersburg, pp. 131–150. IEEE, 1995.
9. F. Makkinga. IDEAL, interlocking design and application language guide and reference. Holland Railconsult, 1994.
10. F. Makkinga and F.J. van Dijk. EURIS-simulation tutorial reference. Holland Railconsult, 1995.
11. D. van der Meij and P. Middelraad. UniSpec. NS Railinfrabeheer, 1996.

Object Oriented Safety Analysis
of an Extra High Voltage Substation Bay

Bartosz Nowicki and Janusz Górski
Department of Applied Informatics, Technical University of Gdańsk
Narutowicza 11/12, 80-952 Gdańsk, Poland
e-mail: {baron, jango}@pg.gda.pl

Abstract. Experiences of application of the object oriented approach to safety analysis of an extra high voltage substation bay are presented. As the first step the object model of the whole application is developed. Then the model is subjected to three safety analysis methods. The analyses are supported by an existing tool. The paper illustrates the application of the proposed methods and also gives some observations on the performance of the tool.

1 Introduction

Object Modelling Technique (OMT) [13] is one of widely accepted object oriented approaches to system modelling and analysis. Basically, it comprises three different models which represent three different views of the system under consideration: the Object Model, the Dynamic Model and the Functional Model. The Object Model concentrates on the structural aspect and represents the system as a collection of object classes and their interdependencies. The Dynamic Model concentrates on the behavioural aspect and, for each class, describes its behaviour in terms of statecharts [6]. The Functional Model is given in terms of data flow diagrams and concentrates on the data processing aspect of the system. Although all three views of OMT are equally important to fully elaborate different aspects of the system, it is the behavioural view which plays the primary role in control dominated applications. Therefore, the behavioural model deserves a special attention during safety analysis.

Industrial applications are often of non trivial complexity and the processes of their modelling and analysis have to be supported by tools. We used Paradigm Plus [1] to support development of Object Models and Statemate 6.11 [7] to support modelling and analysis of dynamic aspects.

The paper consists of five parts. First, an informal description of the extra high voltage substation bay is given. Then the methods applied during safety analysis are briefly presented. Afterwards, selected object oriented models developed during application of those methods are given. Then the results of safety analysis are presented and in conclusion we give an overview of the experiences gathered during our case study.

Due to the space limitations the paper does not include a full description of the safety analysis methods which have been applied. More thorough documentation of the bay case study can be found in [9,10,11,12,14].

2 Extra High Voltage Substation Bay

Object oriented safety analysis was carried out with respect to a line bay of the Mościska 400/110 kV substation. The substation is situated near Warsaw and is an important node supplying energy to the capital city. Its main objective is reconfiguration of the power grid. The substation consists of two busbar systems and eight bays. Our case study focused on the bay number 1 through which the substation is connected to the Miłosna substation.

The aim of the bay is to carry out sequences of switching operations. As the result other objects (e.g. transformers, lines) can be connected to the busbar systems. For instance, the bay number 1 can perform the following operations:

- disconnecting the line from a busbar system,
- connecting the line to a busbar system,
- switching over the line from one busbar system to another .

Switching sequences are carried out by means of:

- circuit breaker - a switching device which is able to switch on, switch off and conduct current,
- disconnector - a switching device which aims at assuring a safe isolating gap in electrical circuit,
- earthing switch - a switching device, used for grounding elements in order to ensure safety during maintenance.

While performing switching sequences the order of operations on switches must be strictly preserved. E.g. disconnecting the line must be performed according to the following sequence:

- breaking off current flow using a circuit-breaker,
- opening the line disconnector to achieve isolation between the disconnected line and the circuit breaker,
- opening the busbar disconnector to achieve the isolation between the circuit breaker and busbars.

If the order is violated and e.g. a disconnector is opened while the line is loaded, the consequences are severe: an electric arc arises between contacts of the disconnector. It is accompanied by high rate optic and acustic phenomena and spray of melted metal. It looks like an explosion and results in destruction of the disconnector. Next, the arc travels to neighbouring phases, resulting in inter-phase short circuits. This can give rise to further consequences, e.g. collapse of a part of the electric power system or personal injury.

The line bay is exposed to the following hazards:

- switching off a line by a disconnector,
- switching on a line by a disconnector,
- closing an earthing switch when a line or busbar system are under voltage.

The substation is planned to be unmanned and the control will be carried out by a computer system. Therefore, safety analysis of the computer based control system must be performed to ensure that its software neither causes nor contributes to any of the above hazards.

3 Object Oriented Safety Analysis Framework

Object models provide a good communication platform between the designers and the application domain specialists and are convenient means for expressing ideas of developers. Object oriented approach is often used for system mission modelling. We postulate that it is worth to investigate suitability of the object oriented to the safety analysis of such systems.

In this section we present three methods of object oriented safety analysis. Each of them addresses a separate safety aspect. The methods are not independent. They co-operate by mutual use of their results. The starting point is the mission oriented model resulting from the OMT analysis stage [13]. We have deliberately extended the existing method of modelling instead of proposing a new one because in our opinion this increases the chances that our approach will be used by practitioners (those who are already familiar with OMT). Instead of proposing a completely new approach we concentrated the effort on extending and strengthening the existing method to adopt it to new problems.

To model developed according the OMT analysis stage represents the system mission. This model can be validated and verified in order to check whether it adequately represents the application and fulfils its requirements. It answers the question „what is the system intended to do?". From the safety standpoint, however, the relevant question is „what is the system prohibited do?". To answer this question the model has to be modified and extended.

Method1: Safety analysis of system mission

The main objective is to reveal design faults of a control system. On this stage the random failures of plant objects are not taken into account.

To enrich the model with the safety aspect we develop what we call the *hazard model*. It explicitly distinguishes between the safe and hazardous states (Fig. 1).

In order to apply this generic model to a specific application we identify *critical objects* (objects the hazard refers to) in the model of the system mission. For a given hazard, the aggregation of critical objects forms the *critical subsystem*. The dynamic model of the critical subsystem and the hazard model shown in Fig.1 are merged to one model which explicitly distinguishes between safe and unsafe states. This model is used to analyse the consistency between the system safety and its mission: the reachability analysis is performed to check whether the hazardous state is reachable within the mission constraints. The detected hazard scenarios provide hints on how to reconstruct the system to ensure safety. More details on the method can be found in [3].

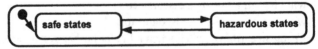

Fig. 1. The generic hazard model.

Method2: Analysis of impact of errors

Method1 assumes that the objects of the plant and the environment are reliable in a sense that they behave as specified. This assumption is not always valid as the plant objects are exposed to random failures and the objects of the environment can violate assumptions concerning their behaviour. Therefore, the system should be systematically examined with the aim of identification of possible faults and checking their impact on safety. The method provides a set of templates of faulty behaviours that are defined as deviations from the normal behaviour. Within the context of a specific application, those templates are validated against possibility of their instantiation in the actual system. Those which are considered significant are then introduced to the model as alternative behaviours. Then we again use the reachability analysis to check whether these faulty behaviours have any impact on safety. If the faults are dangerous the method gives some ideas on how to restore safety either by modifications of the control system or by reconstruction of the plant. More details on this method can be found in [2].

Method3: Safety monitoring

Methods 1 and 2 concentrate on verifying that the system achieves its mission goals within the safety constraints. To strengthen safety guarantees the system can be additionally enriched with a device called *safety monitor*. Its only concern is safety. We have developed a method of systematic synthesis of such safety monitor for a given application. The idea of monitoring [4] is simple: if a potentially hazardous sequence of events is developing in the system, inform the operator or another control system by raising an alarm. A corrective action aiming at safety restoration can be then executed before the hazardous behaviour converts into an accident. The practical approach [5] to safety monitoring is based on the following observation: if the critical subsystem model were stimulated with exactly the same events as the actual system then reaching the hazardous state by the model would mean the hazard in the actual system. Consequently, the model of the critical subsystem constitutes the first version of the safety monitor. The method transforms the critical subsystem model in the following steps:

- *Reduction*: removing all safety irrelevant details from the monitor,
- *Implantation*: ensuring that the monitor is stimulated by only those events that are *measurable* i.e. there are technical means to detect their occurrence,
- *Tuning*: achieving appropriate sensitivity of the monitor: no overlooked hazards, false alarms avoidance and early warning.

4 Object Oriented Model Of the Substation Bay

This section presents some results of modelling of the extra high voltage line bay. More compete presentation can be found in [9,11].

The Object Model

Fig. 2 presents the Object Model of the bay.

310

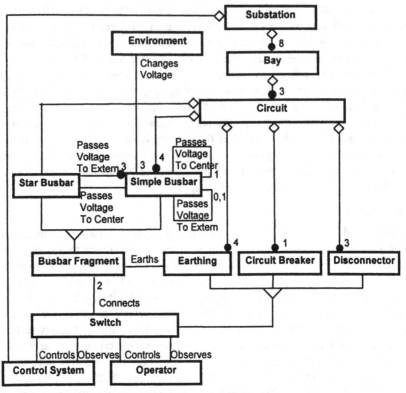

Fig. 2. The class model of the bay.

The meaning of the model is explained in the frame of Fig. 3.

The whole **Substation** consists of 8 **Bays** and the **Control System**. Each **Bay** consists of 3 **Circuits** - one for each phase. The **Circuit** consists of **Busbar Fragments** of two types. The **Circuit** consists of 4 **Simple Busbars** and a **Star Busbar**. The primary aim of **Busbar Fragment** is to pass voltages to the consecutive **Busbar Fragments** what can cause a flow of current. Voltages can be passed in two directions: towards the centre of the **Circuit** and towards external objects. Voltages are passed between **Busbar Fragments** when at least one of them is under voltage and the **Busbar Fragments** are connected by a closed **Switch**. An **Environment** can change the voltage of those **Simple Busbars** which come outside the **Bay**. A **Switch** connects 2 **Busbar Fragments** or a **Busbar Fragment** with earth. Other parts of the **Circuit** are 4 **Earthing Switches**, 3 **Disconnectors** and a **Circuit Breaker**. Each of these devices is basically a **Switch**. The **Earthing Switch** earths the **Busbar Fragment**. **Switches** are controlled by either the **Control System** or an **Operator**. Both the **Control System** and **Operator** observe **Switches** to learn about their actual states.

Fig. 3. Explanation of the object model of the bay.

The Dynamic Model

For each class of the Object Model the corresponding Dynamic Model is developed. Fig. 4 presents the dynamic model of a disconnector and Fig. 5 gives the corresponding explanation (dotted arrows represent faults and are explained in a subsequent part of the paper).

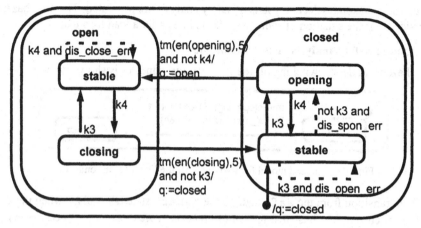

Fig. 4. Dynamic model of a disconnector.

A disconnector can be in either of two states: open or closed. Initially it is in the state closed.stable. The value of the global variable q which is read by busbar fragments and the control system is set to closed. When k3 event comes it moves the disconnector to the state opening. If k4 appears while the disconnector is in the opening state the disconnector returns to the closed.stable state. If however k4 does not appear, then 5 time units after entering opening it moves to the state open.stable (tm(en(opening),5) and not k4) and changes the value of q to open.

When k4 appears while the disconnector is in open.stable it moves to the closing state. If k3 appears while the disconnector is in the closing state the disconnector returns to open.stable state. If however k3 does not appear, then 5 time units after entering opening it moves to the state closed.stable (tm(en(closing),5) and not k3) and changes the value of q to closed.

Fig. 5. Explanation of the dynamic model of a disconnector.

A problem which was encountered during modelling was how to represent the flow of electric current in terms of statecharts. We have developed a protocol which propagates the state „flow of electric current" to all connected busbar fragment objects, as soon as the last and the first in the chain of connected busbar fragments have different voltage potentials.

Dynamic models were developed for the classes shown in Fig.1. It was then verified whether the models meet the mission requirements given in the system specification, e.g. if the state of switches is appropriate after applying the switching sequence of connecting a busbar system to the line. The Statemate tool has been applied during those verifications.

5 Object oriented safety analysis of the substation bay

In this section some selected results of safety analysis are presented. The only hazard considered is the situation of switching off the line under a load by a disconnector.

Method 1: Safety analysis of system mission

The hazard model of switching off the line by a disconnector is shown in the Fig. 6.

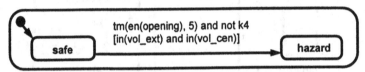

Fig. 6. The hazard model for switching off the line by a disconnector.

The transition from the **safe** state to the **hazard** state takes place when there is a flow of current in a busbar fragment (`[in(vol_ext) and in(vol_cen)]`) and the disconnector is opening (`tm(en(opening),5) and not k4`). There are two critical objects associated with this hazard. Their aggregation forms the critical subsystem (Fig. 7).

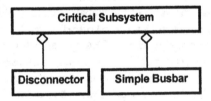

Fig. 7. The class model of the critical subsystem.

Composition of the dynamic models of the simple busbar and disconnector and the hazard model of Fig.6 results in the model consisting of two high-level states: hazardous and safe. The safe state consists of three concurrent states (two of them describe the busbar fragments and the third is related to the disconnector).

Having the hazardous state and transitions leading to this state explicitly modelled provided for performing the reachability analysis. The analysis revealed a design fault in the control system (this fault was then traced back to the incompleteness in the requirements). The fault allowed to connect the line to both busbar systems at the same time. Disconnecting the line from a busbar system results in breaking a current flow between the line and the busbar systems (as the circuit breaker is off) but there is still a flow of equalising current between busbar systems. Opening a disconnector in such a situation led to the hazard. To eliminate the hazard an alternate connection of busbar systems to the line had to be guaranteed. More details can be found in [11].

Method 2: Analysis of impact of errors

The disconnector model presented in Fig. 4 includes transitions represented by dotted lines. They represent *faulty behaviours*. Labels of these transitions include events with the **_err** suffix. They represent the random nature of errors (during analysis we assume that the events enabling those transitions are generated by the environment in a random manner). The requirements specification provides information concerning errors of a disconnector:

- it does not open on command (**dis_open_err**),
- it does not close on command (**dis_close_err**),
- it opens spontaneously without command (**dis_spon_open_err**).

The model with faulty transitions replaces the original model and reachability analysis of hazardous states is performed again. The impact of spontaneous opening of a disconnector is straightforward: if it opens while current flows through it the hazard occurrs. Hewever, we were able to uncover also more complicated hazardous situation which iresulted from two errors of a circuit breaker. More details on the results can be found in [11].

Method 3: Safety monitoring

The details on safety monitor synthesis for the Mościska line bay can be found in [12]. The monitor synthesis involved a series of transformations of the critical subsystem. The monitor model (Fig. 8) was derived from the model of the critical subsystem in the following way:

- it uses concrete instead of generic events and data as it concerns the concrete hazard,
- only measurable events and data are used to observe changes in the actual system,
- it is passive i.e. it does not generate events and modify variables,
- the transition to the **alarm** state initiates from the **closed.stable** state when **k733** appears; it allows to generate the alarm signal before the hazard occurs.

6 Conclusion

In our approach we have exploited two features: object oriented decomposition and behaviour modelling by statecharts. The Object Model concentrates on static structural properties (classes their relationships) and the Dynamic Model defines (in terms of statecharts) the behaviour of the classes. Statecharts appeared to be an adequate formalism to support system safety analysis. During analyses we identified a number of complex situations that potentially could cause hazards. On the other hand any formalism can not ensure safety by itself unless it is used with the defined purpose and in the proper context. In our case the purpose and the context were given by the three methods presented in this paper.

We profited very much from object oriented decomposition. Having a good understanding of what are the boundaries and interfaces of the system under modelling was very important. Obviously the development of individual dynamic models of classes and then assuring proper communication among them is easier then development of a global dynamic model. Some steps of the proposed safety analysis methods work on the level of individual classes rather than on the level of the whole system.

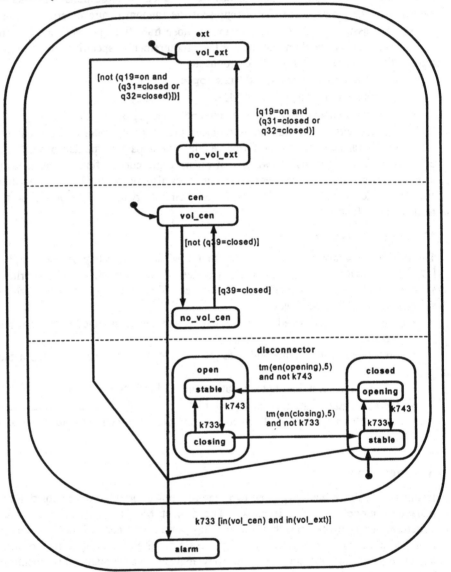

Fig. 8. The dynamic model of the safety monitor.

The proposed methods employ reachability analysis. This way we could identify some highly complicated scenarios of events leading to a hazardous state. Achieving the same result with other techniques (e.g. inspections) seems to be very unlikely.

Although the tool, Statemate, was very useful supporting our work it still has some deficiencies:

- a bug in the tool was revealed (the bug reference number is 15489),
- the metric of model complexity is of little use (time of analysis of different models with the same metric differs from seconds to days),
- the time of analysis grows very fast with the size of models (complexity problem).

To provide for unambiguity of model specifications we have worked out a formal semantics of statecharts using the Z method. This formalisation effort opened a room for exploiting the existing tools supporting Z for performing analyses for those case studies where reachability analysis is inefficient.

Our further plans include carrying out experiments related to application of our methods to safety analysis of a railway signalling system.

References

1. Cadre, *Paradigm Plus. Cadre Edition. User's Guide*, 1994
2. Górski J., Nowicki B., *Object–Oriented Approach to Safety Analysis*, Proc. ENCRESS'95, Springer-Verlag, Bruges (Belgium), September 12–15, 1995, pp. 338-350
3. Górski J., Nowicki B., *Safety Analysis Based on Object-Oriented Modelling of Critical Systems*, Proc. SAFECOMP'96, Springer-Verlag, Vienna Oct. 23-25, 1996, pp. 46-60
4. Górski J., Nowicki B., *Safety Monitor Synthesis Based on Hazard Scenarios*, Proc. ESREL'97, Pergamon, June, 1997, Lisbon, Portugal, pp. 407-415
5. Górski J., Nowicki B., *Object-oriented Safety Monitor Synthesis*, Proc. ENCRESS'97, Chapman&Hall, May 29-30, 1997, Athens, Greece, pp. 121-133
6. Harel D., *Statecharts: A Visual Formalism for Complex Systems*, In Science of Computer Programming 8, 1987, pp. 231-274
7. i-Logix Inc., Burlington, *STATEMATE - Technical Documentation*, 1996
8. *Integration of Safety Analysis Techniques for Process Control Systems*, EC COPERNICUS Joint Research Project 1594, http://www.cs.ncl.ac.uk/research/csr/projects/isat/
9. Nowicki B., Górski J., *Object Oriented Modelling of the Extra High Voltage Substation*, TR ISAT 97/6, ITTI Centre of Software Engineering, Poland, Poznań, April 1997
10. Nowicki B., Górski J., *Object Oriented Modelling of the Extra High Voltage Substation Bay Including Equalising Currents*, TR ISAT 97/16, ITTI Centre of Software Engineering, Poland, Poznań, April 1997
11. Nowicki B., Górski J., *Object Oriented Safety Analysis of the Extra High Voltage Substation Bay*, TR ISAT 97/7, ITTI Centre of Software Engineering, Poland, Poznań, April 1997
12. Nowicki B., Górski J., *Object Oriented Safety Monitor Synthesis for the Extra High Voltage Substation Bay*, Technical Report, Technical University of Gdansk (in preparation)
13. Rumbaugh J., Blaha M., Premerlani W., Eddy F., Lorensen W., *Object-Oriented Modelling and Design*, Prentice Hall Int., 1991
14. Żurakowski Z., *Identification and Preparation of Case Studies - Extra-High Voltage Substation Software Interlocking Case Study*, TR ISAT 97/8, Institute of Power Systems Automation, Poland, Wrocław, December 1996.

Formal Methods III

Petri Nets

Integration of Logical and Physical Properties of Embedded Systems by Use of Time Petri Nets

Francesca Saglietti

Institute for Safety Technology (ISTec) GmbH
Forschungsgelände 85748 Garching Germany
e-mail: saf@istecmuc.grs.de

Abstract. This article aims at emphasising the importance of integrating logical and physical aspects in order to validate requirements and high-level design of safety-related embedded systems. After some introductory remarks motivating the inclusion of continuous process properties into early requirements analysis, it offers a brief survey on some of the existing alternatives. For the purpose of exemplification this contribution focuses on Time Petri Nets, which are extendible beyond binary logic to include physics in terms of real-valued time intervals. The analysis of a real-world example illustrates the applicability of this approach to support the proof or disproof of safety properties, allowing to identify weak assumptions at early design stages.

1   Introduction

1.1 Models and Formal Systems

Embedded systems are conceived

- to *observe* a technical process by sensing physical variables in order to extract information on the internal process state, and

- to *control* the technical process by acting on physical variables in order to (re-) establish an acceptable process state.

As the process to be observed and controlled is subject to physical laws governing reality, the requirements to be defined for a controlled system - including process and embedded computer systems - depend on the human activity of modelling physical reality. In other words, the concepts defining embedded systems are expressed in terms of symbols representing human perception of the objective world. Due to reasons of perception and complexity, modelling has to rely on abstraction: only aspects considered as relevant for the technical process to be controlled are taken into account in the real world representation; this may restrict modelling accuracy. The modelling goals are two-fold:

- to *reproduce* a real entity (the physical process) in a symbolic language, and

- to *anticipate* the pattern of a planned entity (the system to be implemented).

1.2   Verification versus Validation

A formal model is a representation with a well-defined semantics for all of its elements. A formal system is a formal model provided with a calculus, i. e. a set of deductive rules operating on its representation by means of mechanistic inference. Under the assumption of modelling correctness, a formal system provides a rigorous framework for the

- *verification* of logical statements, i. e. for the mathematical derivation of theorems under the hypothesis of predefined axioms.

Being dependent on human perception and experience, however, modelling correctness itself cannot be verified in the framework of a deductive system. It can only be inductively confirmed in the context of the real entity modelled by

- *validation,* i. e. by comparing samples of modelling conclusions with their interpretations in reality.

For this reason, licensing procedures have to distinguish between the following activities of different nature, as illustrated in Figure 1.

Physical Modelling of the Technical Process. This activity lies completely within the domain of physics; it has to be validated (or falsified) by empirical observations based on statistical samples.

Requirements Analysis for the Controlled System. This activity lies at the interface of physics and logic, thus motivating the use of hybrid modelling techniques as those analysed in this article.

Implementation of the Embedded Controller. This activity lies within the logical domain; it can be supported by use of formal methods to provide mathematical proofs of specific properties, e. g. consistency, completeness and model checking at specification level, formal refinement and verification during design and coding phase.

1.3   Further Dualities

Apart from the aspects just considered, the distinction discussed above gives also raise to further considerations on the inherent duality of V&V procedures.

Deterministic versus Probabilistic Dependability Concept. Verification activities are based on a *qualitative* dependability concept in the sense of "capability of service provision"; validation procedures, on the other hand, relate to a *quantitative* dependability concept defined as "probability of service provision". Both concepts refer to predefined operational conditions.

Logical versus Physical Domain. Verification techniques mainly rely on Boolean discreteness within predicate logic frameworks, whereas validation techniques must include continuous physical variables in real-valued domains.

Axiomatic versus Operational Approach. Verification procedures rely on checking particular features in a static way, namely by deduction (regardless of operational options). On the other hand, validation focuses on observations of individual executions meant to reflect particular operational scenarios. Due to their nature, modelling inaccuracies must be *dynamically* detected by testing or tolerated by functional diversity.

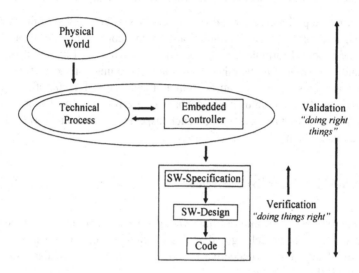

Fig. 1. V&V entities (logical entities in rectangular, physical entities in elliptical margins)

2 Modelling Languages Integrating Logic and Physics

2.1 Need for an Intermediate Modelling Level

Thanks to the flexibility provided by software-based components, the diffusion of embedded controllers in safety-relevant applications is continuously expanding; for similar reasons, also the complexity of safety-critical functionalities is increasing.

The considerable progress achieved during the last decade in the area of formal methods has reduced one main source of faults, namely those caused by erroneous implementation (e. g. see [11]); the growing responsibility of software controllers for complex tasks tends, however, to shift the major source of problems from the actual development phases up towards the earlier phases of requirements analysis.

Some of the main software-related accidents of the last years were related to incomplete or erroneous requirements. The causes were later identified as being partly enforced by inconsistencies between reality and implicit model assumptions, like the following ones.

Causal Assumptions. The braking mechanism of the Airbus aircraft A320 (see [9]) relied on a requirement ("reverse thrust only when touching the ground") modelled by a condition ("reverse thrust only in case of predefined weight on both wheels"), which revealed as non-fulfilling the demands, when only one wheel touches the ground.

Temporal Assumptions. One of the design faults of the radiation machine Therac-25 (see [6], [12] and chapter 4) was activated under particular operating speed conditions (fast re-editing of radiation parameters), unlikely to be reproduced by test cases.

Spatial Assumptions. The definition of the inertial reference system of the Ariane 5 (see [3]) relied on the trajectory values of a previous model (Ariane 4), which differed from the new one with respect to its early horizontal velocity values.

In most cases the problems are not due to actual lack of knowledge of the system to be controlled, but rather to tacit assumptions. In the context of natural language the explicit and repeated formulation of more or less obvious and known details may be tedious and distracting. On the other hand, omitting to mention explicit indications on physical conditions (like the causal, temporal and spatial assumptions mentioned above) may result in the unjustified acceptance of erroneous conclusions. A rigorous notation allowing to take account of such aspects in symbolic form can help to overcome this problem.

2.2 Decidability versus Expressiveness

Depending on their capability of integrating physical and logical properties in a balanced way, hybrid modelling and analysis techniques may differ in terms of their richness or of their formal deductive power, giving raise to a fundamental trade-off between the following features.

Decidability. Exclusively binary, discrete properties allow to be directly translated into Boolean logic. This may include physical conditions, though simplified by a discrete framework. For example, classical fault tree analysis describes the cause of predefined events as conjunction or disjunction of sub-events. Underlying statements are considered as absolute, not allowing for uncertainty degrees. Consequently, language expressiveness is quite poor; on the other hand, the determination of minimal cut sets is decidable (though numerically hard).

Expressiveness. By refining modelling granularity, physical continuity tends to introduce growing sources of uncertainty, for instance due to time, space or causal dependencies. Statements are not considered within an absolute framework anymore, but rather in relation to varying conditions, e. g. in terms of an appropriate modal logic. Extending the notation beyond discreteness to include real-valued intervals (e. g. for expressing time delay) contributes to enrich language expressiveness. Obviously, this may severely limit deductive power resulting in undecidable features.

2.3 Examples

Qualitative Physics. Qualitative expressions may help to represent the characteristic behaviour of entities in a physical environment without requiring an overly-descriptive physical modelling. Quantified relationships among process variables may reveal as impractical, e. g. if absolute figures depend upon a design not yet definitively fixed. A form of abstraction based on causal operators was suggested in [2] and [9].

Dynamic Flowgraph Methodology. DFM (see [4]) is based on multi-state representations of cause-effect and time-varying relationships among system and software parameters. The model is automatically backtracked to produce time fault trees and prime implicants for predefined top events. It supports both the qualitative validation of system design (by early detection of specification faults), and software testing (by systematic selection of critical functional test cases).

Timed & Hybrid Automata. The timed automaton model (see [8]) is a labelled transition system model for components in real-time systems developed for modelling and verifying timing-based computer communication systems. It was extended to a hybrid I/O automaton (see [7]), capable of describing continuous behaviour of real world components in addition to discrete behaviour of computer components.

3 Time Petri Nets

Classical Petri nets provide a well-known, powerful technique to model and analyse:

- *co-operation* of parallel processes sharing common tasks, and

- *concurrency* of parallel processes requiring common resources.

The correct implementation of concurrency has implications on task ordering. In addition, each process may be subjected to absolute time demands (see [10]), like

- *minimum* time delay - action can start at time τ_1 at earliest";

- *maximum* execution time - action must be concluded by time τ_2 at latest".

3.1 Static Properties of TPNs

Like for conventional Petri Nets (PNs), also the static structure of Time Petri Nets (TPNs) consists of a marked bipartite graphs $((P,T), M)$, where

- P denotes a finite set of *places* p representing states,

- T denotes a finite set of *transitions* t representing actions, and

- $M: P \rightarrow N_0$ represents a place *marking* describing momentary states.

TPNs are further characterised by associating to each transition $t \in T$ a static time interval $S(t) := [s_1(t), s_2(t)]$, where $s_1(t), s_2(t) \in Q$ are time indicators for *delay* and action *duration*. Their role is clarified by defining the dynamic behaviour of TPNs.

3.2 Dynamic Properties of TPNs

To reflect the dynamic behaviour of TPNs (slightly simplified from [1]), at any time a variable firing interval $D(t) = [d_1(t), d_2(t)]$ is associated with each transition t. Therefore, the momentary state S of a TPN is given by a pair $S = (M, D)$, where

- M denotes the present place *marking*, and

- D denotes a vector of updated *firing intervals* $(D(t_1),...,D(t_n))$, where $T = \{t_1,...,t_n\}$.

Classical PN-Firing Rule. Transition $t \in T$ is *PN-firable* w. r. t. marking M iff:

each input place of t is marked: $M(p) > 0 \ \forall \ p \in input(t)$.

Assuming $input(t) \cap output(t) = \varnothing$, PN-firing of transition t yields marking $M':P \rightarrow N_0$:

$M'(p) := M(p) - 1 \ \forall \ p \in input(t); M'(p) := M(p) + 1 \ \forall \ p \in output(t)$.

TPN-firability of transition t at time $\tau_{abs} + \tau$. Let τ_{abs} denote a starting time of PN-firability of transition $t \in T$, i.e.:

1. at time τ_{abs} all input states of t are marked: at time τ_{abs} $M(p) > 0 \ \forall \ p \in input(t)$, but

2. not all input states of t are marked shortly before time τ_{abs}:

$\exists \varepsilon > 0: \neg \{\exists$ marking M during $[\tau_{abs} - \varepsilon, \tau_{abs}[: M(p) > 0 \ \forall \ p \in input(t))\}$

Then t is *TPN-firable* at time $\tau_{abs} + \tau$ iff:

1. t is continuously PN-firable in $[\tau_{abs}, \tau_{abs} + \tau]$ with respect to any new marking, i.e.:

$M(p) > 0 \ \forall \ p \in input(t), \ \forall$ marking M during $[\tau_{abs}, \tau_{abs} + \tau]$, and

2. the relative time τ since PN-firability start is in D(t): $\tau \in [d_1(t), d_2(t)]$.

Effects of TPN-Firing of Transition $t \in T$ at time $\tau_{abs} + \tau$. The effects are multiple:

1. a *new marking* $M': P \rightarrow N_0$ as for PN-firing of transition t;

2. a *new firing interval* $D(t_i)$ for $t_i \in T$, according to the following 3 cases $i \in \{1,2,3\}$:

- if t_1 is not PN-firable w.r.t. the new marking M' then $D(t_1) := \varnothing$;

- If t_2 was PN-firable at firing time, without conflict with t,
  and t_2 is still PN-firable after firing t, then $D(t_2) := [\max \{0, d_1(t_2) - \tau\}; d_2(t_2) - \tau]$;

- If t_3 was not PN-firable before and is now PN-firable again,
  or if t_3 is still PN-firable, in spite of conflicts with t, then $D(t_3) := [s_1(t_3); s_2(t_3)]$.

In other words: starting with time τ_{abs}, when a transition t starts being PN-firable, and assuming no other conflicting transition t' firing in the meantime, t may fire *at earliest* after its lower static bound $s_1(t)$ elapses, i. e. at time $\tau_{abs} + s_1(t)$, and *at latest* before its upper static bound $s_2(t)$ elapses, i. e. at time $\tau_{abs} + s_2(t)$.

3.3 Reachability and Boundedness of TPNs

Classical PNs result as restrictions of TPNs in case $[s_1(t), s_2(t)] = [0,\infty[$ $\forall$ t $\in$ T. The extended TPN-structure is more powerful in terms of modelling expressiveness; this benefit, however, is tightly coupled with its higher structural complexity. In other words, the gain in representable information is achieved at the price of a loss in analysability. Fundamental properties supporting net analysis are:

- *TPN-reachability*, concerning the question whether or not a predefined marking is reachable from an initial marking in a finite number of TPN-firing steps, and

- *TPN-boundedness*, concerning the question whether or not a bounded number of tokens is sufficient to represent any reachable marking.

Other than for classical PNs, for TPNs both problems were shown to be undecidable in general (see [5]). Moreover, in case only rational time intervals are considered (i. e. for $d_1(t), d_2(t) \in \mathbf{Q}$ $\forall$ t $\in$ T), both problems can be shown to be equivalent.

4 Application of Time Petri Nets

The aim of this chapter is to demonstrate by means of a real-world example the applicability of Time Petri Nets to model multitasking and to integrate physical – in this case temporal - process parameters to identify critical race conditions. The demonstration will proceed by developing first a graphical specification of the behaviour of the system, by formalising then a safety property for this specification, and finally by attempting at formally proving or disproving that this property holds.

4.1 System Description

The application chosen for demonstration is the computer-controlled radiation therapy machine Therac-25 (see [6]), conceived to allow two different therapeutic modes:

- in *electron* mode the patient is irradiated directly, using bending magnets to spread a beam of moderate energy to a safe concentration; whereas

- in *photon* mode a high rate beam is flattened by an attenuator to produce a uniform treatment.

A major hazard evidently concerns the combination of a high intensity beam with the flattener not being properly placed. The control system relies on several processes (subroutines / human actions), among them the following ones.

Subroutine Datent. *Datent* checks whether the keyboard handler has set mode and energy; it can communicate with the keyboard handling task via a shared variable, which is changed by the keyboard handler to denote completion of data entry. *Datent* calls subroutine *Magnet* for setting bending magnets.

Subroutine Magnet. *Magnet* takes about 8 seconds to set the bending magnets, it calls the subroutine *Ptime* to introduce a time delay during the magnet setting procedures.

Subroutine Ptime. *Ptime* is entered and exited several times during magnet setting. It has to check the presence of editing requests, interrupting the bending process in case of any request (see Figure 2).

The operator. The operator enters mode and energy, and can later edit them separately. The operator can complete editing in less than 8 seconds.

```
Ptime:
1 repeat
2   if bending magnet flag is set then
3     if editing taking place then
4       if mode/energy changed then exit
5   until hysteresis delay has expired
6   clear bending magnet flag
7 return
```

Fig. 2. Routine Ptime (from [6])

As reported in [6], one of the problems which were responsible for dangerous operation was due to the flag cleared by *Ptime* upon its first execution; changes of mode/energy performed during later passes through *Ptime* could not be recognised. If editing was performed particularly fast (in less than 8 seconds), it could be completed before returning to *Datent*, which could not sense its occurrence.

4.2 Modelling by Time Petri Nets

The concurrent execution of *Ptime* and the operator's actions is modelled by the (slightly simplified) TPN shown in Figure 3. It is enriched by inhibiting arcs negating the validity of their input places (see Table 1). Transitions without explicit temporal indications are assumed to occur instantaneously; the only transitions with explicit firing times are:

- $t3(\Delta)$ modelling elapsing of an average hysteresis delay Δ;

- $t7(\Delta')$ modelling editing time, assuming a conservative estimate $\Delta' = [min;max]$.

4.3 Safety Analysis by TPNs

The essential safety property considered here concerns concurrency of editing and magnet bending. Consistency of these tasks can only be ensured if manual parameter changes are always identifiable by the machine controller before beam firing, in

particular if *Ptime* is able to identify any parameter change completed during its execution. In order to check this property, backtracking is applied to the Time Petri Net shown in Figure 1, starting with the critical event "change not detected".
This state is true if P10 (*change detected*) is not reachable, under the condition that any change occurred, i. e. once P9 (*change completed*) is reached. This yields initial condition P9 ∧ ¬P6 for the following backtracking:

$$[P9 \wedge \neg P6] \leftarrow [P8 \wedge \neg (P2 \wedge P5)] \leftarrow [P8 \wedge \neg P2] \leftarrow$$
$$[P7 \wedge \neg (P1 \wedge \neg P0 \wedge \neg P4)] \leftarrow [P7 \wedge (\neg P1 \vee P0 \vee P4)] \leftarrow [P7 \wedge P4]$$

The estimation 8 ∈ Δ' supports the conclusion that within the physical constraints of the application analysed (execution time ≈ 8 s) non-identification of editing changes can indeed occur.

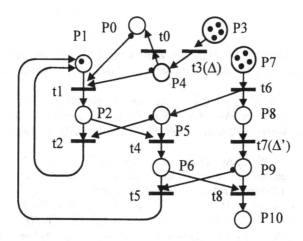

Fig. 3. TPN for routine *Ptime* and operator in Therac-25

Places	and their meaning		
P0	flag cleared	**Transitions**	**and their meaning**
P1	line 2 of *Ptime*		
P2	line 3 of *Ptime*	t0: P4 → P0	clear flag at Δi, i≥2
P3	clock ticks Δi left, i≥2	t1: [P1∧¬P0∧¬P4]→P2	goto line 3 of *Ptime*
P4	alarm set at Δi, i ≥ 2	t2: [P2 ∧ ¬P5] → P1	restart *Ptime*
P5	editing occurred	t3(Δ): P3 → P4	set alarm at Δi, i≥2
P6	line 4 of *Ptime*	t4: [P2 ∧ P5] → P6	goto line 4 of *Ptime*
P7	editing wishes (≥ 0)	t5: [P6 ∧ ¬P9] → P1	restart *Ptime*
P8	editing started	t6: P7 → [P5 ∧ P8]	start change
P9	change completed	t7(Δ'): P8→ P9	conclude change
P10	change detected	t8: [P6 ∧ P9] → P10	exit

Table 1. Explanations to TPN places and transitions shown in Figure 3

5 Conclusion

This contribution aims at encouraging a more diffused use of hybrid (logical and physical) modelling techniques (see Table 2) in the early specification phase of embedded systems, thus supporting integrated V&V activities before implementation.

Entity	Domain	Applicable Techniques
technical process	physical (validation)	informal, e.g. testing, functional diversity
controlled system	physical and logical	both, e.g. qualitative physics, DFM, TPNs
embedded software	logical (verification)	formal, e.g. theorem proving

Table 2. Classification of entities, domains and applicable techniques

References

1. Berthomieu, B., Diaz, M.: Modeling and Verification of Time Dependent Systems Using Time Petri Nets. IEEE Transactions on Software Engineering, Vol. 17. IEEE Computer Society (1991)
2 Coombes, A., McDermid, J., Moffett, J.: Requirements Analysis and Safety: A Case Study using GRASP. Proceedings SAFECOMP'95, G. Rabe editor. Springer-Verlag (1995)
3 European Space Agency: ARIANE 5 Flight 501 Failure Report by the Inquiry Board. Press Release (1996)
4 Garrett C. J., Guarro, S. B., Apostolakis, G. E.: The Dynamic Flowgraph Methodology for Assessing the Dependability of Embedded Software Systems. IEEE Transactions on Systems, Man, and Cybernetics, Vol. 25. IEEE Computer Society (1995)
5. Jones, N. D., Landweber, L. H., Lien, Y. E.: Complexity of some Problems in Petri Nets. Theoretical Computer Science, Vol. 4. Elsevier Science Publishers (1977)
6. Leveson, N. G.: Safeware: System Safety and Computers - A Guide to Preventing Accidents and Losses Caused by Technology. Addison-Wesley (1995)
7. Leeb, G., Lynch, N.: Proving Safety Properties of the Steam Boiler Controller. Lecture Notes in Computer Science, Vol. 11654. Springer-Verlag (1996)
8. Lynch, N.: Modelling and Verification of Automated Transit Systems, using Timed Automata, Invariants and Simulations. Lecture Notes in Computer Science, Vol. 1066. Springer-Verlag (1996)
9. Moffett, J. D., Hall, J. G., Coombes, A. C., McDermid, J. A.: A Model for a Causal Logic for Requirements Engineering. Journal of Requirements Engineering, Vol. 1. Springer-Verlag (1996)
10. Saglietti, F., guest editor: Special Issue on Dependability of Real-Time Software. Real-Time Systems – The International Journal of Time-Critical Computing Systems, Vol. 7. Kluwer Academic Publishers (1994)
11. Saglietti, F.: Dynamic Decision on Checkpointing by Use of Reduced Ordered Binary Decision Diagrams. Proceedings SAFECOMP'97, P. Daniel editor. Springer-Verlag (1997)
12. Thomas, M.: The Story of the Therac-25 in LOTOS. High Integrity Systems, Vol. 1. Oxford University Press (1994)

Safety Verification of Software Using Structured Petri Nets

Krzysztof Sacha

Warsaw University of Technology, Institute of Control and Computation Engineering,
ul. Nowowiejska 15/19, 00-665 Warszawa, Poland

Abstract. A method is described for the analysis and the verification of safety in software systems. The method offers a formal notation for describing the software structure, the means for defining safe and unsafe states of the system and a technique for the software simulation and analysis. The modeling process is based on an extension to Petri nets, which enables the modeler to represent control as well as data processing aspects of the software. The Petri net-based model can be analyzed using the concept of a modified reachability tree or can be used as a framework for a simulated execution. The model can be build in an early phase of the software development process, thus creating the potential for early verification and validation of safety.

1 Introduction

The problem of safety has always played a pivotal role in the development of control systems in such application areas as railway transport, process industry, power plants, etc. The technological shift from traditional hardwired systems towards software-based systems issued a new challenge — it has been recognized that safety analysis should also be incorporated into the software development process and embedded somehow into the software lifecycle. However, the problem of selecting the appropriate methods for safety analysis in software domain has not been solved as yet.

IEC 1508 (draft) standard [1] defines safety in terms of probabilistic measures (the notion of risk). Such a definition encourages two general methods of increasing system safety:

- employing redundant architectures,
- increasing the reliability of components.

The drawback of such an approach within the software domain is, that there are neither the means to measure the software reliability nor even a satisfactory definition. Hence, there are not many methods which can be practically applied to ensure the desired level of software reliability. A short survey of practices and methods which are applied within the software lifecycle in order to enable and to conduct safety analysis for software can be found in [2].

Nevertheless a number of factors have been identified which influence the software reliability. Among them are the following:

- Exact and unambiguous requirement specification.
- Early validation of safety of the specification.
- Credible verification of the design and the implementation against the requirements specification by means of:
  - proof of correctness,
  - testing.

At the current level of the software technology testing cannot guarantee program correctness, while full proofs of correctness are not feasible, as yet. Therefore it seems practical to develop an approach of partial proofs of correctness, i.e. proofs related to selected features which are particularly resistive to testing. Those features correspond to all aspects of interprocess synchronization and communication. The reasoning is such, that a sequential program can effectively be tested. Testing a set of parallel processes is much more difficult.

The goal of this paper is to describe a formal method for the software specification and prototyping which addresses all of the above mentioned problems. The method — called Transnet — offers the potential of formal specification combined with an efficient technique of rapid prototyping and safety analysis. The paper is organized as follows. Section 2 provides the reader with an overview of the method which is based on an extension to Petri nets. Section 3 presents an illustrative example. A description of techniques used for analysis and prototyping is given in Section 4. Timing aspects are considered and formally defined in Section 5. Tools supporting the use of the method and plans for future work are discussed in Conclusions.

2   Overview of the method

Many methods and techniques have been developed for specifying real-time control systems in a formal way. Formal methods are based on mathematical theories, such as: algebra, temporal logic, finite-state machines, functional programming or Petri nets. Transnet is a method which adopts a modified model of Petri nets.

A classical Petri net [3] can be viewed as a bipartite directed graph consisting of nodes which are places and transitions, and oriented arcs. Places are represented graphically by circles, and transitions by bars (or rectangles).The arcs join places to transitions and transitions to places in such a way that neither two places nor two transitions are linked directly. Places of a net can be marked with tokens, drawn as dots. Tokens can move between places as result of transition firings. A transition is enabled, i.e. ready to fire, if all places that input the transition have a token. Firing a transition removes a token from each of its input places and deposits a token in each of its output places. The current distribution of tokens among places which is called a marking, defines the current state of the net.

Petri net is usually interpreted as a control flow graph of a modeled system. Places correspond to conditions within the system, while transitions correspond to actions. A condition can be fulfilled, i.e. marked with a token in the current system state, or not. An action, i.e. a transition firing, can move tokens between places, thus reflecting a change to the system state.

Classical Petri nets are focused entirely on representing the flow of control and provide no opportunity for representing data and time-dependent aspects of the system operation. Hence, various extensions to the basic model have been invented and described in the literature [4–8].

The net model adopted by Transnet [9] restricts the net structure to a composition of three basic building blocks:

- sequential composition,
- alternative selection,
- parallel branching.

This restriction complies with the basic control structures used in program design and implementation. Moreover, it helps in maintaining readability of the specification.

On the other hand, Transnet extends the definition of Petri net by associating (Fig. 1):

- places with variables,
- transitions with data processing functions,
- arcs which lead from places to transitions with Boolean expressions.

The semantics of the extensions to Petri nets is as follows. A transition is enabled if all places that input the transition have a token (classics) and all Boolean expressions associated with the input arcs to the transition evaluate to *true* (extension). Firing a transition removes and deposits tokens as usually, but additionally the function associated with the transition is evaluated and the results are substituted to variables associated with output places. This way, an execution of a net can model the flow of control within the modeled system as well as data values evaluated during the system operation.

A specification of a control system is build as a set of concurrent processes, each of which is modeled by an extended Petri net. A process can be a representation of a system object, such as task or data buffer, or an environmental object, such as discrete model of a physical process. Processes in a specification can cooperate with each other, exchanging messages during a symmetric and synchronous rendezvous, modeled by an **exchange transition** i.e. a transition with input and output arcs belonging to both cooperating processes. A complete specification is formal and executable and therefore can be used as a system prototype.

The introduction of variables and arc expressions changes dramatically the semantics of the model, as the net marking can no longer be used to characterize the state of the model. The real results of the modeled computation are stored as values of variables, while the current marking describes only an internal state of the computation. A more elaborate treatment of this problem is given below.

All processes of a specification are cyclic and run forever. Each process has a distinguished place, referred to as the **terminal place**, which is marked in the inactive state of the process, just between two consecutive cycles of execution. The terminal place holds a token in the initial net marking. The variables associated with the terminal place which are called **terminal variables**, store the results of the computation and retain the process history between the consecutive process cycles. The values of terminal variables are changed at the end of the current process cycle and are stable throughout the next cycle. Other variables do not retain the process history. They comply with the single assignment rule — the idea borrowed from functional languages — and are used only as value-holders which are invalidated when the terminal place of the process receives a token.

The **specification state** is defined as a vector of values of all terminal variables. A sequence of states produced during the net execution, called a **trace**, determines the behavior of the specification. This can be observed from the outside and interpreted by people or devices. The execution of a specification net is indeterministic due to indeterministic scheduling. This implies that a specification net has many traces and the meaning of a specification is characterized by a **trace set**, including all traces that may be produced during the specification net execution. The trace set of a specification can be subject to analysis and validation against the user requirements. This includes also the requirement for system safety.

The method for the specification analysis is based on the construction of the reachability graph — a standard analysis technique developed for various kinds of Petri nets. The initial marking of the net contains a single token in the terminal place of each process. Due to the restrictions imposed on the net structure, the entire net is conservative, hence bounded. Therefore, the reachability graph of the net itself, i.e. without regarding variables, is finite.

Reachability graph of the specification can be analyzed in order to verify the structural correctness of the interprocess communication. This involves examination of the reachability of selected net markings and verification against deadlock. The Boolean expressions associated with arcs can influence the reachability graph in such a way, that the arcs related to conditions which evaluate to *false* become ineffective and can be removed. This enables the modeler to simulate various scenarios of the specification net execution by assuming different values of particular expressions.

3 Example: Railroad Crossing

Consider a railroad crossing equipped with a semaphore (*green — red*) which controls the movement of trains, and a gate (*up — down*) which controls the road traffic. Both devices are controlled by a computer system which receives and processes the information related to the train position. The semaphore is *red* and the gate is *up* in the initial state of the crossing.

A specification of the railroad crossing control system can be split into four parallel activities which can be modeled by a set of four parallel processes (Fig. 1):

- keeping track of the current train position (places $p_1 \ldots p_3$),
- deciding: *red* or *green*, and *up* or *down* (places $c_1 \ldots c_6$),
- operating the semaphore (places s_1, s_2),
- operating the gate (places g_1, g_2).

All processes are cyclic and run forever. The processes communicate with each other to maintain the required state of the railway devices. By convention, arc expressions not shown explicitly in the figure are all equal to *true*.

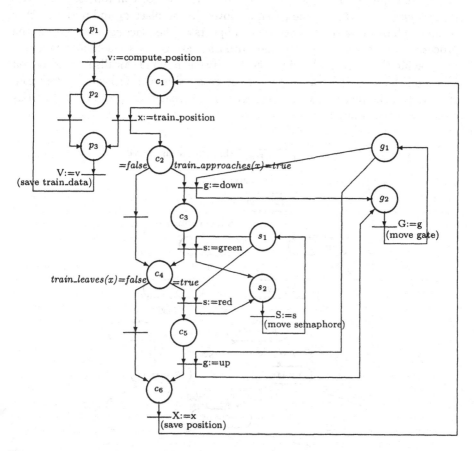

Fig. 1. Transnet model of the railroad crossing control system (terminal variables capitalized, arc expressions in italics, comments in parenthesis)

The first process (p places) models the computation of the current train position. The function *compute_position* can be viewed as a simulator of the train movement or as a procedure which receives the information from the railway track system and maintains the real train position. When the computation is finished, i.e. the place p_2 is marked, the train position is offered to the next process which decides on the necessary action. The communication between both processes is organized in such a way that it cannot block the process which keeps track of the train position — a token can always be moved from the place p_2 to p_3, even if the place c_1 is not marked at the moment.

The decision process (c places) starts with taking the new train position and storing it as a value of the local variable x. Next, when the place c_2 is marked, the process evaluates Boolean expression *train_approaches*, to check whether the train is just approaching the crossing. If this is the case (*train_approaches=true*), two consecutive commands for closing the gate and displaying the green signal on the semaphore are issued and passed to the device controllers. Otherwise (*train_approaches=false*), the token is moved to the place c_4 and nothing other is done. Thus, in both cases the token appears in the place c_4. Afterwards, the process evaluates Boolean expression *train_leaves*, to check whether the train is just leaving the crossing. If this is the case, two commands for displaying the red signal on the semaphore and opening the gate are issued. Otherwise, the token is moved to the place c_6. In the last step the current train position is stored as a value of the terminal variable X.

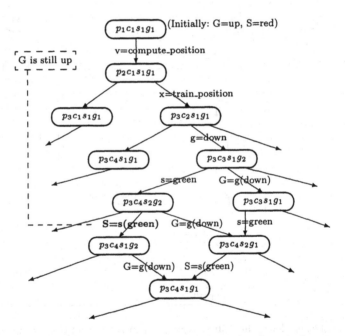

Fig. 2. Part of the reachability graph of the railroad control system

The remaining two processes are device controllers: of the gate and of the semaphore. The gate controller (g places) waits for a command (place g_1 marked), and after receiving the command and storing it as a value of the local variable g (place g_2 marked) it operates the gate accordingly ($G=g$). Thus, the value of the terminal variable G reflects the current state of the gate. The semaphore controller (s places) is nearly identical.

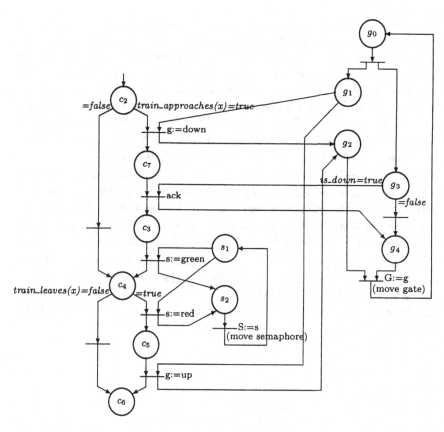

Fig. 3. Part of the modified Transnet model of the railroad crossing control system

It can be noted that the model preserves the parallelism inherent to the problem: the train, the semaphore and the gate are separate devices which operate concurrently, and concurrently with the decision process. A similar problem of modeling a railroad crossing control system by means of Petri nets was considered in [10]. Comparing both models one can note, that Transnet model closer relates to a real design of the control software than to an abstract description of the requirements.

The requirement for safe operation of the railroad crossing devices can be formulated in such a way, that no valuations of terminal variables in which $G=up$ and $S=green$ should appear in any trace of the specification. At the first glance it could seem that this requirement is fulfilled by the specification in Fig. 1, as the commands for moving the gate *down* and for displaying the signal *green* are issued by the decision process consecutively and in the right order. However, a look at the reachability graph (Fig. 2) shows, that a scenario of the net execution is possible which leads directly to the dangerous valuation. The un-safe behavior of the specification results from the possibility of internal delay in both device controller processes.

336

Two solutions can be suggested to eliminate the possibility of reaching the dangerous state, both of which result in a change to the process structure. The first one requires that the gate and the semaphore processes are combined to form a single and sequential control process which can guarantee proper sequencing of the device operation. The other solution is based on a feedback from the gate — the device should be able to signal that the state *down* has been reached. This can be modeled (Fig. 3) by extending the specification net and adding new transitions which synchronize the decision process with the gate controller (synchronization by transition *ack* which can fire only if *is_down=true*).

The dangerous valuation can be reached in the specification in Fig. 1 also in case when the train leaves the crossing. The nature of the problem is similar to the previous one so the solution is also similar — the semaphore should be able to signal the *red* state, and the decision process should postpone opening the gate until the moment in which displaying the red light has been acknowledged.

When the modifications to the model are finished, the correctness of the final specification can formally be proved. Part of the reachability graph shown in Fig. 2 which has been modified in order to reflect changes made to the specification, is depicted in Fig. 4. The un-safe valuation of terminal variables G and S can never be reached.

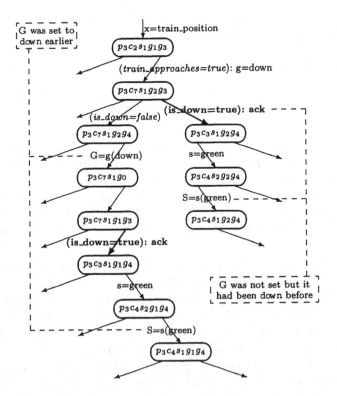

Fig. 4. Part of the modified reachability graph of the railroad control system of Fig. 3

4 Analysis Techniques

The analysis of Transnet specification is based on the analysis of a modified reachability graph of the net. The graph consists of nodes which correspond to the markings of places, and arcs which correspond to transition firings. Boolean arc expressions can influence the shape of the reachability graph in that they can control the firing of transitions which have a common input place. To reflect this influence, each arc of the modified graph is labeled with a name of the firing transition and a name of the Boolean expression which must have evaluated to true in order to enable the firing transition.

It can be noted that the modified graph with all Boolean expressions evaluated to *true* is identical to the classical reachability graph, i.e. the graph with no arc expressions at all. Such a graph represents an indeterministic net in which all conditions in all alternative branches can eventually be fulfilled. The analysis of this graph can help in detecting deadlock conditions due to improper process communication and synchronization. Deadlock can involve the entire specification net or a group of processes (livelock).

The existence of arc expressions extends the scope of analysis and enables the modeler to simulate various scenarios of the specification net execution. This can be done by assuming different values of particular arc expressions, and removing from the reachability graph those arcs which correspond to expressions which have evaluated to *false*. After the removal of selected arcs, the process of graph analysis can be repeated.

The application of the modified reachability graph analysis can be demonstrated using the example railroad crossing control system from the previous section. Consider, e.g., that the gate broke down and cannot be closed (i.e. it remains always in *up* position). This means, that the value of the arc expression *is_down* always evaluates to *false*, and the respective arcs (bold in Fig. 4) should be removed from the modified reachability graph. The remaining graph is safe in that green signal can never be displayed, but at the same time it has a livelock: the decision process is blocked with the token held in the place c_7.

The analysis of the modified reachability graph can be used to verify correctness of the control flow within the specification. In those cases when the processing of data is based on enumerative substitution of values, the reachability graph can also help in the analysis of the results of data processing. This was the case illustrated in the previous part of this section. Otherwise, the processing of data can be validated according to the concept of rapid prototyping.

The specification described in the form of an extended Petri can be executed by simulated execution of the net. Starting from the initial net marking and an initial valuation of terminal variables, a complete trace of the specification can be computed. Due to the inherent parallelism of Petri net the computation is indeterministic. Hence, the experiment can be repeated many times, thus allowing the modeler to investigate different scenarios of the execution. This way the behavior of the specification can be studied and validated. The validation process can include safety requirements which can be described by a set of prohibited values of terminal variables.

5 Timing aspects

Still another extension introduced by Transnet to Petri nets is a mechanism for modeling the flow of time and specifying timing constraints. The extension is very simple and consists of time constants assigned to arcs which lead from places to transitions. The meaning of a time constant Δt is such, that a token must reside in the input place of the arc at least through the time Δt until it can enable the transition pointed by the arc. An arc without an associated time constant is assumed to have the default time value equal to zero.

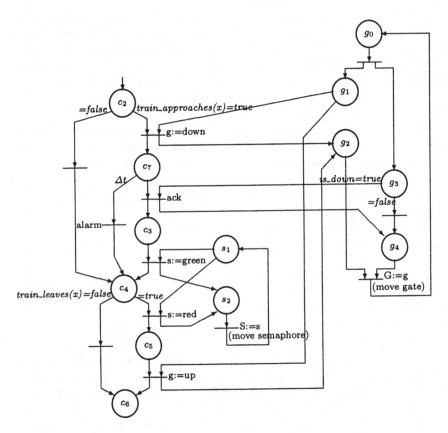

Fig. 5. Part of the model with a timeout

The applications of this time model in Transnet are twofold. First, it is used to define timeouts for potentially infinite operations. Consider, e.g., the model of a railroad crossing system shown in Fig. 3. It has been demonstrated in the previous section that a breakdown of the gate in its *up* position can block the decision process forever, with a token held in the place c_7. To resolve this live-lock of the net, an additional transition is needed to react to the damage (the transition labeled *alarm* in Fig. 5). However, the additional transition should not fire during a regular functioning of the system — this can be forced by assigning a timeout value to the arc which joins the place c_7 with the added *alarm* transition.

The second application of time constants is to model the evaluation time of a function associated with a transition within a process net. One can note that such an evaluation time Δt can be modeled by a construction shown in Fig. 6.

Comparing Transnet model of time to other simple models, which assign time constants to transitions [4] or to places [5], one can note that Transnet model is equally simple, but more expressive. Time constants assigned to arcs can easily model timed transitions (e.g. as in Fig. 6) and timed places. The converse, however, is not true, as the semantics of a timeout can be described by means of time constants assigned neither to places nor to transitions. Moreover, Transnet model of time allows the firing time of a transition to be related separately to the time instants in which tokens are being deposited in each of the input places of this transition.

On the other hand, Transnet model of time is slightly less expressive, but much more simple, than the model proposed in [6] in which time intervals are assigned to transitions. This results from the fact, that Transnet model can describe only lower (but not upper) bound imposed on the firing time of a transition. Such a model matches the characteristics of programming languages and operating system which provide the tools for timeout operations, but do not provide any means to guarantee the upper bound of the execution time.

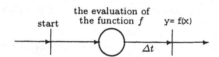

Fig. 6. Evaluation time of a function $f(x)$

Transnet model of time can be defined formally as a finite extension to Petri nets. Having such a definition one can use time-extended Petri net throughout the analysis process, instead of a classical Petri net.

Formally, Petri net can be defined [3] as a four-tuple $C = (P, T, I, O)$ composed of a finite set of places P, a finite set of transitions T, an input function $I : T \longrightarrow 2^P$, and an output function $O : T \longrightarrow 2^P$. It is assumed that the sets P and T are disjoint. A graphical interpretation of both functions is such that the function I defines the arcs which lead from places to transitions, while function O defines the arcs which lead from transitions to places.

A marked Petri net is a pair (C, μ_0) composed of a Petri net C and an initial marking $\mu_0 : P \longrightarrow N$ which assigns natural numbers (with zero) to places. A number $\mu_0(p)$ is interpreted as a number of tokens in the place p. The marking of Petri net can be changed as result of a transition firing. A transition t is enabled in a marking μ if:

$$\mu(p) \geq \#(p, I(t)) \qquad \text{for all } p \in P$$

where $\#(p, I(t))$ equals 1, if $p \in I(t)$, or 0, if $p \notin I(t)$. A transition t enabled in a marking μ can fire. Firing the transition t leads to a new marking μ' defined as follows:

$$\mu'(p) = \mu(p) - \#(p, I(t)) + \#(p, O(t)) \qquad \text{for all } p \in P$$

A marked Petri net is **bounded** if the set $R(C, \mu_0)$ composed of all markings which can be reached from μ_0 by firing transitions is finite. The property of boundedness is of practical importance, as it guarantees, that the net can be analyzed completely by an exhaustive search through the set $R(C, \mu_0)$.

Petri net with timeouts is a three-tuple $K = (C, \mu_0, \tau_0)$ composed of a marked Petri net (C, μ_0) and a function $\tau_0 : P \times T \longrightarrow R$ which assigns rational numbers to arcs leading from places to transitions. A number $\tau_0(p, t)$ is interpreted as a time value which has been assigned to the arc from place p to transition t.

A state of a Petri net with timeouts can be defined as a pair $s = (\mu, \tau)$ composed of a marking μ and a vector of time values τ. The marking μ describes the current distribution of tokens among places. The vector τ describes the current (residual) values of time intervals associated with particular arcs. The size of the vector τ is equal to the number of arcs leading from places to transitions. An entry $\tau(p, t)$ is a rational number which is:

- not defined, if the arc (p, t) is closed, i.e. no token resides in the place p,
- zero, if the arc (p, t) is open, i.e. the place p has continued to be marked with a token at least through the time interval $\tau_0(p, t)$,
- equal to the length of the time interval remaining for opening the arc, if the arc (p, t) is active, i.e. the place p is marked with a token, but not open, as yet.

The execution of a Petri net with timeouts is controlled by the net marking μ and the values of the time intervals in τ. The net executes by shifting time intervals and firing transitions. A transition t is enabled in a state $s = (\mu, \tau)$ if it has all input arcs open, i.e.:

$$\tau(p, t) = 0 \qquad \text{for all } p \in I(t)$$

Let $s = (\mu, \tau)$ be a state of a Petri net with timeouts. The next state $s' = (\mu', \tau')$ can be computed in two steps:

1. If a transition t is enabled in s, then the computation moves to the step 2. If no transitions are enabled in s and Δt is the shortest non-zero time interval in τ, than the execution of the step 1 remains the marking μ unchanged, and shifts all time intervals in τ by subtracting the value Δt. Formally, step 1 computes for all p, t:

$$\text{new } \tau(p, t) = \begin{cases} \tau(p, t) - \Delta t & \text{if } \tau(p, t) \neq 0 \\ 0 & \text{otherwise} \end{cases}$$

The elements of t which were not defined before executing step 1, remain undefined. Step 1 repeats until a transition becomes enabled or all arcs in τ become open or closed.

2. If a transition t_j is enabled in s, then the next step s' is computed for all p, t as follows:

a) $\mu'(p) = \mu(p) - \#(p, I(t_j)) + \#(p, O(t_j))$
b)

$$\tau'(p, t) = \begin{cases} \tau_0(p, t) & \text{if } t = tj \text{ and } \mu'(p) \geq \#(p, I(t_j)) \\ \tau_0(p, t) & \text{if } \mu(p) - \#(p, I(t_j)) < \#(p, I(t)) \\ & \text{and } \mu'(p) \geq \#(p, I(t)) \\ \tau(p, t) & \text{otherwise} \end{cases}$$

It can be noted that states (μ, τ) of a Petri net with timeouts which have the same marking μ can differ from each other only with respect to the values held in vector τ. But from step 1 above results, that those values can never exceed the values stored in the initial vector τ_0. Because all values are rational numbers, hence the number of different values of vector τ is also finite. This leads to the following:

Theorem 1. *A Petri net with timeouts* (C, μ_0, τ_0) *has bounded number of states if and only if marked Petri net* (C, μ_0) *is bounded.*

The theorem is mathematically interested and shows that the analyzability of a Petri net with timeouts relays on the analyzability of the underlying marked Petri net. However, the practical implications are less important, as the state space of Petri net with timeouts is significantly larger than the one of classical Petri net.

It is interesting to observe, that the same proof and the same remark apply to a similar theorem in [6].

Conclusions

Transnet is a method for describing real-time computer systems. It can be used during the specification and preliminary design steps of the software life cycle as well as during the software verification phase [9]. Transnet model of the software structure can also be used for the analysis and the verification of safety. The method offers a formal notation for defining safe and un-safe states of the system and a technique for the software simulation and analysis.

To be practical, the method has to be supported by a set of software tools for creating, analyzing and executing the specification. Central element of the Transnet CASE system is a data base which stores a description of the specification under development. The description can be introduced into computer files by means of a graphical Petri net editor or textual editor. Management tools include decompilers and a browser which can look through the data base and produce a report including the list of processes, the list of exchange transitions, data types, etc.

The net analyzer enables the modeler to build a reachability tree of a Petri net and to answer questions related to deadlock and reachability of selected markings. The net analyzer does not evaluate functions. However, it can be instructed to assume particular values of arc expressions and to modify the tree by removing the arcs associated with expressions assumed *false*.

The net simulator executes the full model of a specification, taking into account data processing functions as well as time values. The problem of coping with huge volume of data produced during the simulation has been solved by exploiting the concept of validation points. A validation point can be identified by a particular net marking or submarking which determine strict points in the net execution. For each validation point a list of variables can be defined. When a validation point is reached during the net execution, the current time and the values of variables are recorded for further analysis.

The drawback of the current CASE system is that it consists of a set of separate programs, part of which have been implemented under DOS and part under Windows. Our current work is directed towards the unification of the system and shaping them in a coherent development environment, with a unified window-based user interface.

Acknowledgments

I wish to thank the anonymous reviewers, who provided comments and suggestions that improved this paper.

The work has been supported by a Warsaw University of Technology statutory grant 504/036, 1998.

References

1. IEC 1508 (draft). Functional Safety: Safety-Related Systems, IEC (1995)
2. Cegiela R., Sacha K., Zalewski A.: Task A3: Safety Analysis for the Software Domain. Copernicus Joint Research Project CP 94 1594 on Integraton of Safety Analysis Techniques for Process Control Systems. IASE. Wroclaw (1997)
3. Peterson, J., L.: Petri net theory and modeling of systems. Prentice-Hall Inc. (1981)
4. Ramchandani C.: Analysis of asynchronous concurrent systems by timed Petri nets. Massachusets Inst. Technol. Tech. Rep. **120** (1974)
5. Coolahan J. E., Roussopoulos N.: Timing requirements for time-driven systems using augmented Petri nets. IEEE Trans. Software Eng. **SE-9** (1983) 603–616
6. Berthomieu B., Diaz M.: Modeling and Verification of Time Dependent Systems Using Time Petri Nets. IEEE Trans. Software Eng. **17** (1991) 259–273
7. Jensen K.: Coloured Petri Nets. Advances in Petri Nets 1986. Brauer W., Riesig W., Rozenberg G. (eds) Springer-Verlag. (1987)
8. Ghezi C., Mandrioli D., Morasca S., Pezze M.: A unified high-level Petri net formalism for time-critical systems. IEEE Trans. Software Eng. **17** (1991) 160–172
9. Sacha K.: Real-Time Software Specification and Validation with Transnet. Real-Time Systems Journal. **6** (1994) 153–172
10. Leveson N. G., Stolzy J. L.: Safety Analysis Using Petri Nets. IEEE Transactions on Software Engineering. (1987)

Reliability

Refinement of Safety-Related Hazards into Verifiable Code Assertions

Ken Wong[1] and Jeff Joyce[2]

[1]Department of Computer Science, University of British Columbia
Vancouver, BC, Canada V6T 1Z4
tel (604) 822-4912 fax (604) 822-5485
kwong@cs.ubc.ca
[2]Raytheon Systems Canada, Ltd.
13951 Bridgeport Road, Richmond, BC, Canada V6V 1J6
tel (604)279-5721 fax (604)279-5982
jjoyce@mail.hac.com

Abstract: This paper presents a process for the stepwise refinement of safety code assertions from identified system hazards. The code assertions are intended for use in system safety verification. The development of the safety code assertions increases the feasibility of using code verification tools such as SPARK Examiner in the safety verification of large software-intensive systems. The process is demonstrated for a hypothetical chemical factory information system.

1. Introduction

An important step in an overall process for the safety engineering of a software-intensive system with safety critical functionality is the verification of the source code with respect to the identified hazards. One difficulty with performing the verification is the large "semantic gap" between the source code and the abstract "system level" concepts/language used to define hazards. To address this problem, this paper outlines a process whereby a safety-related hazard may be systematically refined into verifiable code assertions.

The approach to generating safety code assertions outlined in this paper was originally motivated by our interest in the possibility of using code verification tools such as SPARK Examiner [1] as part of the safety verification of a large software system. Chapter 18 of Leveson's seminal textbook on software safety [3] hints at the possibility of using such tools, but expresses concern about their practical feasibility. Clearly, it would be naive to expect that the safety verification task could be automated by simply feeding the source code for an entire system into a verification tool along with a representation of a safety-related hazard. If code verification tools are to be used in the safety verification of the system, it will be necessary to process the hazard and the source code into a form that the tools can accept as input.

One problem is that the safety-related hazard is likely to be expressed at a much higher level of abstraction, and in a different form, than the assertions expected as input by the code verification tool. The process outlined in this paper addresses this particular problem. There are other problems with using code verification tools for the safety verification of a large software system. The discussion of these problems lies outside the scope of this paper, but in a presentation of our overall approach to safety verification [7] we suggest how many of these other problems may be addressed. This has lead us to conclude that code verifications tools such as SPARK Examiner may indeed be useful in the safety verification of a large software system. Even if such tools are not used, the refinement of a safety-related hazard into a set of verifiable assertions would support other methods of static analysis such as manual inspection.

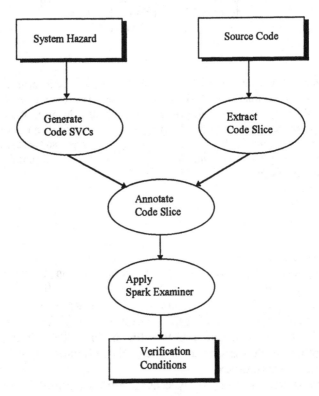

Figure 1: Overall safety verification process.

Our overall approach to the safety verification of large software-intensive systems is shown in Figure 1. This paper focuses on the "Generate Code SVCs" process which appears in the process bubble in the top left side of the figure.

The process for generating source code level "safety verification conditions" (SVCs) bridges the semantic gap between the hazard and source code though a series of refinement steps. This includes the development of SVCs at the system, design and source code level. It is assumed that the safety-critical code is either written in the SPARK Ada subset, or has been translated into SPARK through a process such as that described in [8]. The process for deriving the safety code assertions was developed during research conducted as part of the university-industrial collaborative project, formalWARE [6]. The process is illustrated in this paper with a hypothetical chemical factory information system.

Section 2 outlines some of the difficulties in bridging the semantic gap between the hazards and safety code assertions. The process for developing safety code assertions is presented in Section 3. The chemical factory information system is introduced in Section 4. Each step of the process is then applied to the chemical factory. Section 5 discusses the generation of system level SVCs for the chemical factory information system. The refinement of system level SVCs into design level SVCs is presented in Section 6. This is followed by a discussion of the refinement of design level SVCs into source code level SVCs in Section 7. Section 8 outlines the creation of the safety code assertions from the source code level SVCs. A summary and some conclusions are found in Section 9.

2. Development of Safety Code Assertions

The goal of this paper is to translate system hazards into a set of safety code assertions. A number of difficulties arise when attempting to express the system hazards in terms of code assertions.

2.1 Semantic Gap

System hazards are typically defined at a relatively high level of abstraction. For good reason, the definition of a hazard will be based upon the terminology of the end-user rather than the terminology of the software developer implementing application-level functionality on top of lower layers of software infrastructure and primitives. To perform safety verification of the source code, the definition of the hazard must be mapped to a relationship between elements of the software implementation. This mapping must bridge the "semantic gap" between the terminology used to define the hazard and the terminology of the software developer.

For instance, Section 4.2 of this paper uses the term "invalid temperature" in the definition of a sample hazard for a hypothetical chemical factory information system used as an example in this paper. Ultimately, the hazard must be understood in terms of global variables, sub-program parameters, constants, local variables and other elements of the source code. As revealed later in Section 7.2, the term "invalid temperature" corresponds to a relationship between specific data fields of the various messages passed between components of the software system which implements the chemical factory information system.

Sometimes there may be a high degree of "lexical similarity" between the terminology used to the define the system hazard and the identifiers used as names of elements of the source code implementation. For example, the source code may use a word such as "temperature" as the name of a data field in a message. But in other circumstances, there may not be much lexical similarity between the definition of a hazard and the source code implementation of functionality directly related to this hazard. This may be prevalent in the case of a system which has been developed with an emphasis on abstraction and re-use.

In addition to the challenge of mapping the definition of a hazard to data elements of the source code such as global variables, sub-program parameters, constants, local variables and other elements of the source code, it is also necessary to refine abstract properties such as "invalid" into concrete relationships. Ultimately, these concrete relationships will be defined in terms of combinations of simple arithmetic and logical comparisons between data elements, e.g., "is equal to", "is less than".

2.2 Time and Events

A system hazard often involves a relationship between events over a period of time. This temporal relationship may be apparent in the definition of the hazard or, as demonstrated in Section 5, may be revealed in the derivation of system level SVCs from the hazard definition. The temporality of a relationship is made explicitly by the use of phrases such as "...if the displayed temperature of vessel v is set to d at time t, then at some time no earlier than MAX_SYSTEM_PROPAGATION_TIME milliseconds before t ...".

To make use of tools such as SPARK Examiner, it is necessary to refine these temporal relationships into "non-temporal" assertions which are true or false at specific instants of time in the execution of the software system.

The refinement of temporal relationships into non-temporal assertions depends, in part, on the identification of causal relationships. For instance, it requires analysis of the software implementation to determine that an event such as "the displayed temperature of vessel v is set to d at time t" must have been *caused* by the occurrence of one or more internal events (either as combinations or as alternatives). By means of a search process, these events are chained backwards (in time) to other events. These causal relationships provide a basis for the refinement of the temporal relationships into "non-temporal" assertions.

2.3 "Backward" Expression

Pre- and post-conditions are such that, given the pre-conditions on the input parameters, then the execution of the program should result in the output variables satisfying the post-conditions:

If pre-conditions on input
then post-conditions on output

The hazards, however, are often expressed in a "backward" fashion, beginning with the output, and then specifying the necessary conditions on the input:

If conditions on output

then conditions on inputs

The safety verification condition given as an example in Section 5 is an illustrative example of this "backwards" orientation.

It will be necessary to write the SVCs in a "forward" fashion, in order to arrive at a pre- and post-condition style specification. Often it is possible to obtain a "forward" version of the SVCs from its backward formulation by taking its contrapositive:

If NOT(conditions on input)
then NOT(conditions on output)

This should place conditions on the input into the antecedent of the condition.

3. Process for the Construction of Safety Code Assertions

The safety code assertions are derived from a stepwise process that involves the development of system level, design level and source code level SVCs. If the refinement of the hazard into source code level SVCs is valid, then verification of the source code SVCs is sufficient for the safety verification of the hazard.

The inputs of the process are:

- **System hazards.**
- **Software architecture.**
- **Hazard-related source code.**

The safety code assertions are created for the hazard-related source code. In this paper it is assumed that a representation for the hazard-related source code has been created in the SPARK Ada subset [8].

The output of the process is a combination of SVCs including:

- constraints on variable system parameters or constants - typically expressed as mathematical inequalities, e.g., "X must be refreshed at a greater rate than Y";

- functional correctness conditions on relatively small blocks of source code which lie directly in the critical code path - typically, a pre- and post-condition combination of assertions;

- partial specifications of "peripheral" aspects of the source limited to the minimal assumptions required to carry out safety verification - for example, a limit on the range of the value of the output of a subsystem which does not lie directly in the critical code path.

The refinement process involves the stepwise derivation of system level, design level and source code level SVCs from the hazard definition [5]. The source code level SVCs are translated into SPARK annotations. The steps of the refinement process are:

1. **Generate system level SVCs.** The system is analyzed with respect to the hazard to produce the system level SVCs. They are a set of system constraints that are sufficient to ensure that the identified hazards do not occur. The system level SVCs are generated from the use of a style of reasoning known as "proof by contradiction" to construct a rigorous safety argument [9].

2. **Generate design level SVCs.** The system level SVCs are refined into design level SVCs through analysis of the software architecture. The hazard-related software is partitioned into "functional blocks" of code, and the system level SVCs are mapped into conditions on the functional block's input and output parameters.

3. **Generate source code level SVCs.** The design level SVCs are refined into source code level SVCs through analysis of the source code. The functional block parameters are identified in the source code, and the functional block SVCs are re-written in terms of the source code parameters. The resulting source code level SVCs may also be formalized [5].

4. **Generate safety code assertions.** The source code level SVCs are reformulated in a "forward" fashion and translated into SPARK annotations.

4. Example - Chemical Factory Information System

For illustrative purposes, we consider a hypothetical real-time safety-critical information system for a chemical factory. This is similar to other safety-critical information systems, such as air traffic management [2], in that environmental data is received, processed and displayed to human operators who make critical decisions.

4.1 System Description

The physical layout of the factory consists of a set of reactor vessels each with sensors that record vessel data such as the temperature. The sensors are connected over a LAN to a central server and a set of workstations. The chemical factory distributed information system runs on the central server and the workstations. The information system maintains and processes the vessel information it receives over the LAN, which it then displays on the workstation monitors.

4.2 Safety-Related Hazard

Following a process such as the system safety engineering process outlined in [3], we assume that the display of an "invalid" value as the temperature of a vessel is identified as a system hazard for the chemical factory control and monitoring system.

Hazard: An invalid temperature, D, is displayed for vessel V at time T.

It may be assumed that the identification of this hazard resulted from some earlier analysis which shows that the display of an invalid value as the temperature of a vessel, in combination with other conditions, could lead to a mishap such as a fire or explosion.

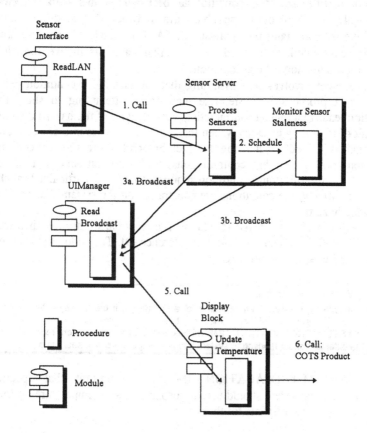

Figure 2: Temperature data flow highlighting the key modules and procedures.

4.3 Hazard-Related Source Code

The safety analysis will focus on a representation of the critical code, which is the output of a process that identifies the hazard-related code, and then translates it into the SPARK Ada subset [8]. The hazard-related source code modules and subprograms are shown in Figure 2. This includes code involved in the processing of sensor updates and the monitoring of stale sensor values.

5. System Level Safety Verification Conditions

The system level SVCs are a set of constraints on the system that are designed to ensure that the system hazards do not occur. The system level SVCs are generated in support of a rigorous argument about the system safety [9]. The approach is similar to the concept of fault tree analysis (FTA) in the sense that that it begins with an assumption that the hazardous condition has occurred and then work "backwards" to systematically cover all of the possible ways in which this condition might have arisen. Like software fault tree analysis (SFTA) [4], a style of reasoning known as "proof by contradiction" is used to show that each disjunctive branch of the argument leads to a logical contradiction.

The argument involves first assuming that the hazardous condition exists. The analysis then proceeds in a stepwise manner by attempting to show that this assumption leads to a logical contradiction. The analysis of the hazard then branches as a result of reasoning by cases. When the analysis branches into one or more cases, each branch is "closed" by showing that each branch leads to a logical contradiction. In the course of generating contradictions, SVCs are introduced. Each SVC is intended to be the minimum condition required to close a particular branch of the analysis. Intuitively, the conditions are constraints on the system that are necessary to avoid the hazard.

The result of such an analysis for chemical factory hazard are five distinct system level SVCs. Full details can be found in reference [9]. The following is an example of one of the five system level SVCs:

Safety Verification Condition:
For all vessels, v, displayed temperatures, d, and times, t, if the displayed temperature of vessel v is set to d at time t, then at some time no earlier than MAX_SYSTEM_PROPAGATION_TIME milliseconds before t the system received a report from the external sensor monitoring system that the temperature of vessel v is d.

MAX_SYSTEM_PROPAGATION_TIME is a constant that specifies the maximum time the system should take to display a vessel temperature on the screen after receiving a sensor update for that vessel.

6. Design Level SVCs

The system level SVCs are refined into design level SVCs through analysis of the software architecture.

6.1 Hazard-Related Functional Blocks

Part of the process of producing a representation of the hazard-related code involves partitioning the relevant software into blocks which are invoked asynchronously. For example, this could be the result of code running in a process on a different computer, or which executes in a different "thread" on the same processor. The resulting "functional blocks" of code may be viewed as procedures with input and output parameters.

The hazard-related functionality for the chemical factory information system partitions into three such functional blocks. The monitoring of sensor staleness is one functional block, and the processing of sensor updates partitions into two functional blocks, LANToBroadcast and BroadcastToDisplay. For example, the LANToBroadcast block involves the reception and processing of LAN messages received from the external sensor monitoring system. LAN messages are read by the procedure ReadLAN and then processed by the procedure ProcessSensors, before being broadcast.

6.2 Functional Block SVCs

The system level SVCs are refined into SVCs for the functional blocks. An important aspect of the refinement is the separation of system functionality and timing issues, into separate functional block SVCs. This allows for the derivation of functional block pre- and post-conditions from the time-independent functional block SVCs.

The system level SVC introduced in Section 5 applies to the propagation of the temperature through the system, which is carried out by the LANToBroadcast and BroadcastToDisplay blocks, with a Broadcast mechanism providing the block communication. As a result, the system level SVC can be refined into design level SVCs involving these relevant functional blocks and the Broadcast mechanism, by extending the rigorous argument.

When performing the refinement, the functional blocks can be viewed conceptually as a procedure with input and output parameters. The system level SVCs are then refined into separate functional and timing conditions, with the system events mapped onto the functional block invocations and output. Furthermore, the functional block becomes the causal agent, i.e., it takes the input and creates the output, which replaces the timing sequence.

An example of a design level SVC for the LANToBroadcast functional block is:

```
LANToBroadcast design level SVC:
For all vessels, v, and broadcast temperatures, d,
if there exists the information that vessel v is d in the output broadcast message, M,
then there exists the information that the temperature of vessel v is d, in the input
LANMessage, L.
```

7. Source Code Level SVCs

The design level SVCs are refined into source code level SVCs, by identifying the functional block input and output parameters, along with any other relevant source code element. In this section we provide a sense of the need for a safety engineer to "dig into" the source code in order to close the semantic gap between the definition of the hazard and the corresponding representation of the SVC in terms of the source code.

7.1 Functional Block Parameters

The input and output parameters of the functional block are determined from examination of the subprograms that make up the block. For example, the main thread of functionality for the LANToBroadcast block is contained in the ReadLAN and ProcessSensor procedures shown in Figure 2. Invocation of the ReadLAN procedure provides entry into the block with a LANMessage Object as input. The ReadLAN procedure then invokes the ProcessSensor procedure, which broadcasts a SensorServer BroadcastMessage as output.

In addition to the input and output parameters for the ReadLAN and ProcessSensor, these procedures have access to package level variables which maintain state information for that package. For example, the SensorServer makes use of the SensorStore Object to maintain a set of sensor readings which are accessed by the ProcessSensor procedure. These are considered "global variables" of the functional block.

7.2 The Source Code Elements

The design level SVC refers to input LAN messages and output broadcast messages, which contains the vessel's temperature obtained by the external sensor monitoring system.

Examination of the LANMessage Object, reveals that updates from the different sensors are maintained in arrays of Sensor Update data records:

```
type LANMessage_SensorUpdate is
   record
      InterpolatedState :
LANMessage_InterpolationRange;
      TemperatureEstab : LANMessage_Temperature_T;
      SensorCodeEstab : LANMessage_SensorCode;
   end record;
```

The TemperatureEstab field maintains the sensor temperature reading, and SensorCodeEstab field maintains the raw sensor code.

Examination of the Broadcast Object, reveals that the updates are maintained in an array of Sensor Objects:

```
type Sensor_Object is
   record
      SID : Sensor_SensorID;
      SensorOperation : Sensor_Operation;
      SensorQuality : Sensor_Quality;
      SensorTemperature : Sensor_Temperature;
   end record;
```

The raw sensor code has been converted and stored as a `SensorID`. The raw temperature reading has been converted and stored as the `Sensor Temperature`.

The design level SVC can now be re-written in terms of these source code elements:

LANToBroadcast Source Code Level SVC:

For all Sensor Objects, s, in output BroadcastMessage, M,

if Sensor Object, s, contains the information SensorID, C, and PresentTemperature, D,

then there exists a SensorUpdate, U, in input LANMessage, L, with the information SensorCodeEstab, C1, which is converted from SensorID, C, and TemperatureEstab, D1, which is converted from D.

---

8. Source Code Assertions

The source code level SVCs include functional correctness conditions which can be expressed as functional block pre- and post-conditions. These pre- and post-conditions can be translated into SPARK annotations.

8.1 Pre- and Post-Condition Style

The functional block SVC is re-written in a "forward" manner by taking the contrapositive form of the condition:

LANToBroadcast Source Code Level SVC (Contrapositive):

For all Sensor Objects, s, in output BroadcastMessage, M,

if NOT(there exists a SensorUpdate, U, in input LANMessage, L, with the information SensorCodeEstab, C1, which is converted from SensorID, C, and TemperatureEstab, D1, which is converted from D)

then NOT(Sensor Object, s, contains the information SensorID, C, and PresentTemperature, D)

The contrapositive form of the functional block SVC can be further refined by using "logical equivalencies". For example, it is possible to move the "NOT" inwards, by using the appropriate logical equivalencies such as:

$$\text{"NOT (there exists ...)"} \equiv \text{"for all (NOT ...)"}$$

The refined contrapositive form of the source code level SVC is then:

LANToBroadcast Source Code Level SVC (Refined Contrapositive):

For all Sensor Objects, s, in output BroadcastMessage, M,

if for all SensorUpdates, u, in input LANMessage, L, with the information SensorCodeEstab, C1, which is not converted from SensorID, C, or TemperatureEstab, D1, which is not converted from D

then Sensor Object, s, does not contain the information SensorID, C, and PresentTemperature, D.

The contrapositive can be determined more precisely by first formalizing the source code level SVC [5]. For this source code level SVC, the entire SVC is a post-condition on the output. In other words, taking the contrapositive form of the source code level SVC did not uncover any pre-conditions.

8.2 SPARK Annotations

At this point, the source code SVCs can be used an input to a code verification process. One possibility is conventional software testing. However, in this paper, we consider the possibility of using a tool-based method based on static verification, in particular, use of SPARK Examiner.

SPARK Examiner may be used to reduce the problem of verifying a "slice" of the code with respect to a source code SVC into a purely mathematical task of verifying a logical expression called a "verification condition". A code verification tool such as SPARK Examiner relieves the human analyst of the task of tracing through the code slice statement-by-statement.

To complete the overall process, the verification conditions must then be verified either by manual efforts or by use of tools such as the SPARK Simplifier and Proof Checker [1].

SPARK annotations make use of the SPARK Ada subset and appears in the code as Ada comments. However, they do not support quantification, so it is not possible to directly express the source code level SVC in the SPARK annotation language. Instead, a "proof function" is defined, ConvertAll, which has the same syntax as an Ada function, and the post-condition is expressed in terms of this proof function:

```
--# function ConvertSensorCode(SC :
LANMessage_SensorCode) return Sensor_SensorID;
--# function ConvertTemperature(T :
LANMessage_Temperature T) return Sensor_Temperature;
--# function ConvertAll(M:LANMessage_Object;
          B:SensorServer_BroadcastMessage;
          L,U:LANMessage_SensorUpdateRange) return
Boolean;

procedure SensorInterface_ReadLAN(Message : in
LANMessage_Object);
--# global in out BroadcastMessage, CurrentSensors;
--# post ConvertAll(Message, BroadcastMessage,
          LANMessage_SensorUpdateRange'First,
          LANMessage_SensorUpdateRange'Last);
```

The proof function can defined as a proof rule:

```
ConvertAll(BM, LM, I, F) may_be_replaced_by
    for_all(u:integer, (I <= u and u <= F) ->
        not (for_all (s:integer, (I<=s and s <=F) ->
            (not(fld_SensorTemperature(element(BM, [u])) =
                ConvertTemperature(fld_TemperatureEstab(element(LM,[s])))
            or not(fld_SensorID(element(BM, [u])) =
                ConvertSensorCode(fld_SensorCodeEstab(element(LM,[s]))))))
```

The proof rule is expressed in the FDL language, which is the required input for the SPARK Proof Checker. For illustrative purposes, the proof rule has been written in a form that closely mirrors the source code level SVC. If a proof of the conditions were to be attempted, it would be possible to re-write the rule in a form more conducive to the proof effort.

9. Summary and Conclusions

A method was presented in this paper for the informal systematic refinement of safety code assertions from system hazards. The assertions are the key program safety invariants, which can then be verified by means such as inspection, testing or code verification. Such a refinement of the hazard allows a tool intended mainly for "correctness verification", such as SPARK Examiner, to be used for "safety verification".

The source code level SVCs (and corresponding SPARK annotations) are not merely superficial re-formulations of the hazards. If the source level SVCs were used for a manual verification process, then we expect the analyst would be at a much greater advantage than if he/she attempted to perform the safety verification by inspecting the code directly in terms of the system level definition of the hazard.

Though the formulation of each step of the refinement involves informal arguments and statements of the resulting conditions, there may be value in partially formalizing some of the steps. For example, formalization of the source code level SVCs would contribute to the care and precision in which the source code elements are identified [5], and help ensure that the contrapositive form of the condition is correctly obtained.

10. Acknowledgments

This work was partially supported by B.C. Advanced Systems Institute, Raytheon Systems Canada, Ltd., and MacDonald Dettwiler. This work is a component of the university-industrial collaborative project, formalWARE.

11. References

1. John Barnes, "High Integrity Ada The SPARK Examiner Approach", Addison Wesley Longman Ltd, 1997.
2. Bruce Elliott and Jim Ronback, "A System Engineering Process For Software-Intensive Real-Time Information Systems", in *Proceedings of the 14th International System Safety Conference*, Albuquerque, New Mexico, August 1996.
3. Nancy G. Leveson, "Safeware: System Safety and Computers", Addison-Wesley, 1995.
4. Nancy G. Leveson, Steven S. Cha, and Timothy J. Shimall, "Safety Verification of Ada Programs using software fault trees", *IEEE Software*, vol. 8, no. 7, pp. 48-59, July 1991.
5. Ken Wong, M.Sc. Thesis, Department of Computer Science, University of British Columbia, 1998.
6. http://www.cs.ubc.ca/formalWARE
7. Ken Wong, Jeff Joyce and Jim Ronback, "Ensuring the Inspectability, Repeatability and Maintainability of the Safety Verification of a Critical System", Department of Computer Science, University of British Columbia, TR-98-06, 1998.
8. Ken Wong, "Looking at Code With Your Safety Goggles On", in *Reliable Software Technologies - Ada-Europe '98*, Lecture Notes in Computer Science, Vol. 1411, Springer, 1998.
9. Jeffrey Joyce and Ken Wong, "Generating Safety Verification Conditions Through Fault Tree Analysis and Rigorous Reasoning", in *Proceedings of the 16th International System Safety Conference*, Seattle, Washington, September 1998.

Conceptual Comparison of Two Commonly Used Safeguarding Principles

Bert Knegtering[1], Aarnout Brombacher[2]

[1] Honeywell Safety Management Systems P.O. Box 116,
5223 AS 's-Hertogenbosch, Netherlands
Bert.Knegtering@Netherlands.Honeywell.com
[2] Eindhoven University of Technology P.O. Box 513,
5600 MB Eindhoven, Netherlands
A.C.Brombacher@wtb.tue.nl

Abstract. Many of today's processes are safeguarded. The objective is to reduce the risk of an out-of-control process to an acceptable level with regard to human safety, environmental safety and economic benefits. Safeguarding systems are applied to obtain the required risk reduction. These systems are "fail safe" or "fault tolerant for safety" (i.e. one failure will not affect the system safety function). System-internal voting determines the overall system action. Two safe guarding architectures are applied in practice.
A comparison study has been done with regard to these architectures and, in particular, to their voting principles.
This study does not include influences of common causes. This paper shows that, for certain parameter values, there is a clear difference in safety performance between these voting principles.

1 Introduction

New international safety standards like ANSI/ISA S84.01 [3], [4] and IEC 61508 [5] have defined Safety Integrity Levels (SILs) to allocate risk reduction factors to four pre-defined safety levels. (see table 1).

Safety functions must lead to a certain risk reduction and can therefore be assigned a specific safety integrity level.

Two principles are commonly used in safeguarding systems: the 2oo3 voting principle and the 1oo2D voting principle. 'D' indicates the integrated failure diagnostics.

Objective of the remainder of this paper is to compare both principles on safety performance.

These two voting principles are compared assuming, identical component failure rates, identical repair rates (Mean Time To Repair), identical diagnostic coverage (DC), identical functional test interval time (TI) and identical environmental circumstances.

Table 1. IEC 61508 safety integrity levels: target failure measures for a safety function, allocated to a safety-related system operating in low demand mode of operation.

Safety integrity level	Low demand mode of operation (Average probability of failure to perform its design function on demand)
4	$\geq 10^{-5}$ to $< 10^{-4}$
3	$\geq 10^{-4}$ to $< 10^{-3}$
2	$\geq 10^{-3}$ to $< 10^{-2}$
1	$\geq 10^{-2}$ to $< 10^{-1}$

The safety performance is calculated for both voting principles expressed in terms of average probability of failure on demand (PFDavg). (For a definition of PFD see paragraph 6).

2 Module failures

Both architectures are built from modules, three for the 2oo3 system, two for the 1oo2D system. Each module can fail in four different ways. The module can "fail to safe" or "fail to dangerous" (i.e. module fails to function), and the failure may be detected or undetected through the built in system diagnostics. If the failure is detected, it may be assumed that the module will be repaired within the "Mean Time To Repair". If the failure is not detected by internal diagnostics, it will be found and repaired during a periodical off-line system test (assuming every failure is found during this test).

Examples

λ^{SD}

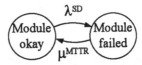

Figure 1. Example safe detected module failure Module failed to safe with rate λ^{SD}, and this failure is detected by internal diagnostics. This failure will be repaired in, for example, 8 hours.

λ^{DU}

Module okay μ^{TI} Module failed

Figure 2. Example dangerous undetected module failure Module failed to dangerous with rate λ^{DU}, and this failure is undetected by the internal diagnostics. The failure will be detected during the off-line periodic system test (for example, once a year).
The repair rate is 1/8760 for TI = 1 year

With: λ^{SD} = module failure rate of safe, detected (SD), failure type

λ^{SU} = module failure rate of safe, undetected (SU), failure type
λ^{DD} = module failure rate of dangerous, detected (DD), failure type
λ^{DU} = module failure rate of dangerous, undetected (DU), failure type
μ^{MTTR} = repair rate for detected failures
μ^{TI} = repair rate for undetected failures

3 The 2oo3 and 1oo2D voting principles

As the voting name indicates, the 2oo3 voting system is built from three redundant modules, against two redundant modules with regard to the 1oo2D voting system. The figures below represent the physical architectures of the systems:

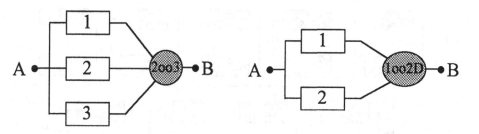

Figure 3. 2oo3 voting system   **Figure 4.** 1oo2D voting system

The 2oo3 voting principle:
The 2oo3 voting system will issue a shutdown command if at least two modules issue a shutdown command. The 2oo3 voting system will fail to perform its intended function on demand if a combination of two failures occur. Both failures will have to be dangerous and undetected (DU) by the system internal diagnostics or one failure has to be dangerous undetected and the other failure has to be dangerous detected (DD). If two dangerous and detected failures occur it is assumed that the system responds in a safe way.

The 1oo2D voting principle:
The 1oo2D system will issue a shutdown command if at least one of both modules issue a shutdown command. The 1oo2D voting system will fail to perform its intended function on demand due to a combination of two dangerous undetected failures, and also due to a combination of a detected failure (safe or dangerous) in one module in combination with a dangerous undetected failure in the other module. Again, if two detected failures occur it is assumed that the system responds in a safe way.

4 Reliability Block Diagrams

The Reliability Block Diagram (RBD) notation (IEC 61078[6]) is used to outline the system reliability.

If the connection between A and B in the RBD's of figures 5 and 6 is open due to a (combination of) failure(s), the system has failed.

As mentioned before, the 2oo3 system comprises three modules, This means that three combinations of dual DU-failures will lead to a system failure. Also in total six combinations of DU and DD failures lead to system failure (see figure 5).

Regarding the failure rates, it can be seen that the 1oo2D RBD has combinations not only of two DU failures but also two combinations of a dangerous undetected failure with a (safe or dangerous) detected failure (see figure 6).

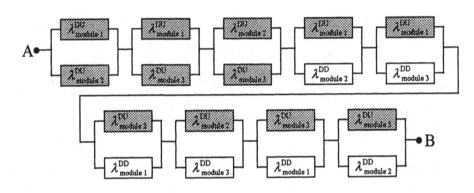

Figure 5. RBD for 2oo3 system voting

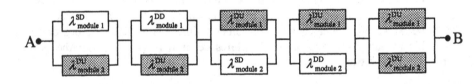

Figure 6. RBD for 1oo2D system voting

In line with IEC 61508 part 6 annex B it is assumed that the probability of a safe failure is equal to the probability of a dangerous failure. Thus, the probability of a combination of a DU-failure with a DD-failure is equal to the probability of a combination of a DU-failure with a SD-failure.

If the RBD's for 2oo3 and 1oo2D are compared, next observation is made:

System	Failure combination	Nr. of combinations
RBD 2oo3	DU-failure & DU-failure	3 combinations
RBD 1oo2D	DU-failure & DU-failure	1 combination
RBD 2oo3	DU-failure & DD-failure	6 combinations
RBD 1oo2D	DU-failure & DD- or SD-failure	4 combinations

- The contribution to the probability of a system failure due to a combination of two DU-failures for the 2oo3 voting principle is expected to be 3 times the probability of the combination of two DU-failures of a system failure for the 1oo2D voting principle.

- The contribution to the probability of a system failure due to a combination of a DU-failure and a DD-failure is expected to be 1.5 times higher for the 2oo3 voting principle than it is for the probability of a system failure due to a combination of an DU-failure and a DD- or SD-failure for the 1oo2D voting principle.

As most systems, specifically designed for safeguarding, have a high diagnostic coverage, the rate of detected failures is significantly higher than the rate of undetected failures.
The important issue, however, is that the detected failures will be repaired "immediately" once they are detected. The probability that the system is affected by such a failure may therefore be smaller than the probability that the safe guarding system is affected with a dangerous undetected failure in applications like the process industries where TI typically is one year or more.

Reliability calculations of both voting principles have been carried out using the Markov modelling technique.
Based on the RBD investigation and validation the reliability expected for the 1oo2D-voting principle is 1.5 to 3 times higher than that for the 2oo3-voting principle.

5 Markov modelling

To calculate the system risk reduction, Markov models (IEC 61165 [7]) are used. Markov modelling is today's most complete technique (Rouvroye et al [1] and Leiming Xing et al [2]).

A Markov model consists of Markov states, which the safeguarding system can adopt. Each state is defined by (a combination of) one or more failures. Transitions between states represent module failures or repair actions.

Figure 7 and 8 represent the graphical state diagram representation of Markov models for both voting principles. State 1 represents the okay-state, where the safeguarding system is free of any failure.

The light-grey states (2 and 3) represent states where the system has a failure but is still able to fulfil its intended safeguarding function. The dark-grey states (4 and 5) represent system states where the system is no longer able to fulfil its intended safety function.

Calculating the probability of dangerous system failure means calculating the probability of the system being in the dark-grey states (4 and 5).

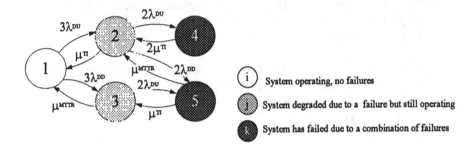

Figure 7. 2oo3 Markov model

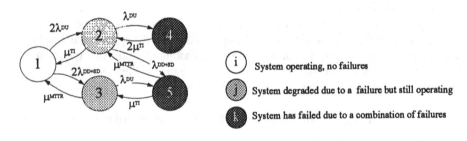

Figure 8. 1oo2D Markov model

Calculation assumptions

- Module failure rates are constant over the life of the system.
- There is no bottleneck with regard to repair crews.
- It is assumed that the total failure rate consists of 50% dangerous failures and 50% safe failures (Assumption matches the assumption made in IEC 61508 part 6, annex B.).
- Each module is considered to be identical, which means identical failure rate
- [λ], identical Mean Time To Repair [MTTR], identical Test Interval [TI] and identical Diagnostic coverage [DC].

- Influences of common causes are not included to avoid pollution of the calculation result. The reason for this is that the main target for the calculation is a comparison of the voting principles.
- Calculation time is set on 1 year, i.e. 8760 hours.

Default calculation values
- Failure rate, $\lambda = 5*10^{-5}$ failures per hour;
- Mean Time To Repair, MTTR = 8 hours;
- Time period functional Test Interval, TI = 1 year;
- Diagnostic Coverage, DC = 95 %.

For every calculation, the parameter settings λ, MTTR, TI, and DC are varied one by one, to obtain an insight into the impact of each parameter on the safety performance.

6 Calculation results

The diagrams below show the PFD average calculated for different values of the mean time to repair, the diagnostic coverage, the failure rate and of the test interval.

The PFD average is defined as the average probability of system failure on demand (IEC 61508[5]), in other words "the average system safety function unreliability". "Average" denotes the mean value during the calculation time.
The risk reduction is denoted by $1/\text{PFD}_{\text{average}}$, thus;

$$\text{architecture comparison factor} = \frac{\text{PFD}_{\text{average}} \ 2\text{oo}3 \ \text{voting}}{\text{PFD}_{\text{average}} \ 1\text{oo}2\text{D} \ \text{voting}} \quad \text{(see also table 2).}$$

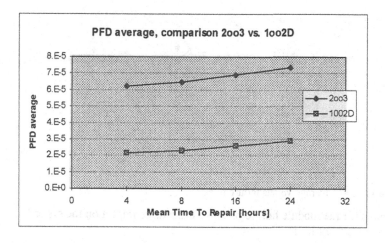

Figure 9. PFD average versus MTTR

Figure 9 shows that the PFD$_{average}$ slightly improves for both voting principles, if the mean time to repair is reduced.

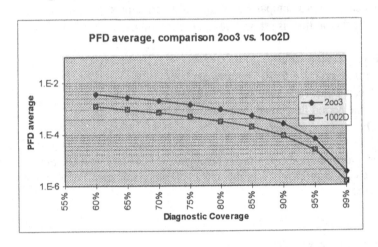

Figure 10. PFD average versus DC

Figure 10 shows that that the PFD$_{average}$ improves greatly, if diagnostic coverage is high.

The conclusion is that variation of the diagnostic coverage has more impact on the system safety performance than, for example, variation of the mean time to repair.

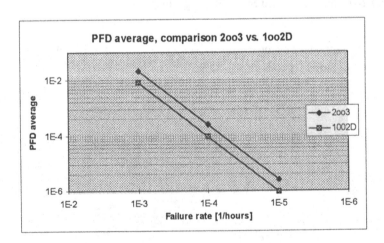

Figure 11. PFD average versus failure rate

The value for the module failure rate also has a large impact on the system performance (figure 11).

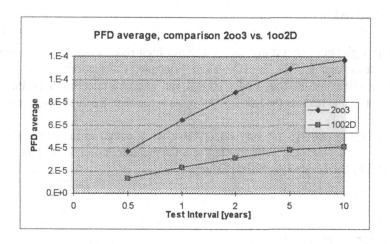

Figure 12. PFD average versus TI

Figure 12: The Markov models use the functional Test Interval (TI) as a repair probability. As the calculation time is set to one year, undetected failures are not found during this year, which means that the probability of the repair rate for this category of failures should be zero. The effect on the calculation is a slightly better safety performance.

MTTR	PFD average 2oo3	1002D	factor:
4	6.02E-05	2.16E-05	2.8
8	6.02E-05	2.31E-05	2.6
16	6.02E-05	2.61E-05	2.3
24	6.02E-05	2.91E-05	2.1

TI	2oo3	1002D	factor:
0.5	3.39E-05	1.37E-05	2.5
1	6.02E-05	2.31E-05	2.6
2	8.37E-05	3.15E-05	2.7
5	1.04E-04	3.85E-05	2.7
10	1.11E-04	4.13E-05	2.7

DC	PFD average 2oo3	1002D	factor:
60%	3.58E-03	1.24E-03	2.9
65%	2.78E-03	9.60E-04	2.9
70%	2.07E-03	7.13E-04	2.9
75%	1.45E-03	5.01E-04	2.9
80%	9.45E-04	3.25E-04	2.9
85%	5.41E-04	1.87E-04	2.9
90%	2.46E-04	8.56E-05	2.9
95%	6.46E-05	2.31E-05	2.8
99%	3.38E-06	1.44E-06	2.3

Lambda	2oo3	1002D	factor:
1E-03	2.08E-02	8.01E-03	2.6
1E-04	2.56E-04	9.19E-05	2.8
1E-05	2.61E-06	9.32E-07	2.8

Table 2. calculation results

7 Conclusions

Even though both systems are able to achieve high risk reduction levels, there is a slight advantage for the 1oo2D voting principle. Calculations for both voting principles demonstrate that, under normal and identical circumstances, the 1oo2D voting principle reduces the risk 2.5 to 3 times better than the 2oo3 voting principle.

The parameter settings are very important when it comes to improving the safety risk reduction. The diagnostic coverage has the greatest impact on the risk reduction followed by the failure rate of the modules.

8 References

1. Leiming Xing, Karl N. Fleming, Wee Tee Loh, Comparison of Markov model and fault tree approach in determining initiating event frequency for systems with two train configurations. Reliability Engineering and System Safety 53 (1996) 17-29, Elsevier Science Limited

2. Rouvroye, J.L., Brombacher A.C., et al, Uncertainty in safety, New techniques for the assessment and optimisation of safety in process industry. SERA-Vol. 4, Safety Engineering and Risk Analysis, ASME, San Francisco, 1995

3. ISA S84, 67 Alexander Drive, P.O. Box 12277, Research Triangle Park, NC 27709.

4. ISA TR84.0.02 version 3 December 1997, 67 Alexander Drive, P.O. Box 12277, Research Triangle Park, NC 27709.

5. IEC 61508, Functional safety of electrical/electronic/ programmable electronic safety-related systems.

6. IEC 61078, Analysis techniques for dependability - Reliability block diagram method, 1991.

7. IEC 61165, Application of Markov techniques, 1995.

A Holistic View on the Dependability
of Software-Intensive Systems

Gerald Sonneck[1], Erwin Schoitsch[1], Lorenzo Strigini[2]

[1] Österreichisches Forschungszentrum Seibersdorf, Seibersdorf, Austria
{Gerald.Sonneck, Erwin.Schoitsch}@arcs.ac.at
[2] Centre for Software Reliability - City University, London, UK
strigini@csr.city.ac.uk

Abstract. This paper gives an example of a holistic, quantitative dependability analysis of a software-intensive system. It demonstrates a way of choosing cost-effective improvements and achieving trustworthy results, even when it may be difficult to get agreement on software reliability data. This is done by identifying those components that are critical for the safety of the whole system. In the case analysed here the software, though extensively used in normal operation, is not critical for the accident scenario considered. Therefore a rough estimate of its failure rate suffices for dependability calculations.

1 Introduction

One of the difficulties for a trustworthy assessment of the dependability of software-intensive systems arises in choosing reliability estimates. For hardware, consensus is usually possible because considerable experience is available, and we have learned to live with (perhaps too conservative) estimates for human behaviour. Opinions on achieved, achievable or demonstrable reliability of software, however, differ considerably - from "according to our models there is about 0.5 faults left in our software" via claimed software failure rates of "less than 10^{-9}/h" to Bev Littlewood's statement at SAFECOMP '95 [1]: "Under quite plausible assumptions, a Bayesian approach to this problem gives us the following: if a system has survived t_0 time units of failure-free operation, there is a 50:50 chance of a further t_0 time units of operation until next failure, e.g. for the flight-critical software, we would need 10^9 hours of failure-free working (i.e. $\cong$ 100 000 years!) to conclude it has a median time-to-failure of 10^9 hours", which means that only modest levels of reliability can be demonstrated.

This does not necessarily mean that software should not be used in systems with high dependability requirements. It rather means that such software-intensive systems should be constructed in such a way that the influence of the software on the dependability of the total system is small.

A method for quantifying this influence is Fault Tree Analysis (FTA) [2], which allows the probability of system failures (so-called top events) to be computed from the failure rates of the components (hardware and software components, operators).

In this paper, a step in the development lifecycle of a safety and security system upgrade using this approach is demonstrated. It should be noted that the configuration described has been constructed only to demonstrate the approach; it is similar to realised configurations, but not identical, so that the numerical results cannot be directly applied to any of these. The aim of this example is to demonstrate a system-level, quantitative analysis encompassing hardware, software and human components. The means for estimating the dependability of individual components will be mentioned for the sake of completeness but not discussed in detail.

2 The Analysed System and Scenario

The analysed system is that part of a safety and security system for buildings which protects rooms against burglary and against fire. These two requirements contradict each other to some extent: security demands that rooms can only be entered and left by authorised people; safety demands that in case of fire the rooms can be entered and left by anybody. The analysed scenario considers both these aspects.

2.1 The Scenario

While passing a room a person, who is not authorised to enter it, smells smoke and enters the room. This is noticed by a sensor, resulting in various actions including the automatic bolting of the door. The fire alarm will cause several actions including the unbolting of the door, so that the person can safely leave the burning room.

The top event for this scenario is therefore: the person cannot leave the burning room. The required lower bound on the mean time to failure (MTTF) for this top event was derived from the total safety and security goals and established to be more than 2000 years - assuming that the initiating event (unauthorised entry because of smoke) takes place once in 10 years.

2.2 Description of the System

We only describe those parts of the system which are relevant for the scenario above. So our system consists of sensors, actuators, hard-wired circuits, the bolt, the computer with software, the control panel, the operator and the power supply.

Normally, the system is run via the computer. Both automatic and manual actions are possible. To provide redundancy for messages that are relevant for dependability, a hard-wired control panel is available; it is independent of the computer and displays summary messages.

Unauthorised entry into a room activates the burglar alarm, which automatically bolts the door. This alarm is also shown on the control panel.

Fire is detected by a smoke detector, which automatically activates the fire scenario (including opening the bolts). Independently, the fire alarm (and its location) is shown on the control panel.

The movement of the *bolt* (close or open) can be electrically activated by:
- the burglar alarm (close)
- the fire alarm via the computer (open) and
- the operator (open or close) via separate, manual controls.

The state of the bolt is indicated on the control panel via fail-safe circuitry.

A *computer* failure might be a hardware or a software failure (or both).

The *operator* takes note of the messages and checks whether the computer has ordered the necessary actions (including opening the bolt). If this is not the case, he can activate them through the control panel. If he notices that the bolt has not opened nonetheless, he can open it manually.

The *power supply* has an emergency supply (cold redundancy).

3 Fault Tree and Component Data

Using all this information, the fault tree for the chosen top event (the person cannot leave the burning room) can be constructed. It consists of the following components (for the sake of clarity only point values of dependability measures are given; the use of confidence levels would not change the main issues of this paper):

Initiating event
eintritt: Unauthorised entry in a room because of smoke; it is assumed that this happens once in 10 years.

Hardware
hw1_com: Computer hardware failure. Experience shows that the reliability of this component is dominated by the mean time to failure (MTTF) of the hard disk of 5 years. The mean time to repair (MTTR) is 9 hours.

hw1_r_el: Electrical failure to open the bolt. The MTTF is 20 years. As this component is inspected once a year the MTTR is dominated by the undetected failures (approximately 0.5 years).

hw1_r_m: Mechanical failure to open the bolt. The MTTF is 10 years, the inspection time one year.

hw1_rauch: Failure of the smoke detector (including the alarm in the control room). This component is fail-safe; only the horn is assumed to have a MTTF of 500 years [3]. The inspection interval is one year.

hw1el: Failure of the public power supply. Experience shows that this happens about once in seven years. The failure is detected immediately, of course, MTTR is one hour.

hw1elnot: Failure of the emergency power supply. The MTTF is 5 years, the inspection interval one year.

Operator

ml_a_f: At fire alarm the operator does not perform the correct action (fire scenario). As the operator is in a stress situation, this is assumed to happen once every ten times.

ml_a_ue: Failure to notice the alarm. Here is no stress, therefore it is assumed to happen in 1% of the cases.

ml_r_f: Failure to open the bolt in case of fire. Once every ten times (stress).

ml_r_ue: Closed bolt not noticed in case of fire. Once every ten times (stress).

Software

sw_f: Software failure. The software performs a simple polling function, so its dependability is described in terms of unavailability. It accumulated 25 operational years without failure since the last release. The Bayesian approach quoted in the Introduction [4] gives a point estimate (mean) for the failure rate of 1 in 25 years. This approach is conservative in considering only observed behaviour, without any additional evidence of quality, but produces a rather "flat" distribution, so we will also consider confidence bounds. The repair time is 24 hours (conservatively, allowing for long latency of failures; restart is normally sufficient for "repair").

Given independence among these component failures, probabilities of failure per demand and unavailabilities can be used together in the fault tree.

4   Results (Base Case)

The first result of a fault tree analysis is a list of the minimal cut sets of the system (a minimal cut set is any combination of components, whose common failure is just sufficient to arrive at the top event). The FTA tool RELVEC [6] was used for all calculations; it uses various approximations which are negligble for our purposes. Our system has 10 minimal cut sets, one of the order two (consisting of two components) and nine of the order three:

```
M I N I M A L   C U T S E T S    (3)
************************************
    1   eintritt  hw1_rauch
    2   eintritt  hw1el      hw1elnot
    3   eintritt  hw1_r_el   m1_r_f
    4   eintritt  hw1_r_m    m1_r_f
    5   eintritt  hw1_r_el   m1_r_ue
    6   eintritt  hw1_r_m    m1_r_ue
    7   eintritt  sw_f       m1_a_f
    8   eintritt  hw1_com    m1_a_f
    9   eintritt  sw_f       m1_a_ue
   10   eintritt  hw1_com    m1_a_ue
```

The next result is the MTTF of the system for this top event, which is calculated to be 660 years. As this is considerably less than the required MTTF of >2000 years, it will be necessary to improve the system. To do this, we have to know the importance of the components for the MTTF of the system.

It is often argued that the largest contribution to the unreliability of a system stems from the cut sets with smallest order - because the probability that n components fail at the same time is greater than that of the failure of n+1 components. This, however, is only true when the failure rates (or the availability figures) of all the components are of the same order. When (as in our system) this is not the case, this method can be very misleading, as the following list of the importance of the cut sets shows (the tool gives unreliability figures over a given time, arbitrarily set to 10,000 hours as the purpose of this step is just to compare the influence of the various components):

```
TSPBASIS  /      top
R E L I A B I L I T Y  T = 10000.0  SHORTEST
*********************************************
   CUT SET                          UNREL       %    CUMUL.
    4   eintritt   hw1_r_m    ml_r_f   4.76E-04  31.19   31.19
    6   eintritt   hw1_r_m    ml_r_ue  4.76E-04  31.19   62.37
    3   eintritt   hw1_r_el   ml_r_f   2.38E-04  15.59   77.97
    5   eintritt   hw1_r_el   ml_r_ue  2.38E-04  15.59   93.56
    1   eintritt   hw1_rauch           9.52E-05   6.24   99.80
    8   eintritt   hw1_com    ml_a_f   1.71E-06   0.11   99.91
    7   eintritt   sw_f       ml_a_f   1.00E-06   0.07   99.97
   10   eintritt   hw1_com    ml_a_ue  1.71E-07   0.01   99.98
    2   eintritt   hw1el      hw1elnot 1.33E-07   0.01   99.99
    9   eintritt   sw_f       ml_a_ue  1.00E-07   0.01  100.00
```

From this list it can be seen that the cut set no. 1 (of the order two) contributes only 6.24% to the unreliability of the system, while the cut sets no. 4 and 6 (both of the order three) contribute more than 31% each. For an efficient improvement of the system it is necessary to use the list which gives the importance of the components:

```
RELIABILITY  I M P O R T A N C E  T = 10000.0   SHORTEST
*****************************************************************
COMP        IMP       %     GROUP     IMP       %    CUMUL.
eintritt   1.00E+0 34.04    eintritt 1.00E+0  34.04   34.04
hw1_r_m    6.24E-1 21.23    hw       9.99E-1  34.02   68.06
ml_r_f     4.68E-1 15.92    m        9.38E-1  31.91   99.98
ml_r_ue    4.68E-1 15.92    sw_f     7.21E-4   0.02  100.00
hw1_r_el   3.12E-1 10.62
hw1_rauch  6.24E-2  2.12
ml_a_f     1.78E-3  0.06
hw1_com    1.23E-3  0.04
sw_f       7.21E-4  0.02
ml_a_ue    1.78E-4  0.01
hw1elnot   8.73E-5  0.00
hw1el      8.73E-5  0.00
```

Here we see that (apart from the initiating event eintritt) the component hw1_r_m (mechanical failure to open the bolt) has the greatest importance. The cheapest way to improve its availability is to decrease the inspection interval from one year to one month - this will be analysed in the next chapter. Alternatively, a parallel-redundant construction of the bolt and its actuation is also possible.

5 Version 1

Version 1 of the analysis differs from the base case only in the component dependability data: the inspection interval of the component hw1_r_m (mechanical failure to open the bolt) is now one month. As the system structure has not changed, the fault tree and the cut sets are the same as in the base case.

For Version 1, the MTTF of the system is about 1500 years, better than in the base case (660 years), but still smaller than the required MTTF (>2000 years). The list of the importance of the components shows two important changes from the base case:

```
TSPV1  /     top
RELIABILITY   I M P O R T A N C E   T = 10000.0   SHORTEST
**********************************************************
COMP        IMP        %     GROUP     IMP       %     CUMUL.
eintritt    1.00E+0  34.99    eintritt  1.00E+0  34.99   34.99
hw1_r_el    7.11E-1  24.88    hw        9.99E-1  34.94   69.93
m1_r_f      4.27E-1  14.93    m         8.58E-1  30.01   99.94
m1_r_ue     4.27E-1  14.93    sw_f      1.64E-3   0.06  100.00
hw1_rauch   1.42E-1   4.98
hw1_r_m     1.42E-1   4.98
m1_a_f      4.05E-3   0.14
hw1_com     2.82E-3   0.10
sw_f        1.64E-3   0.06
m1_a_ue     4.05E-4   0.01
hw1el       1.99E-4   0.01
hw1elnot    1.99E-4   0.01
```

The importance of the component hw1_r_m (mechanical failure to open the bolt) is now only about 5%; the most important component (nearly 25%) is now hw1_r_el (electrical failure to open the bolt), which appears in the two most important cut sets:

```
TSPV1  /     top
R E L I A B I L I T Y   T = 10000.0   SHORTEST
**********************************************
  CUT SET                             UNREL      %    CUMUL.
  3   eintritt  hw1_r_el  m1_r_f    2.38E-04  35.55   35.55
  5   eintritt  hw1_r_el  m1_r_ue   2.38E-04  35.55   71.10
```

Therefore the next step to increase the MTTF of the system is an improvement of the availability of the component hw1_r_el (electrical failure to open the bolt).

6 Version 1a

As in version 1, version 1a differs from the base case only in the data: both the mechanical and the electrical system to open the bolt will now be inspected monthly. Therefore the fault tree and the cut sets are unchanged.

The MTTF of the system for the analysed top event is now about 4150 years. It fulfils the requirement (>2000 years).

From a "holistic" point of view it is interesting to look at the contributions of hardware, software and humans. For this purpose again the list of importance of the components and the component groups is used:

```
RELIABILITY   I M P O R T A N C E   T = 10000.0   SHORTEST
*****************************************************************
COMP       IMP       %    GROUP     IMP       %    CUMUL.
eintritt   1.00E+0  38.39  eintritt  1.00E+0  38.39  38.39
hw1_r_m    3.95E-1  15.16  hw        9.96E-1  38.23  76.62
hw1_rauch  3.95E-1  15.16  m         6.05E-1  23.21  99.82
m1_r_f     2.96E-1  11.37  sw_f      4.56E-3   0.18 100.00
m1_r_ue    2.96E-1  11.37
hw1_r_el   1.97E-1   7.58
m1_a_f     1.13E-2   0.43
hw1_com    7.82E-3   0.30
sw_f       4.56E-3   0.18
m1_a_ue    1.13E-3   0.04
hw1el      5.53E-4   0.02
hw1elnot   5.53E-4   0.02
```

The column GROUP and the following column IMPORTANCE show that the contribution of the hardware (hw) in this system is about 38% and the contribution of the operator is about 23%; the software (sw_f), however, contributes only 0.18%: it affects an action (automatic activation of fire scenario) which is not a "weak link" in the system's response, and it has the operator as a form of diverse redundancy. Hardware components, by contrast, are present in all the redundant paths to achieving the safety action.

This difference in importance also shows itself in the sensitivity of the system MTTF to the availability (or probability of failure on demand) of the component groups, which is shown in the following plots. The ordinates of each plot give the factor (10 - 0.1) by which the measure for the chosen component group is multiplied; the abscissas give the resulting system unavailability and unreliability, allowing us to observe its variation. On the right hand side of the plot, the MTTF is printed for the top event of interest.

For the operator, this sensitivity is rather large: if his unreliability drops by a factor of 0.1, the MTTF of the system will rise to 9100 years; if it rises by a factor of 10 (i.e., the operator is guaranteed to fail on those operations in which he was estimated to fail one time out of ten), the MTTF of the system will drop to 644 years (this is a less accurate result than the others as the FTA tool is not meant to deal with high unreliability values, but the high sensitivity is real):

```
S E N S I T I V I T Y   T = 10000.0   SHORTEST
********************************************
Fr of m                                              MTTF
[years]
0.1-               +*                                  -
9.10E+03
   I                                                   I
0.2-               +*                                  I
7.89E+03
   I                                                   I
0.5-                +*                                 I
6.14E+03
   I                                                   I
1.0-                      +*                           -
4.15E+03
   I                                                   I
2.2-                           +*                      I
2.44E+03
   I                                                   I
4.6-                                    +*             I
1.30E+03
   I                                                   I
 10-                                          +*       -
6.44E+02
   I----------I----------I----------I----------I
  0.1        0.3        1.0        3.0         10
        RELATIVE UNAVAIL (+)   AND UNREL (*)
SENSITIVITY OF RELIABILITY   0.6043
```

Fig. 1. Sensitivity of the reliability of the system to the failure rate of the operator

For the software, however, the sensitivity is very small as shown in Fig. 2. Here the multiplication factor for the failure rate of the software runs from 1 to 100. So the top line gives the previously found system MTTF of 4150 years for a software failure rate of 1 per 25 years. If the 90 % confidence bound (1/2.5 years with this estimation method) is used for the software, the system MTTF will only drop to 3990 years; even using the 99 % confidence bound of 1 per 0.25 years (equivalent to assuming a 0.01 probability of failure on demand) only results in a system MTTF of 2860 year, which is still well above the required 2000 years for this top event.

```
S E N S I T I V I T Y   T = 10000.0   SHORTEST
************************************************
Fr of sw_f                                              MTTF
[years]
   1-                      +*                             -
4.15E+03
   I                                                      I
   2-                      +*                             I
4.13E+03
   I                                                      I
   5-                      +*                             I
4.08E+03
   I                                                      I
  10-                      +*                             -
3.99E+03
   I                                                      I
  22-                      +*                             I
3.79E+03
   I                                                      I
  46-                        +*                           I
3.44E+03
   I                                                      I
 100-                         +*                          -
2.86E+03
   I----------I----------I----------I----------I
  0.1        0.3        1.0        3.0         10
     RELATIVE UNAVAIL (+)   AND UNREL (*)
```

Fig. 2. Sensitivity of the reliability of the system to the failure rate of the software

7   Conclusions

This paper describes an application of fault tree analysis which is routine from the point of view of its form, but interesting in that it crosses the boundaries between the traditional areas of hardware, human and software reliability, demonstrating that analyses limited to each area by itself would be misleading. So, the reported work is an example of the importance of holistic and quantitative analyses for the assessment and especially for cost-effective *improvements* of the dependability of software-intensive systems. These analyses are the only way to determine which components are critical for dependability. For these components, and these only, it is necessary to have somewhat tight estimates of the failure rates, and these are the components which may need improvements. In our example it turned out that the inspection intervals of some of the hardware components should be shortened - a relatively cheap measure; it would have been sheer waste, however, to seek less conservative estimates of the reliability for the software, as the probability of this top event in this particular system is quite insensitive to the software failure rate. The operator, on the other hand, is a critical element in terms of sensitivity, and any doubt that the values chosen are inaccurate in the optimistic direction would require effort to obtain more precise estimates, or design changes.

Any analysis like this depends on the correctness of the assumptions made on its parameters, e.g., on conservative estimates being actually conservative. Arguments about this rely on applying the methods of the specific reliability "areas" (hardware, human, software) to the details of the analysed system. There would thus be more detailed analyses, of which only a terse outline could fit in the space available; but these would remain useless for system-level decisions if not combined appropriately.

The other crucial condition for a trustworthy analysis is that the model used be correct. A critical assumption of any fault tree analysis is of course the independence among the failures of the components. Two orders of precautions apply: detecting and eliminating direct paths of common-cause or propagated failure; and using conservative estimates for individual components to cover positive correlation due to common stress factors [5], [7]. Again, such precautions are not made necessary by the fact that this fault tree mixes hardware, software and human components, but are needed in any application of FTA.

Of course the concrete results depend on the analysed system and accident scenario - in another case the software (or one of its parts), or another hardware or human component may well be the most critical component. This, however, can again only be determined by a holistic and quantitative analysis.

Acknowledgements

This work has been performed in the framework of the European Community research network ΟΛΟΣ - "A holistic approach to the dependability analysis and evaluation of control systems involving hardware, software and human resources" (Human Capital and Mobility Programme, CHRX-CT94-0577), which aims at improving the synergy between the disciplines dealing with hardware, software and human aspects in reliability and safety analysis. The authors are grateful to their colleagues in this network, who provided valuable comments.

References

[1] Littlewoood, B.: "How I learned to start worrying and fear the computer ...", Presentation at SAFECOMP '95, Belgirate, Italy, 11-13 October 1995.

[2] Heidtmann, K.: Zuverlässigkeitsbewertung technischer Systeme, Teubner, Stuttgart - Leipzig, 1997.

[3] IEEE-STD 500-1984: IEEE Guide to the Collection and Presentation of Electrical, Electronic, Sensing Component, and Mechanical Equipment Reliability Data for Nuclear Power Generating Stations, IEEE, New York, 1983 or Wiley, New York, 1993.

[4] Littlewood, B.; Strigini L.: "Validation of Ultra-High Dependability for Software-based Systems", Communications of the ACM, 36, pp. 69-80, 1993.

[5] Hughes, R. P.: "A New Approach to Common Cause Failure", Reliability Engineering, 17, pp. 211-236, 1987.

[6] RELVEC - Reliability Analysis, Technical Research Centre of Finland (VTT), 1986.

[7] Littlewood, B.: "The impact of diversity upon common mode failures", Reliability Engineering and System Safety, 51, pp.101-113, 1996.

Verifying Integrity of Decision Diagrams

Rolf Drechsler

Institute of Computer Science
Albert-Ludwigs-University
79110 Freiburg im Breisgau, Germany
drechsle@informatik.uni-freiburg.de

Abstract

Decision Diagrams (DDs) are the state-of-the-art data structure in CAD of integrated circuits. They are used in many safety critical applications, like verification.
In this paper security aspects of implementation techniques of DDs are discussed. A recursive checksum technique is presented for on-line and off-line checks. These methods are used to verify the integrity of DDs. The correctness of the data structures can be verified by (nearly) no overhead. Experimental results are presented to demonstrate the efficiency of this approach.

1 Introduction

During the last decades, the complexity of *Integrated Circuits* (ICs) has increased exponentially. In the 1970's a typical microprocessor such as the *Intel 8080* consisted of about 5,000 transistors while in 1993 Intel's state-of-the-art processor *Pentium* contains 3.1 million transistors. To handle the complexity of todays circuits the design engineers are totally dependent on *Computer Aided Design* (CAD), i.e., software tools. The capabilities and limitations of CAD tools have crucial impact on the performance and cost of the produced circuits as well as on the resources required to develop a circuit. Consequently, CAD for ICs is a very important and increasingly growing research area.

In many tasks during the design process *Decision Diagrams* (DDs) are used: Most common synthesis tools for logic optimization (two-level and multi-level) are based on *Binary Decision Diagrams* (BDDs) [5] (see e.g. [8, 7, 23, 20]). Especially for the verification step many different DD types, i.e. extensions of BDDs, have been introduced [16, 12, 6, 11, 14].

Since ICs are nowadays used in many safety critical applications it is very important to make DD packages not only as fast and memory efficient as possible [2, 18, 17, 13], but also as *secure* as possible. So far the security aspect for DDs has not been considered.

For "simple" data structures like linked lists and binary (search) trees good techniques are known for secure implementations [22, 1, 4].

The security aspect becomes even more important when current trends, like parallel implementations of DD packages [21], are considered. These implementations use complicated communication protocols and it is well-known that several of these protocols contain bugs (see e.g. [15]).

Recently a *Recursive Checksum Method* (RCM) has been introduced in [4] for trees. Since most DD packages are based on recursive operations the RCM can directly be applied to DDs. The use of the RCM also helps during the implementation of a DD package, since many errors in the memory management can be detected very early.

In this paper we consider methods for guaranteeing the integrity of DDs by on-line and off-line checks. We consider different fault types, like *Copy Faults* (CFs) and *Memory Faults* (MFs) [4]. We show that the RCM can also be applied successfully to graphs. The implementation is discussed, i.e. the RCM can be integrated in DD packages by (nearly) no overhead: Since most DD packages are based on recursive synthesis operations, like *If-Then-Else* for BDDs [5, 2], the recursive checksum computation can be incorporated with no additional cost (in contrast to other data structures [1, 4]). We give results on fault injection experiments for BDDs that show that all of the assumed errors can be detected at very low cost, i.e. our method can be implemented without any memory overhead (in clever implementations like [17]) and the runtime overhead is less than 5% on average.

The paper is structured as follows: In Section 2 we briefly review the definitions of DDs. In Section 3 we discuss the fault model considered in this paper. Section 4 describes our approach to handle the security aspect. Implementation aspects and experimental results are given in Section 5 and 6. Finally, the results are summarized.

2 Decision Diagrams

We now introduce basics of DDs. We focuses less on a mathematical exact description, instead we want to give an informal description that helps the reader to get an impression of the underlying data structure. For more details see [10].

The best known DD type is the *Binary Decision Diagram* (BDD) [5]. The description in the following is mainly based on BDDs, but all results directly transfer to other DD types, e.g. DDs including edge values [16, 6, 11].

All DDs are graph-based representations, where at each (non-terminal) node labeled with a variable x_i a decomposition of the function represented by this node into two subfunctions (the *low*-function and the *high*-function) is performed. Furthermore, the underlying graph is *reduced* and *ordered*, i.e. all redundant nodes are removed and the variables occur in the same order on all paths of the DD, respectively.

E.g. for BDDs the following decomposition is considered:

$$f = \overline{x}_i f_{low(v)} + x_i f_{high(v)}$$

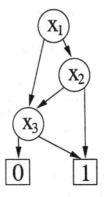

Fig. 1. BDD for $f = x_1 x_2 + x_3$

(f is the function represented at node v, $f_{low(v)}$ ($f_{high(v)}$) denotes the function represented by the *low*-edge (*high*-edge) of v. The recursion stops at terminal nodes labeled with 0 or 1.

Example 1. In Fig. 1 the reduced ordered BDD for function $f = x_1 x_2 + x_3$ is given.

For the representation of a node the pointer to the *low-* and *high*-function has to be stored. Further memory is needed for the index of the node and the reference counter.

Additionally, to store edge values for DDs (where this is allowed) memory is needed. It is straightforward to integrate this in the approach that is presented in the following but we restrict ourselves w.l.o.g. to BDDs.

Finally, we briefly consider the typical synthesis operation on DDs: The synthesis of two DDs is carried out by performing a recursive call on subgraphs. For BDDs a sketch of the recursive *If-Then-Else* (ITE) algorithm from [2] is given in Fig. 2. Similar algorithms can be considered for word-level DDs [6, 11].

3 Fault Model

In this section we briefly discuss some aspects of the fault model. As already pointed out in [22] there is no general agreement how to measure the robustness of a storage data structure.

Simple errors that should be detected are errors in single bits or words, i.e. if the contents of a memory cell is modified by a fault.

Additionally, in this paper we consider the fault model from [4]: We allow two kinds of memory errors in our model, i.e. *Copy Faults* (CFs) and *Memory Allocation Faults* (MAFs). Obviously, many other "real-world" faults are also covered by this model.

```
ite(F,G,H) {
        if (terminal case) return result;
        if (computed-table entry (F,G,H) exists) return result;

        let xᵢ be the top variable of {F,G,H};

        THEN  = ite(F_{x_i}, G_{x_i}, H_{x_i}) ;
        ELSE  = ite(F_{\bar{x}_i}, G_{\bar{x}_i}, H_{\bar{x}_i}) ;

        if (THEN == ELSE) return THEN;

        // Find or create a new node with variable v and sons THEN and ELSE
        R = Find_or_add_unique_table(xᵢ,THEN,ELSE);

        // Store computation and result in computed table
        Insert_computed_table({F,G,H},R);

        return R;
}
```

Fig. 2. ITE-algorithm

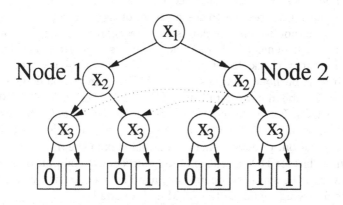

Fig. 3. Example for copy fault

Copy faults: Copy the contents of one node into an other node.
Memory allocation faults: Memory is allocated that has already been used by an other node.

Example 2. An example for a CF is given in Fig. 3. For simplicity the non-reduced BDD of Example 1 is given. If the contents of Node 1 is copied into Node 2 the dotted pointers result. Obviously, the function being represented is changed.

Obviously, CFs can not be captured by checksum computations that do not consider the environment of the node, since the node itself is valid but has a wrong location. This fault may result from a wrong address to which data is written back. MAFs often occur during software development, since efficient implementations of DDs often overload the memory management of the operating system [2, 17]. (For more details on CFs and MAFs see [4].)

4 Security Aspects

DDs are used in more and more applications were security is a very important aspect, e.g. verification. Thus, there is a need for secure data structures.

The simplest idea to make data structures securer is to store each component several times. (Notice that in that way some kind of memory faults, like MAFs, can also not be detected.) The idea of multiple storing also leads to the ability of not only error detecting, but also error correcting data structures. These topics have been studied for "simpler" data structures like linked lists (see e.g. [22]). Storing the same information several times obviously results in large memory overhead. Also the access time per node would drastically increase for DDs, since several pointers have to be handled. (E.g. during sifting [19] often several thousand pointers have to be redirected.)

In the following we restrict to the problem of error detection.

A general method for making data structures more secure is the use of checksums, i.e. for each element a characteristic value is computed. The simplest example is the parity check. But this method has the drawback that errors that result from neighborhood relations (as e.g. MAFs) can not be detected.

We now describe in more detail the *Recursive Checksum Method* (RCM) that we apply to DDs: For each node a checksum c is computed that results from the checksums c_l and c_r of the left and right son of the node and from a node internal information. Here we make use of the index of the node. (We will see in the following that for DDs methods based on recursive computations can easily be integrated in the synthesis operations, like ITE (see Section 2 and 5).)

For the following we define the RCM c of a node by

$$c = (c_l + c_r + variable\_index) \quad mod \quad m, \tag{1}$$

where m denotes an integer number and *variable_index* of a BDD node v is i iff v is labeled with variable x_i[1]. Obviously, the choice of m largely influences the quality of the checksum. The larger m is chosen the more memory is used to store the information, but the more secure the DD gets.

Example 3. If $m = 2$ then only a parity check is performed.

Remark 1. For DD types allowing edge values these values have also to be incorporated in the checksum.

---

[1] Here we choose a very simple function so that the description remains simple.

We now consider two main problems: We want to detect errors on-line and we want to check the integrity of a given DD by off-line tests.

On-line check: The on-line check verifies the correctness of the node during each access. This is done by recomputing the checksum of the successors during each access. Additionally, each information that is obtained by a look-up in the computed table is checked. Due to the recursive nature of the synthesis procedures on DDs and of the RCM the checksum computation can easily be incorporated in the program code. (For more details see Section 5.)

Off-line check: The check for integrity can be performed by a *depth-first-search* algorithm starting from the roots of the DD. At each node (starting at the terminals) the checksum is recursively computed. Then a comparison to the checksum value stored in each node is carried out. If a comparison fails an error is detected.

Using these on-line and off-line techniques also the software development can be simplified tremendously. As mentioned above many DD packages overload the memory management of the operating systems. Using the on-line check many errors can be detected very early. If (due to performance reasons) the on-line check is not desired during normal operation of the package it can easily be switched off. (This also offers the possibility to operate DD packages in a *debug mode* and in a *normal operation mode*.)

One further advantage of an off-line check on DDs is that the nodes are referenced several times (in contrast to trees). Thus, there is a high probability to detect errors with only a small number of encoding bits (see experiments in Section 6).

One problem that is not considered in this paper is the aspect of faulty computations, e.g. what happens, if the checksum computation is wrong? Previous work has proposed the term of safe and unsafe memory for other data structures. These results can directly be transfered to graphs and DDs. (For more details see e.g. [1, 4].)

5 Implementation

We now briefly discuss how the RCM of the previous section can be implemented in a DD package. (For the rest of this section we assume that the reader is familiar with basics about the implementation of DD packages.)

In the following we restrict ourselves to the ITE operator used for BDDs. (For other DD packages based on recursive synthesis analogous modifications can be given.) Only minor modifications have to be performed to integrate the approach in a given DD package:

– An additional (integer) value must be included in the description of a node. At this point also a short integer or only a few bits can be used, but with smaller number of memory the data structure becomes less secure (see Section 6). It depends on the designer of the data structure to determine the

optimal trade-off for his application: Is security or memory overhead more important?
- During the recursive ITE calls the checksum has to be computed. Since ITE also works recursively only a constant overhead per node has to be invested. For each node that is newly created the checksum c is computed as described in the previous section.

Example 4. For ITE-based BDD packages after each computation of the nodes THEN and ELSE (see Fig. 2) the checksum of these new nodes is verified. Thus also erroneous modifications of bits (or even words) in a node can be detected. Additionally, after each successful lookup in the unique table the node is checked for correctness.

Remark 2. In usual DD packages some bits are often unused, e.g. in the BDD package from [17] two bits per pointer have no functionality. Since in each node two pointers are stored, i.e. the pointers for the low- and high-function, four bits are unused.

6   Experimental Results

In this section we present results of some fault injection experiments. All experiments have been carried out on a preliminary BDD package implementation on a *SUN SPARCstation 4*. An upper node limit of 250.000 was used.

Several symbolic simulation runs were considered for the combinational parts of the sequential benchmarks from [3]. For the ordering of the variables the initial ordering of the inputs as they occur in the benchmark description was used.

In the first set of experiments we considered the on-line check method, i.e. we check the data structure during the symbolic simulation. We inserted a fault by randomly changing the contents of one variable in a node. Thus, we not only considered bit faults, but also word faults that correspond to multi-bit faults. (Notice that this fault can also be detected by a conventional checksum approach. Recursive computation does not influence the result.) We use Formula (1) for the recursive computation of the checksum[2]. During each run one fault is inserted. In some cases this fault does not have to modify the result, e.g. if the fault occurs in a redundant part of the circuit during the symbolic simulation. But nevertheless the on-line check detects that something might be damaged. In Table 1 a 1 (0) denotes that the error was (not) detected. Each column denotes a different value for m. As can easily be seen only a few bits are needed to detect all errors in the package during the symbolic simulation of these benchmarks, i.e. only 3 bits are needed to encode the 5 values.

We now focus on the off-line check for CFs and MAFs. In a second experiment we considered a successful symbolic simulation and started with a *depth-first-search* computation. We randomly inserted faults by the following procedure:

---

[2] More sophisticated computation methods could obviously even improve the quality of the result.

name	$m = 2$	$m = 3$	$m = 4$	$m = 5$
s00208	0	0	1	1
s00298	1	1	1	1
s00344	0	0	1	1
s00400	0	0	1	1
s00444	0	0	1	1
s00510	0	1	1	1
s00641	0	0	0	1
s00713	0	0	0	1
s00820	0	0	1	1
s00832	0	0	1	1
s00838	0	0	0	1
s00953	0	0	0	1
s01238	0	0	1	1
s01423	1	0	1	1
s01488	0	1	1	1
s01494	0	1	1	1

Table 1. On-line check

name	pointers	faults	$m = 2$	$m = 3$	$m = 4$	$m = 5$
s00208	8	1	0	0	1	1
s00298	8	2	1	1	1	1
s00344	10	1	0	0	1	1
s00400	10	2	0	0	1	1
s00444	10	2	0	0	1	1
s00510	10	1	0	1	1	1
s00641	10	6	1	0	1	1
s00713	10	5	1	0	1	1
s00820	10	1	0	0	1	1
s00832	10	1	0	0	1	1
s00838	10	1	0	0	0	1
s00953	10	2	1	0	1	1
s01238	10	0	0	0	0	0
s01423	10	2	1	0	1	1
s01488	10	1	0	1	1	1
s01494	10	3	1	1	1	1

Table 2. Off-line check

During the construction we stored a pointer's address for fault insertion at about each 50th node creation (up to a maximum of 10 pointer addresses)[3]. In the second and third column of Table 2 we give the information about the number of faults considered. *pointers* (*faults*) denotes the number of addresses stored (faults inserted). Again we considered different values for m. The results are given in the succeeding columns of Table 2. Once more it can be seen from the table that only 3 bits are needed to detect all faults. (For benchmark *s01238* no faults have been inserted, since all stored pointers are not present in the representation of the outputs.) Even an encoding of 2 bits is able to detect most faults. This results from the fact that often the same node is referenced several times. Such during each access there is the possibility to detect the fault.

As can be seen from our experiments only 3 bits are needed to detect all faults. Thus, following Remark 2 no memory overhead results for efficient DD package implementations from incorporating the RCM. In our implementation the runtime overhead was less than 5% on average.

7 Conclusions

Security aspects of *Decision Diagrams* have been discussed. Since DDs are used in more and more safety critical applications there is a need to also make the implementation of the DD package as secure as possible.

In this paper a first step in this direction has been performed: Fault models for other data structures have been considered for DDs. The method of *recursive checksum* computation has been applied to DDs and has been integrated in on-line and off-line checks. It has been demonstrated by fault injection experiments that these methods are able to identify memory errors during the operation of a DD package. A check for the whole DD for integrity can also easily be performed. These methods can be integrated with only little overhead with respect to runtime and no overhead with respect to memory.

If is focus of current work to extend the ideas discussed in this paper to DD packages that also allow dynamic minimization algorithms, like sifting [19, 9]. Furthermore, aspects of secure DDs will be extended to not only error detection but also error correction.

Acknowledgment

The author likes to thank Bernd Becker and Nicole Drechsler for their helpful comments.

---

[3] The problem was that in this way we mostly stored enough pointers so that at least some were also present in the final result, i.e. during a symbolic simulation many nodes are created that are not needed for the representation of the outputs. Thus, errors in these nodes could not be detected by the off-line test.

References

1. N.M. Amato and M.C. Loui. Checking linked data structures. In *Int'l Symp. on Fault-Tolerant Comp.*, pages 164–173, 1994.
2. K.S. Brace, R.L. Rudell, and R.E. Bryant. Efficient implementation of a BDD package. In *Design Automation Conf.*, pages 40–45, 1990.
3. F. Brglez, D. Bryan, and K. Kozminski. Combinational profiles of sequential benchmark circuits. In *Int'l Symp. Circ. and Systems*, pages 1929–1934, 1989.
4. J.D. Bright, G.F. Sullivan, and G.M. Masson. Checking the integrity of trees. In *Int'l Symp. on Fault-Tolerant Comp.*, pages 402–411, 1995.
5. R.E. Bryant. Graph - based algorithms for Boolean function manipulation. *IEEE Trans. on Comp.*, 35(8):677–691, 1986.
6. R.E. Bryant and Y.-A. Chen. Verification of arithmetic functions with binary moment diagrams. In *Design Automation Conf.*, pages 535–541, 1995.
7. O. Coudert. Two-level logic minimization: an overview. *Integration the VLSI Jour.*, 17(2):97–140, 1994.
8. O. Coudert, H. Fraisse, and J.C. Madre. A breakthrough in two-level logic minimization. In *Int'l Workshop on Logic Synth.*, page P2b, 1993.
9. R. Drechsler and B. Becker. Dynamic minimization of OKFDDs. In *Int'l Conf. on Comp. Design*, pages 602–607, 1995.
10. R. Drechsler and B. Becker. *Binary Decision Diagrams - Theory and Implementation*. Kluwer Academic Publishers, 1998.
11. R. Drechsler, B. Becker, and S. Ruppertz. K*BMDs: A new data structure for verification. In *European Design & Test Conf.*, pages 2–8, 1996.
12. R. Drechsler, A. Sarabi, M. Theobald, B. Becker, and M.A. Perkowski. Efficient representation and manipulation of switching functions based on ordered Kronecker functional decision diagrams. In *Design Automation Conf.*, pages 415–419, 1994.
13. S. Höreth. Implementation of a multiple-domain decision diagram package. In *CHARME*, Chapman & Hall, pages 185–202, 1997.
14. S. Höreth and R. Drechsler. Dynamic minimization of word-level decision diagrams. In *Design, Automation and Test Europe*, pages 612–617, 1998.
15. R.P. Kurshan. *Computer-Aided Verification of Coordinating Processes*. Princeton University Press, 1994.
16. Y.-T. Lai and S. Sastry. Edge-valued binary decision diagrams for multi-level hierarchical verification. In *Design Automation Conf.*, pages 608–613, 1992.
17. D.E. Long. *Long-Package Sun Release 4.1 Overview of C Library Functions*. 1993.
18. S. Minato, N. Ishiura, and S. Yajima. Shared binary decision diagrams with attributed edges for efficient Boolean function manipulation. In *Design Automation Conf.*, pages 52–57, 1990.
19. R. Rudell. Dynamic variable ordering for ordered binary decision diagrams. In *Int'l Conf. on CAD*, pages 42–47, 1993.
20. C. Scholl. Multi-output functional decomposition with exploitation of don't cares. In *Design, Automation and Test Europe*, pages 743–748, 1998.
21. T. Stornetta and F. Brewer. Implementation of an efficient parallel BDD package. In *Design Automation Conf.*, pages 641–644, 1996.
22. D.J. Taylor. Error models for robust storage structures. In *Int'l Symp. on Fault-Tolerant Comp.*, pages 416–422, 1990.
23. B. Wurth, K. Eckl, and K. Antreich. Functional multiple-output decomposition: Theory and implicit algorithm. In *Design Automation Conf.*, pages 54–59, 1995.

Author Index

Springer
and the
environment

At Springer we firmly believe that an international science publisher has a special obligation to the environment, and our corporate policies consistently reflect this conviction.

We also expect our business partners – paper mills, printers, packaging manufacturers, etc. – to commit themselves to using materials and production processes that do not harm the environment. The paper in this book is made from low- or no-chlorine pulp and is acid free, in conformance with international standards for paper permanency.

Springer

Lecture Notes in Computer Science

For information about Vols. 1–1428

please contact your bookseller or Springer-Verlag

Vol. 1466: D. Sangiorgi, R. de Simone (Eds.), CON-CUR'98: Concurrency Theory. Proceedings, 1998. XI, 657 pages. 1998.

Vol. 1467: C. Clack, K. Hammond, T. Davie (Eds.), Implementation of Functional Languages. Proceedings, 1997. X, 375 pages. 1998.

Vol. 1468: P. Husbands, J.-A. Meyer (Eds.), Evolutionary Robotics. Proceedings, 1998. VIII, 247 pages. 1998.

Vol. 1469: R. Puigjaner, N.N. Savino, B. Serra (Eds.), Computer Performance Evaluation. Proceedings, 1998. XIII, 376 pages. 1998.

Vol. 1470: D. Pritchard, J. Reeve (Eds.), Euro-Par'98: Parallel Processing. Proceedings, 1998. XXII, 1157 pages. 1998.

Vol. 1471: J. Dix, L. Moniz Pereira, T.C. Przymusinski (Eds.), Logic Programming and Knowledge Representation. Proceedings, 1997. IX, 246 pages. 1998. (Subseries LNAI).

Vol. 1473: X. Leroy, A. Ohori (Eds.), Types in Compilation. Proceedings, 1998. VIII, 299 pages. 1998.

Vol. 1474: F. Mueller, A. Bestavros (Eds.), Languages, Compilers, and Tools for Embedded Systems. Proceedings, 1998. XIV, 261 pages. 1998.

Vol. 1475: W. Litwin, T. Morzy, G. Vossen (Eds.), Advances in Databases and Information Systems. Proceedings, 1998. XIV, 369 pages. 1998.

Vol. 1476: J. Calmet, J. Plaza (Eds.), Artificial Intelligence and Symbolic Computation. Proceedings, 1998. XI, 309 pages. 1998. (Subseries LNAI).

Vol. 1477: K. Rothermel, F. Hohl (Eds.), Mobile Agents. Proceedings, 1998. VIII, 285 pages. 1998.

Vol. 1478: M. Sipper, D. Mange, A. Pérez-Uribe (Eds.), Evolvable Systems: From Biology to Hardware. Proceedings, 1998. IX, 382 pages. 1998.

Vol. 1479: J. Grundy, M. Newey (Eds.), Theorem Proving in Higher Order Logics. Proceedings, 1998. VIII, 497 pages. 1998.

Vol. 1480: F. Giunchiglia (Ed.), Artificial Intelligence: Methodology, Systems, and Applications. Proceedings, 1998. IX, 502 pages. 1998. (Subseries LNAI).

Vol. 1481: E.V. Munson, C. Nicholas, D. Wood (Eds.), Principles of Digital Document Processing. Proceedings, 1998. VII, 152 pages. 1998.

Vol. 1482: R.W. Hartenstein, A. Keevallik (Eds.), Field-Programmable Logic and Applications. Proceedings, 1998. XI, 533 pages. 1998.

Vol. 1483: T. Plagemann, V. Goebel (Eds.), Interactive Distributed Multimedia Systems and Telecommunication Services. Proceedings, 1998. XV, 326 pages. 1998.

Vol. 1484: H. Coelho (Ed.), Progress in Artificial Intelligence – IBERAMIA 98. Proceedings, 1998. XIII, 421 pages. 1998. (Subseries LNAI).

Vol. 1485: J.-J. Quisquater, Y. Deswarte, C. Meadows, D. Gollmann (Eds.), Computer Security – ESORICS 98. Proceedings, 1998. X, 377 pages. 1998.

Vol. 1486: A.P. Ravn, H. Rischel (Eds.), Formal Techniques in Real-Time and Fault-Tolerant Systems. Proceedings, 1998. VIII, 339 pages. 1998.

Vol. 1487: V. Gruhn (Ed.), Software Process Technology. Proceedings, 1998. VIII, 157 pages. 1998.

Vol. 1488: B. Smyth, P. Cunningham (Eds.), Advances in Case-Based Reasoning. Proceedings, 1998. XI, 482 pages. 1998. (Subseries LNAI).

Vol. 1489: J. Dix, L. Fariñas del Cerro, U. Furbach (Eds.), Logics in Artificial Intelligence. Proceedings, 1998. X, 391 pages. 1998. (Subseries LNAI).

Vol. 1490: C. Palamidessi, H. Glaser, K. Meinke (Eds.), Principles of Declarative Programming. Proceedings, 1998. XI, 497 pages. 1998.

Vol. 1493: J.P. Bowen, A. Fett, M.G. Hinchey (Eds.), ZUM '98: The Z Formal Specification Notation. Proceedings, 1998. XV, 417 pages. 1998.

Vol. 1495: T. Andreasen, H. Christiansen, H.L. Larsen (Eds.), Flexible Query Answering Systems. IX, 393 pages. 1998. (Subseries LNAI).

Vol. 1496: W.M. Wells, A. Colchester, S. Delp (Eds.), Medical Image Computing and Computer-Assisted Intervention – MICCAI'98. Proceedings, 1998. XXII, 1256 pages. 1998.

Vol. 1497: V. Alexandrov, J. Dongarra (Eds.), Recent Advances in Parallel Virtual Machine and Message Passing Interface. Proceedings, 1998. XII, 412 pages. 1998.

Vol. 1498: A.E. Eiben, T. Bäck, M. Schoenauer, H.-P. Schwefel (Eds.), Parallel Problem Solving from Nature – PPSN V. Proceedings, 1998. XXIII, 1041 pages. 1998.

Vol. 1499: S. Kutten (Ed.), Distributed Computing. Proceedings, 1998. XII, 419 pages. 1998.

Vol. 1501: M.M. Richter, C.H. Smith, R. Wiehagen, T. Zeugmann (Eds.), Algorithmic Learning Theory. Proceedings, 1998. XI, 439 pages. 1998. (Subseries LNAI).

Vol. 1502: G. Antoniou, J. Slaney (Eds.), Advanced Topics in Artificial Intelligence. Proceedings, 1998. XI, 333 pages. 1998. (Subseries LNAI).

Vol. 1503: G. Levi (Ed.), Static Analysis. Proceedings, 1998. IX, 383 pages. 1998.

Vol. 1504: O. Herzog, A. Günter (Eds.), KI-98: Advances in Artificial Intelligence. Proceedings, 1998. XI, 355 pages. 1998. (Subseries LNAI).

Vol. 1508: S. Jajodia, M.T. Özsu, A. Dogac (Eds.), Advances in Multimedia Information Systems. Proceedings, 1998. VIII, 207 pages. 1998.

Vol. 1510: J.M. Zytkow, M. Quafafou (Eds.), Principles of Data Mining and Knowledge Discovery. Proceedings, 1998. XI, 482 pages. 1998. (Subseries LNAI).

Vol. 1511: D. O'Hallaron (Ed.), Languages, Compilers, and Run-Time Systems for Scalable Computers.

Vol. 1512: E. Giménez, C. Paulin-Mohring (Eds.), Types for Proofs and Programs. Proceedings, 1996. VIII, 373 pages. 1998.

Vol. 1513: C. Nikolaou, C. Stephanidis (Eds.), Research and Advanced Technology for Digital Libraries. Proceedings, 1998. XV, 912 pages. 1998.

Vol. 1514: K. Ohta,, D. Pei (Eds.), Advances in Cryptology – ASIACRYPT'98. Proceedings, 1998. XII, 436 pages. 1998.

Vol. 1516: W. Ehrenberger (Ed.), Computer Safety, Reliability and Security. Proceedings, 1998. XVI, 392 pages. 1998.

Vol. 1518: M. Luby, J. Rolim, M. Serna (Eds.), Randomization and Approximation Techniques in Computer Science. Proceedings, 1998. IX, 385 pages. 1998.